Labor Histories

The Working Class in
American History

A list of books in the series
appears at the end of this book.

Labor Histories

Class, Politics, and the
Working-Class Experience

EDITED BY

ERIC ARNESEN,

JULIE GREENE, AND

BRUCE LAURIE

University of Illinois Press

Urbana and Chicago

© 1998 by the Board of Trustees of
the University of Illinois

Manufactured in the United States of America
I 2 3 4 5 C P 5 4 3 2 I

This book is printed on acid-free paper.

Library of Congress Cataloging-in-Publication Data

Labor histories : class, politics, and the working-class
experience / edited by Eric Arnesen, Julie Greene, and
Bruce Laurie.
p. cm. — (The working class in American history)
Includes bibliographical references and index.
ISBN 0-252-02407-9 (cloth : alk. paper)
ISBN 0-252-06710-X (pbk. : alk. paper)
1. Labor—United States—History—Congresses.
2. Working class—United States—History—Congresses.
3. Labor movement—United States—History—Congresses.
4. Trade-unions—United States—History—Congresses.
5. Labor policy—United States—History—Congresses.
I. Arnesen, Eric. II. Greene, Julie, 1956- . III. Laurie, Bruce.
IV. Series.
HD8057.L28   1998
331'.0973—dc21   97-45358
CIP

For David Montgomery

Contents

Preface

THIS BOOK ORIGINATED in a conference held in June 1993 at the University of Pittsburgh at Greensburg, Pennsylvania. More than forty labor historians gathered there for three days to share their work, to discuss their discipline and its future, and to socialize with old friends. This relaxed conference provided the opportunity to celebrate and reflect upon the influence of David Montgomery, an extraordinary teacher and scholar in the field of labor history. As graduate students either at the University of Pittsburgh or at Yale University, the historians present, plus many others who could not attend, had worked with Montgomery as their advisor and mentor. As a group our interests ranged widely, blending an emphasis on labor with political, social, cultural, or gender methodologies, yet David Montgomery's influence provided a common thread that united us.

As a scholar, David Montgomery has bucked both the trendy specialization and the fascination with social science methodology that together heavily influenced the profession after the mid-1960s. Indeed, no "new labor historian" has brought a more capacious perspective to the field than Montgomery, and few have been more prolific. His first essays in the early 1960s on mid-nineteenth-century radicalism adumbrated key aspects of his now-classic *Beyond Equality: Labor and the Radical Republicans* (1969). He followed this initial body of work with a set of articles on the origins of the labor movement in northeastern port cities and the particular experiences of Irish handloom weavers in antebellum Philadelphia. The late 1960s and early 1970s saw Montgomery producing essays on the shop floor, immigrant labor, and managerial reform between the Civil War and World War II, which later constituted the heart of his influential *Workers' Control in America* (1979), as well as several historiographical interventions and commentaries on the labor scene, past and current. *The Fall of the House of Labor* (1987), arguably his most deeply researched and intellectually ambitious work, went beyond *Workers' Control* by exploring the travail of casual workers and machine tenders, and by probing labor politics at the national level in a more systematic way. And just when it appeared as if he had left the nineteenth century for good, he returned to it from the fresh perspective that informs the highly relevant and resonant *Citizen Worker: The Experience of Workers in the United States with Democracy and the Free Market during the Nineteenth Century* (1993).

While it is impossible to represent the complexities of such an enormous body of work in this short space, it is fair to say that four themes define its special signature. One is the enduring significance of class strife as a driving force of American history. Class, to Montgomery, has always appeared in the form of relationships between labor and capital, not some abstract power governed by the iron laws of the market nor derived from a static position within the economy. Montgomery sees working-class consciousness as forged at the workplace and as underlying other sources of identity rooted in race, gender, or ethnicity, or shaped by the community. A closely related theme claims that class conflict itself derives mainly, though not exclusively, from the chronic tension between labor and capital over control of the production process. This contest over "workers' control" may well constitute the centerpiece of Montgomery's scholarship since the late 1960s.

Montgomery's earliest and most recent writings clearly reflect a third theme: the enduring importance of ideology, both as a motivating force and as a means of mediating class relationships, if not so much at the workplace then surely in the political area. As for politics, a fourth and final theme, Montgomery placed it at the center of his work from the beginning, long before critics of the new labor history argued for bringing the state back in. His respect for the centrality of politics is surpassed only by his skepticism of theoretical convention and love for narrative. Montgomery's desire to tell a good story can be seen in a range of themes, from the persistent attempts made to criminalize plebeian forms of leisure, to the struggles of textile hands for a ten-hour day in the Civil War era, to the efforts machinists made in the early twentieth century to outlaw scientific management. No reader of Montgomery's engaging essays and books can help but appreciate his evocation of class politics not only as electoral activity but also as public policy.

In one sense, then, the ensuing essays represent a body of work in honor of David Montgomery, their intellectual and political inspiration. Montgomery's pedagogy has involved a clear vision of egalitarian and politically informed engagement, yet his hallmark as a teacher has been his genuine openness and wide-ranging appreciation for the multitude of questions that labor history addresses. Over the years Montgomery's students have explored diverse historical problems and methodologies, producing essays and monographs that branched away from their mentor's focus in important ways. Such eclecticism also informs this book, which coincidentally evolved to become not a traditional festshcrift but rather an exploration of the thematic and methodological diversity which characterizes United States working-class history as the current century draws to an end.

We've acquired a great many other debts in working on this project. We are grateful to all the scholars who attended the 1993 conference, sharing their scholarship and ideas with one another and in that way providing such a rich beginning for this book. For their work organizing that conference we're indebted to James Barrett, Peter Gottlieb, Kathryn Oberdeck, Shelton Stromquist, and especially to Cecelia Bucki and Mark McColloch. An informal group emerged out of that conference to discuss possible follow-up projects, and its members played an invaluable role in shaping the book which resulted. In addition to the six scholars just mentioned, that group included Ileen DeVault, Priscilla Murolo, and Peter Rachleff. We owe a very great deal, of course, to this book's contributors. It has been a privilege to work with each one of them.

Financial support for this ongoing project came from the University of Missouri at Kansas City, the University of Pittsburgh at Greensburg, the Institute for the Humanities and the Great Cities Institute at the University of Illinois at Chicago, the University of Massachusetts, and the University of Colorado. We thank each of these institutions. We have been blessed with a remarkably supportive and generous editor, Richard Wentworth at the University of Illinois Press, whose suggestions and advice have been invariably on the mark. Patricia Hollahan has provided us with skillful copyediting and helpful suggestions in the final stages of preparing the manuscript for publication. Finally we each thank our families for their support and encouragement: Katrin Schultheiss and Rachel Arnesen, James Maffie, and Leslie and Becca Laurie.

Introduction

JULIE GREENE, BRUCE LAURIE,
AND ERIC ARNESEN

THERE HAS NEVER EXISTED a direct relationship between the state of organized labor and the state of labor history. The Progressive Era that spawned the Wisconsin school of labor history grudgingly tolerated the American Federation of Labor and aggressively fought against the self-activity of the great mass of industrial workers. Thirty years later, when these industrial workers came together in the drama that gave rise to the Congress of Industrial Organizations, they still had not found their own historians. This paradox continued into the 1960s, when the rise of the new labor history paralleled the beginnings of organized labor's steady decline. Though the future of this paradoxical disjuncture is far from clear, there are preliminary signs of renewed ferment within both the labor movement and the field of labor history, suggesting healthy intellectual and organizational engagement with problems both have long avoided.

Labor's revival, however, is far from certain, for formidable obstacles now confront American workers. Since the 1970s, a revived anti-labor ideology among corporate managers has spawned an industry of consultants to prevent unionization and to roll back the hard-won gains of the unionized sector. The increasing globalization of the economy has allowed corporations to indulge their historic preference for low-wage, nonunion, and powerless labor, this time located abroad, where workers often toil in sweatshops, maquiladoras, and investment zones under repressive conditions. At the same time, the threat of future relocation often serves as an effective club against worker protests at home. Continued deindustrialization and capital flight, as well as a technological revolution based on information processing, threaten to erode further the nation's unionized manufacturing base and to create even more low-wage, nonbenefit, and often temporary jobs in the expanding service sector. Political conservatism in both the Democratic and Republican parties has made the state the partner of capital not only in its search for new markets and cheap labor but also in its recent anti-union crusade.

An increasingly diverse working class, composed of different racial and ethnic groups and large numbers of women, has emerged amid this economic transformation. This diversity poses organizing challenges the AFL-CIO has not fully addressed. The historic transition of power in 1995 from the old guard, represented by labor bureaucrat Lane Kirkland, to the new, represented by reformer John Sweeney, augers well for the revival of labor organizing and militancy, as do reform movements in numerous unions. But such revival remains only a possibility.

In contrast, the new labor history, now over four decades old, remains a vital and growing field. Building on the pioneering work of David Montgomery, David Brody, Melvin Dubofsky, and Herbert Gutman, new labor historians have meticulously chronicled a history of working-class activism and resistance to industrialization and corporate control in a larger struggle for industrial democracy. Workers' agency, shop floor culture, traditions of radicalism, the evolution of trade unions and labor movements, workers' racial and gender ideologies and practices, and workers' community and family life—these are but a few of the subjects that have commanded the attention of a generation of scholars. Over the past decade or so, labor historians have subjected their field to intense scrutiny: the critical issues raised by historians focusing on politics, race, and gender, in particular, have spurred practitioners to formulate new questions and research projects. This newer work has enriched our understanding of three key themes in working-class history: politics and the state, class and culture, and institution building and labor activism. Presenting new scholarship in these three major areas, this book seeks to capture the energy and new interpretations that have marked the new labor history in recent years.

Despite the divergent fates of labor history and the labor movement, some observers believe that organized labor's fall has implications for the historical study of unions and the working-class past. Those who have written the labor movement's (premature) obituary have also questioned the future of labor history. In these conservative times, the cynicism of some journalists and scholars has soared to a new level, as they project their own pessimism about the prospects for social change today onto the past. This volume aims to counter these impressions and to assert the vitality, relevance, and significance of the field and its basic concepts.

The essays in *Labor Histories* advance the basic argument that class has been and remains a central category of analysis, indispensable to the study of working people and the broad drama of United States history itself. It is important to dispel certain notions, recently popular among critics of labor history, about the concept of class. Let us begin by stating what it is *not*. First, in these essays class neither implies a specific set of beliefs nor dictates a particular organizational or ideological response. Throughout American history, working people have advanced a variety of perspectives, visions, and agendas informed by class. In some cases, these have resembled the more "classical" formulations, with their emphasis on conflict between workers and employers, a belief in a labor theory of value, and the like; in other cases, workers set themselves apart from their social "betters" by adopting a more diffuse sense of group identity, anchored at the workplace or in the community, sometimes mediated by ethnic or racial identity.

Second, class is not merely a discursively constructed phenomenon best understood in relation to language, a position increasingly popular in some academic quarters. To isolate language from the material conditions in which it is produced or to regard the "material" as merely discursively constructed itself obliterates analytical distinctions between forms of knowledge and the conditions of their production; it also risks replacing one form of determinism with another. And third, class is not a direct reflection of material conditions, unmediated by culture and language. Social, political, religious, and discursive experiences necessarily inform the "content" of class in historically specific contexts.

What, then, is class? The meanings and significance ascribed to class over the last 150 years have been so rich as virtually to defy categorization. Its origins, for scholars ranging from Marx and Weber to Eric Olin Wright, are anchored in capitalist economic development. Whether people control their own and others' labor power and whether they possess the power to make decisions about the division of labor are issues that today inform scholarly understanding of class and class relations. Class may give rise to certain outlooks and dispositions that are widely shared and that impart a social, political, moral, and/or religious significance.

Most new labor historians, including those in this book, do not associate a consciousness of class or class formation with one's position in the production process or in the larger economy. They instead treat class as a historical process in which the agency of workers themselves features prominently, if not exclusively or without constraint, and which embodies social, cultural, and political aspects. Following English historian Edward Thompson, in speaking of class we mean a "body of people who share the same congeries of interest, social experiences, traditions, and value system, who have a disposition to behave as a class, to define themselves in their actions and in their consciousness in relation to other groups of people in class ways."[1] Eschewing any form of determinism, the contributors to this volume contend that class and class experience are not one-dimensional or unidirectional. Class pervades all aspects of social experience—family and gender relations, neighborhood, politics, race relations, and associational life; it infuses the realms of production and consumption, the work experience, family and community life, politics, social life, ideology, and culture in all its forms. Class and class consciousness in turn bear the imprint of the social relations of the workplace, the character of state policy, and gender, race, ethnicity, and region.

These are not remarkable assertions. For decades, labor historians have insisted on the specificity of working-class experiences in their exploration of the manifestations of class in American life. Yet to reassert and refine this argument is important at the end of the twentieth century, for in the academy and in popular perception it has become fashionable to dismiss class as a dated, reductionist, or romantic construct. In the broader culture, the promotion of the United States as a classless society, the unprecedented economic growth of the post–World War II era "American Century," and the myth—and reality—of social mobility have all contributed to the popular belief that "class" is a thing of the past, applicable perhaps to distant decades or to Europe. In the academy, historians who equate "class" with classical Marxist definitions have not had a difficult time in finding it largely absent in the American past: no classical class consciousness, no class.

Not all scholars have employed such caricatured definitions or rejected alternative definitions of class out of hand; in fact, the broader concept remains central to much work in not only labor history but women's and more recently African-American history as well. Even as we write, class is again gaining currency in popular discourse, as media, political candidates, and pundits grapple with how our new economy has produced a growing gap between rich and poor; how increasing numbers of Ameri-

cans and the newest immigrants are "losers" in current economic transformations; how unemployment, economic insecurity, and stagnant and
even downward social mobility are affecting ever larger numbers of people; and how vast numbers of people—particularly inner-city African
Americans—have been completely excluded from the economy. Although
the denial of class divisions and tensions remains prominent in contemporary political analysis, the reality of class lurks persistently just below
the explanatory surface. We suggest that scholarly attention to the history of class in the United States and its relationship to race, gender, and
ethnicity will prove ever more important in the years ahead.

Politics and the State

The American economy does not operate independently of politics: labor markets, working conditions, and employment relations have always
been constrained by legal assumptions or codes that themselves expressed
particular assumptions, values, and interests that were forged through
political contestation. The first theme of *Labor Histories* focuses on ways
working men and women historically have experienced and influenced
American political structures and political culture. This has taken many
different forms. Workers have built independent parties and embraced
alternative movements of populism, socialism, and communism; they also
have joined enthusiastically in torchlight parades for Republican and
Democratic candidates and built alliances with major parties in hopes of
gaining leverage. Regardless of the particular form it takes, however, the
relationship between workers and the political sphere has never been one-
sided. If the state has shaped labor relations, limited workers' tactics, and
intervened decisively in labor conflicts, working people too through their
beliefs, decisions, choices, and actions—inside and outside formal mainstream or alternative political parties—have profoundly influenced American policies and political culture.

Mainstream political historians have traditionally focused little attention on the working-class experience or on class as a force in the making
of political consciousness and activities. The dominant school of political
historiography during the 1960s and 1970s slighted class in favor of ethnic, religious, and cultural factors as affecting popular politics in the nineteenth and early twentieth centuries.[2] More recently, a "state-centered"
methodology has grown popular among historians and social scientists
interested in the connection between government and society. Led by
scholars such as Theda Skocpol and Stephen Skowronek, this approach

holds that the central government bureaucracy—or the state—operates autonomously as a causal agent in United States society, economics, and politics. It rejects approaches in the tradition of social history as mistakenly "society-centered." This methodology has won a large following, as scholars from fields long dominated by social history have seized the opportunity for taking politics and the state seriously.[3] Even labor history has felt the effect of the state-centered methodology. Works in the field encouraged by Skocpol's call to "bring the state back in," such as William Forbath's recent book, have contributed richly to our understanding of the state's impact on labor.[4] Yet often in a state-centered methodology, the role played by ordinary working Americans in constructing and contesting political relationships tends to get lost. This makes the relationship between class, politics, and the state harder to understand.

The traditions of the new labor and social history are a necessary corrective to attributing excessive primacy to the state in explorations of class and politics. Although new labor historians have lavished far more attention on community and workplace settings than on politics, a growing number of historians have begun integrating working-class politics into their work.[5] Among the diverse approaches pursued by these and other scholars, a constant element can be observed: each anchors his or her scholarship not in the putative autonomy of state actors and institutions but rather in concrete social and economic relationships. Their work is informed by notions of class and class formation that stress working men and women's agency in the rich variety of political and social environments in which they lived.

No easy assumptions can be made about the precise relationship between class and politics in American history. In this country class influences are often so mingled with racial, ethnic, gender, and regional elements as to be hardly distinguishable. Socialist and labor parties have never attracted more than a fraction of working Americans. A united class vote has never existed, whether in support of the major or third parties. There exists no singular working-class political culture. Nor can one argue that state power affects the entire working class in the same way. Perhaps because of these limitations, earlier scholarship on the subject often took Werner Sombart's famous query—"Why is there no socialism in America?"—as a starting point, and thereby posed a negative question instead of assessing the actual relationship that did exist between different groups of working people and politics. This sort of binary opposition—either workers join a socialist or labor party, or else they possess no class-based political identities whatsoever—misses the rich and complex worlds of working-class political consciousness and associations that most often fall somewhere between those two poles.

It is helpful to delineate three key elements in working people's political universe: political activities, political culture and consciousness, and the state. In each case a broad definition is required that is open to a wide range of experiences and influences. Our understanding of political activity, therefore, would include not only campaigning, torchlight parades, and other partisan activities but also strikes, food riots, and other forms of collective expression. By political culture and consciousness we mean those languages and beliefs about the political and social order, citizenship, and the state, and the cultural forms and styles working people use to voice those beliefs. Finally, by the state we mean government bureaucracies and courts as well as the actions taken by politicians, civil servants, military officials, and judges that influence workers' lives.

In each of these areas the relationship and the influences exerted are multidirectional. Working people and their struggles to achieve a better life are unquestionably affected by the political options available at any given time. For example, the state sets parameters around the labor movement in different ways, depending on its character at any given moment and the particular nature of its class alliances. A great deal hinges on the disposition of the courts to constrain worker activity or the inclination of political officials to repress it by calling out the police, militia, troops, or all three. The political climate can also be decisive. The major parties can impede or encourage independent politics depending on their response to worker initiatives. Yet working men and women play a profound role in creating American politics as well. The state emerges and takes on a particular character as diverse social groups, workers among them, express their political vision and pressure the government to respond to their demands. The precise nature of American political culture at any given time results from a dynamic interaction of workers and other Americans to received ideas. For example, the courts and major parties, two institutions that for long periods studiously avoided acknowledging the class-based needs and interests of working people, began changing by the early twentieth century at least in part because of pressure those workers exerted.

Finally, understanding the complex relationship between class and politics means that we cannot study the working class in isolation. Working men and women engage not only with the structures of American politics; they also engage, and often do battle, with other social groups—including other workers, middle-class associations, politicians, employers, and reformers. The jostling over diverse and sometimes contradictory demands has generated much of the substance of American politics.

Class and Culture

The new labor history first distinguished itself sharply from earlier schools of historical and sociological scholarship on labor through its treatment of culture. Industrial relations specialists and historians in the tradition of the "old" labor history focused their attention on a strata of white male skilled workers without much of a life outside the workplace and union hall. Rarely did they depict labor's domestic life, associational activities, or leisurely doings that the new labor historians identified as "culture" and proceeded to place at the center of their work. For these earlier writers, culture was assumed to be synonymous with high culture and thus beyond the capacity of ordinary people. Work was for the poor, culture for the rich.

Echoes of this narrow, economistic perspective have not completely disappeared from the historical literature and are pervasive in the popular media. Recent surveys of working-class families in rust-belt cities and towns, for instance, invariably depict an erstwhile male auto or steel worker stranded by capital flight and forced to patch together a living wage from a service job that yields a fraction of his previous income, from his wife's earnings, and in the worst of cases from the take of teenage children. (Who can forget Michael Moore's condescending portrait of a Flint, Michigan, woman whose rabbits served as more than pets for her family, in *Roger and Me?*) Such a pathetic picture is our contemporary equivalent of muckrakers' depictions of impoverished immigrant families a century ago. There is not much culture in this tableau other than an explicit or implied culture of poverty—and usually no culture at all.

The new labor history made workers' culture a centerpiece of much of its analysis.[6] Building on the work of Edward Thompson, labor historians explored the development of distinctive working-class cultures in a variety of settings. While they understood culture to be ineluctably conditioned by the material circumstances in which people found themselves, they also recognized that it was no mere reflection of purportedly objective forces. Culture was a resource; it was adaptive and interpretative, something that workers themselves forged in the course of living their lives and making sense of their world. They were hardly immune from the larger society's dominant culture, to be sure. But neither were they its passive recipients. Workers brought culture to the workplace when they engaged in wage or other forms of labor. Their class experiences on and off the job informed their culture, which was itself expressed in many arenas. There was no single "key" to understanding workers' beliefs and behaviors nor a single, privileged place for finding and studying it. Not just the workplace but the saloon, union hall, church, fraternal lodge, dance hall, public square, and city street were all sites where workers tried to understand their world, where they celebrated or mourned, relaxed or shared their hopes and fears, expressed their visions of a better life, or simply enjoyed each others' company.[7]

Much of this work on culture has been salutary, suggesting the ways in which people's consciousness is necessarily complex. Take the case of popular religion: It was not inherently a bulwark of capitalism or the "opiate of the masses," in Marx's derisive phrase. Its more subtle observers have shown the same evangelical Protestantism that figured so centrally in the formation of early industrial discipline also made workers more aware of the sharpening distinction between work and leisure and of the value of time itself. Time-conscious workers became more protective of what they thought to be their time—"our own time," as they called it—and demanded more of it in what proved to be a century-long fight from the 1830s to the 1930s for the ten- and then the eight-hour workday. Neither did ethnic consciousness always fragment working-class America into warring factions or linguistic or nationality groups (although it certainly did that too at times). Class and ethnicity often reinforced one another, strengthening both a consciousness of class and working-class organization.

Current explorations of working-class cultures have begun to leave behind earlier, romantic celebrations of workers' resistance or oppositional values to examine critically the precise values, attitudes, and discourses workers employed and the roles they played in their evolving notions of their own social identities.[8] Working-class activists may have carefully cultivated "movement cultures" with explicit political agendas, such as the Knights of Labor and the CIO, which strove to incorporate workers of various backgrounds, skill levels, and to some extent different races and genders. But they also at times nurtured cultures of male and white chauvinism that not only excluded women and blacks but weakened or thwarted the working-class organization they sought to achieve.

Culture and class, then, should be treated as inextricable elements in historical analysis. Yet in some hands, cultural analysis has drifted from its material moorings and achieved an authority of its own that can only be described as a kind of cultural determinism. Similarly, emphasis on class without regard to culture represents a retreat into the past, a return to a cold, formalistic Marxism or to the sterile assumptions of industrial relations specialists, neither having much relevance to the modern world.

Institution Building and Labor Activism

A final organizing theme of this book deals with the diversity of working-class movements and organizations. The dynamics of capitalist industrialization undermined traditional forms of labor while creating new ones, generating profound insecurity and impoverishment for some and economic opportunity and advancement for others. They posed challenges to workers, who responded in a multitude of ways—by organizing associations to counter the influence of employers, by seeking accommodation with elites, by migrating, or by just getting by. If some embraced the ethos of acquisitivism and individualism, many others sought refuge in forms of mutuality and community that offered a different yardstick by which to measure self-worth, value, and the economic system itself.

From the eighteenth century through the present, American workers have built and influenced a wide array of organizations and movements. The range of such groups reflected the diversity of the working class itself, embracing not merely craft and industrial unions but farmer/tenant protest associations and utopian socialist bodies of the antebellum era, organized and unorganized movements by former slaves to achieve a modicum of independence and dignity in slavery's aftermath, socialist and communist parties, ethnic fraternal lodges, and churches as well. Whatever their response to the oppressions and opportunities they faced, workers have brought distinctive perspectives into their organizations.

Just as there has never been a homogeneous working class in the United States—in terms of workers' experiences, outlooks, or goals—logically there has never been a single or unified working-class movement. As David Montgomery has argued, "instead of listening for the 'voice of the working class,' . . . we must be attuned to many voices, sometimes in harmony, but often in conflict with one another."[9] The themes of unity and fragmentation have long been of interest to historians of American labor, and the verdict seems clear: No single "class interest" has been shared by all members of the American working class.[10] Different groups of workers have competed against one another just as others have cooperated; workers' unity was always fragile, provisional, and ultimately temporary. Such qualified solidarity among workers and the very belief in a unified or unifiable working class, then, did not spring out of some inexorable logic of capitalist development. Rather, unity has always been an aspect of an affirmative project, something that labor activists sought to build.

And yet, even that project of unification and the fostering of a political self-awareness was itself rarely a universal one. At most times throughout American history, the vision of class has been profoundly complicated by—and indeed constituted by—other competing loyalties, identities, and solidarities. Just who would be organized or welcomed into the fellowship of labor? What constituted membership in a bona fide working class? Ethnicity, religion, skill, gender, and race all figured prominently in the definitions of class and class organization advanced by working-class activists and their rank and file in nineteenth- and twentieth-century America.[11]

Skilled, white, native-born artisans in the mid-nineteenth century found some workers without the necessary strength, virtue, or ability to warrant inclusion in their organizations. Some of them joined in the vicious assaults on African Americans, ridiculed women unionists, and scoffed at the unskilled. A century later, many skilled AFL craftsmen in the early 1930s rejected as the "rubbish at labor's door" the first- and second-generation southern and eastern Europeans who made up a growing segment of mass production industries. In each case, skill and ethnicity fused into a particular definition of what it was to be an American worker: skill and membership in particular ethnic groups made one a worker, capable of defending oneself and worthy of participation in an organization or movement of comrades; those without skill or the proper ethnic pedigree were not fellow workers or even potential allies but real or assumed threats to be ignored, excluded, or fought. During the nineteenth century, however, both white native-born and immigrant workers found some common ground in their shared hostility toward African-American workers—antebellum slaves or postbellum freed men and women. Similarly, white male workers were never of one mind about women's participation in the "family" or waged economy or the labor movement. Shared concepts of women's subordinate place, the family wage, and working-class domesticity infused their beliefs and practices across lines of race, ethnicity, and skill.

Three important points require emphasis in an analysis of workers' organization in United States history. First, the impulses toward unity, carefully fostered by members of the "militant minority," are significant in their own right and their achievements impressive, given the countervailing tendencies of fragmentation and the heterogeneity of the working class. The Knights of Labor in the mid-1880s, the Industrial Workers of the World in the first and second decades of the twentieth century, the Congress of Industrial Organizations in the late 1930s, and even the American Federation of Labor during World War I were remarkable for their efforts to minimize or even break down barriers between groups of workers and for their expansion of the definitions of solidarity. Second, an appreciation of solidarity must not detract from an understanding of its limits or of the constraints imposed on workers by their own self-definitions. The Knights of Labor's expansive vision of a commonwealth of virtuous producers, for example, may have tentatively included African Americans, but it remained firmly anchored in the anti-Asian ideologies of the era, leading most Knights to reject out of hand Chinese membership; similarly, it enthusiastically embraced women's participation, but channeled it in gender-specific directions with its promotion of new forms of working-class domesticity.

And third, even under the best organizational and ideological conditions the forces arrayed against workers' movements have always been considerable. To focus exclusively on workers' ideologies, movements, and practices—crediting workers with the ability to achieve their goals or holding them wholly responsible for their own failures—abstracts working-class struggles from the very contexts in which the battles were fought. Workers' movements confronted fierce opponents: employers, their associations, and usually the state, often in an economic environment that proved inhospitable to begin with. Working-class organizations never functioned in an economic or political vacuum, whether they were internally divided or united, however imperfectly. Labor history has remained appropriately steadfast in its examination of class power, rarely forgetting that workers' movements were often fought tooth and nail by those with an invested stake in their failure. The very ferocity of so much industrial conflict in the nineteenth and twentieth centuries, as well as the persistence of constant localized struggles in workplaces and communities to define the conditions of work and life, should remind us that a tremendous amount was at stake, something of which participants—if not all historians today—were keenly aware.

To say that the history of the American working class is complex and multifaceted is not to say that it is a history of resignation or despair. It is one thing to recognize such complexity, quite another to say that complexity prevails. One is reminded here of the initial composition of the CIO and its depiction by early historians. The latter predictably gave us a straightforward account of the federation's institutional life and heroic struggles, overlooking and perhaps even excusing attitudes of rank and filers in most CIO affiliates that relegated women and blacks to subordinate roles, or no roles at all in the worst circumstances. Most such affiliates no longer resemble their former selves. All of those in the industrial sector, like the United Automobile Workers, are considerably smaller, and reflect the cultural diversity and greater women's presence that characterizes modern America. Most recent work on the United Automobile Workers addresses not only the union's racist past and more inclusive present but also the efforts to overcome its chauvinism, partly from enlightened activists and mostly from blacks and women themselves.[12] This richer and more complicated interpretation suggests that real achievements are often born of flawed and imperfect organization. It also suggests that progress rarely comes in linear fashion as the old Whigs and modern positivists believe. More often it is episodic, and usually incomplete. This book helps explain why.

Notes

1. For contemporary and historical understandings of class, see: Anthony Giddens and David Held, eds., *Classes, Power, and Conflict: Classical and Contemporary Debates* (Berkeley: University of California Press, 1982), and especially the essay by Erik Olin Wright titled "Class Boundaries and Contradictory Class Locations," 112–29. A useful rendering of class is Ira Katznelson, "Working-Class Formation: Constructing Cases and Comparisons," in Katznelson and Aristide Zolberg, eds., *Working-Class Formation: Nineteenth Century Patterns in Western Europe and the United States* (Princeton: Princeton University Press, 1986), 3–44; E. P. Thompson's definition of class comes from his "The Peculiarities of the English," in Ralph Miliband and John Saville, eds., *Socialist Register 1964* (London: Merlin Press, 1966), 357.

2. See for example Richard Jensen, *The Winning of the Midwest: Social and Political Conflict, 1888–1896* (Chicago: University of Chicago Press, 1971); Paul Kleppner, *The Cross of Culture: A Social Analysis of Midwestern Politics* (New York: Free Press, 1970); Kleppner, *Continuity and Change in Electoral Politics, 1893–1928* (New York: Greenwood Press, 1987).

3. Theda Skocpol, "Bringing the State Back In: Strategies of Analysis in Current Research," in Peter B. Evans, Dietrich Rueschmeyer, and Theda Skocpol, eds., *Bringing the State Back In* (New York: Cambridge University Press, 1985), 3–37; Theda Skocpol, *Protecting Soldiers and Mothers: The Political Origins of Social Policy in the United States* (Cambridge: Harvard University Press, 1992); Stephen Skowronek, *Building a New American State: The Expansion of National Administrative Capacities, 1877–1920* (New York: Cambridge University Press, 1982).

4. See for example William Forbath, *Law and the Shaping of the American Labor Movement* (Cambridge: Harvard University Press, 1991). For other approaches see Melvyn Dubofsky, *The State and Labor in Modern America* (Chapel Hill: University of North Carolina Press, 1994), and Christopher L. Tomlins, *The State and the Unions: Labor Relations, Law, and the Organized Labor Movement in America, 1880–1960* (New York: Cambridge University Press, 1985).

5. David Montgomery, *The Fall of the House of Labor: Workplace, the State, and American Labor Activism, 1865–1925* (New York: Cambridge University Press, 1987); Amy Bridges, *A City in the Republic: Antebellum New York and the Origins of Machine Politics* (Ithaca: Cornell University Press, 1987); Sean Wilentz, *Chants Democratic: New York City and the Rise of the American Working Class, 1788–1850* (New York: Oxford University Press, 1984); Leon Fink, *Workingmen's Democracy: The Workplace, the State, and American Politics* (Urbana: University of Illinois Press, 1983); Michael Kazin, *Barons of Labor: The San Francisco Building Trades and Union Power in the Progressive Era* (Urbana: University of Illinois Press, 1987), 3–7, 277–90; Mari Jo Buhle, *Women and American Socialism, 1870–1920* (Urbana: University of Illinois Press, 1981). A fine summary of the growing literature on labor politics is David Brody's essay, "The Course of American Labor Politics," in *In Labor's Cause: Main Themes on the History of the American Worker* (New York: Oxford University Press, 1993), 43–80.

6. The first major statement by a historian of United States labor is, of course, Herbert G. Gutman, "Work, Culture, and Society in Industrializing America, 1815–1919," *American Historical Review* 78 (1973): 531–88. The first major collection of essays in this genre is Milton Cantor, ed., *American Working-Class Culture: Explorations in Labor and Social History* (Westport, Conn.: Greenwood Press, 1979). A number of monographic works in this spirit quickly followed, most of which focused on a single town or city. See Bruce Laurie, *Working People of Philadelphia, 1800–1850* (Philadelphia: Temple University Press, 1979); Wilentz, *Chants Democratic*. Later work built on David Montgomery's seminal article, "Workers' Control of Machine Production in the Nineteenth Century," *Labor History* 17 (1976): 486–509. See especially Susan Porter Benson, *Counter Cultures: Saleswomen, Managers, and Customers in American Department Stores, 1890–1940* (Urbana: University of Illinois Press, 1986). For more recent work of this kind, see Richard Stott, *Workers in the Metropolis: Class, Ethnicity, and Youth in New York City* (Ithaca: Cornell University Press, 1990), and Robert Weir, *Beyond Labor's Veil: The Culture of the Knights of Labor* (University Park: Pennsylvania State University Press, 1996).

7. Roy Rosenzweig, *Eight Hours for What We Will: Workers and Leisure in an Industrial City, 1870–1920* (New York: Cambridge University Press, 1983); Kathy Peiss, *Cheap Amusements: Working Women and Leisure in Turn-of-the-Century New York* (Philadelphia: Temple University Press, 1986).

8. See, for example, Ava Baron, ed., *Work Engendered: Toward a New History of American Labor* (Ithaca: Cornell University Press, 1991); David Roediger, *The Wages of Whiteness: Race and the Making of the American Working Class* (New York: Verso, 1991).

9. Montgomery, *Fall of the House of Labor*, 1.

10. See, for example, Richard Jules Oestreicher, *Solidarity and Fragmentation: Working People and Class Consciousness in Detroit, 1875–1900* (Urbana: University of Illinois Press, 1986); James R. Barrett, *Work and Community in the Jungle: Chicago's Packinghouse Workers, 1894–1922* (Urbana: University of Illinois Press, 1987); Ruth Milkman, *Gender at Work: The Dynamics of Job Segregation by Sex during World War II* (Urbana: University of Illinois Press, 1987).

11. See, for example, Dana Frank, *Purchasing Power: Consumer Organizing, Gender, and the Seattle Labor Movement, 1919–1929* (New York: Cambridge University Press, 1994); Eileen Boris, *Home to Work: Motherhood and the Politics of Industrial Homework in the United States* (New York: Cambridge University Press, 1994); Roediger, *Wages*

of Whiteness; Eric Arnesen, *Waterfront Workers of New Orleans: Race, Class, and Politics, 1863–1923* (1991; reprint, Urbana: University of Illinois Press, 1994); Alexander Saxton, *The Indispensable Enemy: Labor and the Anti-Chinese Movement in California* (Berkeley: University of California Press, 1971); Michael K. Honey, *Southern Labor and Black Civil Rights: Organizing Memphis Workers* (Urbana: University of Illinois Press, 1993); Daniel Letwin, *The Challenge of Interracial Unionism: Alabama Coal Miners, 1878–1921* (Chapel Hill: University of North Carolina Press, 1997); Devra Weber, *Dark Sweat, White Gold: California Farm Workers, Cotton, and the New Deal* (Berkeley: University of California Press, 1994).

12. Nancy Gabin, *Feminism in the Labor Movement: Women and the United Auto Workers, 1935–1974* (Ithaca: Cornell University Press, 1990); Kevin Boyle, *The UAW and the Heyday of American Liberalism 1945–1968* (Ithaca: Cornell University Press, 1995); Nelson Lichtenstein, *The Most Dangerous Man in Detroit: Walter Reuther and the Fate of American Labor* (1995; reprinted as *Walter Reuther: The Most Dangerous Man in Detroit* [Urbana: University of Illinois Press, 1997]); Thomas J. Sugrue, *The Origins of the Urban Crisis: Race and Inequality in Postwar Detroit* (Princeton: Princeton University Press, 1996).

Part 1

Politics and the State

Chapter 1

Land and Freedom

The New York Anti-Rent Wars and the
Construction of Free Labor in the
Antebellum North

REEVE HUSTON

THE SOCIAL IDENTITY of mid-nineteenth-century Northerners centered on the belief that their region was uniquely friendly to "free labor." Variants of this idea informed the ideologies of the northern Democratic and Republican parties and left a powerful imprint on Northerners' understanding of the sectional crisis and the Civil War.[1] Recently, a number of historians have sought out the origins of this idea. They argue that a new conception of free labor emerged during the early nineteenth century from the efforts of courts, urban employers, and intellectuals to legitimize the emerging system of wage labor. As slavery, indentured servitude, and apprenticeship fell into decline and the number of wage workers expanded, courts and employers drew increasingly sharp lines between wage labor, which they depicted as "free," and "unfree" class relations based on personal subordination. They defined free labor as a contractual relationship between juridical equals in which employees could not be physically compelled to fulfill their agreements. As long as wage contracts were uncoerced and employees were free to quit, this relationship could legitimately entail dramatic inequalities of power, subjecting workers to the "order, control, and direction" of their bosses.[2] From the 1830s on, employers and intellectuals linked this conception of free labor to a celebration of capitalist growth as guaranteeing the dignity of labor, equal economic opportunity, and social mobility for the sober and industrious. For them, free labor was labor that was free to prosper according to individual merit in a competitive capitalist economy. Workers offered their own, competing definitions of free labor, which found champions in politics. But the courts' and employers' conception gained political and legal hegemony and found its fullest expression in the ideology of the Republican party.[3]

This interpretation offers a compelling account of how conflicts over wage labor helped create new ideals of freedom. But it errs in attributing the origins of these ideals *entirely* to conflicts over wage labor.[4] Both Republicans and northern Democrats saw petty proprietorship among farmers as the cornerstone of free labor, and Republicans backed up their commitment to independent farming by placing the land question, in the form of a homestead act, at the center of their ideology and program.[5] It is worth asking whether these elements of free-laborism, like the Republicans' legitimization of wage labor, emerged out of social conflict, and what part farmers played in creating these ideas. A good place to start is with the chronic conflicts over land during the early nineteenth century. From New York to Kansas, antebellum farmers fought to defend their land claims from landlords, speculators, mortgage holders, and railroads.[6]

It is also worth asking whether economic and social change affected farmers' vision of free labor. Christopher Clark and others have shown how northeastern farmers increased their production for market, shifted from account book to cash exchange, and made increasing use of wage labor on their farms in the half-century before the Civil War. Their work reveals both that rural Northeasterners played a critical role in industrial capitalist development before the Civil War, and that farmers' experience of capitalism was significantly different from that of urban workers and entrepreneurs.[7] Although Clark has examined changes (as well as significant continuities) in farmers' economic morality during this transformation, no one has yet explored changes in husbandmen's more formal political and economic ideology. A close look at farmers' movements for land during the antebellum period can provide important insights into how the rural majority thought about and contended with capitalist development and how, in doing so, they contributed to broader contests over the meaning of free labor.

Tracing the rural origins of free-labor ideology has important implications for the broader field of antebellum labor history. Labor historians' tendency to focus on propertyless wage earners offers a narrow definition of "labor" that would have seemed alien to most antebellum workers. Nearly two-thirds of the economically active population of the United States worked in agriculture in 1860.[8] Though farmers had different experiences than wage earners, large numbers of both groups continued to think of themselves as members of the "producing classes" well into the nineteenth century. This shared sense of identity often masked conflicting interests and agendas, but it nonetheless informed the ideology and politics of groups like the National Reform Association, the Farmers' Alliance, and the Knights of Labor.[9]

Simply including farmers' voices will not complete our understanding of the origins of free-labor ideology, however. This ideology found its fullest expression and greatest social impact in politics, an arena in which the major political parties had disproportionate power to determine ideas and programs. Most studies either overlook party activists' part in the creation of free-labor thinking, portray them as directly reflecting social reality, or depict them as transmitting the ideologies and interests of key class constituencies.[10] But politicians did not just reflect social reality. They helped *create* it, by offering their constituents powerful conceptual frameworks with which to interpret their experience.[11] These frameworks were not dictated by any one constituency. Political historians have argued that the major parties were heterogeneous coalitions, each uniting members of many classes, regions, and ethnic and religious groups under a single partisan banner. Such parties were complex organizations, steered by an increasingly professional leadership class whose interests often diverged from the needs of their constituents. Amy Bridges, Harry Watson, Ronald Formisano, and Joel Silbey argue that politicians reshaped the demands of constituents to fit the requirements of coalition building and the needs of party organizations.[12] Although these historians eschew a close analysis of ideas in favor of examining the ways in which party leaders dealt with specific popular sentiments and demands,[13] we can use their approach to gain insight into the relationship between popular belief and party ideology. In doing so, we can show how party leaders *created* an ideology of free labor, rather than merely transmitting it.

This essay examines farmers' and party activists' part in redefining "free labor" during the 1840s and 1850s by focusing on the New York Anti-Rent Wars, the largest farmers' movement in the United States before the 1870s. Some 260,000 men, women, and children—over 8 percent of New York's population—lived on scores of estates along the Hudson, Delaware, and Mohawk rivers. These estates ranged in size from 6,000 to 750,000 acres. Tenants leased their farms in perpetuity, for a number of years, or as long those named in the lease remained alive. Beginning in 1839, many of these farmers built a movement that aimed at destroying these estates and distributing the land among themselves.[14] Though New York's system of leasehold tenancy was virtually unknown in other states after the Revolution and the Anti-Rent Wars were sui generis, the wars themselves were enormously influential in their own right. Before the effective demise of their movement in the 1850s, the anti-renters elected scores of local and state officials, provided the swing votes that elected a governor, and helped write a new state constitution. The politicians influenced by their movement included such nationally influential figures as William Seward, Horace Greeley, Ira Harris, and Martin Van Buren. In addition, although the specific labor system in which the anti-renters worked was unusual, their general concerns were not. Demands for land, as well as fierce opposition to economic and cultural subordination to a patrician class, came from farmers and workers throughout the antebellum North.[15] Finally, New York's leasehold communities after 1820 experienced many of the same economic and social changes that swept through much of the rural Northeast. The Anti-Rent Wars provide one example of how farmers grappled ideologically and politically with their integration into a broader capitalist economy.[16]

In New York's leasehold district, a recognizable ideology of free labor emerged not in conflicts over wage labor but in a four-way struggle over land. Leasehold tenants, conservative politicians, reformist party activists, and urban land reformers each elaborated their own vision of "free labor." Politicians and reformers drew on new ideas about labor and freedom being formulated in the cities and the courts, but had to address the ideas of the anti-renters. Out of this interaction, reform politicians forged a largely new and ultimately triumphant ideology that reconciled farmers' aspirations to liberal political economy and replaced older, authoritarian visions of class relations with an expansive, producerist vision of capitalist development.

Aside from their lease obligations, tenants were like other farmers in the Northeast. Those with long-term leases enjoyed certain property rights in their farms, and leasehold communities included prosperous and poor farmers, as well as professionals, artisans, manufacturers, and landless laborers. But their relations to their landlords were distinctive. The leasehold system embodied the contractual freedom and legal equality that became the norm in the decades after the American Revolution. At the same time, it was governed by an attenuated version of the paternalism and hierarchy that had marked colonial and early national society. Legally, landlord-tenant relations rested on the formal equality of the contract. Tenants got the use of the land in exchange for an annual rent; they were free to sell out and move on at any time. Both landlord and tenant infused this contractual interchange with deference and mutual obligation. During the 1780s and 1790s, both groups participated in a theater of subordination. One prospective tenant prefaced his request for a site on which to build his house with the hope that "your Worship does not take Ill [to hear me], patiently considering, my boldness to your Worship. . . . I must Confess my Self, to be below your Worship." Though such groveling disappeared in the early nineteenth century, tenants continued to doff their hats and speak in reverential tones before their landlords.[17] For their part, proprietors practiced individual "leniency" toward their subordinates, offering abatements to those tenants who made a good-faith effort to meet their obligations. They provided land to very poor families free of charge and granted financial support to churches and schools. Above all, they refrained from prosecuting tenants for unpaid rents. Landlords routinely dunned and cajoled leaseholders, but seldom sued them.[18]

These habits of benevolence and deference declined during the 1820s and 1830s when landlords, who were falling increasingly into debt, began prosecuting their tenants for their unpaid rents. In 1839, the landlord Stephen Van Rensselaer died, leaving debts worth $750,000 and a will that directed his executors to pay his obligations by collecting his tenants' overdue rents. Renters on his estate organized a movement that aimed at ending Van Rensselaer's and other landlords' claims to their estates. The movement spread rapidly, claiming tens of thousands of supporters in eleven counties by late 1845.[19]

The anti-renters adopted a threefold strategy. They organized town and county anti-rent associations that oversaw a boycott on rent payments; collected funds; educated the tenantry and the public through publications, meetings, picnics, and dances; and coordinated a legal campaign against the proprietors. They formed the "Indians"—armed and disguised bands of boys and young men who intimidated and assaulted those who did business with the landlords and drove off officers of the law who entered the estates to prosecute tenants. Finally, leasehold militants lobbied the legislature and, in 1844, created their own political organization. In some counties, the anti-rent "party" nominated independent candidates for state and local office; in others, they selected their candidates from among the nominees of the major parties. Through these organizations, insurgents published five newspapers, stopped rent collection on most estates, and elected scores of public officials.

The anti-renters articulated a vision of "free labor" that left no room for the paternalist subordination under which they had lived for generations. Their vision drew on a long tradition of agrarian belief and practice, but marked a turning point in that tradition. From the earliest colonial settlements, northeastern farmers embraced John Locke's view of property rights in a state of nature: wilderness land rightfully belonged to those who "improved" it by clearing trees, breaking cropland, and constructing houses, fences, and barns. These ideas found powerful political expression in numerous back-country conflicts following the Revolution. While members of the gentry saw property in land as originating in the grant of land by a sovereign (king, federal government, state legislature, Indian sachem) and subject to transmission through sale of legal title, frontier farmers insisted that property was created by the labor that improved the land. They believed that independent proprietorship was the natural status of free men, and that as long as unimproved land existed, everyone willing to improve it had a claim to a portion of it.[20]

Farmers on a handful of New York estates drew on these ideas about property in resisting landlord rule during the 1750s, 1760s, 1790s, and 1810s.[21] Moreover, they put agrarian concepts into everyday practice well into the nineteenth century. Squatting was common on New York's estates during the eighteenth century, and squatters believed that their improving occupation gave them a legitimate claim to the soil. In 1785, Harmon Best, a squatter, found that Daniel Moon had bought the farm he had occupied and partially improved. When Moon moved in, Best threatened to eject him "unless I will give him one hundred dollars for his possession." Population growth and landlord pressure made squatting less common after 1790, but tenants continued to hunt, fish, run their stock, and cut timber on unoccupied land, in accordance with the widespread notion that natural resources on unimproved land belonged to those who expended the labor to take them.[22]

During the 1820s and 1830s, however, economic change in the leasehold communities began to weaken these agrarian traditions. Improved roads and the growth of manufacturing villages and small-scale industries provided new markets, and leasehold farmers responded by increasing their production for sale. At the same time, soil depletion and competition from western wheat-growing areas compelled leasehold farmers to switch their focus from grain cultivation to sheep raising and dairying. New agricultural practices allowed the majority of tenants to achieve a new level of comfort, as increased production for market allowed them to make unprecedented amounts of money and gave them access to new consumer goods. But rising land prices and the turn toward sheep and dairy farming made farming more capital intensive. Young men found it harder to accumulate the land, equipment, buildings, and livestock needed to begin farming on their own.[23] As a result, wage labor and subtenancy became important features of the leasehold economy. By 1850, one-third of farm families in the leasehold towns of Westerlo and Roxbury had at least one live-in servant or laborer.[24]

These developments conspired to create a crisis on the common lands of the estates. Population growth after 1780 simultaneously reduced the area open to expropriation of timber, game, and mast and increased the number of people taking those resources. Steamboat lines and rural manufacturers proliferated, creating an enormous new demand for wood, bark, and charcoal. The result, according to David Ellis, was the "ruthless destruction" of local forests. In this context, individuals' right to take resources from common lands became charged with controversy. Numerous tenants bought timber lots to assure themselves of a wood supply, only to become embroiled in conflict with neighbors who cut at will. Similar conflicts emerged over the grazing of livestock. Beginning in the first decade of the nineteenth century, residents flooded town clerks with complaints about neighbors' livestock breaking into their crop enclosures. Some tenants demanded legal restrictions on the use of the commons, but failed to effect consensus on the issue. Between 1804 and 1828, the Rensselaerville town meeting debated on a yearly basis whether to allow sheep, hogs, and cattle to roam at large, with no clear policy emerging. Ordinances prohibiting the roaming of hogs in one year were repealed in the next, only to be reinstated again a few years later. Rensselaerville permanently outlawed the roaming of hogs, horses, sheep, and horned cattle in 1828; other towns continued to allow it, with varying restrictions, into the 1850s.[25]

New York's leasehold tenants thus began a campaign against landlord domination as new forms of inequality appeared and as agrarian traditions pitted neighbor against neighbor. Tenants' vision of free labor bore the marks of these circumstances. Anti-renters embraced agrarian notions of freedom, but omitted earlier challenges to dominant conceptions of property. Like earlier agrarians, they linked freedom to property ownership, economic independence, security, and control over the products of their labor. Drawing on a widespread rural and working-class belief in the labor theory of value, they argued that freedom rested on each producer's ability to control the fruits of his labor. Joseph Hoag of Delaware County wrote that "The idea that a man must be compelled to toil, and still be

under the stern necessity of remitting to another the effects of his labors
to support him in opulence and luxury, is revolting to every principle of
American liberty."[26] Freedom also depended on economic security. Again
and again, anti-renters denounced the landlords' power of eviction, which
robbed them of a life's labor and the privilege of being rooted in a familiar place, connected to kin and community. Eviction, one militant wrote,
deprived tenants of "their only means of subsistence and [left] them to
become wandering vagrants in the country."[27]

Free labor also meant freedom to trade. Anti-renters condemned the
quarter sale—a lease provision that allowed landlords to take a portion of
the proceeds (usually a quarter) when a tenant sold his farm. This practice, they believed, infringed on their right to sell the products of their
labor. As one farmer put it, "the tenants have not the right to trade on their
own earnings." Similarly, militants on Livingston Manor denounced as
"unrepublican" the provisions in their leases that required them to sell
their surplus at the proprietor's stores and to take their grain to the landlord's mills. They demanded the right to trade where they wished. In defending free trade, the anti-renters celebrated active commerce, but not
the speculative risk and specialized division of labor that increasingly
marked northern commercial life. Instead, they sought a social order in
which producers directly exchanged the products of their labor with one
another. A Columbia County farmer wrote to *Young America*, a newspaper of the New York City land reform movement, that with the impend-
ing triumph of the anti-renters, "your mechanics in the cities might soon
get village sites, where they could come among us and manufacture their
articles, for which we would exchange our produce, saving between us the
expenses of *rent* and *transportation*."[28]

For the anti-renters, any threat to these basic economic freedoms endangered other liberties. The landlords' claim to the fruits of tenants' toil
created large concentrations of wealth which, in turn, gave them unnatural power over their subordinates. One casualty of this imbalance was
cultural equality and the right to dignity. One militant complained that
tenants were "ground down . . . below the dignity of serfs. Their farms,
their hard earnings, their all, are held at the option of a man brought up
in luxury." Because of their powerlessness, leasehold farmers "must plod
their way yearly with trembling steps and enter the halls of his lordship,
bending and bowing . . . to solicit the favor of enjoying their property."[29]
This inequality also endangered republican government. Tenant activists
drew on republican fears of concentrated wealth to argue that the landlords' wealth and power gave them the means to suborn legislators and

to subordinate tenants to their political will. Ejection, one militant wrote, was "a powerful instrument in the hands of one man for bending his fellow man to his own will, and making him subserve his own selfish, political, or mercenary interest."[30]

Thus the anti-renters believed that freedom depended on the ability of each producer to control the products of his toil. This essential freedom secured all others: economic security, freedom to trade, cultural equality, and political independence. It, in turn, depended on universal, individual, freehold landownership. The anti-renters of Delaware County put it well: "In all free governments, it is essential that the people themselves be free. They cannot be free unless independent. . . . To be completely sovereign, they must individually be the lords of the soil they occupy, and hold it freely, subject to no superior but the people themselves." Universal landownership would place all who labored on an equal footing, freeing them from the personal humiliations that were the lot of the poor. It would guarantee to all who labored dignity and prosperity, and a place in a vibrant commercial economy—an economy defined by simple exchange between producers. This class equality rested on the subordination of women and children. The anti-renters, in defending the rights of citizens and producers, defined both of those categories as exclusively male. They sought to do away with "unnatural" class hierarchies, and to retain the "natural" hierarchies of sex and age. Women and children would remain subordinated to male householders; the householders themselves would meet one another in the marketplace and in politics as equals, without a superior class to expropriate the products of their labor or control their votes.[31]

This social vision drew heavily on Revolutionary-era beliefs that free men were ordained by God to be independent proprietors, and it injected a troubling element into antebellum political debate. The Democrats, and the Jeffersonians before them, had long insisted that widespread landownership best secured individual freedom. But neither party had insisted that *all* laborers own the means of production. With important constituencies among urban workingmen and small employers, few Democratic leaders dared proclaim that the propertyless were not free. Instead, both the Jeffersonians and the Jacksonians pursued policies that sought to make property ownership as widespread as possible. To do more would be to throw into question the existing definition of property.[32] Yet the anti-renters baldly insisted that to be propertyless was to be unfree and that in a free society all men must own land. This clearly implied that great land holdings had no place in a free society—for if all men owned land, who would labor on such estates?

Yet only a minority of anti-renters embraced fully the implications of their own definition of freedom. Where their agrarian forebears had based their challenge to great estates on a rival conception of property, most insurgents embraced the prevailing belief that property in land derived from legal title that could be traced to a grant from the sovereign. They did challenge their landlords' right to the land by claiming that estate titles were fraudulent and by demanding a law enabling them to challenge those titles in court. In addition, they called for laws taxing landlords' rent income and abolishing the proprietors' right to seize tenants' personal property in payment for rent. The challenge to landlords' titles posed a bold threat to the leasehold system, but it could not ensure universal access to land. Although tenants denounced the leasehold system for allowing a few men to expropriate the labor of thousands of producers, few challenged the definitions of property that made such land holdings possible. Thus "Clermont" of Columbia County stated that large landed estates "tend . . . to make the many . . . serfs and vassals of the few," but insisted that the tenants "do not ask for a division of lands. They say if the lords do, in fact, *own* the lands as they claim, they alone have a right to dispose of them."[33]

The chasm between the anti-renters' social vision and their specific proposals resulted from tenants' failure to come to terms with agrarian traditions in the context of disappearing common lands and growing wage labor and subtenancy in the leasehold communities. Amidst endemic conflict between tenant owners of unimproved land and neighbors who extracted resources from those lands, any suggestion that labor could establish a right to land risked dividing the movement. Such an idea would also sit uncomfortably with the growth of alienated labor in the leasehold towns. Leasehold militants kept an unbroken silence over whether local conditions violated their social vision. When they invoked the labor theory of value to defend their improvements from the claims of the landlords, the only productive labor they recognized was that of leaseholders. The muscle and sweat of hired laborers that helped create those improvements went unacknowledged. The question of whether laborers had a claim to the products of their labor, or whether their relationship to their employers undermined the dignity and equality due them as citizens, went unasked. Tenants entered their struggle with the landlord when they were poised uncomfortably between older, agrarian ideals and newer realities. As a consequence, their social vision remained ambiguous, evasive, and contradictory.

Nonetheless, the tenants' movement posed a formidable challenge to the property rights of the landlords and to an established system of labor.

As such, it inspired fierce opposition from two factions in New York politics: the conservative Whigs and radical Democrats (also known as Barnburners). Landlords had long been important constituents in both groups, and leaders of these factions embraced in principle what landlords and tenants had practiced until recently: contractual, market-based intercourse infused with hierarchy and deference. Daniel Dewey Barnard, the most prominent defender of the leasehold among the Whigs, denounced the idea that men were naturally equal in anything except civil and political rights. Society, he argued, was an organic entity, with different orders held together by reciprocal obligations and common purpose. At the height of the Anti-Rent Wars, he wrote that "there must be orders in society, and diversity of employment, and diversity of condition; and there must be a State, and subjects of the State, and somebody to command and somebody to obey."[34] James Fenimore Cooper, a Democrat and the most prominent defender of the landlords, could not have agreed more. In 1838, a year before the tenants' movement began, he launched a full-scale defense of hierarchy and deference. In a natural social order, he argued, "equality of condition is rendered impossible. One man must labor, while another may live luxuriously on his means; one has leisure and opportunity to cultivate his tastes, to increase his information, and to refine his habits, while another is compelled to toil, that he may live. One is reduced to serve, while another commands." He insisted that Americans learn to defer to the superior knowledge and refinement of gentlemen.[35] After the outbreak of tenant resistance, Cooper published the *Littlepage Manuscripts*, a fictional trilogy that depicted the leasehold system as a natural and beneficent hierarchy. When tenants complained that leasehold tenures denied them the equality due to citizens, Cooper responded that "the column of society must have its capital as well as its base." The relationship between landlords and tenants was "entirely natural and salutary," for it promoted the prosperity of poor farmers, advanced the "civilization" of the country, and encouraged progress in agriculture. Such beneficence sprung from the willingness of wealthy landlords to devote "their money, knowledge, liberality, feelings, and leisure" to the improvement of the soil.[36]

Cooper, Barnard, and others combined this organic vision with a staunch commitment to capitalist progress. They uniformly championed commercial and industrial growth, viewing the leasehold system as essential to a healthy commercial economy. They saw no tension between liberal political economy and a hierarchical social order; indeed, they believed the one arose inevitably from the other. Like his fellow Democrats, Cooper embraced a liberal social vision in which legal and political equals strove to accumulate wealth in a competitive free market. But where most Democrats believed that this order would result in a rough social equality among all white men, Cooper argued that innate differences of talent and industry would produce different degrees of wealth, education, and cultivation. And these, in turn, created orders in society, each with its own duties and obligations.[37] Daniel Dewey Barnard also rooted his defense of hierarchy in the liberal fundamentals of private property, freedom of contract, and economic competition.[38] Along with Cooper and other conservatives, he believed that the main danger of the anti-rent movement lay in its threat to these fundamentals. He denounced the tenants' efforts as "a CONCERTED, PRACTICAL REPUDIATION of . . . rents, and of the obligations, or contracts, under which they are payable." Their principles, he warned, "strike directly, not at one kind of property, but at all property," thereby endangering agricultural, commercial, and industrial progress.[39]

The landlords' allies shared their vision of an organic, hierarchical society rooted in liberal economics with other northern elites—notably large-scale manufacturers. Heirs to the Federalists' organicism and fear of disorder, these later paternalists tied their forebears' ideas to a firmer faith in economic competition and social mobility, and often to evangelical Protestantism. They sought to turn the institutions of a rapidly expanding capitalist economy into academies of order. Theirs was a distinctive, patrician vision of capitalist development, one that differed significantly from the more egalitarian vision espoused by entrepreneurial master artisans and small manufacturers.[40]

At the heart of this patrician capitalism lay a definition of free labor that affirmed the legal equality of the laborer while allowing for authoritarian relations between classes. Drawing on employment-law doctrines recently formulated by the courts, the defenders of the leasehold system held that any labor relationship entered into voluntarily was both free and binding. The judiciary committee of the 1844 state assembly insisted that despite the "objectionable" nature of certain provisions of the leases, the legislature could do nothing about them. Landlords and tenants "have agreed and consented to them, and no matter how onerous the burthen may be, they have no right to expect relief at the hands of the State from a contract voluntarily entered into." Behind this reasoning lay a distinct notion: that freedom amounted to the formal equality between the parties to a contract. As Daniel Dewey Barnard argued, landlords and tenants "stood upon their contracts, and, as contracting parties, they stood before the law of the land upon a footing of perfect civic equality." Liberty was to be measured not by the conditions of labor or the degree of personal autonomy possible within a set of social relations but by the ability of an individual to enter into an agreement without coercion.[41]

Despite the opposition of conservatives, the anti-renters found numerous allies in the major political parties and among reformers. Liberal Whigs, conservative Democrats (also called Hunkers), and activists from the National Reform Association, a land reform organization based in the New York City journeymen's movement, all offered support. Help from all three groups increased dramatically after 1844, when the anti-renters' entry into electoral politics gave them significant clout at the ballot box. These allies did not simply bring the anti-renters' vision of free labor into politics. Instead, they reshaped that vision to conform to the ideologies and pragmatic needs of their organizations. The result was not one anti-rent vision of free labor, but three.

One of the tenants' most popular allies was Thomas Ainge Devyr, an Irish expatriate, former radical Democratic editor, and founding member of the National Reform Association. Devyr, who served as editor of the anti-rent *Albany Freeholder* in 1845 and 1846, linked the insurgents' desire for universal landownership to the National Reformers' attack on a cornerstone of capitalist social relations—private property in land. Natural law, he argued, had bequeathed to every man a natural right to as much land as he and his family could till. He insisted that land was not a commodity but was God's gift to humanity, to be used, but never owned, by its cultivators. Neither the "book of Nature or the Book of God," he wrote, "sanctions that 'right of property' from which flows all this human suffering." Nature had supplied all people "with the wants of humanity" and "the hands of humanity to win for themselves a lodging and a bed and board. . . . *Here* is the hungry belly, and the arm willing to work. *There* is the soil, mutely courting the hand of cultivation."[42]

Behind Devyr's attack on private property in land lay an agrarian version of Adam Smith's economics. "The law of supply and demand," he insisted, "is a most harmonious *and regulating* law, provided man has the option of 'supplying' his wants from the soil." Once land was guaranteed to all, individuals would be free to accumulate commodities—the products of human labor—but not land. Individual landholdings would be limited to the amount a single family could till. A free market under these circumstances would turn all of society into "one vast system of cooperation" that would benefit all producers.[43] Devyr's social vision provided no analysis of exploitation through wage labor; indeed, he insisted that wage labor would be beneficial once land was guaranteed to all. He joined tenant militants in keeping silent regarding wage labor and subtenancy in the leasehold district. But on the question of landed property, he translated the tenants' desire for land, security, and exchange into a radical vision of free labor premised on a "natural right" to the soil.[44]

Devyr and his fellow National Reformers won the support of a significant minority of anti-renters. In 1844, anti-rent leader John J. Gallup welcomed the National Reformers' idea of a "union" of the two movements: "You will find hearty cooperation in this whole region." Between 1845 and 1851, over a dozen town anti-rent associations formally affiliated with the New York City reformers. Many more supported the radicals' ideas without joining their organization. Scores of letters to the anti-rent and National Reform press endorsed the notion that each citizen had a natural right to the land. Numerous meetings demanded a constitutional limit on the size of individual landholdings as well as the distribution of the public domain in small lots, free of charge, to landless settlers.[45] Unlike most anti-renters, these militants embraced and extended the agrarianism of the Revolutionary-era back-country rebels.

Like Devyr, the Whig and Democratic activists who supported the anti-renters shared their constituents' desire to abolish what they saw as an anachronistic and unrepublican labor system. But they also sought to wean those constituents from the contagion of "agrarianism." These activists hailed from the liberal faction of the Whigs and conservative wing of the Democrats, factions that John Ashworth describes as constituting a "liberal capitalist consensus" in antebellum politics. Their representatives consistently sought to tie the anti-renters' aspirations to a vision of society in which private property, economic competition, and social mobility created boundless economic progress. Just as important, the Whigs among these politicians began to embrace the antislavery cause when they took up the anti-rent banner.[46] As they engaged in both struggles, these politicians began to forge a new, syncretic vision of free labor.

All party allies concurred in the anti-renters' equation of landownership and freedom. Ira Harris, a liberal Whig who represented the anti-renters in the state legislature, declared that "in proportion as the land . . . is distributed among the people, that people and that country are free."[47] Like their constituents, these leaders believed that landownership would provide the cultivators of the soil with control over the fruits of their labor, economic security, individual autonomy, dignity, and political independence.[48] They insisted, however, that broad-based ownership derived from a competitive market economy, not from agrarian reform. The main evil of the leasehold system, they agreed, was that it stifled individual initiative, undermining productivity and economic progress. Robert Watson, an anti-rent legislator allied with the Democrats, argued that insecurity of tenure and the quarter-sale destroyed the natural tendency of people to promote the public good by pursuing private gain. Rather than enriching their soil through careful cultivation, they "taxed it to the uppermost. . . . No works of utility, improvement, and of elegance will be constructed with an idea of being enlarged hereafter."[49] Just as distressing was the tendency of the leasehold to hinder what one legislative committee called "a free exchange of the lands." As a result, the committee complained, leasehold tenures "tend to restrain labor from seeking, through shifting employments, its most advantageous application, and to repress the disposition, the habit, and the opportunities of enterprise."[50]

According to party reformers, individual enterprise and the free flow of land and labor to their most efficient uses would best ensure an extensive distribution of land. Watson offered the anti-renters a vision of free labor in which young, landless men would work as laborers in order to accumulate the capital with which to begin farming on their own. These early years would instill industry, economy, and sobriety in a young man, for "every dollar he can spare will go to pay for his farm." Once he purchased a homestead, security of property would spur his energies: "the young freeholder is constantly . . . making improvements upon his farm, for he knows he is providing a happy home for himself and his children."[51] Harris also insisted that competition and social mobility were the sole legitimate mechanisms for distributing land. "The real estate of a country," he said, "should be left free to center, where it sooner or later will, if competition and enterprise are left free to operate unobstructed, in the hands of the industrious and prudent. Every attempt to interrupt this natural course of things is contrary to the true interests of a *republican* community."[52]

This formulation honored the primary concerns of manor tenants— control over the fruits of their labor, economic security, dignity, personal autonomy, and political independence. But Harris and Watson subordinated these aspirations to the larger objectives of economic competition, social mobility, and free enterprise. Thus they transformed the anti-renters' conception of freedom as land, security, equality, and exchange into the freedom to compete and prosper in a buoyant capitalist economy. In their vision, nothing was guaranteed but the freedom then being endorsed by the courts and by economic elites: civic equality, self-ownership, and control over one's body and labor.[53]

Reformist Whigs and Democrats thus placed the anti-renters' vision of free labor on the narrowest possible foundation. They envisioned a world in which economic security and the full enjoyment of the fruits of one's labor were the rewards of hard work and social mobility, not rights guaranteed to all producers. Ira Harris's ideal that land should concentrate in the hands of the "industrious and prudent" carried the corollary that some producers would be landless, albeit because of their own shortcomings.

These assumptions soon translated into policy. In 1846, the state legislature acceded to two of the anti-renters' demands, passing laws taxing landlords' rent income and abolishing their right to seize tenants' personal property as payment for rent. The bills applied only to lands leased for more than ten years, thus indemnifying a large number of leasehold estates from their provisions. The committee that drafted these bills rejected the anti-renters' belief that any domination of one class by another violated American freedom. "The most objectionable feature" of landlord-tenant relations, they wrote, was not that they allowed some citizens to expropriate the fruit of the other citizens' labor, but that they "are perpetual." Short-term leases, on the other hand, were adapted "to the peculiar and temporary circumstances of the parties"; as such, they "no doubt exist beneficially." Where anti-renters envisioned a society in which every man worked for himself on his own land, the committee made clear that the relationship of landlord and tenant, employer and employee, was not in itself oppressive. What saved it from being so was the promise of social mobility.[54]

This limited conception of freedom also contained an expanded vision of capitalist development. Robert Watson, Ira Harris, and their Whig and Democratic colleagues sought to make individual landholding as widespread as possible, and insisted that unbridled capitalism best served that aim, rather than concentrating the soil in a few hands. Through this formulation, reformers wedded the anti-renters' desire for a society of freeholders to a belief that social mobility would solve economic inequality and a faith in the distributive powers of a capitalist economy. They sought to link popular defenses of producers' rights to a conviction that equality, prosperity, and republican government would best be preserved by the emerging capitalist economy. This was not entirely a new synthesis; we can see an early version of it in the thinking of the Jeffersonian Republicans.[55] But it continued to be re-created in social and ideological conflict as entrepreneurs and political leaders justified capitalist social relations to audiences championing producers' rights. Such conflicts were common in the decades before the Civil War. Only a decade before, urban master artisans had forged a similar synthesis to defend their new workshop practices from the challenges of an emerging labor movement. These ideas provided a powerful challenge to conservatives' celebration of hierarchy, and would soon become the ideological centerpiece of the new Republican party—their ideology of free labor.[56]

Whig and Democratic leaders also linked this conception of freedom to new policy initiatives. In 1845 and 1846, now competing with the National Reform Association for control of the tenants' movement, they appropriated the radicals' defense of a "natural right" to the soil. But they made it safe for capitalist enterprise by applying it not to land already held as private property but to the vast public lands of the West. As one Whig wrote, "man has a certain 'inalienable right,' not only to 'life, liberty, and the pursuit of happiness,' but also to a sufficiency of the common elements, by God created *and not already appropriated* to render the first inalienable right operative."[57] By 1846, every anti-rent legislator had endorsed one of several proposals to distribute the public lands of the West in small lots to settlers, at minimal or no charge. None of these proposals restricted future sales or the accumulation of large tracts of the public domain. Along with urban and western party politicians, these leaders outlined what would become another central element of the Republican party program: the Homestead Act.[58]

This cautious vision of free labor was far from triumphant in the 1840s. Conservatives challenged reformers' power in both parties, while National Reformers vied with them for the support of the tenantry. Most tenants supported Harris, Watson, and their fellow reformers because of their political effectiveness; their social vision overlapped only partly with that of their leaders. The vast majority of tenants concurred in the Whigs' and Democrats' conception of land as a commodity; several defended the right of individuals to accumulate land without limit. "William Tell" of Rensselaer County ridiculed his fellow anti-renters' call for restrictions on individual accumulation of land. The majority of anti-renters, he argued, supported the right of a man to own any amount of property "accumulated through his own honest industry." But not a single militant publicly endorsed Harris's and Watson's belief that economic competition and social mobility would guarantee widespread access to land.[59]

The triumph of Whig and Democratic reformers came through political struggle, and can be attributed to two factors: superior political resources and the political conflict over slavery. In 1845 and 1846, Thomas Devyr broke with Whig and Democratic anti-renters and began a campaign to unite tenant militants and National Reformers in a new agrarian party. His campaign aroused the opposition of Hunkers and Whigs. Charles Bouton, the Hunker editor of the *Albany Freeholder*, fired Devyr for his political challenge, depriving him of the largest newspaper audience among tenants. Devyr formed the *Anti-Renter*, which proved a feeble rival to the *Freeholder*. In 1846, Devyr's supporters and other insurgents united in an effort for an independent anti-rent nomination for governor. Their efforts presented an obstacle to Ira Harris, who planned to use the anti-rent vote to elect John Young, a liberal Whig, for governor. Harris packed local anti-rent conventions with Whig regulars, assuring Young's nomination at the state convention. The National Reformers threw together a "Free Soil" ticket in the final days of the campaign, only to go down to defeat. Young triumphed in the November election, and Devyr, broke and demoralized, left for his former home on Long Island.[60]

Conservatives offered a far more formidable challenge to the reformers. Beginning in 1845, Barnburners and conservative Whigs in several counties created bipartisan "Law and Order" tickets in opposition to the anti-renters and their allies in the parties. Opposition spread to the state Whig party, where between 1846 and 1850 conservatives carried on a vitriolic campaign against the liberals' alliance with the anti-renters. When John Young won the anti-rent nomination for governor, conservative Whigs turned against him in the state election. James Watson Webb's *New York Courier and Enquirer* denounced Young's lukewarm support for anti-rentism as "the most bare-faced attempt at LEGISLATIVE ROBBERY—the most manifest outrage on vested rights, that has ever been brought forward in any civilized community." In 1850 the conservative revolt led to a permanent breach in the party. Backed by landlord money, conservatives pointed to the liberals' support for anti-rent, anti-slavery, and other reform causes as evidence of their desire to "dissolve the Union of the States," "prostrate all law and order in the dust," and "resol[ve] . . . society into its original elements." This campaign culminated in the Silver-Gray movement, which bolted the 1850 Whig convention and hastened the demise of the Whig party. The Silver Grays presented their ticket as the "Anti-Disunion Ticket. Anti-Abolition, Anti-Seward, Anti-Weed, Anti-Anti-Rent, Anti-Demagogueism."[61]

As this factional conflict peaked, the anti-rent movement fell into decline. Increased intraparty conflict convinced conservatives and reformers in both parties of the necessity of silencing the leasehold controversy. James Brooks, a New York City conservative, warned the 1848 Whig convention that the anti-rent excitement "was a two-edged sword, and it would cut whoever touched it." Politicians of all stripes agreed; from the end of the 1840s on, they carefully avoided taking a public stand on the issue. At the same time, the rural economy recovered from the depression of 1837–46, bringing renewed prosperity to the leasehold district. In the face of political stalemate and economic opportunity, large numbers of tenants turned to individual and market-oriented strategies for ensuring their independence. Tenants intensified their specialization in dairy and sheep raising and increased production for market, while engaging in powerful campaigns to outlaw the sale of alcohol and build wooden turnpikes. Growing numbers of tenants embraced an individual solution to the anti-rent conflict as well: they began buying their farms from the landlords. In 1852, the state anti-rent convention collapsed into partisan squabbling, and the *Albany Freeholder*, the last surviving anti-rent newspaper, closed its doors. The movement survived in a few scattered towns, but its power on the state and county level was at an end.[62]

The conception of free labor forged during the leasehold conflict survived the movement's collapse and decisively defeated the conservatives' social vision. Many of the key actors in this development were former tenant militants and their Whig allies. During the late 1840s and 1850s, the liberal Whigs' opposition to the westward spread of slavery won them increasing popular support in New York state. After 1855, the liberals helped form the Republican party, which gained control of the state legislature and the governorship in 1856. Former allies of the anti-renters like William Seward, Horace Greeley, and Ira Harris became key Republican leaders. On the local level, one-time agrarian activists figured prominently in founding the new party. In Delaware County, a tenant later recalled, the anti-renters "united with the old Whigs and the Abolitionists and formed a new party under the name of the Republican party." In Albany County, nearly a quarter of the delegates to Republican conventions during the 1850s had once been insurgents.[63] Their party, like the Whig and Democratic anti-rent leaders, embraced a conception of free labor that wedded petty proprietorship to vigorous capitalist development.

The end of the Anti-Rent Wars and the Republicans' rise to power marked the provisional triumph of one vision of "free labor" over several others. By the 1850s, the conservatives' celebration of hierarchy had been displaced by a new consensus that valued social mobility, vigorous enterprise, and a widespread distribution of property as the economic foundations of a free society. Even the judges who refused to entertain challenges to the landlords' titles subscribed to this new consensus. Justice Wright, in dismissing a suit against the owners of Livingston Manor, agreed that the leasehold system was "antagonistical to free institutions," "retard[ed] the accumulation of property," "paralyz[ed]" the energies of tenants, and undermined their "innate sense of independence."[64] Similarly, the major parties defeated the National Reformers' insistence on the natural right of each producer to an equal share of the land. These rival conceptions were not annihilated, however. Conservatives' vision of free labor as subordination sanctioned by contracts remained the centerpiece of labor law for the rest of the century, a product of the courts' application of the English law of master and servant to American labor relations.[65] And plebeian demands for an equal distribution of the land survived in labor circles, only to resurface after the Civil War.[66]

The anti-renters' hope for universal landownership went down to defeat as well, due partly to the ambivalence of its champions but mostly to the strength of its opponents. Leasehold militants had never made clear *how* they wished to achieve their society of freeholders. The fact that the majority embraced a conception of property that rested on paper title contributed to the failure of that vision. During the anti-rent wars, leasehold militants stood poised between an older, agrarian vision of free labor and newer conceptions more compatible with a capitalist social order. Thomas Devyr and the National Reformers offered new, noncapitalist ways to realize old dreams, and many embraced them. But the political power of the Hunkers, liberal Whigs, and Republicans determined the outcome. So did their need to retain the loyalty of tenants. During the 1840s and 1850s, a producer-friendly vision of capitalist development triumphed in New York's leasehold district.

The late 1840s and 1850s marked a critical era in the formation of northern discourses of free labor. The Anti-Rent Wars played a critical part in that process, both because of their extent and because of the national influence of New York's political leaders. More importantly, they exemplified a broader process in which militant farmers placed the land question at the center of political debate, forcing the major political parties to come to terms with their demands and their conception of free labor. The definitions of free labor and the contours and outcome of the struggle doubtless varied from place to place. But the experience of New York's leasehold district indicates that the vision of "free labor" that triumphed by 1860 was forged largely through political struggle, in which both farmers and politicians played a creative role.

Notes

1. Eric Foner, *Free Soil, Free Labor, Free Men: The Ideology of the Republican Party before the Civil War* (New York: Oxford University Press, 1995); Bruce Levine, *Half Slave and Half Free: The Roots of the Civil War* (New York: Hill and Wang, 1992); John Ash-

worth, "Free Labor, Slave Labor, and the Slave Power: Republicanism and the Republican Party in the 1850s," in Melvyn Stokes and Stephen Conway, eds., *The Market Revolution in America: Social, Political, and Religious Expressions, 1800–1880* (Charlottesville: University Press of Virginia, 1996), 128–46.

2. Robert J. Steinfeld, *The Invention of Free Labor: The Employment Relation in English and American Law and Culture, 1350–1870* (Chapel Hill: University of North Carolina Press, 1991); Christopher Tomlins, *Law, Labor, and Ideology in the Early American Republic* (New York: Cambridge University Press, 1993), 223–92, quotation on 225.

3. Sean Wilentz, *Chants Democratic: New York and the Rise of the American Working Class, 1788–1850* (New York: Oxford University Press, 1984), 145–254, 271–86, 299–389; Bruce Laurie, *Artisans into Workers: Labor in Nineteenth-Century America* (New York: Hill and Wang, 1989), 47–112; David Montgomery, *Citizen Worker: The Experience of Workers in the United States with Democracy and the Free Market during the Nineteenth Century* (New York: Cambridge University Press, 1994); Foner, *Free Soil*, ix–xxxix, 11–39.

4. The sole exception is Eric Foner, who examines the place of land and petty proprietorship in the thought of Republican party leaders. But since Foner's study focuses on political leaders, it understandably does not discuss the actions and beliefs of farmers themselves, or their impact on the ideology of free labor. Nor does it examine the impact of the land question on Republican ideology, except insofar as it served Republican leaders' ideas about social mobility and wage labor (Foner, *Free Soil*).

5. Ibid.; Ashworth, "Free Labor," 133–38.

6. See, for example, Paul Wallace Gates, *The Farmer's Age: Agriculture, 1815–1860* (New York: Holt, Reinhart, 1960); Gates, *Fifty Million Acres: Conflicts over Kansas Land Policy, 1854–1890* (Ithaca: Cornell University Press, 1954); Gates, *History of Public Land Law Development* (Washington, D.C.: Government Printing Office, 1968); Allan G. Bogue, "The Iowa Claim Clubs: Symbol and Substance," *Mississippi Valley Historical Review* 45 (1958–59): 231–53; Paul Evans, *The Holland Land Company* (Buffalo: Erie County Historical Society, 1924); Charles Brooks, *Frontier Settlement and Market Revolution: The Holland Land Purchase* (Ithaca: Cornell University Press, 1996); Roy Robbins, *Our Landed Heritage: The Public Domain, 1776–1936* (Princeton: Princeton University Press, 1942).

7. See especially Christopher Clark, *The Roots of Rural Capitalism: Western Massachusetts, 1780–1860* (Ithaca: Cornell University Press, 1990); Winifred Barr Rothenberg, *From Market-Places to a Market Economy: The Transformation of Rural Massachusetts, 1750–1850* (Chicago: University of Chicago Press, 1992); Allan Kulikoff, *The Agrarian Origins of American Capitalism* (Charlottesville: University Press of Virginia, 1992), 13–95; Jonathan Prude, *The Coming of Industrial Order: Town and Factory Life in Rural Massachusetts, 1810–1860* (New York: Cambridge University Press, 1985); Robert A. Gross, "Culture and Cultivation: Agriculture and Society in Thoreau's Concord," *Journal of American History* 69 (1982): 42–61.

8. U.S. Department of Commerce, Bureau of the Census, *Statistical History of the United States, from Colonial Times to the Present* (reprint, Stamford, Conn.: Fairfield Publishers, n.d.), 74. The concept of "economically active" was constructed in such a way as to render the labor of most women and children invisible, and these figures reflect those exclusions. See Jeanne Boydston, *Home and Work: Housework, Wages, and the Ideology of Labor in the Early Republic* (New York: Oxford University Press, 1990).

9. Wilentz, *Chants Democratic*; Helene Sara Zahler, *Eastern Workingmen and National Land Policy, 1829–1862* (New York: Columbia University Press, 1941); Leon Fink, *Workingmen's Democracy: The Knights of Labor and American Politics* (Urbana: University of Illinois Press, 1983), esp. 3–17; Lawrence Goodwyn, *Democratic Promise: The Populist Moment in America* (New York: Oxford University Press, 1976).

10. Wilentz, *Chants Democratic*; Foner, *Free Soil*, 12–15, 31, 38; Montgomery, *Citizen Worker*, 58, 71, 144–45.

11. Jean H. Baker, *Affairs of Party: The Political Culture of Northern Democrats in the Mid-Nineteenth Century* (Ithaca: Cornell University Press, 1983), 21–22, 23–24, 261–354; Joel Silbey, *The American Political Nation, 1838–1893* (Stanford, Calif.: Stanford University Press, 1991), 74, 127–28.

12. Amy Bridges, *A City in the Republic: Antebellum New York and the Origins of Machine Politics* (1984; reprint, Ithaca: Cornell University Press, 1987); Silbey, *American Political Nation*; Harry L. Watson, *Jacksonian Politics and Community Conflict: The Emergence of the Second American Party System in Cumberland County, North Carolina* (Baton Rouge: Louisiana State University Press, 1981); Watson, *Liberty and Power: The Politics of Jacksonian America* (New York: Farrar, Straus, and Giroux, 1990); Ronald P. Formisano, *The Transformation of Political Culture: Massachusetts Parties, 1790s–1840s* (New York: Oxford University Press, 1983).

13. The sole exception to this is Ronald Formisano's brief but brilliant analysis of the ways in which the Massachusetts Democrats appropriated and transformed the Workingmen's Party's critique of concentrated economic power. See Formisano, *Transformation of Political Culture*, 271–75.

14. The standard studies of the Anti-Rent Wars are Henry Christman, *Tin Horns and Calico: A Decisive Episode in the Emergence of Democracy* (New York: Henry Holt, 1945); David Maldwyn Ellis, *Landlords and Farmers in the Hudson-Mohawk Region, 1790–1850* (Ithaca: Cornell University Press, 1946). See also John Reeve Huston, "Land and Freedom: The Anti-Rent Wars, Jacksonian Politics, and the Contest over Free Labor in New York, 1785–1865" (Ph.D. dissertation, Yale University, 1994).

15. On farmers' struggles for land, see n. 6 above. On farmers' and workers' efforts to free themselves from patrician domination, see Wilentz, *Chants Democratic*, 23–103; Montgomery, *Citizen Worker*, 13–51; Alan Taylor, "Agrarian Independence: Northern Land Rioters after the Revolution," in Alfred F. Young, ed., *Beyond the American Revolution: Explorations in the History of American Radicalism* (DeKalb: Northern Illinois University Press, 1993); Taylor, *Liberty Men and Great Proprietors: The Revolutionary Settlement on the Maine Frontier, 1760–1820* (Chapel Hill: University of North Carolina Press, 1990).

16. Clark, *Roots of Rural Capitalism*; Prude, *Coming of Industrial Order*; Gross, "Culture and Cultivation."

17. Anthony (?) to Abraham Ten Broeck, 13 Sept. 1782, box 53, folder 6, Van Rensselaer Manor Papers, New York State Library, Manuscripts Division, Albany, N.Y.; *Albany Freeholder*, 30 April, 13 Aug., 17 Sept. 1845. On post-Revolutionary struggles for recognition of poor men's dignity and equality, see Gordon S. Wood, *The Radicalism of the American Revolution* (New York: Alfred A. Knopf, 1992), 231–43; Alfred F. Young, "George Roberts Twelves Hewes (1742–1840): A Boston Shoemaker and the Memory of the American Revolution," *William and Mary Quarterly*, 3d ser., 38 (1981): 561–62; Joyce Appleby, *Capitalism and a New Social Order: The Republican Vision of the*

1790s (New York: New York University Press, 1984), 51–78; Alfred F. Young, *The Democratic Republicans of New York: The Origins, 1763–1797* (Chapel Hill: University of North Carolina Press, 1964).

18. Ledgers A and B, Van Rensselaer Manor Rent Books, New York State Library, Manuscript Division, Albany, N.Y.; petition of Woodstock inhabitants to Robert R. Livingston, quoted in Alf Evers, *Woodstock: History of an American Town* (Woodstock, N.Y.: Overlook Press, 1987), 110; "Statement of Jonathan Brown in the case of James Aiken of Rensselaer County for Stephen Van Rensselaer," n.d., box 115, Van Rensselaer Manor Papers; Daniel Moon to Abraham Ten Broeck, 6 May 1785, folder 15, Ten Broeck Family Papers, Albany Institute of History and Art, Albany, N.Y.; John O. Gordon, *An Historical Sermon Preached in the Presbyterian Church, Rensselaerville, New York, July 2nd, 1876* (Albany: Van Benthysen and Sons, 1876), 12; William Bertrand Fink, "Stephen Van Rensselaer: The Last Patroon" (Ph.D. dissertation, Columbia University, 1950), 170–72.

19. Huston, "Land and Freedom," 242–312.

20. William Cronon, *Changes in the Land: Indians, Colonists, and the Ecology of New England* (New York: Hill and Wang, 1983), 56–57, 73, 77; Taylor, "Agrarian Independence," 222–25.

21. Taylor, "Agrarian Independence," 222–23; Huston, "Land and Freedom," 98–101.

22. Daniel Moon to Abraham Ten Broeck, 6 May 1785, Ten Broeck Family Papers; Abel French to Abraham Ten Broeck, 9 June 1806, ibid.; Van Rensselaer Rent Books, Book A, 759; Evers, *Woodstock*, 105, 160–70.

23. Leases on most leasehold estates were perpetual or long-term. On these estates, farmers had the right to sell their improvements; once the supply of unimproved tenant farms disappeared in the 1810s and 1820s, becoming an independent farmer meant buying the farm of a tenant. The purchaser, of course, would remain obligated to pay rent to the landlord.

24. Manuscript Federal Census, Population, Westerlo, Albany County, N.Y., 1850; ibid., Roxbury, Delaware County, N.Y., 1850; Martin Bruegel, "The Rise of a Market Society in the Rural Hudson Valley, 1780–1860" (Ph.D. dissertation, Cornell University, 1994), 14–15, 37–39, 117–213; George Holcolm Diary (typescript), 1830, Manuscripts Division, New York State Library, Albany, N.Y.; Work Record/Diary, Delhi, N.Y., 1830, Delaware County Historical Association, Delhi, N.Y. For a fuller discussion of these trends, see Huston, "Land and Freedom," chap. 3.

25. James H. Thompson Diary, 29 June, 19 July 1839, New York State Historical Association, Cooperstown, N.Y.; Rensselaerville Town Minute Book, 1795–1833, microfilm copy at New York State Archives, Albany, N.Y.; Town of Westerlo, Town Board Minutes, Apr. 4, 1815–Apr. 12, 1870, microfilm copy at New York State Archives; Town Book of the Town of Roxbury, vol. 1 (1799–1844), microfilm copy in the Delaware County Clerk's Office, Delhi, N.Y., 35–37; Evers, *Woodstock*, 126, 160–70; Ellis, *Landlords and Farmers*, 210.

26. *Albany Freeholder*, 13 Aug. 1845. On popular uses of the labor theory of value, see Wilentz, *Chants Democratic;* Taylor, "Agrarian Independence"; William Manning, *The Key of Liberty: The Life and Democratic Writings of William Manning, "A Laborer,"* *1747–1814*, ed. Sean Wilentz and Michael Merrill (Cambridge, Mass.: Harvard University Press, 1993).

27. *Albany Anti-Renter*, 4 Oct. 1845. See also ibid., 23 July 1845.

28. "A Tenant" to Sheriff Michael Artcher, 9 Sept. 1839, in *New York Senate Documents* 1840, No. 70:31; *Albany Freeholder*, 7 May, 27 Aug. 1845; *Young America*, 4 Jan. 1845.

29. *Albany Freeholder*, 25 Mar. 1846. See also ibid., 25 June, 13 and 27 Aug., 17 Sept. 1845, 1 Apr. 1846.

30. *Albany Anti-Renter*, 4 Oct. 1845.

31. *Albany Freeholder*, 25 Mar. 1846. For a full discussion of the gender, age, and racial exclusions in the anti-renters' vision of freedom, see Huston, "Land and Freedom," 336–48, 377–78, 381–82.

32. Drew R. McCoy, *The Elusive Republic: Political Economy in Jefferson's America* (Chapel Hill: University of North Carolina Press, 1980), 185–208; John Ashworth, *"Agrarians" and "Aristocrats": Party Political Ideology in the United States, 1837–1846* (Cambridge: Cambridge University Press, 1987), 21–52, 87–111.

33. *Albany Freeholder*, 27 Aug. 1845.

34. Daniel Dewey Barnard, *Man and the State: Social and Political* (New Haven: B. L. Hamlen, 1846), 46.

35. James Fenimore Cooper, *The American Democrat: A Treatise on Jacksonian Democracy* (1838; reprint, New York: Funk and Wagnalls, 1969), 39, 84–87.

36. James Fenimore Cooper, *The Chainbearer* (1845; reprint, New York: G. P. Putnam's Sons, n.d.), v; Cooper, *The Redskins, or, Indian and Injun* (1846; reprint, New York: G. P. Putnam's Sons, n.d.), x–xi.

37. Cooper, *American Democrat*, 39, 42–43, 70–76. On most Democrats' tendency to tie liberalism to an egalitarian social vision, see Ashworth, *"Agrarians" and "Aristocrats,"* 21–34.

38. Barnard, *Man and the State*, 17–22.

39. *New York Assembly Documents* 1844, No. 183:8–15; Daniel Dewey Barnard, *The "Anti-Rent" Movement and Outbreak in New York* (Albany: Weed and Parsons, 1846), 4, 15–17, 24.

40. On the social vision of large-scale manufacturers, see Prude, *Coming of Industrial Order*, 110–16; Cynthia J. Sheldon, *The Mills of Manayunk: Industrialization and Social Conflict in the Philadelphia Region, 1787–1837* (Baltimore: Johns Hopkins University Press, 1986), 100–115; Anthony F. C. Wallace, *Rockdale: The Growth of an American Village in the Early Industrial Revolution* (New York: W. W. Norton, 1972), 296–337, 350–471; T. W. Dyott, *An Exposition of Moral and Mental Labor, Established at the Glass Factory of Dyottville, in the County of Philadelphia* (Philadelphia: n.p., 1833); Robert F. Dalzell, *Enterprising Elite: The Boston Associates and the World They Made* (Cambridge, Mass.: Harvard University Press, 1987). On the social vision of the Federalists, see Linda K. Kerber, *Federalists in Dissent: Imagery and Ideology in Jeffersonian America* (Ithaca: Cornell University Press, 1970); James Roger Sharp, *American Politics in the Early Republic: The New Nation in Crisis* (New Haven: Yale University Press, 1993); Alan Taylor, *William Cooper's Town: Politics and Persuasion on the Frontier of the Early American Republic* (New York: Alfred A. Knopf, 1995). On the social vision of small manufacturers, see Wilentz, *Chants Democratic*, 35–42, 145–53, 271–86.

41. *New York Assembly Documents* 1844, No. 183:21; Barnard, *"Anti-Rent" Movement*, 14. On this definition of freedom in the courts, see Tomlins, *Law, Labor, and Ideology*, 223–92. For a dissenting view of the courts' construction of freedom in employment relations, see Steinfeld, *Invention of Free Labor*, 73–93, 138–72.

42. *Albany Freeholder*, 14 May 1845.

43. *Albany Freeholder*, 4 June 1845.

44. See ibid., 7, 14, 21 May, 18 June 1845; *Albany Anti-Renter*, 31 Jan. 1846.

45. Letter of John J. Gallup in *Young America*, 1 June 1844; *Albany Freeholder*, 17 Sept. 1845, 21 Jan., 25 Feb., 26 Aug. 1846; *Albany Anti-Renter*, 14, 21 Feb. 1846 and passim; *Young America*, 9, 23 Aug. 1845, 21, 28 Feb., 7 Mar. 1846 and passim, 1844–46; *Equal Rights Advocate*, 15 July 1846.

46. Listings for the New York Anti-Slavery Society in *Hoffman's Albany Directory*, 1839–46; Ira Harris, *Abolition of Distress for Rent: Remarks of Mr. Ira Harris of Albany, upon the Bill to Abolish Distress for Rent* (Albany, N.Y.: Freeholder, 1846), 23; Ashworth, "Agrarians" and "Aristocrats," 132–74.

47. Harris, *Abolition of Distress*, 5.

48. Ibid., 3, 20; speeches of Robert Watson in *Albany Freeholder*, 4 June, 9 July, 20 Aug. 1845; *New York Assembly Documents* 1846, No. 156:7.

49. *Albany Freeholder*, 28 May, 4 June 1845. See also *New York Assembly Documents* 1846, No. 156:7–8; Harris, *Abolition of Distress*.

50. *New York Assembly Documents* 1846, No. 156:7–8. See also Harris, *Abolition of Distress*; Watson's speeches in *Albany Freeholder*, 28 May, 4 June 1845.

51. *Albany Freeholder*, 20 Aug. 1845.

52. Harris, *Abolition of Distress*, 7.

53. Steinfeld, *Invention of Free Labor*, 73–93, 138–72.

54. *New York Assembly Documents* 1846, No. 156:7–8.

55. Appleby, *Capitalism and a New Social Order*.

56. Wilentz, *Chants Democratic*, 271–86; Laurie, *Artisans into Workers*, 51–57; Foner, *Free Soil*, 11–39.

57. *Albany Freeholder*, 17 Dec. 1845 (emphasis added).

58. *Equal Rights Advocate*, 19 Aug., 2, 9, 23 Dec. 1845; *Albany Freeholder*, 28 Jan., 24 June, 17, 30 Dec. 1846; *Albany Anti-Renter*, 14 Feb. 1846; *Young America*, 4 Oct. 1845; Harris, *Abolition of Distress*, 11.

59. *Albany Freeholder*, 14 May 1845 and passim, 1845–52.

60. Ibid., 6 Aug., 30 Sept. 1845, 14 Oct., 25 Nov. 1846; *Young America*, 9 Aug. 1845; *Albany Anti-Renter*, 17 Oct. 1846 and 1845–46, passim; *Equal Rights Advocate*, 7, 21 Oct., 11 Nov. 1846; Thomas Ainge Devyr, *The Odd Book of the Nineteenth Century, or, Chivalry in Modern Days, A Personal Record of Reform — Chiefly Land Reform, for the Last Fifty Years*, 2 vols. (n.p.: privately printed, 1882), 2:50–51; Christman, *Tin Horns and Calico*, 272–73.

61. *New York Courier and Enquirer*, reprinted in the *Equal Rights Advocate*, 5 Aug., 21 Oct., 25 Nov. 1846, and in *Albany Freeholder*, 14 Oct. 1846; *New York Express*, reprinted in *Equal Rights Advocate*, 21 Oct. 1846; *New York Tribune*, reprinted in *Albany Freeholder*, 11 Nov. 1846; *Albany Atlas*, 3 Nov. 1846; *Albany Freeholder*, 29 July, 12 Aug., 2 Sept. 1846, 6 Nov. 1850; *Albany Daily State Register*, 27 Mar., 2 Oct. 1850; DeAlva Stanwood Alexander, *A Political History of the State of New York*, 2 vols. (New York: Henry Holt, 1906), 2:145–58, 205–42.

62. *New-York Daily Tribune*, 16 Sept. 1848. For a discussion of political stalemate, economic and cultural change, and the decline of the anti-rent movement, see Huston, "Land and Freedom," 515–88.

63. H. J. Munger, "Reminiscences of the Anti-Rent Rebellion" (typescript), New-York Historical Association, Cooperstown, N.Y. Lists of delegates and officers at Republican conventions are drawn from the *Albany Evening Journal*, 1855–60. The lists

of convention delegates and officers were compared to lists of anti-rent activists in Albany County drawn from the *Albany Freeholder* and *Albany Anti-Renter,* 1845–46. For a full discussion of the relationship between the anti-renters and the New York Republicans, see Huston, "Land and Freedom," epilogue.

64. *Livingston Manor Case. Opinion of Mr. Justice Wright, in the Case of the People* agt. *Hermon Livingston. Supreme Court-Columbia County* (Hudson, N.Y.: Hudson Gazette, 1851), 17.

65. Tomlins, *Law, Labor, and Ideology,* 223–92.

66. Eric Foner, "Class, Ethnicity, and Radicalism in the Gilded Age: The Land League and Irish-America," in Foner, *Politics and Ideology in the Age of the Civil War* (New York: Oxford University Press, 1980), esp. 168–79; Ronald Yanosky, "Seeing the Cat: Henry George and the Rise of the Single-Tax Movement, 1879–1890" (Ph.D. dissertation, University of California at Berkeley, 1993).

Chapter 2

The "Fair Field" of the "Middle Ground"

Abolitionism, Labor Reform, and the Making of an Antislavery Bloc in Antebellum Massachusetts

BRUCE LAURIE

THE RISE OF Joseph Tinker Buckingham is the stuff of American legend. Born in 1779 to a shoemaker-turned-tavernkeeper in Windham, Connecticut, Buckingham started at the bottom of New England's social order. His father's death in 1782 left a brood of ten children and a scrappy but impoverished mother, who struggled to hold her family together until succumbing to an inevitable breakup, in which young Joseph and his siblings were bound out to relatives, friends, and farmers or mechanics. Joseph became the ward of a farmer until age sixteen, when he began an apprenticeship in a Walpole, New Hampshire, newspaper shop. With a toehold on the ladder of artisan respectability, he continued his apprenticeship in Greenfield, Massachusetts, and in 1800, like countless other aspiring artisans, left the provinces for the promise of bustling Boston. In the Hub City he worked first as a journeyman, sometimes as a superintendent, and always with the intent of setting up on his own. An autodidact with a flair for popular literature, admiration for Masonry, and love for controversy, he started several magazines that combined literary criticism and political opinion, only to see them fail, one by one; he did not enjoy his first success until the early 1820s when his *New England Galaxy and Masonic Journal* found a sustaining readership. The *Galaxy* gave Buckingham a name in publishing circles and a celebrity that drew him ever closer to the centers of political power. He formed a friendship with Daniel Webster, then an ambitious political newcomer, who helped arrange financial backing for Buckingham's *Boston Daily Courier*, which soon became the preferred organ of mechanics with National Republican politics. This stint as editor and part-owner of the *Courier* earned him the sobriquet of "the most independent editor of his time."[1]

Buckingham's independent spirit faced a severe test in spring 1832. For the second time in seven years, Boston's skilled workers went on strike for a ten-hour day. The story of this standout, as well its predecessor and successor in 1825 and 1835, has been told many times.[2] The city's wealthiest merchants crushed all three work stoppages, threatening to sack journeymen on strike and cancel the contracts of master craftsmen.[3] What concerns us here is the bearing of men like Buckingham amid the labor unrest. Master mechanics divided on the question of shortening the workday. One group lined up with the merchants against the journeymen, either because they feared for their jobs or because they shared the entrepreneurial ethos of their social betters.[4] James L. Homer, a publisher by trade and outspoken foe of unionism, told a gathering of mechanics in 1836 that the ten-hour movement was a "ridiculous project" out of place in the United States and in his shop, where journeymen put in fifteen-hour days, he said, "with apparent cheerfulness."[5]

Buckingham himself represented master craftsmen more skeptical of Homer's entrepreneurialism and supportive of the aggrieved journeymen.[6] During the 1832 strike he planted a reporter in an emergency meeting of merchants at the Exchange Coffee House, and then published his story. The "Spectator" asserted that the shipwrights' and caulkers' grievances "ought to be remedied." As he saw it, the dispute exposed the merchants' and shipowners' arrogance, unilateralism, and insistence on "imposing their own terms." Ridiculing the merchants' hypocrisy, jealousy of power, and "selfishness which blinds the intellect as well as hardens the heart," "Spectator" closed with a plebeian's interpretation of the uses of organization. "The spirit of association," he argued, "has extended itself to the industrious employments, and it is too late to repress it now. Merchants were regarded as a degraded class by the Federal Aristocracy. They raised themselves by *association*. The laboring class will accomplish . . . what the merchants have done—*by association*."[7]

This was not the first time Joseph Tinker Buckingham tangled with Brahmin Boston, nor would it be the last. In the early 1820s he had closely identified with the Middling Interest, a splinter group of populist mechanics and shopkeepers.[8] By the late 1820s he was back on good terms with political regulars, working with the National Republicans and then the Whigs. But as the brouhaha over the ten-hour movement indicates, Buckingham's stubborn independence made for stormy political relationships. His acceptance of the Whiggish order was always conditional; it strained to the breaking point in the mid-1840s, when he broke for good, not only with the Whigs but with the two-party system itself, joining the Free Soilers, then the American Republicans, and then the Republicans.[9]

What are we to make of Buckingham's politics? Two points should be underlined straightaway. First, while he was something of a political maverick, he was in no sense an eccentric out of step with Boston mechanics. A leading journalist, he was also a prominent member, then president, and finally official chronicler of the Massachusetts Charitable Mechanic Association, the most important fraternity of mechanics in the Bay State.[10] Kindred associations in other New England cities and towns consisted of master mechanics fully in accord with Buckingham's views on the ten-hour day.[11] Such mechanics shared an abiding belief in what David Montgomery aptly calls the "community-of-interest ideal."[12] Rooted in the fraternalism of craft production, this ideal attenuated the impact of the market on employer and employee by stressing mutuality of interest, reciprocity, and amicable resolution of differences through conciliation and compromise. Both sides were expected to respect one another, and observe each others' needs, as economic men and as husbands, fathers, and citizens. In the hothouse of Bay State industrialism, the community-of-interest ideal cut in two directions simultaneously. It drew master mechanics closer to journeymen and farther from merchant capitalists, who abused craftsmen and upset the harmony of their shops. Second, a large and swelling group of Bay State mechanics cut their activist teeth in the abolitionist movement of the 1830s or in the political antislavery movement of the 1840s. Such mechanics proved to be the most reliable friends of the ten-hour movement after the early 1840s. They infused antislavery politics in Massachusetts with the zeal and fervor of labor reform, creating a strong if unstable alliance with workers in the name of challenging the "lords of the lash and the lords of the loom."[13] Popular antislavery in Massachusetts, therefore, did not emerge inevitably from the inchoate antislavery feelings of free laborers and their allies; instead popular leaders deliberately cultivated such sentiment in the political fluidity of the late antebellum years. This essay discusses the evolving political outlook of such reformers, along with their project of building a popular political bloc on the foundation of labor reform and antislavery.

∂

The partnership of labor reform and antislavery in the mid-1840s was dimly perceptible a decade earlier. Though skilled workers belonged to antislavery societies in Bay State manufacturing towns, their unions were more concerned about conditions in mills and workshops. The New England Association of Farmers, Mechanics, and Other Working Men, and the Boston Trades' Union, the leading regional and local workers' organizations, respectively, drew membership with ambitious manifestos on labor reform and the ten-hour day, not with antislavery oratory. Labor's journalists and leaders were another matter. The *New England Artisan*, official organ of the New England Association in the early 1830s, reprinted abolitionist tracts, condemned anti-abolitionist violence, and considered itself "friends of the colored people," slave and free.[14] Slavery also troubled some readers of the labor press. "A Democrat" once assailed the well-dressed mob that beat William Lloyd Garrison as nothing more than "wine-soaked . . . turtle-fed aristocrats" and Southern sympathizers.[15]

It is difficult to gauge the impact of events like the Garrison mobbing, and harder still to assess the more subtle force of the written word. We simply do not know how individuals responded to arguments of the kind put forth by "Democrat." We can be more certain that his antislavery idiom was popular abolitionism's signal contribution to the abolitionist movement. In a follow-up letter written several months later in 1835, "Democrat" insisted that inequality in the North and South took different forms but traced to the common source of "natural sympathy between the Northern aristocrat and Southern planter," who shared an affinity for "luxury and pride" and for "slavery." He called aristocratic planters and haughty cotton manufacturers "lords of the lash and the lords of the loom," helping to coin the slogan that would become synonymous with popular antislavery in the 1840s.[16]

By that point the institutional framework of labor reform and political dissent had changed radically. The state's fledgling labor movement, severely weakened by the failed ten-hour drives in 1832 and 1835, simply vanished in the aftermath of the 1837 panic. Its abolitionist movement survived the lean years of the late 1830s but at the cost of unity. Tactical and strategic differences between moral suasionists and political activists split the movement in the late 1830s between the Garrisonians and the followers of Joshua Leavitt and others who formed the Liberty party. Movement stalwarts and fellow travelers associated with both causes likewise reassessed their positions. Joseph Buckingham, for instance, repudiated the ten-hour movement in the mid-1840s, if we can judge from his remarks to labor reformers working for a legal limitation on the workday in mills and factories. Buckingham told the reformers that he considered the hours of work a subject of bargaining between employer and employee, and not a matter to be settled by lawmakers.[17]

One of the more noteworthy features of this stage of the ten-hour movement, apart from the heavy involvement of women, was the support rendered by a faction of antislavery men in the Liberty party.[18] This party was never a monolithic force but a coalition of moral reformers dubious of the labor movement, on the one hand, and labor radicals perhaps best represented by Elizur Wright, Jr., on the other. Wright broke with the Garrisonians over their close association with the evangelical church and abstention from politics.[19] He also developed a social perspective and companionate strategy for broadening the base of the movement that further estranged him from Garrisonianism. Wright spoke a social idiom in contrast to Garrison's moralisms, and thought about abolitionism in political terms. He observed in the mid-1830s that the "head and tail of society have been strongly connected in acting the part of the South. Purse-proud aristocrats and penniless profligates," he said with the recent anti-abolitionist riots in mind, "have united in the work of opposing the abolitionists, each according to his ability and talents." He couldn't imagine "converting these parties, till we can change the interests of the one, and take away the grog of the other," which seemed unlikely in any event. As we might expect of a man in flight from his evangelical heritage, Wright didn't think much of intensified recruitment within the church; he likewise dismissed the upper class of "merchants, the politicians" as corrupted "by Southern trade and companion-ship." The movement would have better luck with the "honest, hard-handed, clear-headed, free laborers and mechanics of the North," who in concert with the "yeomanry," would "identify their interests with those of the slave." This "middle ground," he believed, was a "fair field."[20]

Wright shared the rural New England origins and evangelical background of many fellow abolitionists—but little else. Born in village Connecticut, he followed his father's footsteps to Yale with the intention of preparing for the ministry; instead, he sought work as a teacher after graduation in 1826, then in the early 1830s signed on as a field-worker for the American Anti-Slavery Society. From the late 1830s, he moved in several directions at once, evolving into an outspoken atheist, an expert in life insurance and amateur mathematician, and a spunky journalist, as well as political insurgent. Wright didn't let abolitionism restrict his social vision. And while he never strayed very far from the community-of-interest outlook he had articulated in the 1830s, he never fully embraced the bourgeois, free laborist beliefs of mainstream abolitionism, or the more sharply drawn class focus of the region's most radical workers. He stood poised between these positions in a kind of independent radicalism that proved more consonant with the perspective of labor radicals than with the entrepreneurialism of manufacturers.

Wright's was not the radicalism of instant conversion. His politics owed much to his initial religious impulses, relationships with politicians, and perhaps above all else personal experience in Europe in a period of political ferment. His Yankee Protestantism imparted a heartfelt idealism and profound animus for both the materialism of the idle rich and moral failings of the poor. Encounters with the sons of Southern planters at Yale reinforced this perspective, as did the social composition of the Boston mob that roughed up Garrison. In the wake of Garrison's beating, Wright, then secretary of the American Anti-Slavery Society, wrote off the upper and lower classes as hopelessly corrupted by material interests and alcohol, respectively, and urged the strategy of mobilizing the middling ranks against the "Slave Power." The young abolitionist at first thought of the "middle ground" in the literal social terms of mechanics and yeomen, but gradually expanded this vision to include the region's laboring people.[21] He began to think better of workers as abolitionist sentiment spread following the Garrison mobbing. If the modest influx of working people seemed cause for new optimism, so did the ten-hour movement of the 1830s. Although Wright opposed unionism at this time, the short-hours movement revealed that the same upper-class Bostonians with the strongest ties to the South were the most uncompromising opponents of the ten-hour day. The workers and master mechanics behind the movement, moreover, were not riffraff and rabble but perfectly respectable family men in fear of their own degradation.

This sympathetic image of workers became more compelling when Wright toured England in 1844. The past few years had been as hard on him as any other ordinary white American. The six-year depression had ruined myriad businesses and given workers a long dose of unemployment. Through it all Wright had no steady work, only intermittent jobs as a bookseller and journalist as well as a causal laborer reduced to farming a tract of rented scrub land in Dorchester to feed his needy family. He also translated LaFontaine's *Fables*. In hopes of pitching the book to a European audience he set sail in early 1844 on a stipend from Leavitt, landing first in Ireland and then moving on to England.[22] As his recent biographer correctly observes, Wright was strongly affected by the poverty of the Irish peasant and English industrial worker; he was also moved by the antislavery activity, ten-hour sentiment, and support for free trade coursing through England's industrial districts. At Coventry he heard the Irish Repealer Daniel O'Connell deliver an impassioned speech on the poverty of migrant laborers toiling in the "harvest-fields of England for the most scanty wages. . . . I did not look to see if there were streamlets on other faces," he wrote in his column for Leavitt's *Emancipator*, "I noticed afterwards there had been some on mine."[23] He later met a host of reformers and took special notice of patricians fighting for a legally prescribed ten-hour workday. These were formative experiences that deeply impressed Wright with new appreciation for the possibilities of coalition politics in the American antislavery movement, and for the value of following reform politics in England and on the Continent.[24] The Elizur Wright who returned to Boston in 1844 was a worldlier man of some political sophistication.

A key aspect of Wright's perspective in the 1840s has been misunderstood. A recent biographer correctly distinguishes him from the single-issue abolitionists, only to lump him together with middle-class free laborists. It is true, as this argument goes, that Wright was something of an American exceptionalist convinced the conditions in the United States made it possible to avoid the class strife of the Old World.[25] He would reconcile differences between capital and labor by erasing the line between employer and employee.[26]

It is one thing to demonstrate that Wright and his associates promoted class harmony, quite another to interpret this policy as middle-class radicalism. To associate Wright with such a tradition is to miss the larger implications of his thought. Many of Wright's companions wound up as middle-class radicals in the 1860s, and a decade later several ended their public life as conservative Democrats or Liberal Republicans. That said, it is essential to keep their own history in mind. In the 1840s and 1850s they were youngish men of modest means and dissident politics, not aging reformers disillusioned with the promise of Reconstruction, wary of labor militancy, and increasingly responsive to business interests. They simply lost faith in labor reform, that is, in replacing the institutions of mainstream capitalism with the institutions of cooperation.[27] In fact, not long after he returned from Europe, Wright used his newly formed *Boston Daily Chronotype* to distance himself from free laborism. Nowhere is this clearer than in his pronouncements on free trade. Again and again, Wright explained that his free trade stance did not make him an ally of Locofoco Democrats or their patrons in the mercantile community. He favored free trade because protectionism amounted to an unfair tax on the poor and middling classes, and represented an insidious industrial policy that inexorably concentrated capital in fewer hands. Tariffs protected capital, not labor, in his view. Nor did his belief in free trade extend to other spheres of economic activity; it did not mean license to do as one saw fit in the marketplace.[28]

Wright's tour of England helped convince him that unrestrained growth was the source of inequality, not its cure. He claimed as much in an 1844 piece that listed the lessons he drew from the struggle for the Factory Acts, the third and last of which was that "the production of wealth in a country, by no means insures a larger participation in the products of industry by the mass of the people."[29] What to do? He doubted that "Christianity . . . [would] soften the hearts of the capitalists, and incline them to give more than the market price for labor, either in the shape of increasing . . . wages or diminishing the work." Nor did he expect much from work stoppages. Strikes seldom succeeded and usually backfired, but at least pointed in the "right direction" insofar as they embodied organization.[30] Wright proposed several alternatives, from establishing cooperative workshops to land reform that would reduce competition and restore a measure of economic independence.[31]

A ten-hour law became the centerpiece of Wright's program for labor. Timing helps us explain why. His tacit support for a ten-hour day turned active and energetic in the mid-1840s partly because of the rebirth of the working-class movement on its behalf. Though women led the charge, the movement did include the very kind of men Wright hoped to enlist in the Liberty party. The fact that the women of milltown Massachusetts couldn't vote did not deter him; he had recently witnessed fellow British abolitionists plead their cause to workers who couldn't vote, either. Perhaps the English movement served as a kind of model for him. There is little doubt that the promise of greater leisure time for self-improvement held great appeal to a republican theorist like Wright, who as early as the 1830s had expressed fears of an ignorant and desperate proletariat. The English experience and closer contact with the highly literate women of Lowell alleviated such apprehensions and drew him into the fray. Finally, and in sharp contrast to free laborism, Wright had come around to the view that workers deserved the protection of government because of their dependence and vulnerability. As he argued in 1846, it was the duty of government "to see that the republic takes no damage. It is its business to look particularly after the weak."[32]

Abolitionist involvement in the ten-hour movement intensified perceptibly during the mid-1840s. Wright editorialized for factory regulation and addressed ten-hour groups in Lowell and other industrial towns, which then endorsed him for public office.[33] Such formal interchange and mutual support elevated the partnership between antislavery and labor reform to a much higher plane.

Most historians emphasize differences between Wright's Libertyites and the Free Soilers. Conventional wisdom treats the Liberty party as a minor political force unworthy of much attention, with a deep but narrow base in evangelical communities, and as more of an abolitionist than antislavery expression, that is, a party that would do away with slavery and not merely contain it. Free Soilers, according to this view, were a more formidable party with a broader following and a more pragmatic position on slavery, preferring containment over abolition. In addition, the Free Soilers are usually depicted as more critical of planters than sympathetic to slaves or free blacks.[34] Such distinctions make sense. Bay State Libertyites never garnered more than 10 percent of the vote, a puny proportion by comparison to the Free Soilers' impressive 25 percent. They did run better in evangelical villages than the Free Soilers, who had an advantage in rural towns regardless of religious preference.[35] In addition, Liberty men seem to have been friendlier to the slaves, though there is strong evidence that Massachusetts Free Soilers didn't share the racism of some of their New York colleagues.[36] Nonetheless, these parties had some common features. First, the Liberty party gradually established beachheads in industrial towns after 1844 thanks, as we have seen, to the work of such party leaders as Wright. This suggests that the party cleared a path for Free Soilism in the commonwealth's industrial places.[37] Second, and closely related to the first point, Free Soilism in Massachusetts mobilized plebeian voters because it spoke to both local and national issues at once. It addressed widespread fears of the Slave Power, as well as popular grievances of a political and economic sort. Free Soil lawmakers pushed for the secret ballot to protect citizen workers from the intimidations of Whiggish industrialists.[38] They called for political reapportionment that would strengthen rural towns at the expense of what party activists increasingly referred to as the Money Power in Boston, helpmate of the Slave Power.[39] At the political level, Free Soilism gave voice to the resentment felt by master craftsmen and small employers like Buckingham for merchant elites. Indeed, its antislavery spirit proved to be the most acceptable outlet for popular antipathy to the commonwealth's political and industrial establishment. More poignant still for our purposes, the party picked up where the laborist wing of the Libertyites left off on the legalization of the ten-hour day, forming the Coalition government that controlled or strongly influenced state politics from 1851 to 1853.[40] No other third party of the period invested such importance in shortening the workday.

By the same token no phase of the ten-hour movement was as complex as the one that spanned the late 1840s and early 1850s. It spread from Boston's machine shops to the corporate factories of Lowell and independent mills in smaller towns. The momentum swept in third-party men, first Free Soilers and Coalitionists and then American Republicans, who moved the battlefield from the workshop and factory to the campaign hustings and the General Court. By the mid-1850s, the ten-hour day was the norm in the old handicrafts, and in most metallurgical pursuits. The textile hands who had started the movement had to settle for an eleven-hour day and longer dinner breaks.[41]

Mass activity pulsated between 1846 and 1851 in eastern foundries and machine shops.[42] Boston machinists prevailed on the strength of a short strike in October 1851.[43] It was such an important milestone to the men at two large shops in South Boston that they marked its first anniversary with a procession, followed by a dinner and then a fireworks display.[44] Worcester machinists celebrated in a way that was congruent with the fraternalism of the city's master mechanics. Several years earlier, in 1844, a mechanics' meeting took note of sharpening unrest on shop floors over irregular work schedules and long hours, and endorsed a shorter and uniform workday. Regular hours, they reasoned, would make production runs more predictable, and fewer hours at work would improve the health and morals of employer and employee. Such masters "unanimously" adopted the "eleven hour system," and then in the early 1850s established a ten-hour day.[45] Ruggles, Nourse, Mason & Company, a leading maker of agricultural implements in Worcester, adopted the new policy in fall 1851, following a petition from their hands. The following February the workmen presented their employers with a rosewood clock "elaborately carved and elegantly furnished," with an engraving on the pendulum that read:

Ten Hours
presented to
Messrs. Ruggles, Nourse, Mason & Co.
By the Workmen in their Employ
Oct. 16, 1851[46]

Such flexible firms in Worcester and Boston, however, did not confer the ten-hour day as a gift with no strings attached. They gave with one hand and took with the other, tightening rules and increasing oversight. The "least idleness," it was said, constituted "sufficient reason for . . . discharge. No one is allowed to spend more than five minutes in conversation with any workman, and no unnecessary delay of any kind is permitted."[47]

It would be equally misleading to dismiss all ten-hour employers as calculating businessmen who responded to pressure from workers and then made them pay. A good number of them were ideologues genuinely enamored of the community-of-interest ideal. They believed that excessive toil did violence to body and soul; that it was possible and indeed desirable to reduce and possibly eliminate class tensions by meeting their workers halfway; that to strike the pose of the taskmaster was to reproduce the oppression of the plantation and the cotton mill that Yankee mechanics found so abhorrent.[48] Likewise Elizur Wright, who ran his newspaper shop on a ten-hour regime and not at all on Sunday, bragging in early November 1850 that it was the city's only Sabbatarian publishing house because it put out a Sunday edition on Saturday for "spiritual improvement" and gave journeymen the day off.[49] On Thanksgiving Day a few weeks later, Wright's grateful journeymen sent him a turkey, together with the following poem:

> To Mr. Wright
> with the respects of the "Chronotype Typos"
> Frank and free as thy writings are
> Is the gift our feelings send thee;
> But not as rich as thy mind's bazaar,
> Nor large enough to offend thee.
> It springs from the hearts whose every beat
> Is gladdened by thy "mighty pen,"
> We love to mark thy spicy sheet,
> And gladly greet it back again.
> If "flower" of speech be missing here
> Then let the "flour" we send suffice,—
> And if our "proof" should "foul" appear,
> We're always ready to revise.[50]

Such fraternal feeling was precisely what erstwhile Libertyites and Free Soilers had sought to promote. By the early 1850s, however, they concluded that voluntary activity had reached its limits. Now they had the choice of either joining the swelling ranks of factory workers poised for still more job actions or leading a quieter movement for a political solution. To labor reformers with Wright's outlook, this was no choice at all.

The leadership of the last and most political phase of the ten-hour movement derived from the antislavery vanguard in the Bird Club.[51] Formed in the late 1840s by paper manufacturer and temperance reformer Frank Bird, this clique of journalists and politicians became the kitchen cabinet of the "radical Republican establishment."[52] Its great asset, according to a recent scholar, was single-minded devotion to an antislavery party. As a result, club members had no consistent philosophy or position on other issues, and were indifferent to reform politics in state government.[53] This is true only in part. Bird and his men were a heterodox group including free laborists, unfriendly to working-class politics, as well as labor radicals like Wright. Very few, however, watched state politics from the sidelines. Three of its earliest (and perhaps charter) members—James M. Stone, William S. Robinson, and Wright himself—were the titular heads of the recrudescent ten-hour movement.

Each of these men came to the movement and the Free Soil party by different routes. Wright's is already known.[54] His new comrade, William S. Robinson, was new to labor reform. A printer by training and journalist by trade, Robinson ran a Whig paper with a temperance slant in Concord during the 1830s, then went to Lowell to work for William Schouler's *Courier*, where he met and in 1848 married Harriet Hanson, later author of the 1898 memoir *Loom and Spindle; or, Life among the Early Mill Girls.*[55] Robinson warmed to labor in part because of his own simple origins and early career as all-around printer and journalist. When he moved to Lowell, he learned of labor's plight close up and developed genuine sympathy for its workers. Their cause became his once Robinson and fellow Free Soilers vied for political power. In Lowell, as in other industrial towns, third party politics was impossible without labor reform, and labor reform was impossible without a ten-hour plank.

This lesson wasn't lost on James M. Stone, the other Bird Club member who also straddled the line between antislavery and labor reform. Stone, like Robinson, was a printer and journalist, but from another political shore. A radical Democrat and temperance advocate, he moved to Worcester in the mid-1840s to take over a temperance paper affiliated with the laborist faction of the local Washingtonian movement.[56] A year or so later he accepted a political appointment in the Boston Customs House, indicating strong ties to the party establishment, but not blind loyalty since he was a Free Soiler in 1848. Stone didn't share Wright's enlightened views on race, and was a labor advocate earlier than Robinson.[57] He knew, as they did, however, that to be a credible Free Soiler in the Bay State's industrial districts was to be a ten-hour man.

The multiple political affiliations of Wright, Robinson, and Stone cannot be stressed enough. Here, after all, were three members of the Bird Club, antislavery's central command when it was a mere cabal, who were interchangeable with labor reform leadership in mid-century Massachusetts. In their hands, labor advocacy and antislavery were mutually reinforcing, not mutually exclusive. The period in which the labor and anti-slavery movements "talked past" one another, in Eric Foner's apt formulation, had finally ended.[58] A pageant sponsored by Free Soilers in Worcester in late June 1848 gave real and symbolic expression to this union of labor reform and antislavery. Elizur Wright reported that a huge crowd from "hill and dale, counter and workshop, plough and loom" formed a great antislavery column, which merged in the downtown with two hundred workmen from the "great plough establishment of Ruggles, Nourse, & Mason," the same men who would present their employers with the ten-hour clock in 1852. At the town commons the party faithful heard speeches from Joshua Leavitt, Amasa Walker, and others, and then elected delegates to the (founding) Free Soil convention at Buffalo. William S. Robinson, an organizer of the affair, was on the podium that afternoon, and was among those who offered three cheers for none other than Joseph Tinker Buckingham in appreciation for quitting the (Cotton Whig) *Courier.*[59]

No one expected Buckingham to assume much of a role in this ten-hour movement. Nearly seventy years old, he never had much talent for organizing anyway and had already come out against ten-hour legislation. This was work for younger men, for the likes of Stone, who in 1851 formed Ten Hour State Convention, with help from Wright, Benjamin Butler, and other Free Soil/Coalition lawmakers and party operatives. Stone's ubiquitous cadre did a good bit of electoral work, encouraging local committees to endorse Coalition candidates or make support for office-seekers from mainstream parties contingent on voting for a ten-hour bill.[60] Elections in milltowns during the early 1850s, wrote a historian of the movement, "regularly turned on this issue."[61]

Ten-hour leaders stressed three themes on the stump and in flyers. They invoked the republican axiom that (male at least) factory hands were also citizens who could not possibly fulfill their civic obligations. The unremitting toil of the mill thwarted self-improvement required of responsible citizenship and put public order at risk by creating a desperate underclass. Long hours sowed "ignorance, vice and crime," claimed a labor speaker in the textile village of Oxford.[62] A convention report written by Stone in 1852 added that mill drudgery "robs the laborers of their *right* of moral and intellectual culture."[63] It had to press the economics of his case because manufacturers had mounted a scare campaign that featured threats of layoffs and wage cuts.[64] Stone's elaborate riposte accused the manufacturers of intimidation and dishonesty, and argued that a ten-hour day would bring greater prosperity, not disaster, to factory communities. He reasoned that trimming the workday in mechanized factories effectively pared the labor supply, which drove up wages in the short run. Labor would benefit in the long run because improved morals and manners attendant on more leisure necessarily improved living standards and consumption habits.[65]

The political aspect of labor reform's argument ranged more widely. It reflected, first of all, the Free Soil tenet that fair and just government protected the weak and restrained the strong. Such a principle took on special significance in the context of a legal day's work because the weak were women without a formal political voice and wholly at the mercy of powerful corporations.[66] Free Soil politicians sometimes confessed that cutting the workday helped consolidate their ranks in the state's industrial districts.[67] They even developed political terminology for their industrial strategy, referring to factories that adopted the ten-hour day and reliably voted Free Soil as "Coalition Shops."[68] The movement also offered Free Soilers a platform to assail the immorality of the lords of the lash, as well as the lords of the loom. George W. Benchley, a major Free Soil politician from Worcester, once wagged an accusing finger at Whig opponents in the state house, thundering that "When the question, presented to the Cottoncrat, concerns men versus money, money is certain to attain his suffrage."[69] The "money power," read the state convention's 1852 report, had an "insatiable appetite" for "centralization" and, so Free Soiler politicians said again and again, a horrific romance with the "slave power."[70]

As such rhetoric would suggest, and recent historians of the movement indicate, this was a man's theater of war. The women who had figured so prominently in the drive of the previous decade were either marginalized by the men or dropped out voluntarily, or both.[71] Machinists dominated the movement in places like Worcester, and largely displaced spinners and weavers in Lowell.[72] This heavy presence of metal workers explains why a local observer wasn't challenged when he characterized labor reformers in the 1850s as the "elite" of the working class.[73]

It also goes a long way toward explaining the course of the movement's last phase. Metal workmen, after all, were a labor aristocracy that enjoyed rather more leverage at the point of production than textile operatives.[74] In fall 1851, shop meetings in machine factories and shipyards in the Hub City produced a rash of ten-hour strikes, which ended in a couple of weeks with mixed results.[75] Though many shops in Charlestown and Boston instituted a ten-hour day, a few tried to renege a year later and nearly all in other locales successfully held out.[76]

This labor unrest had great political ramifications. Free Soil leaders set aside their opposition to strikes and generally lent moral support in party organs. The *Commonwealth* reported these events and the firings they sometimes entailed, insisting that tactical excess in a good cause was excusable, ten hours being "quite a sufficient allowance of toil, we should think."[77] Its columnist chided owners who used the new work regimen to cut wage scales or stiffen work rules.[78] Other party men took a stronger hand, for though men like Wright and Henry Trask had taken an active interest in labor, there is good reason to believe that it was these strikes that stirred a larger circle, and indeed brought in the Free Soilers as a party on the side of labor. It seems hardly coincidental, for instance, that the initial meetings of Stone's state convention took place in October 1851, coincident with the machinists' strikes.[79] Nor is there much doubt that the example of the Boston machinists inspired ten-hour committees in the belt of metal shops from Lawrence through Lowell and down to Worcester. There in fall 1852, not long after the second state convention meeting, the Boston Associates and independent operators of machine shops in five cities and towns suddenly cut their hours to eleven from twelve or twelve and a half. Just about a year later, the Boston men extended this policy to their textile centers; independents in other places followed suit.[80]

It was in this flux of worker mobilization, Free Soiler support, and employer liberalization that the ten-hour day insinuated itself into Bay State politics. No state issue, and no national ones except the Fugitive Slave Act and the Kansas-Nebraska Act, carried such a potent political charge. Coalitionists elevated the ten-hour day to the top of their agenda, to coequal status with the secret ballot. Both issues, party activists rightly believed, would help break the Whig grip on industrial centers.[81] The Coalition surged in those places in the elections of 1851 and 1852. A shaken Whiggish commentator plaintively asked in the aftermath of the 1851 poll "where would the Coalition be today without the manufacturing city of Lowell, and the town of Fall River?"[82]

The observer had a point. Election returns reveal impressive Free Soil strength in major factory towns. Free Soilers tripled the Liberty proportion in 1848, gathering 29 percent in the state as a whole. Their vote fluctuated downward to 21 percent through 1851, climbed back to 27 percent in 1852, and then fell to 24 percent a year later. Free Soilism did appreciably better in select shoe manufacturing centers and in the metal towns of the central corridor. The party ran behind the statewide average in smaller cotton towns with enduring paternalistic traditions and growing concentrations of Irish immigrants. Such places as Chicopee in the west and Waltham in the east cast a stingy Free Soil vote. It did much better in textile towns with large concentrations of Yankee workers, factories with weak or flagging paternalistic policies, and muscular ten-hour movements. Free Soilers in the Essex county textile hamlets of Amesbury and Salisbury consistently outpaced the ticket; in Lowell, Fall River, and New Bedford they surpassed it by 3 to 12 points in the early 1850s. The party clearly deepened its base among factory workers in frontline industrial towns.[83]

Coalition lawmakers used their newfound strength to make ten hours a legal day's work. Their influence varied to the rhythm of the labor movement, rising in 1851–52 to a peak in 1853, and then falling off sharply in 1854. In 1852 William S. Robinson, now a Free Soil representative from Lowell, reintroduced a bill defeated in the 1850 session that went down to defeat 48 to 117.[84] The vote energized party operatives, who redoubled efforts in the ensuing electoral campaign. In 1853 Robinson's new floor leaders easily pushed through a new bill.[85] The problem came in the Senate, where Whigs and rural Democrats passed a substitute, with a clause that permitted individuals to make their own bargains with employers through private contracts. This provision, popular with nearly all regular politicians and free labor ideologues, was anathema to Robinson's Free Soilers, who voted not to concur when the bill came before their body.[86] As 1853 drew to a close, Coalitionists returned to their districts to find the ten-hour movement in eclipse, their party in shambles, and their own careers in danger. The fall elections reflected the silence of the streets, as Whigs regained their hold on the legislature, and on major industrial districts as well. Lowell, the prize of the Coalition in the previous poll, returned to the Whig fold.[87]

What had gone wrong? The Coalition was not united on labor reform. Had it been so there would have been a ten-hour law in 1852, and more likely in 1851, when it enjoyed a majority in the House. Rural Coalitionists and those from small towns with frail ten-hour movements and paternalistic companies bitterly fought reform.[88] Conscience Whigs in the Coalition, many of them upper-class men, opposed a legally prescribed workday.[89] In addition, politicians and workers were outflanked by shrewd and wily employers. For every collegial employer like Wright in Boston, or Ruggles, Nourse, Mason & Co. in Worcester, there were many more recalcitrants who fired labor activists and threatened everyone else with wage reductions, layoffs, and other punishments.[90] An observer insisted that in 1855 Lowell's "corporation managers" simply bought the opposition.[91] Several historians of Massachusetts politics have since accepted this interpretation.[92] There is no doubt that textile manufacturers intimidated their workers, intensified their lobbying after 1850 (concentrating on the Senate in 1853), and resorted to bribery. Still, from the perspective of the workforce, the decisive factor proved to be management's calculated gamble on granting an eleven-hour day in 1852 and 1853. This timely compromise thwarted the ten-hour movement by dividing its rank and file. It neutralized the metal workmen, who were the political backbone of the movement, and widened the gender divide that had been slowly growing since the collapse of the second ten-hour movement in the late 1840s.[93] Some machinists, it is true, pressed on into 1854 and 1855. A good number, however, took what they got in 1852, and then settled into a defensive posture.[94]

Textile hands acted similarly, and were considerably more vocal about it. Nearly two years after the shift to an eleven-hour day in 1853, operatives were still of mixed minds. A small minority opposed any legislation whatever, while another group, clearly larger and probably scattered but strong in Fall River, favored reform.[95] A third group, based largely in Lowell but represented in Lawrence as well, preferred the machinists' solution of defending the gain of 1853.[96] These workers feared a return to a twelve- or thirteen-hour day, a fear that gained credibility when, in March of 1855, in the midst of the legislative debate, textile hands in Manchester, New Hampshire, struck to resist an extension of the workday. The strike convinced a Lawrence operative and doubtless scores of others that "our fears are not without foundation."[97] The Manchester strike, and widespread expectations of layoffs, argued strongly for accepting the compromise of an eleven-hour day.

The final chapter in the antebellum movement was written in 1855, not by Free Soilers but by Know Nothings. Recent work on the nativists indicates they were more complex than the anti-Catholic zealots most historians have thought them to be. They were a loose and fractious coalition of three groups, one of which consisted of political novices animated by anti-Catholicism and suspicion of active government in all realms except cultural proscription. Another embraced former Whigs (and possibly some Democrats) who retained the economic conservatism of their previous affiliation. The third and largest bloc included former Free Soilers and independent radicals, who gave the movement the antislavery ethos recent scholarship has begun to stress, as well as its labor reform elan. Thus, in 1855, the nativist House approved a ten-hour bill by 181 to 81, but the Senate again rejected it, this time by a resounding 11 to 26.[98]

The 1855 session was one of the busiest in the history of the commonwealth. It dealt not only with all manner of legislation to restrict the rights of immigrants but also with several antislavery bills. A nativist senator questioned some backbenchers for concentrating on such antislavery matters as a personal liberty bill and the removal of a pro-Southern judge. He did not oppose such laws and wished to "say, that I honor the man whose sympathies are so enlarged." He applauded the effort to give the slave-on-the-run personal liberty and asked only the same for the operatives "who are deprived the right to regulate their own employment, the right to command some of their own time."[99] No Free Soil radical would have disagreed.

The shared political biographies of Elizur Wright, William Robinson, and James Stone speak to several aspects of the relationship between labor politics and antislavery. They tell us that in Massachusetts the leadership of politicized antislavery and labor reform were synonymous, that the most forceful opponents of slavery in state politics were also labor's most consistent advocates. These reformers were not the elite or middle-class free laborists depicted in much of the historical literature. Such a description fits Richard Dana, Jr., or Henry Wilson and other Free Soil and Republican stalwarts in Massachusetts, and with good reason. Dana and John Palfrey were scions of the commonwealth's first families, closely akin to David B. Davis's bourgeois reformers who measured social relationships in general against the yardstick of chattel slavery. To them, self-possession *was* the foundation of freedom, and the legal protections of citizenship and economic individualism its guarantor. Small wonder that their wing of Free Soilism and Republicanism embraced the pervasive spirit of entrepreneurial individualism.[100]

Wright, Robinson, and Stone, and perhaps even Buckingham in youth were not bourgeois men in the usual sense of the term. Robinson and Bird drifted in that direction after 1870.[101] Such disillusionment, however, came late in life, and several years after they had effectively withdrawn from public affairs. It is highly misleading, not to say ahistorical, to read the politics of their golden years into the politics of their youth and middle age. We might think of these men as a generation that spent an experimental infancy in the Jackson years, matured into radical reformers in the 1840s and 1850s, and wavered during the Civil War and Reconstruction, tilting first toward radical Republicanism and then toward the conservatism of laissez-faire liberalism. Only two of the activists discussed above—Buckingham and Wright—do not fit this pattern. Buckingham espoused a cautious version of the community-of-interest ideal to begin with, moderated his views on labor reform as early as the 1840s, and died before the onset of the Civil War; Wright remained pretty much of an intrepid radical.[102]

Two things distinguished Wright and his set from Dana's. Wright and his comrades were ordinary men, mechanics who never rose to great wealth or achieved gentility. Such a pedigree put them in closer social proximity to manual workers than bourgeois antislavery activists, and left a strong influence. For if there was anything that set Wright apart from Dana, it was pride in work and belief in the dignity of manual labor. This is why we should be wary of including the Wrights of antebellum America in the great, amorphous middle class. In social terms, these men are best considered as middling not middle class, and in ideological terms as radical not free laborist, because they rejected the cardinal principles of free laborism for a more fraternal worldview rooted in the collaborative customs of the workshop and the reciprocity of the New England village.

Their relationship with labor, organized and otherwise, was complicated. The community-of-interest ideal for them was not a rhetorical device or ideological ornament. Instead, it was freighted with standards of fairness and expectations of interdependence, and with the notion that honorable employers followed through. They were also consistent insofar as they granted their own workers a ten-hour day, labor's central demand in this period. That some of them traded shorter hours for tighter discipline does not vitiate the point that so-called Coalition employers conceded what the cotton manufacturers steadfastly resisted throughout the antebellum years. There were limits, of course, to managerial flexibility. These employers accepted some form of unionism, or worker representation, but drew the line at class conflict. They tolerated strikes against the "cottoncrats," but not against fellow craftsmen in the trades. This could be and often was a source of tension in the cities of the Middle Atlantic states with their relatively well-organized and independent-minded workers. But it was not such an encumbrance in New England and in Massachusetts especially, where workers were not so well organized, and even when they were, persistent traditions of craft fraternalism made for more inclusive organizations. In this respect, it is important to recall that every major labor organization in antebellum Massachusetts brought together middling reformers and small employers with workers. The community-of-interest ideal, then, was not imposed on workers from without; it was part and parcel of regional convention.

It was also implicit in the vision of the Free Soilers, one of the most important and underestimated insurgencies of this period. The Free Soil party was not the single-issue party depicted in the historical literature, nor was it divorced from everyday life at the local level. In a recent work Robert Fogel makes two observations on the Free Soilers that cut to the core of antislavery politics in the turbulent 1850s. First, he argues that the party stood aloof from the "mushrooming labor movement" and showed "little interest in linking their antislavery demands, which centered on who would control the federal government, with the class issues that raged at the local level."[103] Second, and by extension, he tells us that the party stalled because it failed to do what the Kansas-Nebraska Act did, namely, draw workers into direct confrontation with the Slave Power. The first claim simply does not apply to Massachusetts, where in the 1840s Free Soil politicians like Wright courted organized labor and labor leaders like William Field Young, William West, and Sarah Bagley were in fact antislavery activists. As for the second point it, too, must be qualified if we consider the ten-hour movement. Ten-hour campaigners in the Bay State simply did not construe theirs as a one-dimensional struggle for labor, so much as a two-dimensional struggle for labor and against the "cottonocracy," that is, the minions of the planters. Such derisive language is instructive. Cotton, in the minds of Free Soilers and Libertyites before them, was the dirty word of the period, and what united the lords of the lash and the lords of the loom. Massachusetts workers fully realized the local character of labor oppression; after all, they had struggled for the greater part of thirty years, starting in 1825, to quit work at sunset, only to be stymied again and again by the state's leading merchant capitalists and industrialists. The longer that struggle dragged on the clearer it became that local capitalists were morally bankrupt men, the clients of Southern slavers. Thus, the Free Soilers and their predecessors in Wright's wing of the Liberty party helped draw workers into indirect conflict with the Slave Power by way of the Money Power.

Notes

The research for this work was supported by a grant from the National Endowment for the Humanities in collaboration with the American Antiquarian Society, 185 Salisbury Street, Worcester, Mass.

1. Gary J. Kornblith, "From Artisans to Businessmen: Master Mechanics in New England, 1790–1850" (Ph.D. dissertation, Princeton University, 1983), 291–349. Also, Kornblith, "Becoming Joseph T. Buckingham," in Howard B. Rock, Paul A. Gilje, and Robert Asher, eds., *American Artisans: Crafting Social Identity, 1750–1850* (Baltimore: Johns Hopkins University Press, 1995), 123–34; and Joseph Tinker Buckingham, *Per-*

sonal Memoirs and Recollections of Editorial Life, 2 vols. (Boston: Ticknor, Reed, and Fields, 1852). The quotation is in Allen Johnson and Dumas Malone, eds., *Dictionary of American Biography* (hereafter *DAB*), 22 vols. (New York: Charles Scribner's Sons, 1937), 3:227–28.

2. Susan M. Kingsbury, ed., *Labor Laws and Their Enforcement* (London: Longmans, Green, and Co., 1911), 3–22; John R. Commons et al., *History of Labour in the United States*, 4 vols. (New York: Macmillan, 1918–35), 1:158–62, 298–301, and 306–25; David R. Roediger and Philip S. Foner, *Our Own Time: A History of American Labor and the Working Day* (Westport, Conn.: Greenwood Press, 1989), 1–79; and Teresa Anne Murphy, *Ten Hours' Labor: Religion, Reform, and Gender in Early New England* (Ithaca: Cornell University Press, 1992), 32–56.

3. Murphy, *Ten Hours' Labor*, 43–46. See also Ronald P. Formisano, *The Transformation of Political Culture: Massachusetts Parties, 1790s-1840s* (New York: Oxford University Press, 1983), 227–37, and David Brody, "Time and Work during the Early American Industrialism," *Labor History* 30 (Winter 1989): 5–46.

4. Formisano, *Transformation of Political Culture*, 229–30. See also John R. Commons et al., eds., *Documentary History of American Industrial Society*, 10 vols. (Cleveland: Arthur H. Clark Co., 1910–11), 6:76–77.

5. James Lloyd Homer, *An Address Delivered before the Massachusetts Charitable Mechanic Association on the Celebration of their Tenth Triennial Festival* (Boston: Homer, Palmer, and Joseph T. Adams, 1836), 17.

6. See, for instance, Kornblith, "From Artisans to Businessmen," 514–35. See also George W. Light, "A Plea for the Laboring Classes," *New England Magazine* (1835): 429–33, and *Boston Mechanic and Journal of the Useful Arts* (Dec. 1835): 143–44.

7. *Boston Courier* (hereafter *BC*), 2 June 1832.

8. Formisano, *Transformation of Political Culture*, 181–87 and 192–93.

9. See *DAB*, 3:227–28.

10. Joseph Tinker Buckingham, comp., *Annals of the Massachusetts Charitable Mechanic Association* (Boston: Crocker and Brewster, 1853).

11. The best treatment of such mechanics is Kornblith, "From Artisans to Businessmen," 514–35.

12. See David Montgomery, *Beyond Equality: Labor and the Radical Republicans, 1862–1872* (New York: Knopf, 1967), 114–34.

13. For a different interpretation of this discourse see David Roediger, *The Wages of Whiteness: Race and the Making of the American Working Class* (New York: Verso, 1991), esp. 43–92.

14. See, for instance *New England Artisan*, 20 Sept. 1832, and 10 Jan. 1833. For more examples of this rhetoric see *Boston Daily Reformer* (hereafter *DR*), fall editions, 1835. The most suggestive secondary works on popular or working-class abolitionism are Leonard L. Richards, *"Gentlemen of Property and Standing": Anti-Abolition Mobs in Jacksonian America* (New York: Oxford University Press, 1970); John Jentz, "The Antislavery Constituency in Jacksonian New York City," *Civil War History* 27 (June 1981): 101–22; Edward Magdol, *The Antislavery Rank and File: A Social Profile of the Abolitionists' Constituency* (Westport, Conn.: Greenwood Press, 1986); and Debra Gold Hansen, *Strained Sisterhood: Class and Gender in the Boston Female Anti-Slavery Society* (Amherst: University of Massachusetts Press, 1993).

15. *DR*, 28 Oct. 1835.

16. Ibid., 8 Dec. 1835.

17. *Newburyport Herald,* 3 Nov. 1846.

18. See Thomas Dublin, *Women at Work: The Transformation of Work and Community in Lowell, Massachusetts, 1826–1860* (New York: Columbia University Press, 1979), and Murphy, *Ten Hours' Labor,* for recent interpretations of the ten-hour movement in the 1840s.

19. Lawrence B. Goodheart, *Abolitionist, Actuary, Atheist: Elizur Wright and the Reform Impulse* (Kent, Ohio: Kent State University Press, 1990), and Philip Green Wright and Elizabeth Wright, *Elizur Wright: The Father of Life Insurance* (Chicago: University of Chicago Press, 1937).

20. American Anti-Slavery Society, *Third Annual Report* (New York: Wm. S. Dorr, 1836), quotations on 59 and 81–82.

21. Ibid., 81–82. Also Goodheart, *Abolitionist, Actuary, Atheist,* 66–68.

22. Goodheart, *Abolitionist, Actuary, Atheist,* 121–22.

23. *Emancipator,* 24 Apr. 1844. Also ibid., 1 May and 10 July 1844.

24. See, for instance, *Boston Daily Chronotype* (hereafter *BDC*), 22 July 1846, 11 Nov. 1847, 25 Apr. 1848, and 23 Aug. 1849.

25. Goodheart, *Abolitionist, Actuary, Atheist,* esp. 130–33.

26. Ibid., 130–31. Also see *BDC* in 1848 passim for Wright's interpretation of European revolution. Also ibid., 3 Aug. 1846, 22 Aug. and ff. 1848, and 16 and 23 Aug. 1849. On cooperatives in this period see Edwin Charles Rozwenc, *Cooperatives Come to America: The History of the Protective Union Store Movement, 1845–1867* (Mt. Vernon, Iowa: Hawkeye-Record Press, 1941).

27. The most systematic treatment of such radicals in this period is Montgomery, *Beyond Equality,* which not only associates radicalism with the individualism other historians have since emphasized. It also observes that radical Republicans constituted a "generation," a point that scholars of radicalism have overlooked. My point here is that the men who would emerge in the 1860s as Montgomery's radicals, were more youthful in the 1840s and 1850s and more radical. We are viewing them at an earlier stage in their life cycle.

28. *BDC,* 13 Mar. 1846, 26 May 1846, 15 and 17 July 1847, and 24 Feb. 1848.

29. *Emancipator,* 1 May 1844.

30. *BDC,* 23 July 1846.

31. Ibid., 17 Dec. 1847.

32. Ibid., 13 Aug. 1846. Also ibid., 8 Nov. 1847.

33. Reinhard O. Johnson, "The Liberty Party in Massachusetts, 1840–1848: Antislavery Politics in the Bay State," *Civil War History* 28 (Sept. 1982): 237–65, esp. 245–46 and 255–56. Also *BDC,* 13 Aug. 1846, and 23 Sept. 1847.

34. James Stewart, *Holy Warriors: The Abolitionists and American Society* (New York: Hill & Wang, 1976), 97–123.

35. See Johnson, "Liberty Party in Massachusetts," 255–56, and Carl Siracusa, *A Mechanical People: Perceptions of the Industrial Order in Massachusetts, 1815–1880* (Middletown, Conn.: Wesleyan University Press, 1979), esp. 251–56.

36. See Eric Foner, "Racial Attitudes of the New York Free Soilers," in Foner, *Politics and Ideology in the Age of the Civil War* (New York: Oxford University Press, 1980), 77–93. There was some variation on racial attitudes among Massachusetts Free Soilers, just as there was in New York, but there is compelling evidence that as a group

the Bay Staters were quite racially enlightened. The racial attitudes of Massachusetts Free Soilers is the subject of a paper in progress.

37. The best analysis of this is Johnson, "Liberty Party in Massachusetts." Also see, Siracusa, *Mechanical People*, 80–81, 182–207, and 253–56; and Formisano, *Transformation of Political Culture*, 321–43.

38. On the secret ballot see Formisano, *Transformation of Political Culture*, 335–38; Michel Brunet, "The Secret Ballot Issue in Massachusetts Politics 1851 to 1853," *New England Quarterly* 26 (Sept. 1952): 254–62, and Siracusa, *Mechanical People*, 182–87. The best national treatment of the Free Soilers continues to be Richard H. Sewell, *Ballots for Freedom: Antislavery Politics in the United States, 1837–1860* (New York: Oxford University Press, 1976). More recent work on the state level, as cited above, leaves a richer and more complex picture of a reform party, and not a single-issue crusade.

39. Kevin Sweeney, "Rum, Romanism, Representation, and Reform: Coalition Politics in Massachusetts, 1847–1853," *Civil War History* 22 (June 1976): 116–37.

40. Ibid. See also *Worcester Daily Spy* (hereafter *WDS*), 18 Sept. 1849, 12 Jan. 1851, and 1 Sept. 1851, as well as *Commonwealth*, 24 May 1851 and 18 June 1853.

41. See, for instance, Roediger and Foner, *Our Own Time*, 77–79, and Kingsbury, *Labor Laws and Their Enforcement*, 89.

42. *BDC*, 20 and 22 June 1847.

43. Roediger and Foner, *Our Own Time*, 66–68. See also *BDC*, 6, 9, 13, 23, and 24 Oct. 1851.

44. *Boston Atlas* (hereafter *BA*), 4 and 6 Oct. 1852.

45. *State Sentinel and Worcester Reformer* (hereafter *SSWF*), 19 Apr. 1844.

46. *WDS*, 21 Feb. 1852.

47. *Commonwealth*, 23 Oct. 1851.

48. See, for instance, *The Hours of Labor. Address of the Ten Hours State Convention, held in Boston, September 30, 1852, to the People of Massachusetts; together with a Report and Bill* . . . (Boston: n.p., 1852), esp. 1–3. Also *Commonwealth*, 2 Jan. 1852; *WDS*, 5 Sept. 1853; and Kingsbury, *Labor Laws and Their Enforcement*, 79–80.

49. *BDC*, 4 Nov. 1850.

50. Ibid., 27 Nov. 1850.

51. On Bird see Donald B. Marti, "Francis William Bird: A Radical's Progress through the Republican Party," *Historical Journal of Massachusetts* 11 (June 1983): 82–93.

52. Dale Baum, *The Civil War Party System: The Case of Massachusetts, 1848–1876* (Chapel Hill: University of North Carolina Press, 1984), esp. 82 and ff., quotation on 3.

53. Ibid., 28–29 and 145–46.

54. Ibid., 85–86, and *Commonwealth*, 1 Jan. and 25 Nov. 1851, and 26 May 1852.

55. Harriet Hanson Robinson, *Loom and Spindle: or, Life among the Early Mill Girls* . . . (Boston: T. Y. Crowell, 1898). On Robinson see Edward T. James et al., eds., *Notable American Women: A Biographical Dictionary*, 3 vols. (Cambridge, Mass.: Belknap Press, 1971), 3:181–82. Also Claudia Bushman, *"A Good Poor Man's Wife": Being a Chronicle of Harriet Hanson Robinson* (Hanover, N.H.: University Press of New England, 1981).

56. Stone remains a shadowy and elusive figure. For his obituary see *Boston Evening Transcript*, 20 Dec. 1880. Also *SSWF*, 25 May, 7 June, and 13 Sept. 1844, for a hint of

his politics. These editorials lead one to doubt the saintly portrait of him in Kingsbury, *Labor Laws and Their Enforcement*, 61–62.

57. *SSWF*, 13 Sept. 1844.

58. Eric Foner, "Abolitionism and the Labor Movement," in Foner, *Politics and Ideology*, 61.

59. *BDC*, 30 June 1848.

60. Roediger and Foner, *Our Own Time*, 65–79 and ff., and Kingsbury, *Labor Laws and Their Enforcement*, 54–89.

61. Kingsbury, *Labor Laws and Their Enforcement*, 70.

62. *WDS*, 5 Aug. 1853.

63. *Hours of Labor*, 2. Also, *WDS*, 14 Feb. 1852.

64. See, for example, *WDS*, 23 Mar. 1854. See also Kingsbury, *Labor Laws and Their Enforcement*, 71–74.

65. *Hours of Labor*, 4–6.

66. Ibid., 7–8.

67. See *WDS*, 5 Aug. and 1 Oct. 1853, and *Lowell Daily Advertiser*, 15 Mar. 1853.

68. *Lowell American Citizen* (hereafter *LA*), 3 Mar. 1853. Also, Kingsbury, *Labor Laws and Their Enforcement*, 76.

69. *WDS*, 11 Jan. 1854.

70. *Hours of Labor*, 8. See also *WDS*, 18 Sept. 1849, and *Commonwealth*, 24 May and 6–7 Aug. 1851.

71. See, for instance, Murphy, *Ten Hours' Labor*, 222–25. Also Dublin, *Women at Work*, 200–202, and Lori Ginzberg, *Women and the Work of Benevolence: Morality, Politics, and Class in the Nineteenth Century United States* (New Haven: Yale University Press, 1990), 98–132.

72. At the local level each ten-hour committee brought together Free Soil and later nativist politicians with male workers from the leading occupations in a particular place. In Lowell, Fall River, and other textile towns, the working-class members were from the cotton and woolen industries. In Worcester, by contrast, the most active ten-hour advocates from the working class were machinists, armorers, and industrial blacksmiths, some of whom had accumulated substantial property holdings. Worcester ten-hour leaders Henry Benchley, an armorer by trade, and Charles Whittemore, a machinist, each owned $3000 in real property, according to the 1850 census. See *WDS*, 19 Feb. 1852, and 1 Oct. 1853, and U.S. Census Bureau, *Seventh Census, Population Schedule*, mss (1850). Also Dublin, *Women and Work*, 200–202, and *Commonwealth*, 1 Oct. 1852.

73. *WDS*, 11 Nov. 1854.

74. On the social standing of metal workers see Bruce Laurie et al., "Manufacture and Productivity: The Making of an Industrial Base, 1850–1880," in Theodore Hershberg, ed., *Philadelphia: Work, Space, Family and Group Experience in the Nineteenth Century* (New York: Oxford University Press, 1984), 43–92. On their shop-floor practice see David Montgomery, "Workers' Control of Machine Production in the Nineteenth Century," *Labor History* 17 (1976): 486–509.

75. *Commonwealth*, 6, 9, 13, and 23 Oct. 1851. Also ibid., 4 Oct. 1852.

76. *LA*, 3 Jan. and 10 Mar. 1853.

77. *Commonwealth*, 9 Oct. 1851.

78. See, for instance, ibid., 23 Oct. 1851.

79. Kingsbury, *Labor Laws and Their Enforcement*, 65.

80. Ibid., 89–90.

81. Formisano, *Transformation of Political Culture*, 336–43. Also Siracusa, *Mechanical People*, 80–81, 184–85, and 198–201, and appendix to table C-1, 253–56.

82. *BA*, 27 Nov. 1851.

83. Siracusa, *Mechanical People*, table C-1, 253–56. These figures, reproduced from Siracusa's tabulations, derive from gubernatorial races.

84. Kingsbury, *Labor Laws and Their Enforcement*, 85–87. One assumes that Coalitionists joined the opposition in the House since they had a majority in the body.

85. Ibid., 87–88. Also *WDS*, 18 and 21 May 1853.

86. *LA*, 12 Apr. 1853, and *Commonwealth*, 18 May 1853.

87. See Siracusa, *Mechanical People*, table C-1, 253–56.

88. Formisano, *Transformation of Political Culture*, 337.

89. See, for instance, Richard H. Abbott, *Cotton and Capital: Boston Businessmen and Antislavery Reform, 1854–1868* (Amherst: University of Massachusetts Press, 1991), 10–27, and n. 98.

90. See *Commonwealth*, 29 Aug. and 11 Nov. 1851 and 8 June 1853. Also *WDS*, 22 Nov. 1851.

91. See Charles Cowley, *Illustrated History of Lowell* (Boston: Lee & Shepard, 1868), 149.

92. See also Formisano, *Transformation of Political Culture*, 340, and John R. Mulkern, *The Know-Nothing Party in Massachusetts: The Rise and Fall of a People's Movement* (Boston: Northeastern University Press, 1990), 112.

93. See Dublin, *Women at Work*, 200–202, and Murphy, *Ten Hours' Labor*, 191–225.

94. And with reason, since regional employers, including the federal government agency with jurisdiction over Boston's shipyards, sought to extend the workday. See, for instance, *LA*, 3 Jan. 1853. Also ibid., 10 and 19 Mar. 1853.

95. The best forum for worker attitudes in this period was the *Boston Daily Bee* (hereafter *BDB*), a leading nativist sheet that printed a revealing series of letters from labor advocates and activists in the first half of 1855. See ibid., 29 Mar. and 4 Apr. 1855. To judge from an exchange between Harriet Farley and a critic, it would seem that some Yankee women continued to oppose reform. See *BDC*, 13 and 18 May 1848, and David A. Zonderman, *Aspirations and Anxieties: New England Workers and the Mechanized Factory System, 1815–1850* (New York: Oxford University Press, 1992), 258–59. Most scholars agree that the newly arrived Irish also opposed reform in this period. See Dublin, *Women at Work*, 145–64 and 198–207.

96. *BDB*, 16 Feb., 15 and 27 Mar., and 11 Apr. 1855. Also ibid., 28 Mar. 1855.

97. Ibid., 27 Mar. 1855. On the Manchester strike see *Boston Evening Traveller*, 21, 22, and 29 Mar. 1855, and *Worcester Transcript* (hereafter *WT*), 7 Apr. 1855.

98. *WT*, 25 Mar. 1855. *Boston Daily Advertiser*, 24–25 Mar. and 4, 11, and 16 Apr. 1855. See also *BA*, 11, 13, and 14 Apr., 1855. On the nativists see Mulkern, *Know-Nothing Party in Massachusetts*; Tyler Anbinder, *Nativism and Slavery: The Northern Know Nothings and the Politics of the 1850s* (New York: Oxford University Press, 1992); and Mark Voss Hubbard, "Populism and Public Life: Antipartyism, the State, and the Politics of the 1850s in Connecticut, Massachusetts, and Pennsylvania" (Ph.D. dissertation, University of Massachusetts at Amherst, 1997).

99. The speaker is Elihu Baker. See *Boston Post*, 14 Apr. 1855. Also E. C. Baker, *Speech of the Honorable E. C. Baker, of Middlesex, upon the Bill to Regulate the Hours of Labor in Incorporated Establishments. . . .* (Boston: William White, 1855), 5.

100. See David B. Davis, *The Problem of Slavery in Western Culture* (New York: Oxford University Press, 1966), 342–61. On the Republicans' entrepreneurial spirit, see Montgomery, *Beyond Equality*, 114–34, and Eric Foner, *Free Soil, Free Labor, Free Men: The Ideology of the Republican Party before the Civil War* (New York: Oxford University Press, 1970), esp. 11–39.

101. See Baum, *Civil War Party System*, 89–91 and 145–47. Also Marti, "Francis William Bird."

102. On Wright's later years see Goodheart, *Abolitionist, Actuary, Atheist,* 141–202.

103. Robert Fogel, *Without Consent or Contract: The Rise and Fall of American Slavery* (New York: W. W. Norton & Co., 1989), 369–70.

Chapter 3

Dinner-Pail Politics

Employers, Workers, and Partisan Culture
in the Progressive Era

JULIE GREENE

DURING THE EARLY twentieth century anti-union employers organized
into the National Association of Manufacturers (NAM) embarked on an
unprecedented bid for political power. They wanted, first, to defeat trade
union efforts to win labor reforms and political influence, and second, to
build an alliance with the Republican party, and especially with its conservative wing. To achieve these goals they targeted working-class voters
who, they believed, could be persuaded to vote for conservative, anti-union
candidates. The open shop employers hired an experienced agent, Martin Mulhall, who created an organization of conservative workers and
otherwise hustled the vote for his bosses. Mulhall sought to teach Republican politicians that businessmen, not union leaders, control the labor
vote: "I have been preaching for months to these people that the shopmen and thinking mechanics are not controlled by the jawsmiths of any
labor union, but the man that treats them well and gives them employment and good wages is the one they seek for advice."[1]

Mulhall's project provides a rare opportunity to explore the evolving
relationship between party politics, conservative employers, and the working class during the Progressive Era. Typically one enters a shadowy world
of rumor and innuendo when seeking to assess employers' political arse-

nal in the fight against labor. But thanks to charges of scandal and corruption against the NAM during the early years of Woodrow Wilson's presidency, we have a comprehensive picture of its political activities from 1902 until 1913. The accusations, made by the NAM's own Martin Mulhall, provoked lengthy investigations by both Houses of Congress, and the records they generated allow us to examine the nature and extent of the NAM's political war against labor.[2]

The politics of the NAM emerged from and reflected a dramatic transformation of American political culture. The nineteenth-century world of partisan politics faded after 1896, as scholars such as Walter Dean Burnham, Samuel Hays, and Richard McCormick have described, and closely contested elections, unwavering party loyalties, and campaign politics based upon mass entertainment declined. By the Progressive Era party structures and traditions weakened in discernible ways. Citizen participation in electoral politics fell, and factionalism divided the Republican and Democratic party organizations during this period, as progressive and conservative wings battled for ascendancy. Last but not least, the parties faced unprecedented challenges as the presidency grew in power and as new organizations, commonly known as interest groups, emerged to contest their power. The latter introduced a different range of political rivalries as they jockeyed against each other and against the political parties for influence and power.[3]

Yet for all the significance of the rising interest groups, it is important not to exaggerate the parties' decline. The structure and culture of the party system weakened but remained durable. At least three factors helped the partisan culture withstand its challengers. First, the extra-party organizations, while often more innovative in attempting new strategies, lacked the parties' experience. Second, one-party hegemony characterized most regions of the United States. The South remained solidly Democratic while the Republicans dominated much of the Northeast and Middle West, and parts of the Far West.[4] Third, although the parties could not stave off key political reforms during the Progressive Era, they did control the character of those reforms. The major parties managed to lose little when their representatives passed laws shaping the electorate or limiting the ability of alternative parties to compete electorally. Even as the electorate shrank in size and as the major parties grew less attractive to Americans, independent or socialist alternatives to those parties were ironically being closed down.

These developments generated highly fluid political relationships, and they raise several questions. Exactly how did interest groups establish a power base: did they work in opposition to the parties, or in alliance with them? Interest groups pushed the parties to compete on a prosaic level of concrete issues like liquor, the open shop, and women's suffrage. How did issue politics mesh with the loyalties established in the era of partisan dominance? Did these new political relationships improve the political avenues available to specific social groups or classes?

This essay will use the NAM's political project of the early twentieth century to explore political contestation during a time of transformation. More than a battle between labor and capital, this was also a clash between partisan structures and traditions on the one hand, and an emergent, more issue-focused political culture on the other. My thesis is that traditional partisan culture, although declining, remained strong, highly resilient, and ultimately triumphant during the Progressive Era. Partisan structures and traditions defined what was politically possible even as a new, group-oriented system emerged. The essay will begin by looking broadly at the open shop movement across the nation, sketching its origins, its early focus on congressional lobbying, and its entrance into electoral politics. Then it will shift into a closer look at the race dearest to the NAM leaders' hearts, the 1908 gubernatorial campaign in Indiana.

America's Open Shop Drive

The great depression of the 1890s caused rising unemployment, widespread bankruptcies, falling wages, and low profit margins. When recovery began in 1897, both workers and employers moved to stabilize their positions in case of further economic crisis. Unions grew rapidly between 1898 and 1904. The American Federation of Labor's membership soared from 280,000 workers to more than 1.6 million, and its presence reached into new trades and regions. These successes represented the most impressive period of sustained growth in labor's history to that time. For their part, businessmen moved rapidly toward consolidation, picking up on organizational innovations begun in the 1880s. The merger movement of 1898 to 1904 swallowed over two thousand companies to create approximately two hundred trusts.[5] Well-to-do businesspeople independent of the trusts responded with their own version of a merger movement, rapidly creating employers' associations across the nation. Trade associations, industry-specific organizations, and chambers of commerce all flourished after 1897, as did groups focused on protecting the tariff or encouraging wider foreign markets.[6]

The new organizational strengths of workers and employers intensified conflict on shop floors. Strikes became endemic between 1898 and 1904, more than doubling the frequency of the previous five years, and the number of workers involved in strikes saw a comparable rise.[7] Particularly in industries such as the metal and building trades, militant workers saw economic recovery as a chance to recoup losses in wages and basic conditions during the depression. Nonetheless the Murray Hill agreement of 1900 between the National Metal Trades Association and the International Association of Machinists, proudly supported by the National Civic Federation (NCF), broke down within a year to mutual recrimination.[8]

By 1903 the new employers' associations advocated treating trade unions with unbending hostility. Quickly their strategy flowered into a widespread social movement among American employers, supplanting the collaborative tactics favored by the NCF to become the most popular business solution to workplace conflict. The most influential movements could be found in cities like Chicago, Denver, Indianapolis, Pittsburgh, and Detroit. Anti-union employers stressed rhetoric of Americanism, liberty, and independence, and criticized the unions' "tyranny" over innocent working men. As a journalist portraying the movement observed: "Without the aid of non-union men . . . the employers would fight without troops. The ease with which they enlist non-union workmen is eloquent proof of the unpopularity of many unions in their own field."[9]

Employers' associations also drew on a common storehouse of tactics. They used lockouts to preempt strikes and organized nonunion workers into protective societies offering housing and safe travel to work. They enlisted as many employers as possible, using pressure tactics to recruit new affiliates. They also used labor bureaus to ensure an ample supply of workers, as well as strikebreakers and blacklists to control their employees.[10]

Meanwhile the open shop drive recruited several powerful adherents among the national associations. By 1905 the National Metal Trades Association, the United Typothetae, the National Founders' Association, and the National Erectors' Association had all adopted a hostile, anti-union approach to industrial relations.[11] The greatest victory of the burgeoning open shop drive by far, however, lay in winning over the National Association of Manufacturers in 1902.

Founded in Cincinnati in 1895, the NAM spent its early years advocating increased foreign trade, pressing especially hard for the Nicaraguan canal and its control by the United States government. Three members of the NAM, all open shop leaders in their respective communities of Indianapolis, Dayton, and St. Louis, sought to transform the association into the national representative of the employers' anti-union movement. In 1902 this faction elected its man, David Parry of Indianapolis, to the presidency, and he rapidly refocused the young NAM. At the 1903 convention Parry formalized the association's hostility toward labor in a fiery speech, reviling the union movement as "a mob-power, knowing no master except its own will." Afterwards NAM delegates unanimously adopted a "Declaration of Principles" that established the association's position on labor issues. It opposed any acts interfering with the personal liberty of employers or employees. Simultaneously, under Parry's leadership the NAM journal, *American Industries,* became the open shop's leading voice. In the next years, members favoring a conciliatory approach to labor relations drifted away, while employers attracted to its anti-union focus flooded into the organization.[12]

By 1904 the NAM led the nation's anti-union movement, and "Parryism" became a common synonym for the open shop drive. As a contemporary put it, Parry was "rapidly becoming one of the most important personages of the day, for he is at the forefront of a movement which has more social significance than any other at the present time."[13] Parry created two other open shop organizations: the Citizens' Industrial Alliance (a broad organization open to any person opposed to unions) and the National Council for Industrial Defense (an affiliated group responsible for the NAM's work on legislation). By 1908 the NAM boasted three thousand institutional members nationwide.[14]

Basing cooperation on the labor issue allowed NAM leaders to build a broader coalition of employers than possible otherwise. In the midst of divisive tariff battles in 1909 the NAM secretary wrote, "It is surprising how many of our members take issue with us on everything except the labor question. This tariff situation should be a warning to our leaders to never undertake anything that is not directly connected with the labor question. On that the manufacturers are a unit. The minute you get away from it there is no unity."[15] It was precisely the opposition to organized labor, in short, that molded American employers into an effective social movement.

The firms most active in the open shop drive, including those in the NAM, were typically large, locally based manufacturers. As Robert Wiebe described the movement, its adherents were wealthy businessmen a cut below the trusts.[16] Parry himself, an Indianapolis carriage-maker employing one thousand workers, personified this trend. At the same time, the open shop drive embraced a wide range of employers. As an Omaha trade unionist declared in 1904, "every bank, every retail store, every wholesale house, every railroad official, and every contractor is in the wreckers' association. There are, no doubt, seven hundred men in it."[17]

The ascendancy of anti-unionism, as opposed to more conciliatory trade agreements, could be seen even in the NCF's 1903 convention to discuss the open shop drive. The meeting was a professed failure, according to William English Walling: "Instead of the peace talk of the previous conferences, every employer favored the open shop, and every union man opposed it." In following years the NCF avoided the issue of the open shop as strenuously as the NAM emphasized it.[18]

Open Shop Politics and Congressional Lobbying

The NAM brought political activity as well as greater visibility and more resources to the open shop movement. Its leaders immediately tackled the sphere of federal legislation, in order to block labor reforms desired by the union movement. They launched a campaign to influence the U.S. House of Representatives and to build alliances with those congressmen, usually Republicans, who were least friendly to labor.

The NAM's new political activism confronted a new form of labor politics. In 1895 AFL president Samuel Gompers embarked upon a campaign to win labor's demands through political activity. The AFL's program at first employed only traditional lobbying tactics, and its goals similarly reflected the circumscribed agenda of a trade union federation. Rather than demanding broad social legislation, the AFL focused upon two main issues: reforming the labor injunction (the source of great injustice toward workers and their unions, Gompers felt), and an eight-hour law for government employees.[19]

Despite such narrow goals, AFL leaders committed themselves fully to their political program and invested great time and effort in it. Gompers moved the Federation headquarters from Indianapolis to Washington, D.C., and established a permanent legislative committee. By 1900 the AFL engaged in diverse lobbying activities at the federal level: for example, it worked against unfavorable legislation and drafted new versions of bills and found sponsors for them.[20] Finally between 1900 and 1903 the AFL seemed to inch closer to a position of influence with Congress. Federation leaders successfully opposed efforts to expand antitrust legislation (so that unions might be prosecuted under its purview) in 1900.[21] More importantly, they came tantalizingly close to victory on two key goals. Three years in a row the House of Representatives passed the anti-injunction and eight-hour bills desired by the AFL, though each time the Senate defeated them. Also during this period the AFL saw Congressman John Gardner of New Jersey, considered one of labor's best friends in the House of

Representatives, appointed to the critical chairmanship of the Labor Committee.[22]

By the first years of the twentieth century AFL leaders, confident of their influence with House members, shifted their attention to winning over senators. But at this moment the NAM launched its own lobbying program, and the AFL's political momentum abruptly ended.

The NAM began its agitation in the autumn of 1902, soon after David Parry's election to the presidency, by targeting the AFL's eight-hour bill. NAM leaders sent a letter and a pamphlet presenting "Thirty Three Reasons" against the bill to nearly nine thousand manufacturers and government contractors, encouraging opposition to it. The employers' activism influenced the Senate committees: although they again reported the bills favorably, amendments supported by open shop employers significantly weakened each bill.[23]

Next, NAM leaders targeted labor's stronghold in the House of Representatives. At the center of their strategy stood the new Speaker of the House, Joseph Cannon, a powerful "standpatter" who looked kindly upon an alliance with anti-labor employers. Representatives of the NAM conferred with Cannon to ensure probusiness appointments to the House Committee on Labor.[24] Then NAM leaders mobilized to control as many of them as possible, contacting employers in each congressman's home district.

Richard Bartholdt, a St. Louis congressman and a member of the Labor Committee, exemplified the NAM's success at lobbying Congress. In November 1903 James Van Cleave of St. Louis reported that Adolphus Busch, the prominent St. Louis brewer, "practically holds Mr. Bartholdt in the hollow of his hand . . . [and Bartholdt] dances like a jumping jack whenever Mr. Busch pulls the string." NAM political agent Marshall Cushing soon wrote the Anheuser-Busch Brewing Company to discuss the House Labor Committee and the need for congressmen who were not "afraid of the labor vote." Within a few months the NAM had, through Busch, an indirect line of communication with Congressman Bartholdt.

This relationship proved fruitful for anti-union employers during hearings on the eight-hour bill held by the Labor Committee in 1904. The NAM sought to draw out the hearings as a way to kill the bill. Upon the NAM's request, Busch instructed Bartholdt to extend the hearings for three or four more weeks. The tactic succeeded, and the bill never came up for a vote.[25] The employers and their congressional friends had good reason to bottle up bills in committee. Congressman Littlefield of Maine, a top NAM ally, once remarked that if the Judiciary Committee had reported labor's bills, the House of Representatives would certainly have passed them by a large majority. As Secretary Cushing described his tactics in an internal memo to NAM field-workers, "A week ago we demanded hearings and got them and now the game is to string them out indefinitely. . . . We get the witnesses to come, put other organizations to the front, . . . canvas the Committee secretly, bring pressure to bear secretly."[26]

As a result of the NAM's campaign, the AFL suffered a sudden reversal of its political fortunes even as its leaders intensified their political efforts. The House Judiciary Committee held hearings on the anti-injunction bill in 1903, 1904, and again in 1905, but the bill never left committee. Introducing the bill in 1904, Congressman Grosvenor of Ohio described the impact of the employers' political campaign. The very same bill had been before Congress for years, and had repeatedly passed the House almost unanimously, he noted. Yet now "a frantic, senseless, hysterical outcry goes up from all over the country that this bill, if passed, is to strike down some great principle of law that the country depends upon for its salvation."[27] Nor was this a temporary setback. The AFL would not achieve another legislative victory until the Republicans lost control of Congress in 1910.

Electoral Politics and the NAM

This legislative stalemate escalated the conflict between the AFL and the NAM, as both groups aggressively entered electoral politics between 1904 and 1910. In 1906 AFL leaders began a mass campaign to elect supportive politicians. Years later Gompers noted the NAM's influence in this historic shift: "it was necessary to break the strangle-hold which enabled organized employers to control legislation. In order to get action by Congress, I knew we had to make an appeal to congressmen and that no appeal would be stronger than a threat of action at the ballot box."[28] Like the NAM, the Federation fought electorally for goals the major parties seemed unwilling or unable to pursue. Yet even as AFL leaders exerted a new independence in politics, they kept a close eye on the Democrats and aspired to a closer and more fruitful relationship with party leaders.

NAM leaders entered into a similar relationship with the Republicans. Before 1908, NAM political strategy relied largely on "gumshoe" tactics: that is to say, a quiet bribing of workers, discreet distribution of political leaflets, and efforts to sabotage opponents. In 1907 as James Van Cleave, the St. Louis owner of Buck's Stove and Range Company, assumed the NAM presidency, Martin Mulhall became the NAM's chief political agent. Mulhall authored a new political script, taking the organization beyond lobbying and into realms normally associated with the political parties. He entered electoral politics, worked to mobilize voters, and influenced the selection of candidates. NAM leaders borrowed heavily from the campaign spectacles developed by the parties, for example, organizing torchlight parades and fife and drum corps. Yet they blended that culture with their traditional gumshoe arsenal.

The NAM's new political agent had himself received training in the workshop of party politics. While most NAM officials had roots in businessmen's circles, Mulhall had been a Republican operative for decades, beginning in the early 1880s as an organizer for William McKinley's senatorial campaign. In 1888, a campaign infamous for its political corruption, the Republican National Committee appointed Mulhall to its committee targeting labor and Irish-Americans.[29] In 1902, Mulhall came to the NAM's attention. He had organized conservative workers in Baltimore into a group he called the Workingmen's Protective Association. Mulhall's abilities to mobilize workers behind conservative causes appeared useful, as did his experience in party politics. For the next eight years, he served as lobbyist, campaign worker, and strikebreaker for the NAM. In several cities new branches of his Workingmen's Protective Association supplied strikebreakers and conservative activists. Mulhall also helped his bosses lobby top Republican leaders by securing appointments or arranging visits.[30]

Tired of the dirty work of strikebreaking and political bribery, Mulhall hoped to build legitimate working-class support for the Republican party.[31] The campaigns of 1908 gave him his opportunity, as Mulhall undertook a battle for workers' votes in congressional and gubernatorial campaigns in New Jersey, New York, Pennsylvania, Ohio, Maryland, Missouri, and Indiana, and supported the campaign of Republican presidential nominee William H. Taft.[32] The most important battle, however, involved the governorship of Indiana. Except for brief trips to the east coast Mulhall spent the campaign season in Indianapolis, directing the NAM's nationwide political effort from there.

The state of Indiana loomed large in American politics. The competitiveness that characterized political races there, with the winning party (usually Republican) rarely receiving more than 51 percent of the vote, gave the state influence in deciding the outcome of national races. As a result, the national parties spent a great deal of time and money on Indiana, often nominating a Hoosier for president or vice president. Thus the race for the Indiana governorship emerged as one of the most closely watched state battles in 1908.[33]

The region also stood at the forefront of the employers' open shop drive. Indianapolis was home not only to NAM activist David Parry but also to the Employers' Association of Indianapolis (EAI), an influential open shop organization created in 1904. By 1908 the EAI had established open shops in the metal and building trades. What had once been headquarters to the trade union movement was on its way to becoming, in the words of a union activist, "The graveyard of union aspirations; the scabbiest hellhole in the United States."[34]

In 1908 Indiana's open shop battle moved full force into the race for governor. The AFL and the Indiana State Federation of Labor mobilized behind Democratic candidate Thomas Marshall, while the employers supported Republican James E. Watson. Why did the open shop activists risk so much on one campaign? Not only were they strong in Indiana, they were also tied closely to Republican nominee James Watson. A leading conservative in the Indiana Republican party, Watson stood second only to Charles Littlefield of Maine among the NAM's congressional friends. Elected to Congress in 1894, Watson became majority whip—and hence right hand of Speaker Joseph Cannon—in 1901, and served in that capacity until 1908, when he stepped down to run for governor. And like Cannon, Watson strongly supported the employers in their fight against labor.[35]

At stake in this campaign, as the NAM leaders saw it, lay the future of Republican conservatism. This is why they worked harder for Cannon and Watson than for Taft, who bore the stigma of Rooseveltian progressivism. Furthermore, with this campaign the NAM made its most ambitious bid for legitimacy and power within the Republican party. As NAM secretary Schwedtman wrote to Mulhall: "your campaign in Indiana should mark a new departure from old campaign methods. Once the politicians understand that they will have to reckon with us, and . . . that they need not be afraid of having their connection with us known, they will be most careful to consult us in all important State and National movements."[36]

Defeating Watson became a top priority in the AFL's campaign program. Under the leadership of Speaker Joseph Cannon, no bills favorable to labor had come up for a vote in the last session. This made it difficult to identify congressmen worthy of support based only upon their voting record. Instead, labor focused on the chain of power in Congress that killed their bills at committee level. This meant an attack on such congressmen as Speaker Cannon, his whip James Watson, and chairmen such as Charles Littlefield of the Judiciary Committee. While Gompers characterized Cannon as the "Mephistopheles of American politics," he deemed James Watson "the Faust who helps to despoil the American people's rights."[37] Gompers himself conducted a four-day train tour of the state that autumn. Accompanied by state and national labor leaders, he made dozens of speeches and inspired local activists, who blanketed towns with leaflets and fliers. Thousands of workingmen greeted Gompers and his comrades wherever they stopped.[38]

The major political parties energetically appealed to working people throughout 1908. Democrats stressed the need for anti-injunction legislation—the same issue emphasized by Gompers and the AFL—and attacked the Republicans as unfriendly to unions and working people. Republicans focused on economic prosperity. Continuing a theme they had adopted in 1896, the GOP promised that only *they* could deliver a healthy economy, in part through reliance on the high tariff. As candidate Watson put it, the Republican party seeks to "keep wages high, to keep factories open, and to keep hopes in the hearts of the workmen." Democrats and labor activists pointed to the recent recession to challenge Republican claims about prosperity. In the context of closed factories and unemployed workers, Gompers declared to Indiana factory workers, "Dangling a dinner pail in the faces of honest workingmen is a shame." Yet Gompers and the Democrats provided no positive program other than injunction reform.[39]

Gompers's Indiana tour unleashed a vicious attack with a strong nativist accent. Republicans charged that Gompers was a foreigner who dictated to American workers. An "American Workingman" wrote in the Republican-affiliated *Indianapolis Star* of his humiliation at seeing the great AFL, an organization of native-born Americans, "being ruled and reigned by a foreigner," and an English Jew at that. As Watson habitually concluded his attacks on Gompers, "Every laboring man who respects himself will stand up and defend the right to vote as he pleases."[40] Such charges led Gompers regularly to exhibit his naturalization papers during political meetings, and to confess his personal political evolution: "I have never been . . . [a Democrat] and am not now. A long time ago I was a Republican, but I'm not guilty now."[41]

In a campaign so dominated by appeals to labor, Watson's effort among workingmen became particularly important. The Republican candidate spoke more often to labor crowds than to any other group. Just before election day Watson added regular noonday factory meetings to his schedule, speaking at foundries and machine shops. Indianapolis's Republican newspaper reacted with daily editorials, articles, and letters to the editor addressing labor issues or attacking the unions' political role.[42]

The key to the Republican labor campaign lay with Martin Mulhall and the NAM's organizing among manufacturers and workers. Mulhall began his work by meeting with state Republican leaders, who asked that the NAM take responsibility for mobilizing working-class voters. After conferring with his bosses at the NAM, Mulhall accepted the challenge.[43] Joining forces with David Parry, C. C. Hanch (proprietor of Nordyke and Marmon Manufacturing Co. and vice president of the Indiana branch of the NAM), and Captain John Gowdy (representing the Republicans), Mulhall recruited firms throughout the state to join forces with them and contribute money to Watson's campaign.[44]

Attention then shifted from financing to building an organization of workers that would support Watson for governor. Hanch urged manufacturers throughout the region to handpick worker representatives from their own factories for the new organization: "it is essential that you be careful in your selection, as the operatives must be thoroughly trustworthy and worthy of your confidence."[45] At the first meeting of employees on 11 September, Mulhall happily observed that: "The men who were selected by the employers, were . . . high-grade, intelligent, well-appearing mechanics." By October Mulhall reported that more than one hundred workers attended the meetings and were performing a number of services. They recruited co-workers to support the Republican ticket and canvassed workplaces to determine the magnitude of the Republican vote. Taking down the names and addresses of those brave enough to confess plans to vote the Democratic, Socialist, Prohibition, or Independent tickets, Mulhall's operatives then delivered packets of political leaflets to them, in hopes of bringing them around to the Republicans.[46]

The new organization, named the Workingmen's Protective Association (or WPA—the same name given to other organizations created by Martin Mulhall throughout the country) presented itself as a legitimate workers' endeavor. A letter to manufacturers described it as an organization "in which the employer has no say for this is a workingmen's organization."[47] Claiming to represent eight thousand wage earners, the WPA stressed in another piece of campaign literature: "At heart we have only the best interests of the working people, of which we are a part." It urged workers not to be "intimidated or coerced or sold out to the Democratic party" by anyone who preaches "class hatred—the classes against the masses." At the same time the NAM instructed members not to mention the group or its activities to any person, "since the most effective results can be accomplished . . . by quiet activity."[48]

Next the WPA reached out to the vast mass of industrial workers by creating Republican factory clubs. At Nordyke and Marmon, a plant with some five hundred employees, WPA loyalists formed both a Taft-Sherman-Watson club, with 350 members, and a uniformed drum corps of thirty men. All across town Republican clubs, with fife, drum, and bugle corps, sprang up, particularly in factories owned or managed by members of the Employers' Association of Indianapolis.[49]

With the manufacturers' committee active, the WPA hustling votes, and Republican clubs established in many factories, the NAM had laid a strong foundation for its political campaign. As a climax Mulhall orchestrated a series of grand industrial parades. Almost each week during the last stages of the campaign, workers marched on behalf of Republican candidates. When presidential nominee William H. Taft visited, or when James Watson came to town, thousands of workingmen punctuated the event with a dramatic procession from the factories of Indianapolis.[50]

The NAM activists saw these industrial parades as their crowning achievement. David Parry viewed Mulhall as "certainly a trump and pastmaster in political art. Of course our Democratic friends have been howling like a pack of hurt hounds, . . . but they have gotten on to the conditions too late to stop our purpose." Mulhall reported to NAM headquarters that the parades had achieved their purpose. Now the NAM activists had only to wait confidently for election day when, they knew, Watson would win the governor's election.[51]

The Results of the Employers' Campaign

Unfortunately for Mulhall and the NAM, Democrat Tom Marshall soundly defeated Watson for the governorship. In an otherwise narrow election, Marshall won by nearly fifteen thousand votes out of a total of some seven hundred thousand. For the first time since 1893 the Democrats took control in Indiana. The Democrats also won eleven out of thirteen seats in Congress, a majority in the lower house of the state legislature, and the offices of lieutenant-governor and superintendent of public instruction. Yet the Republicans won the presidency in Indiana and swept most other state offices.[52] Voters had specifically repudiated the Republican gubernatorial ticket; the Democrats had their best results in fifteen years; and the open shop employers lost their biggest gamble. How did this happen?

NAM leaders could not overcome three major obstacles. First, while the NAM worked to inject issue politics into the 1908 campaign season, they competed against other issues and other group demands that undermined their campaign. Second, the parties' shifting fortunes and the historic loyalties of the electorate in Indiana both independently influenced the course of politics in 1908. And third, the NAM leaders had targeted a working class that had its own ideas about whom to vote for and why. A closer look at Indiana politics, and especially at the NAM campaign in Indianapolis, illustrates these dynamics.

During the Progressive Era, Indiana still exhibited many characteristics associated with the political culture of the Gilded Age. Partisan loyalty continued to bc worn like a proud badge, the newspapers still marched to a partisan beat, and as recently as 1897 the state had passed a law requiring voters to state their party affiliation to poll takers.[53] Historically the parties divided the state between them, with Democrats dominating in southern counties and some cities, especially where brewing interests were strong, and the Republicans enjoying hegemony in the northern counties and in most manufacturing areas. Southern Indiana was a region of poorer farms, with large concentrations of German Americans, where discontent was common. Northern Indiana, on the other hand, was wealthier, more populous, and more Yankee.[54]

Indiana Democrats, like their counterparts across the country, had struggled to overcome factionalism since the depression of the nineties split the party over currency issues. Every election since 1892 had been a bruiser for the Democrats, and in 1904 the party sunk to its lowest point. But in 1908 party fortunes improved, as Democrats settled on a little-known, small-town lawyer named Thomas Marshall for their gubernatorial candidate, a witty man who thrilled the convention by refusing to run until the convention pledged to unite in support of his candidacy. Marshall himself perfectly typified the partisan culture of his era. A Democrat's Democrat, Marshall stuck with his party in 1896, remaining loyal to William J. Bryan and his party ideals when few in the state did. Regarding his own party loyalty Marshall once quipped: "There are a great many things which I believe that I know are not so; for instance, I believe that the Democratic party is always right." A fundamentalist Presbyterian, Marshall was a complicated figure who refused to force his religion on others, had married a Catholic, and raised their son Catholic to please his wife. A one-time alcoholic, then a teetotaler, he nonetheless opposed prohibition.[55]

Though Republicans had enjoyed a long period of unity and electoral success in Indiana, tensions within the party had been growing. By 1908 the party's progressive faction was quite strong, having elected a reformist governor, J. Frank Hanley, in 1904. An old-fashioned Republican, Hanley fought "immoral behavior" in a crusade against gambling, tobacco, and, most importantly, alcohol. In the spring of 1908 Governor Hanley, who was not running for reelection, convinced state Republicans to adopt a plank endorsing local county option. This proposal allowed the mostly rural supporters of temperance to outlaw liquor for an entire county, despite the opposition of urban voters. In September Hanley called a special session of the general assembly to pass the county option law—and succeeded by a narrow margin.[56]

Hanley's crusade against liquor had peaked even as the Republican convention chose its next gubernatorial candidate from the party's conservative wing. James Watson disliked prohibition. By pushing hard for county option amidst a gubernatorial election, Hanley revealed his determination to get rid of alcohol even if it allowed Democrats into the statehouse. The Republicans' split over moral reform greatly weakened their 1908 campaign. To a friend Albert Beveridge called Watson a liar, a man who represented "a regime which had cut the throat" of progressive Republicans. Hanley told Watson he was "morally unfit" to be governor, and departed the state at the height of the 1908 campaign to lecture on the evils of alcohol.[57]

Indiana's 1908 gubernatorial campaign thus shaped up as one in which liquor and traditional partisan loyalties competed for influence. What then of labor? The NAM campaign helped push workers into the Democratic camp and linked labor and liquor together with traditional loyalties into a bundle that defeated the Republican ticket.

Analysts agreed after the election that the labor vote had been critical. As the Republican *Indianapolis News* put it, workers "were determined to strike a blow, they wanted to show their strength, and they have done so." The NAM clearly united organized labor against the Republican ticket. Conservative employers miscalculated in believing that their public campaign would gain them acceptance among Republicans as a legitimate political power. Instead their strategy only exposed political coercion, which in turn angered many workingmen and alienated Republican party leaders.

Democratic and union leaders relentlessly publicized rumors of WPA activity. A Democratic newspaper speculated about the "Mysterious Letters" sent to coerce and intimidate workers in the large factories. Within days they traced the letters to Mulhall, operating out of an office adjoining that of the Indianapolis Employers' Association. Mulhall thickened the muddy waters by declaring he was working for the Republican National Committee. The situation grew more explosive in the following days as every group involved in Mulhall's schemes (the Republican National Committee, the Indianapolis Employers' Association, and the NAM) denied any association with him. But labor leaders and journalists soon pieced together the evidence and demonstrated that Mulhall was indeed connected to all three organizations. The scandal proved to many workers that Watson and the open shop employers were in league with one another. Labor newspapers grew vehement in their condemnations of Watson, and activists blanketed the state with circulars warning workers about Mulhall's activities "in conjunction with labor-crushing employers." As the circular noted, "No wage worker with a trace of American patriotism in him will countenance this effort . . . to rob him of his franchise."[58]

Indiana's voting returns suggest how partisan loyalty combined with the issues of liquor and labor to defeat the Republican gubernatorial ticket in 1908. County returns demonstrate remarkable consistency in partisan associations: the south remained overwhelmingly Democratic, while the north remained Republican.[59] Voting in working-class districts followed a regional and trade unionist axis. Northern cities with weak labor movements tended to vote Republican (as in Gary and East Chicago), while southern towns where labor was stronger tended to vote Democratic. Vanderburgh county in southern Indiana's mining region, with Evansville as its major city, provides a useful example. Historically it voted Republican, and in 1908 the trend continued *except* when it came to the governorship: for that office Vanderburgh went Democratic by some three hundred votes. Several other Republican mining counties of southwestern Indiana likewise supported the Democrat Marshall for governor in 1908.[60]

The key to gauging the impact of the NAM campaign, however, lies with Marion County, the home of Indianapolis and Mulhall's headquarters. Historically Republican, Marion County responded to Mulhall's campaign by voting Democratic across the board in 1908 except for one office—the presidency. In that case county residents supported Republican candidate William Taft.

The economy of Indianapolis included a diverse range of manufacturing establishments, with an emphasis on slaughtering and meatpacking, foundries and machine shops, automobiles, flour and grist milling, and publishing. Small-scale industry—for example, furniture-making—continued to play an important economic role.[61] Relatively few immigrants lived there, and "old" immigrants far outnumbered those from southern and eastern Europe. In 1910 native-born whites born to native parents made up nearly two-thirds of the city's population (64.5 percent). Immigrants from northern and western Europe (England, Scotland, and Sweden, for example) constituted 63 percent of Indianapolis's foreign-born residents. Far more prominent among the population, in short, were native-born whites, Germans, and other old immigrants, and African Americans.[62]

These statistics sketch the rough outlines of Indianapolis's working class. But when the NAM or the AFL spoke of "labor" they didn't typically mean the entire working class. For Indianapolis AFL activists, "labor" meant members of the city's thirty-eight unions, which represented skilled, white, and native-born men. Germans played a leading role in the city's labor movement. NAM leaders, on the other hand, targeted workers in the largest industrial establishments—meatpacking plants and automobile and carriage factories, for example, whose owners led the Employers' Association of Indianapolis. These firms employed large numbers of old and new immigrants.[63]

African-American workers did not fit smoothly into the calculations of either labor or the employers. Rarely employed in the large factories targeted by the NAM, Indiana blacks nonetheless participated in the Republican campaign in large numbers. Mulhall's industrial parades often included an entire division of African Americans. African-American clubs in support of the Republican ticket sprang up, including some organized along occupational lines (for example, the Hotel Waiters' Republican Club and the Coachmen's Club). Yet the regular Republican machinery, not the NAM, reached out to these workers. These workers would not likely be attracted to the Democratic ticket in any case, given its white supremacist posturing. Hoosier John Kern, Democratic candidate for vice president in 1908, proudly bragged that he'd not received a single African-American vote in a previous election: "I was elected by the white vote, but defeated by the ignorant nigger vote." The *Indianapolis World*, a black newspaper, carefully reminded its readers of these and similar Democratic sentiments during the 1908 campaign.[64]

Ward-level voting returns suggest how different segments of Indianapolis's working class reacted to the campaign of 1908. Table 3.1 demonstrates the distribution of its ethnic groups in 1910. Manufacturing in Indianapolis centered in the southern and western parts of town (wards nine through fifteen), the same region that contained most workers. Immigrants in Indianapolis gathered primarily into the twelfth, thirteenth, and fifteenth wards. In ward thirteen lay the heart of the German community, both first- and second-generation. Sizeable numbers of Germans also lived in the ninth, tenth, eleventh, and twelfth wards. The largest number of new immigrants resided in one corner of the twelfth ward, commonly called the "Foreign District." Two smaller communities provided a home for new immigrants: Hungarians, Slovenes, and Irish lived in Haughville in the fifteenth ward; and in the eleventh ward, primarily an area of Germans and Irish, there also resided small groups of Italians and Greeks.[65]

Table 3.1. Indianapolis: Ethnicity by Ward in 1910

Ward	Native-born White	Foreign-born	Native-born, Foreign Parents	African American
1	13,340	993	2,737	2,941
2	10,968	700	2,241	899
3	7,646	657	1,878	3,920
4	16,257	843	2,744	3,141
5	4,688	865	1,732	3,497
6	5,344	970	1,079	2,549
7	8,950	995	2,254	788
8	7,690	710	1,842	1,053
9	16,734	1,441	4,632	500
10	13,856	1,422	4,011	851
11	8,677	1,627	3,391	291
12	4,910	2,882	2,423	296
13	9,616	3,014	6,674	272
14	8,404	529	1,309	300
15	13,113	2,119	2,473	518
	150,193	19,767	41,420	21,816

Source: *Thirteenth Census of the United States*, vol. 2, *Population*, 1910, 574.

Table 3.2 suggests that workers turned out strongly for the Democratic party. Although the evidence is incomplete (native-born workers with native parents are unfortunately the most difficult to trace), there is a clear correlation between the most upper-class, Yankee neighborhoods (wards two, three, six, and eight) and Republican voting trends. African Americans voted solidly for the Republican party throughout this period.[66] Conversely, ethnic Indianapolis, and especially the German heartland in the southern part of town, voted strongly Democratic. It is difficult to distinguish between the voting patterns of new and old immigrants. Both groups were well represented in ward twelve, for example, but citizenship rates were much higher among Germans than among the new immigrant ethnic groups. Still, the evidence suggests that when they voted, new immigrants and old more likely voted Democratic.

These trends do not represent a pure reaction against the employers' activities. In such a German town, for example, it is impossible to separate the liquor issue from pro-labor sentiment. But the numbers indicate how concerns over liquor and labor, together with partisan traditions, constituted obstacles to the NAM leaders' plans. The NAM targeted above all first- and second-generation immigrants working in the largest factories. Since 1896 immigrants had voted Republican in increasing numbers, yet they remained linked predominantly to the Democratic party. Attracting them to the Republican party became even more difficult in Indiana's

Table 3.2. Indianapolis: 1908 Voting Returns by Ward

Ward	President		Governor	
	Bryan	Taft	Marshall	Watson
1	2,357	2,681	2,487	2,575
2	1,448	2,389	1,650	2,192
3	1,163	2,983	1,399	2,750
4	2,177	3,120	2,317	3,002
5	1,319	1,832	1,395	1,762
6	1,258	2,220	1,432	2,048
7	1,807	1,983	2,027	1,764
8	1,115	2,026	1,305	1,841
9	2,676	2,120	2,866	1,942
10	2,879	1,970	3,056	1,813
11	2,526	1,554	2,673	1,414
12	2,017	1,176	2,277	920
13	348	1,312	3,660	1,145
14	1,383	1,148	1,403	1,145
15	788	517	812	495

Source: Indianapolis Star, 5 Nov. 1908.

Note: Ward level returns are unavailable for parties other than the Republican and Democratic. In Marion County the prohibition candidates for president and governor received 839 and 761 votes respectively, while the Socialist candidates for president and governor received 1075 and 876 votes (*Report of the Secretary of State of Indiana,* 1908).

1908 campaign once the party focused on moralistic issues like prohibition. First- and second-generation German immigrants illustrate this dynamic. As a key group that rejected the Democrats for Republicans during and after the election of 1896, Germans might have provided rich support for Watson.[67] Ward thirteen, for example, with the greatest concentration of Germans, did overwhelmingly support Taft for the presidency. Yet these workers, the heart of Indianapolis's working class and a group that opposed prohibition, were pushed back to the Democratic side by the 1908 campaign and turned out in large numbers for Marshall.

Conclusion

While busily mobilizing workers into pro-Republican parade formations, Martin Mulhall had bragged he would prove that workingmen look to their employers, not "the jawsmiths of any labor union," for political advice. Instead the anti-union employers' experiment, to bring workers into the Republican camp and make a public bid for political power, ended in humiliation. In 1910 the NAM leaders virtually shut down their electoral strategy. They sent Mulhall into fewer than half a dozen contests and allowed only the most discreet tactics. Noisy torchlight parades had become an embarrassment to the NAM leaders. Their failure suggests the difficulties involved in forging a new politics based on group or class demands.

The NAM's first political project involved lobbying congressmen to oppose the demands of organized labor. Here they enjoyed a quick and full success as the House of Representatives, which had been growing friendly to labor, suddenly turned against the AFL. Congress would remain deaf to labor's pleas for reform until the Democrats took control in 1910. The NAM's next and more ambitious tactic, entering electoral politics to influence workers' voting behavior and thereby prove itself a useful ally to conservative Republicans, took the employers into far more dangerous territory. Now they confronted obstacles not only in the form of organized labor but also in well-established party structures and traditions.

Frustrated by a system that did not seem sufficiently vigorous in representing the interests of its constituency, NAM leaders wanted to rise above the parties and work independently as agents of the open shop employers. Yet as they struggled to transcend the party system, NAM leaders worked within a political culture shaped and defined by the parties. Even the employers' political style suggests the contradiction: Mulhall was caught between the gumshoe tactics of bribery and corruption developed by employers for busting unions and the classic party techniques of torchlight parades and fife and drum brigades. Ultimately, torn between the two styles, Mulhall cracked and confessed his sins to party leaders in the Senate and House of Representatives.

The NAM's project did not result in a new alliance with the Republican party. To the contrary, Republican leaders had already doubted the usefulness of anti-union employers before 1908, but that explosive campaign magnified for them the full dangers of alliance with the open shop movement. They might profit from employers' politics but the relationship had best remain private: voters could be alienated if the open shop drive became visibly associated with the Republican party. Labor's political power might not be as great as some unionists liked to think, but neither was it as insignificant as the open shop proponents preached.

On a broader level, the NAM's political work during the Progressive Era reminds us that conflicts between labor and capital never operated in a vacuum. The political parties powerfully shaped the context in which groups like the NAM and the AFL mobilized, even as their popularity declined. Voters in Indianapolis, particularly when apprised of the NAM's machinations, rejected the employers' candidate as too closely identified with a particular group interest. AFL leaders typically succeeded little better at attracting voters to support their candidates. Group or class demands alienated voters accustomed to more traditional appeals to nation, duty, and party. Understanding the political fortunes of workers and employers thus requires close attention to the resilient role played by the structures and culture of the party system.

Notes

For their advice and suggestions on this essay I am very grateful to Eric Arnesen, James Barrett, David Brody, Robert Cherny, Dana Frank, Bruce Laurie, David Montgomery, and especially Leon Fink. I am also indebted to the National Endowment for the Humanities for financial support provided through its Fellowship for College Teachers.

1. See Martin Mulhall to Frederick Schwedtman, 17 and 24 Oct. 1908, U.S. Senate, *Maintenance of a Lobby to Influence Legislation: Hearings before a Subcommittee of the Committee on the Judiciary*, 63d Cong., 1st sess., 1913 (hereafter cited as *Maintenance*), vol. 2. pt. 2, 2227 and 2264; David Parry to Schwedtman, 17 Oct. 1908, *Maintenance*, vol. 2, pt. 2, 2230.

For background on the open shop drive see Robert Wiebe, *Businessmen and Reform: A Study of the Progressive Movement* (Cambridge, Mass.: Harvard University Press, 1962); Clarence Bonnett, *Employers' Associations in the United States* (New York: Macmillan, 1922); William C. Pratt, "The Omaha Business Men's Association and the Open Shop, 1903–1909," *Nebraska History* 70 (Summer 1989): 172–83; Thomas Klug, "Employers' Strategies in the Detroit Labor Market, 1900–1929," in Nelson Lichtenstein and Steven Meyer, eds., *On the Line: Essays in the History of Auto Work* (Urbana: University of Illinois Press, 1988), 42–72; Philip Foner, *History of the Labor Movement in the United States*, vol. 3: *The Policies and Practices of the American Federation of Labor, 1900–1909* (New York: International, 1955); and David Montgomery, *The Fall of the House of Labor: The Workplace, the State, and American Labor Activism, 1865–1925* (New York: Cambridge University Press, 1987), 269–75.

2. The best single source on the congressional investigations is Robert Hunter, *Labor in Politics* (Chicago: Socialist Party of America, 1915).

3. For an introduction to these changes in American politics see Walter Dean Burnham, "The System of 1896: An Analysis," in Paul Kleppner et al., *The Evolution of American Electoral Systems* (Westport, Conn.: Greenwood Press, 1981), 147–202. See also Samuel Hays, "Political Parties and the Community-Society Continuum," in William N. Chambers and Walter Dean Burnham, eds., *The American Party Systems: Stages in Political Development*, 2d ed. (New York: Oxford University Press, 1975), 152–81; Michael McGerr, *The Decline of Popular Politics: The American North, 1865–1928* (New York: Oxford University Press, 1986); and Richard McCormick, *From Realignment to Reform: Political Change in New York State, 1893–1910* (Ithaca: Cornell University Press, 1981).

4. See Burnham, "System of 1896," 181.

5. Selig Perlman, "Upheaval and Reorganisation," in John Commons et al., *History of Labour in the United States*, vol. 2 (New York: Macmillan, 1918), 522; Alfred Chan-

dler, *The Visible Hand: The Managerial Revolution in American Business* (Cambridge, Mass.: Belknap, 1977), 332.

6. Wiebe, *Businessmen and Reform*, 16–41.

7. Lewis L. Lorwin, *The American Federation of Labor: History, Policies, and Prospects* (Washington, D.C.: The Brookings Institution, 1933), 58–63; see also Paul Douglas, "An Analysis of Strike Statistics, 1881–1921," *Journal of the American Statistical Association* 18 (Sept. 1923): 866–77; and Leo Wolman, *The Growth of American Trade Unions, 1880–1923* (New York: National Bureau of Economic Research, 1924).

8. Montgomery, *Fall of the House of Labor,* 259–69; Selig Perlman, *History of Trade Unionism in the United States* (New York: Macmillan, 1922), 163–88.

9. Isaac Marcosson, "The Fight for the 'Open Shop,'" *World's Work* 11 (Dec. 1905): 6956–65; John Keith, "The New Unions of Employers," *Harper's Weekly* 48 (23 Jan. 1904): 130–34. See also: "Freedom in Kansas City," *American Industries* 1 (15 July 1903): 15; J. West Goodwin, "Sedalia's Citizens' Alliance and Others," *American Industries* 1 (1 Aug. 1903): 13–14; and James C. Craig, "How Colorado Had to Fight, and Fought and Won," *American Industries* 2 (16 May 1904): 5–6.

10. Klug, "Employers' Strategies in the Detroit Labor Market." See also Klug, "The Roots of the Open Shop: Employers, Trade Unions, and Craft Labor Markets in Detroit, 1859–1907" (Ph.D. dissertation, Wayne State University, 1993).

11. Bonnett, *Employers' Associations in the United States*, 24; Philip Foner, *History of the Labor Movement*, 3:39–40.

12. Wiebe, *Businessmen and Reform*, 27–29; Bonnett, *Employers' Associations in the U.S.*, 301–2; Albert Steigerwalt, *The National Association of Manufacturers, 1895–1914* (Ann Arbor: Graduate School of Business Administration, University of Michigan, 1964), 109–15.

13. Keith, "New Unions of Employers," 131; see also Ray Stannard Baker, "Organized Capital Challenges Organized Labor," *McClure's Magazine* 23 (July 1904): 282.

14. Albion G. Taylor, *Labor Policies of the National Association of Manufacturers* (Urbana: University of Illinois Press, 1928), 18; "For Free Industrial Conditions: Through the Citizens' Industrial Association," *American Industries* 2 (16 Nov. 1903): 3–4.

15. Frederick Schwedtman to James Emery, 5 Feb. 1909, *Maintenance*, vol. 3, pt. 2, 2635.

16. Wiebe, *Businessmen and Reform*, 13–14.

17. F. A. Kennedy to Gompers, n.d., *American Federationist* (hereafter cited as *AF*) 11 (June 1904): 507–8; Bonnett, *Employers' Associations in the United States*, 341.

18. William English Walling, "Can Labor Unions Be Destroyed?" *World's Work* 8 (May 1904): 4755–58. For more on the social character of the NAM and its rival the NCF, see James Weinstein, *The Corporate Ideal in the Liberal State, 1900–1918* (Boston: Beacon, 1968); and Montgomery, *Fall of the House of Labor,* 272–75.

19. On the AFL's political evolution see Julie Greene, *Pure and Simple Politics: The American Federation of Labor and Political Activism, 1881 to 1917* (Cambridge: Cambridge University Press, 1998); and Marc Karson, *American Labor Unions and Politics, 1900–1918* (Carbondale: Southern Illinois University Press, 1958).

20. Frank Valesh, "Alleged Anti-Trust Laws," *AF* 4 (Apr. 1897): 25–26; Andrew Furuseth et al., AFL Legislative Committee, to the AFL Executive Committee, *AF* 7 (July 1900): 193–210.

21. Gompers, "Relative to Trust Legislation," *AF* 7 (May 1900): 134–35; Furuseth et al. to Gompers and the AFL Executive Council, 11 June 1900, *AF* 7 (7), July 1900, 193–210.

22. Charles Nelson and James Grimes, "AFL Legislative Report," *AF* 11 (Apr. 1904): 314–15; Gompers' testimony before the House Committee on Labor, *AF* 11 (July 1904): 589–601; Samuel Gompers, *Seventy Years of Life and Labor: An Autobiography*, 2 vols. (New York: E. P. Dutton, 1925), 2:232–33.

23. Marshall Cushing to David Parry, 20 Dec. 1902; David C. Meehan, Ironclay Brick Co., Columbus, to J. B. Foraker, 15 Dec. 1902. Both documents are in *Maintenance*, vol. 1, pt. 2, 50–54 and 42–43.

24. Cushing to N. W. Kendall, New Haven, 7 Dec. 1903, *Maintenance*, vol. 1, pt. 2, 144–45; J. D. Spreckles to Cannon, 2 Dec. 1903, *Maintenance*, vol. 1, pt. 2, 136–37.

25. Van Cleave to Cushing, 25 Nov. 1903, 128–29; Cushing to Dear Sir at Anheuser-Busch, 7 Dec. 1903, 145; Cushing to Adolphus Busch, 5 Mar. 1904, 269; Busch to Cushing, 5 Mar. 1904, 270. All documents are from *Maintenance*, vol. 1, pt. 2.

26. Cushing to "The Boys on the Firing Line," 8 Mar. 1904, *Maintenance*, vol. 1, pt. 2, 274–75; Bonnett, *Employers' Associations in the United States*, 324.

27. Quoted by Gompers in his testimony on the bill before the House Judiciary Committee, *AF* 11 (15 July 1904): 6–7. The AFL's eight-hour bill was also killed at the committee level during this period. See Gompers, "Juggling with the Eight Hour Bill," *AF* 11 (May 1904): 396–97.

28. Gompers, *Seventy Years*, 2:241–42.

29. For Mulhall's early political career, see J. C. Delaney to Whom It May Concern, 21 Mar. 1907, *Maintenance*, vol. 3, pt. 1, 2845; J. W. Babcock, Vice Chair, Republican Congressional Committee, to Schuyler S. Olds, 14 Mar. 1894, *Maintenance*, vol. 3, pt. 1, 2844.

30. No signature [Cushing] to Mulhall, 9 June 1905, *Maintenance*, vol. 1, pt. 2, 491; Mulhall's testimony in *Maintenance*, vol. 3, pt. 1, 2499 and 2894; Mulhall to Frederick Schwedtman, 7 Sept. 1908, *Maintenance*, vol. 2, pt. 2, 1979–80; and Mulhall to George Shanklin, 7 Sept. 1908, *Maintenance*, vol. 2, pt. 2, 1573–74.

31. See Mulhall's testimony in *Maintenance*, vol. 3, pt. 1, 2475 and 2521–23; and Cushing to Mulhall, 13 Oct. 1904, *Maintenance*, vol. 1, pt. 2, 426–27.

32. Mulhall to Henry Loudenslager, 21 Aug. 1908, *Maintenance*, vol. 2, pt. 2, 1915; Mulhall to Schwedtman, 11 Sept. and 23 Oct. 1908, *Maintenance*, vol. 2, pt. 2, 2003–7 and 2259; Schwedtman to H. B. Anthony, 22 Oct. 1908, *Maintenance*, vol. 2, pt. 2, 2257; Mulhall's financial account, 31 Oct. 1908, in *Maintenance*, vol. 2, pt. 2, 2319; and his testimony in *Maintenance*, vol. 2, pt. 1, 2943–44.

33. John H. Madison, *The Indiana Way: A State History* (Bloomington: Indiana University Press, 1986), 208–10; Charles S. Hyneman, C. Richard Hofstetter, and Patrick F. O'Connor, *Voting in Indiana: A Century of Persistence and Change* (Bloomington: Indiana University Press, 1979), 83–111; and Philip R. VanderMeer, *The Hoosier Politician: Officeholding and Political Culture in Indiana 1896–1920* (Urbana: University of Illinois Press, 1985).

34. Bonnett, *Employers' Associations in the United States*, 499–532; Orlando B. Iles and Andrew J. Allen, *Labor Conditions and the Open Shop in Indianapolis*, pamphlet published by the Associated Employers of Indianapolis, Inc., 1920, Indiana State Library,

Indianapolis. See also Sidney Fine, *Without Blare of Trumpets: Walter Drew, the National Erectors' Association, and the Open Shop Movement, 1903–1957* (Ann Arbor: University of Michigan Press, 1995).

35. James E. Watson, *As I Knew Them: Memoirs of James E. Watson* (Indianapolis: Bobbs-Merrill, 1936), 13, 27, and 56.

36. Schwedtman to C. W. Post, 2 Nov. 1908, *Maintenance*, vol. 2, pt. 2, 2323; Schwedtman to Mulhall, 14 Oct. 1908, *Maintenance*, vol. 2, pt. 2, 2206; Van Cleave to Parry, 27 Aug. 1908, *Maintenance*, vol. 2, pt. 2, 1939; and Schwedtman to Mulhall, 3 Nov. 1908, *Maintenance*, vol. 2. pt. 2, 2325.

37. Gompers is quoted in "Democrats Sway State Federation," *Indianapolis Star*, 1 Oct. 1908, 1.

38. Edgar Perkins to Gompers, 10 Oct. 1908, *American Federation of Labor Records: The Samuel Gompers Era*, microfilm ed. (Glen Rock, N.J.: Microfilming Corporation of America, 1979) (hereafter cited as *AFL Records*), reel 68; O. P. Smith to Gompers, 4 Nov. 1908, *AFL Records*, reel 69; Samuel Gompers to Edgar A. Perkins, 6 Oct. 1908, *AFL Records*, reel 68; "Gompers in Indiana," *Union*, 24 Oct. 1908, 1; "Gompers in Indiana," *Indianapolis Star*, 17 Oct. 1908, 5.

39. "Gompers in Indiana," 5; "Watson Lauds Taft," *Indianapolis Star*, 21 Oct. 1908, 14; "'Full Dinner Pail Empty' Says Bryan," *Indianapolis Star*, 23 Oct. 1908, 2.

40. An "American Workingman," to the Editor, *Indianapolis Star*, 6 Oct. 1908, 6; "City Gives Watson Assuring Ovation," *Indianapolis Star*, 17 Oct. 1908, 1 and 4.

41. "Democrats Sway State Federation," *Indianapolis Star*, 1 Oct. 1908, 1.

42. For a sample of Watson's work among labor see "Hold Noon Meetings," *Indianapolis Star*, 13 Oct. 1908, 3; "Workingmen Hear Watson," *Indianapolis Star*, 15 Oct. 1908, 4. To follow the *Indianapolis Star*'s appeals to workingmen, see "Business in the Elections," 8 Oct. 1908, 6; and "Gompers and the Labor Vote," 18 Oct. 1908, 6.

43. Mulhall to J. P. Bird, 14 Aug. 1908, 1883; Schwedtman to Mulhall, 17 Aug. 1908, 1895–96: both in *Maintenance*, vol. 2, pt. 2.

44. The following citations all come from *Maintenance*, vol. 2, pt. 2: Schwedtman to Mulhall, 17 Aug. 1908, 1835–38; Mulhall to Schwedtman, 25 and 27 Aug. and 7 Sept. 1908, 1929–30, 1940–41, and 1979–80; David Parry to James Van Cleave, 26 Aug. 1908, 1935.

45. C. C. Hanch to Dear Sir, 26 Sept. 1908, 2127–29; Nordyke and Marmon Co. to Dear Sir, 3 Nov. 1908, 2326; both *Maintenance*, vol. 2, pt. 2.

46. Mulhall to Schwedtman, 22 Sept. 1908, 2093; C. C. Hanch to Dear Sir, 26 Sept. 1908, 2127; C. C. Hanch to Dear Sir, 26 Sept. 1908, 2046–47. All *Maintenance*, vol. 2, pt. 2.

47. C. C. Hanch to Dear Sir, 26 Sept. 1908, *Maintenance*, vol. 2, pt. 2, 2126 and 2046–48.

48. Workingmen's Protective Association to Dear Sir, 21 Oct. 1908, 2246; A. J. Allen to Dear Sir, 1908, 2129. Both in *Maintenance*, vol. 2, pt. 2.

49. Mulhall to Schwedtman, 15 Sept. and 7 Oct. 1908, *Maintenance*, vol. 2, pt. 2, 2041 and 2152.

50. Mulhall to Schwedtman, 23 Sept., 7 and 17 Oct. 1908, *Maintenance*, vol. 2, pt. 2, 2099, 2152, and 2230; "Thousands Parade and Cheer Senator," *Indianapolis Star*, 1 Nov. 1908, 11.

51. Mulhall to Schwedtman, 17 and 24 Oct. 1908, 2227 and 2264; David Parry to Schwedtman, 17 Oct. 1908, 2230; all *Maintenance*, vol. 2, pt. 2.

52. For voting returns see the *Report of the Secretary of State of Indiana, 1908*, Indiana State Library, Indianapolis.

53. VanderMeer, *Hoosier Politician*, 24–28.

54. See Clifton Phillips, *Indiana in Transition: The Emergence of an Industrial Commonwealth, 1880–1920*, vol. 4 of *The History of Indiana* (Indianapolis: Indiana Historical Society, 1968), 4.

55. On Marshall see his well-written memoirs, *Recollections of Thomas R. Marshall: A Hoosier Salad* (Indianapolis: Bobbs-Merrill, 1925); and Charles M. Thomas, *Thomas Riley Marshall: Hoosier Statesman* (Oxford, Ohio: Mississippi Valley Press, 1939), the quote is on 36.

56. Labor's opposition to Watson was hardened by the Republican party position on liquor: both the state federation and the Indianapolis Central Labor Union strongly condemned the local county option bill, arguing that it would cost workers' jobs and violate individuals' rights to drink as they please ("Politics Menaces Life of Federation," *Indianapolis Star*, 2 Oct. 1908, 1). On the Republicans and liquor see Phillips, *Indiana in Transition*, 97–101; Mulhall to Schwedtman, 15 Aug. 1908, *Maintenance*, vol. 2, pt. 2, 1887; [Mulhall] to Ferdinand [Schwedtman], 17 Aug. 1908, *Maintenance*, vol. 2, pt. 2, 1889–90; [Mulhall] to J. P. Bird, 14 Aug. 1908, *Maintenance*, vol. 2, pt. 2, 1883; Mulhall testimony, *Maintenance*, vol. 3, 2828.

57. Lawrence M. Bowman, "Stepping Stone to the Presidency: A Study of Thomas Riley Marshall's 1908 Indiana Gubernatorial Campaign" (Ph.D. dissertation, University of Kansas, 1967), 19–20, 166.

58. "Against Mulhall's Campaign," *Indianapolis News*, 15 Oct. 1908, 3; "Political Circulars to Employes Are Traced," *Indianapolis News*, 7 Oct. 1908, 3; "Colonel Mulhall and the Manufacturers' Association—A Fable," *Union*, 10 Oct. 1908.

59. *Report of the Secretary of State of Indiana*, 1900, 1904, and 1908, Indiana State Library, Indianapolis.

60. Mining counties that supported Marshall included Vigo, Clay, Owen, Greene, Sullivan, Knox, Dubois, Martin, Vanderburgh, and Posey; those that supported Watson were Vermillion, Parke, Daviess, Pike, Gibson, Warrick, and Spencer (*Report of the Secretary of State of Indiana*, 1908).

61. U.S. Department of Commerce, Bureau of the Census, *Thirteenth Census of the United States, Taken in the Year 1910*, vol. 9: *Manufactures* (Washington, D.C.: Government Printing Office, 1912), 184; see also Ruth C. Crocker, *Social Work and Social Order: The Settlement Movement in Two Industrial Cities, 1889–1930* (Urbana: University of Illinois Press, 1992).

62. Those native born to parents of foreign or mixed parentage represented 17.7 percent of the population, immigrants made up only 8.5 percent, while African Americans composed 9.3 percent. Furthermore, Germans vastly outnumbered other ethnic groups in the immigrant community: 38 percent of first-generation immigrants and 54 percent of second-generation immigrants were of German ethnicity. The Irish made up Indianapolis's second-largest ethnic group (16 percent of first- and 23 percent of second-generation immigrants). These statistics are based on the *Thirteenth Census of the United States*, vol. 2: *Population*, 1910, 546.

63. *Trades Unions of Indianapolis: Their History and Biographical Sketches of Leading Union Officers and Prominent Public Men*, prepared under the auspices of the Indianapolis Central Labor Union, Indianapolis, 1896. For a breakdown of occupations worked by different ethnic and racial groups see the U.S. Department of Commerce, Bureau of the Census, *Tenth Census of the United States*, vol. 4: *Occupations* (Washington, D.C.: Government Printing Office, 1880), 556–58.

64. Emma Lou Thornbrough, *The Negro in Indiana: A Study of a Minority* (Indianapolis: Indiana Historical Bureau, 1957), for her discussion of the *Indianapolis World* see 27; and Thornbrough, *Since Emancipation: A Short History of Indiana Negroes, 1863–1963* (Indianapolis: Indiana Division, American Negro Emancipation Centennial Authority, 1964,); *Indianapolis Star*, 1 Sept. and 16 Oct. 1908.

65. Besides the census volumes already cited, see Crocker, *Social Work and Social Order*; George Theodore Probst, "The Germans in Indianapolis, 1850–1914" (M.A. thesis, Indiana University, 1951); James J. Divita, *The Italians of Indianapolis: The Story of Holy Rosary Catholic Parish, 1909–1984* (Indianapolis: Holy Rosary Parish, 1984); Divita, *Slaves to No One, a History of the Holy Trinity Catholic Community in Indianapolis on the Diamond Jubilee of the Founding of Holy Trinity Parish* (Indianapolis: Holy Trinity Parish Rectory, 1981); Thornbrough, *Negro in Indiana*; Robert Barrows, "A Demographic Analysis of Indianapolis, 1870–1920" (Ph.D. dissertation, Indiana University, 1977); Frederick Kershner, "A Social and Cultural History of Indianapolis, 1860–1914" (Ph.D. dissertation, University of Wisconsin, 1950); and L. M. Campbell Adams, "An Investigation of Housing and Living Conditions in Three Districts of Indianapolis," *Indiana University Bulletins* 8 (Sept. 1910).

66. Thornbrough, *Negro in Indiana*, 10–33.

67. Richard Jensen, *The Winning of the Midwest: Social and Political Conflict, 1888–1896* (Chicago: University of Chicago Press, 1971), 291–96.

Chapter 4

Class Wars

Frank Walsh, the Reformers, and the Crisis of Progressivism

SHELTON STROMQUIST

RARELY HAVE THE "causes of industrial unrest" been so publicly and searchingly scrutinized as they were in the volatile hearings of the U.S. Commission on Industrial Relations (USCIR) from 1913 to 1915. Even more rarely have the divisive results of such an investigation been so forthrightly aired. While the outcome was not foreordained, the investigation took place in an atmosphere of heightened class conflict that focused the public's attention on the enduring problem of class and raised the stakes in the commission's recommendations. The Progressive movement, deeply invested in the efficacy of such investigations as a means of restoring harmony between classes, watched the process unfold with great interest and deepening concern.

The turmoil within the USCIR is well known. However, despite the attention historians have lavished on it, the implications of the commission's undertaking for the fate of the Progressive movement and for the nature and meaning of progressivism itself have not been adequately explored. More was at stake than competing traditions of intellectual investigation, or what Leon Fink has termed a split between "agitators" and "engineers." Historians, attentive to the call for "industrial democracy" that emanated from the commission's majority, have underestimated the extent to which class partisanship divided Progressive reformers. Graham Adams, Jr., who defined the period as "an age of industrial violence," noted the commitment of Progressives to promoting social harmony. But while identifying the divisions that splintered the commission, he failed to connect them with schisms in the wider Progressive movement.[1]

This essay highlights a deep ideological division among Progressives that this episode reveals with stunning clarity. Some reformers advocated class-conscious support of labor's interest, while others professed a commitment to promote class harmony through programs of social amelioration. Frank Walsh, the commission's vigorous chairman, came to view labor's interest as paramount and concluded that "no alleged or actual altruism of more fortunately circumstanced classes will avail to remove existing injustices." Instead, he argued that any constructive work must be "in the hands of men representing the interests of workers and directed to fitting the workers to exercise an ever-increasing measure of control over the industry in which they are engaged."[2]

The broad coalition of reformers that conceived the USCIR took a different view. These reformers envisioned a society of self-directed individual citizens—a "classless" people in a democratic polity purged of corrupting influences.[3] While forging links to an earlier republicanism shorn of its competing and contradictory claims, Progressives saw themselves in resolutely modern terms, as agents of an efficient and democratic order.[4] Shaken, like so many Americans, by the bitter class conflict of the late nineteenth century, they sought to invent social machinery for overcoming class polarization. To that end they advocated varied forms of industrial conciliation, social amelioration, uplift, Americanization, and democratic reform. While they believed some degree of social inequality was inevitable and were troubled by the presence of unassimilable and racially distinct "others," they confidently pursued reforms to heal the most dangerous social divisions and "improve the race."[5] Most Progressive reformers did not imagine a society that was literally without class differences but a people among whom class differences were of diminishing importance and not a basis for political mobilization.

Their movement achieved unprecedented breadth and coherence in the years 1911 and 1912.[6] Its vital center lay in an extensive network of reform organizations and their intellectual allies. They aggressively pursued public policy initiatives at local, state, and national levels. Two accomplishments in 1912–13 signified the reform movement's growing influence. First, the reformers persuaded two administrations, one Republican and one Democratic, to undertake a major investigation of the "causes of industrial unrest" using the favored instrument of a public commission staffed by experts. Second, by crafting a program of "Industrial Minimums" at the June 1912 meeting of the National Conference of Charities and Corrections and promoting it through the leading reform journal, *The Survey*, reformers proved instrumental in shaping the platform of the Progressive party. They brought to that autumn's presidential campaign a revivalist spirit that promised social regeneration through a realignment in American politics.[7]

For a reform movement committed to fostering class reconciliation, the resurgence of class conflict was troubling. After 1909, class warfare again disrupted the industrial peace in ways that reformers could not ignore. Mass strikes and even violent pitched battles became not simply a "western" problem but a symptom of renewed national crisis. With the strikes of immigrant garment workers in New York and Philadelphia and steelworkers at McKees Rocks, Pennsylvania, a "revolt of the laborers" gathered steam and threatened potentially to undermine the edifice of reform at the very moment reformers acquired the influence needed to reshape public policy and politics at the national level.[8] This class warfare, on a scale comparable to the crisis years of the late nineteenth century, gave the reformers' efforts to reconcile the interests of labor and capital new urgency. If the renewed conflict did not threaten to destroy the Progressive movement, it caused many to question the movement's unifying premise.

From massive outbreaks in 1909, conflict spread during the next two years to new centers and reached new levels of violence. On 1 October 1910, a powerful bomb exploded in the *Los Angeles Times* building, during a bitter strike of structural ironworkers, killing twenty persons and setting the stage for a divisive and ultimately disastrous campaign to defend the accused McNamara brothers, officials of the union. A large strike among Chicago garment workers erupted in the fall of 1910, followed by a general strike on the Harriman railroad lines in 1911, and the Lawrence textile strike in early 1912. Then followed bitter strikes of West Virginia coal miners, Paterson silk workers, and Colorado coal miners in 1912 and 1913. Labor conflict attended by significant violence seemed to spread unchecked from one mass production center to another, taking root especially among new immigrant unskilled workers.[9]

Social Reform and Class Conflict

The rising levels of class conflict particularly troubled an influential network of social reformers who, in many ways, formed the core of the Progressive movement. They had sought to rehabilitate American democracy by mobilizing citizens without regard to class in a campaign to root out what Edward Devine termed the "obnoxious and pauperizing features of an imperfect environment which society can change by conscious social effort." A new consciousness of class now threatened that project. Speaking for his fellow editors of *Charities and the Commons*, Devine argued in 1908 that a set of "more or less isolated . . . conquerable evils," not a "bad system," was the problem to be addressed. The "attack on insanitary tenements, tuberculosis, and child labor" had been mounted, "as if it were worth while to overcome them even while private property and wages and profits remain in evidence as essential features of our industrial system."[10] Graham Taylor appealed to workers to rise above their narrow interests. He had seen the signs of an "awakening of the wage earners of our country . . . to the consciousness of their class interest," but he professed to see a more widespread "awakening of the mass to move together to claim and conserve the rights and interests common to the whole community." Taylor believed that the labor movement must abandon its parochial interest in wage earners alone "by being broadened into taking more public spirited views."[11] John Graham Brooks called upon organized labor to "enter upon its heavy task of leading the fight against a party tyranny." He noted that "no class (if that word must be used) has so much at stake in all this as the wage-earner."[12]

In the fall of 1911, more than a year after the fatal explosion at the *Los Angeles Times* building, the accused McNamara brothers confessed to the crime. While the labor movement had largely stood by the brothers despite the case that was mounted against them, the social reformers viewed the bombing itself and the defense of the accused with alarm. The confessions loosed an agonized torrent of sentiment urging class reconciliation. The reformers called for an industrial commission to investigate the causes of industrial unrest and recommend new "laws and methods for industrial adjustment." Paul Kellogg, editor of *The Survey*, expressed the consensus view of the twenty-nine reformers who participated in the magazine's forum, entitled "Larger Bearings of the McNamara Case." "The situation," he wrote, "is too much freighted with the public well-being to be left to contending forces to keep striking false balances." Speaking on behalf of the interest of "the whole people," he asserted that "we must give structure to fair play; reality to justice; and buttressed channels to those economic forces which, when they work at cross-purposes, jam up the currents of our national life."[13] While differences in emphasis abounded among the reformers who were queried on the meaning of the McNamara case, nearly all stressed the need for recognition of labor, for eliminating "predatory" organization among labor and capital, and for addressing the underlying conditions that produce violence.[14]

Investigating the "Causes of Industrial Unrest"

During the last weeks of December 1911, a remarkable group of social reformers gathered in the offices of *The Survey* in New York to consider how the deepening problem of industrial unrest might be solved. Jane Addams presided over the first meeting, which included Kellogg, Lillian Wald, Florence Kelley, Rabbi Stephen Wise, Samuel McCune Lindsay, and John Haynes Holmes. Succeeding meetings expanded the circle to include other settlement workers, the director of the Russell Sage Foundation, and the secretary of the National Child Labor Committee.[15] In a petition to President Taft, delivered on 30 December, the group made its case for a commission to investigate industrial relations. This self-styled Industrial Relations Committee drew on a favored remedy when it called for a legislated commission "to investigate, study and consider the grave problems" that faced the nation. "The American people as a whole must think these things through. . . . We need more light. . . . Today, as fifty years ago, a house divided against itself cannot stand. We have yet to solve the problems of democracy in its industrial relationships and to solve them along industrial lines."[16] The outbreak of the Lawrence textile strike in early January gave the petition even greater urgency.

During the succeeding months, the campaign for an industrial relations commission gathered steam.[17] Legislation submitted by President Taft, in response to the reformers' petition, moved slowly through Congress, shepherded at every stage by the Industrial Relations Committee and its network of supporters. When President Taft finally signed the law on 23 August 1912, the battle shifted to the composition of the commission.[18] Taft's selection of undistinguished public members and his failure to appoint either a woman or a respected social scientist annoyed the reformers, who urged that ratification of the panel be postponed until the new president, Woodrow Wilson, could name his own.

Wilson's nominees were more acceptable to the reformers, largely because he included John R. Commons from the University of Wisconsin, whom Kellogg cited as "the one man in America, who, as economist and investigator, has thought out industrial reforms, as statesman has drafted them into laws . . . and as administrator has practically enforced those laws." But the two other public members had not been among those the committee identified. Mrs. J. Borden (Florence) Harriman, a wealthy New

York City reformer, was, by her own account, regarded by Florence Kelley as "a comparative amateur." And Frank Walsh, a Kansas City attorney, named by Wilson to chair the commission, was well outside the primary orbits of reform in New York and Chicago, a Wilson supporter in the election, and at least in the East comparatively unknown.[19]

Walsh brought to the work of the commission an unusual mix of western partisan politics and rough-and-tumble reform, colored by his own experience with poverty and reform in Kansas City. As his friend and colleague Dante Barton noted, he was well prepared for the "technical part" of the commission's work, but "he is better fitted for the fight that lies ahead—for the human side of it." From a boyhood that taught him "what life is at its hard angles," Walsh had developed a deep hatred of poverty as "an unnecessary evil."[20] Having taught himself the law, he had practiced as an attorney in Kansas City since 1889. His practice gradually became entwined in the webs of local social reform, as did his activity in the Democratic party. By the early twentieth century he was moving toward a career in public service that included membership on the city's Tenement Commission, the Board of Civil Service, and Kansas City's pioneering Board of Public Welfare, designed, as Barton noted, to make "private charities unnecessary." Walsh fought running battles with the state Democratic party machine and helped elect reform governor Joseph Folk in 1904. He was recruited in 1912 by Woodrow Wilson's campaign to form a Bureau of Social Service that looked toward promoting a broad program of reform after the election.[21] Walsh brought to his chairmanship of the commission views on labor that were already well developed. As he told George Creel, "I feel very strongly that the commission should not be conceived as an arbitration board or a smelling committee. . . . It is *causes* that we are after, not *symptoms*."[22] Although publicly Walsh expressed views on labor conflict seemingly consistent with a tradition of industrial conciliation that had deep roots in the Progressive movement, privately he agreed with the sentiments of close political allies from Kansas City who argued "that our present industrial system should be placed on trial."[23]

During the two years of hearings that crisscrossed the country and produced, at times, acrimonious encounters with corporate titans and ameliorist reformers, Walsh came to embody a labor progressivism that directly challenged the ideal of class harmony. That ideal fired the imaginations of reformers like Paul Kellogg, Jane Addams, and Edward Devine, who had fought to create an industrial relations commission and saw themselves as its architects.[24] By the spring of 1915, deep into public hearings on the causes of industrial unrest, Walsh pleaded with reformer Edward J. Ward,

"For heaven's sake, don't accuse me publicly of being a 'constructive states-man.' Phrases and terms constantly take on new meanings. In the indus-trial field, at the present time, a constructive statesman might be defined as one who would substitute statutes for wages, with the chloroforming of public opinion as a byproduct." He belittled "the Wisconsin Idea" pro-pounded by John R. Commons and Charles McCarthy and criticized their legalistic approach to investigation whereby "fundamentals remain large-ly untouched."[25]

The press and members of the reform community greeted the appoint-ment of the U.S. Commission on Industrial Relations with great fanfare. Yet in the cautious maneuverings behind the scene, potential division and a certain wariness was evident even at the outset. Frank Walsh had a close-knit circle of Kansas City reformers and publicists whom he enlisted to project his vision of industrial reform. L. A. Halbert, superintendent of the Kansas City Board of Public Welfare, wrote to congratulate his former colleague on his nomination. Halbert expressed the conviction that Walsh would go to the "heart of the problem." His views directly contradicted those of the Progressives who had fashioned the commission: "I hope that the Commission will not give much time to health, safety and comfort in factories, or to industrial education, or anything of that sort but will go directly at the question as to how much voice the laborers should have in determining the conditions under which they will earn their living. . . . I believe that our present industrial system should be placed on trial by this Commission and you are just the man to conduct the trial." Walsh agreed with "the spirit of your kind expression" which "would be what would give me cause to do it."[26]

Walsh's most revealing discussion of his intentions for the commission came in correspondence with his close friend George Creel, who was preparing a major profile of Walsh for *Colliers'* magazine. Walsh empha-sized that "we are going into conditions more than specific troubles, and that if our investigation results in placing our whole industrial system upon trial and endorsing or condemning it, that this Commission ought to do so in brave and definite terms." While expressing profound frustration that the court system and the Supreme Court majority "are our real rulers," he asked that Creel adopt a "judicious note" but not "conceal a real sen-timent I have with regard to these questions of industrial relations." He expressed support for Commons's practical idea to put the commission's ideas in the form of proposed legislation. But his emphasis was clearly on the agitational value of such a strategy. "I believe that out of this that we could get up a people's lobby that would be something worthwhile."[27]

Even as Walsh and his closest colleagues devised strategies for the forthcoming hearings, key reformers from the Industrial Relations Committee, who had been largely responsible for creating the commission, moved
to embrace and guide Walsh's initial efforts. Paul Kellogg assembled the
collective wisdom of the reform community for the commission's edification. He reminded Walsh and his colleagues that "no member of the
committee which agitated for the legislation was named on the commission." But, he suggested, "as a volunteer body it is in a good position to
follow up the work and cooperate in exploring the field which in its conception, gave fire to the movement from the start." The diverse contributors to another symposium sponsored by *The Survey* were, he intimat-
ed, "indicative of the closeness with which the work of this new body will
be followed."[28]

The commission began its work amidst great anticipation. Almost immediately a division of responsibilities developed between two branches
of the commission's work: public investigation through hearings directed
at shaping public opinion and "scientific" inquiry through the preparation of detailed reports designed to influence the drafting of legislation.
The hearings, presumably, would build public support for legislation that
would result from investigation. Commons recalled that this division of
responsibilities in fact sprang from his own conversation with Walsh in
Kansas City. "He had charge of the public hearings . . . with his own staff.
I had charge of the staff of investigators appointed on my recommendation." Commons believed the hearings were "of much importance, although the witnesses merely stated their opinions and interpretations,"
whereas his experience with the National Civic Federation and the Wisconsin Industrial Commission had convinced him that he could work more
effectively in "private conference between the leaders of organizations in
reaching agreements by conciliation." These agreements could result in
"detailed recommendations to Congress on future legislation."[29] These
differences in perspective, present at the outset, would grow over the next
two years, revealing a fundamental schism among reformers.

Progressives Divided

From the outset the commission's work was colored by the continuing
labor crisis. Investigators fanned out across the country against the back-
drop of labor conflict that gave heightened urgency to their mission. Even
before the first hearings opened or the preliminary reports of investigators were filed, violence broke out in the coalfields of Colorado. By early

spring that conflict, culminating in the Ludlow massacre, cast a shadow of deepening bitterness and class polarity across the path of the commission and brought home the enormous chasm that still divided labor and capital.[30]

The commission was, nonetheless, slow to organize itself.[31] Research director W. Jett Lauck supervised four divisions of expert investigation amidst concerns, articulated especially by Commons, about his inattentiveness to the commission's work. Formally scheduled hearings did not begin until early April in Washington and focused on two areas—trade agreements and efficiency systems—of prime concern to Commons and the industrial relations experts whom he had been instrumental in assembling.[32] By mid-April, Commons finally persuaded Walsh to replace Lauck. The issue went deeper than a mere personnel matter; at stake was the nature of the investigation itself and the remedies that might be proposed.

Charles McCarthy, a leading proponent of the "Wisconsin Idea," had testified, at Commons's behest, before the commission in late December about the "method" of investigation. He drew directly on his Wisconsin experience, where for the previous thirteen years, he noted, "all constructive work, every piece of it, has been under my charge." McCarthy articulated a very specific conception of "constructive work." Surveying past experience with investigatory commissions, he argued that faulty methods had been adopted. "In the early days when an investigation was started like this they would bring in almost all kinds of testimony to get at the facts and then that testimony would result in a great many volumes. You would not have anything left afterwards." Instead, McCarthy proposed they "get the consensus of what there is on the subject first." Select a few "very fundamental things which will lead to something else afterwards." Then put men trained for these subjects onto the investigation. And finally, "ask a trained body of draftsmen, constructive workers . . . to show us plans of some kind upon which you can work." New legislation, drafted by experts on the basis of carefully planned investigation, was the end to which all work of such commissions should strive. McCarthy had outlined in striking form the program favored by Commons and the reformers who had promoted the commission.[33]

While the investigatory work under Jett Lauck did get under way, McCarthy and Commons remained concerned that the commission continued to place too much emphasis on public hearings. In April McCarthy advised Walsh that "the Commission will have to do some thorough research work before it gets through with its investigations." He urged that

Lauck and other heads of the divisions for investigations be sent up to Wisconsin "to consult with Commons and myself. We could go over his entire plan. . . . In the drafting of bills and so forth, Commons and I could get a group around here which would be glad to discuss them." He foresaw concerted investigation and new legislation in the areas of social insurance, industrial education, minimum wage, and immigration.[34]

In early May, McCarthy received word of Lauck's resignation as director of research, and, after months of hinting at his availability, McCarthy offered himself as director of research. Drawn to this "great statesmanlike program of social betterment," and aware of the "question of administration" before the commission, he boldly asserted, "I have come to the conclusion that the only thing that can be done with it is for me to take hold of it in some way."[35] McCarthy's offer reached Walsh at a very low moment. He had just received word that Lauck "is talking very viciously about our Commission; that it is a 'political frame-up'; that all our work is futile; that we do not wish to do any constructive [work]." McCarthy's offer found him in a receptive disposition.[36]

McCarthy moved quickly to assume responsibility for the commission's research program. He argued, as had Commons, for better distributing commission resources by cutting down on hearings and providing more adequate funding for research. His predisposition went in the direction of "constructive work" and legislated institutional change. Among the first crises he faced was the continuing financial predicament that threatened the completion of the work. Lauck urged McCarthy not to plan on getting additional funds from Congress, but to seek to control as large a share of the remaining funds for expert investigations as possible. The struggle over the remaining funds would continue and intensify during the remaining months of McCarthy's tenure with the commission.[37]

McCarthy also confronted increasing tension between the commission and the reform community. He wanted to understand the courts' ineffectiveness in situations like Colorado and "work out of it some constructive ideas." A national mediation board or commission of some sort was, in his view, the solution: "If people have no way of getting complaints settled, if favoritism exists, then we might as well make up our minds that they are going to organize and make a state within a state. If they cannot do this by mere organization, they will do it by force. The more justice exists, the less need there will be for force."[38] These same ideas had been voiced in a conference with the "Survey crowd." The meeting attended by McCarthy included Paul Kellogg, Jeremiah Jenks, Florence Kelley, Ben Lindsey, and John Glenn.[39] The group emphasized "the attitude of courts and inequality before the law as the main cause of unrest and violence." Although the conference ended harmoniously, McCarthy was well aware how attentively the commission was being watched and criticized by the reform community.[40]

McCarthy received confidential communications from William Leiserson, one of the commission's principal investigators and a student of Commons and McCarthy, regarding Leiserson's attempts to see Jane Addams and "Mrs. Robins" in Chicago and his extensive discussions with *The Survey* crowd in New York. Leiserson met for three and a half hours with Kellogg, whom he believed was persuaded "that we were going to do a big thing." Florence Kelley was also initially skeptical, "she like Devine was laboring under some delusions as to what you and Wisconsin stood for"—that "we would recommend giving to administrative boards full power to fix any standards whatever and would have minimums set by statute." Assured that this was not the case, she was relieved. Leiserson believed that Kellogg and Edward Devine had gotten an erroneous impression of the character of the commission's work from their inquiry the previous winter.[41] Thus, McCarthy found himself perched uneasily between alternative conceptions and programs for the commission. He soon found the ground beneath his feet eroding

From August 1914 until the final reports were issued a year later, a series of intersecting dramas played out within the commission that highlighted the underlying divisions among Progressives over the industrial unrest that had swept across the United States. Substantive differences over the sources of unrest were central to the conflicts. Was it to be explained by the psychology of workers, the failure of legal institutions, the absence of effective state regulation, or, as Walsh and his allies came to believe, the distribution of wealth and power? The nature of the "constructive work" needed to remedy those problems also caused division. What role would be played by careful, scientific investigation, the drafting of precise and enforceable legislation, or, alternatively, by mobilizing public outrage and opinion and creating a new politics of labor? Concretely, the split within the commission over the relative importance of investigatory work or public hearings polarized the staff and led to a severe rupture. The reformers who retained a proprietary interest in the work of the commission grew increasingly vocal in their criticism. Controversy over the Rockefeller Foundation's own industrial investigation, announced in September 1914, and over the relationship between the commission and the philanthropists and their social-work allies—what Walsh came to call the "Charity Trust"—further alienated the reformers. These bitter divisions would be reflected in the multiple final reports of the commission and would color subsequent assessments of the fruits of its investigation.[42]

Rockefeller and the "Charity Trust"

An issue of great symbolic consequence surfaced in early October and magnified other divisions in the commission's work. The Rockefeller Foundation had announced an investigation of its own, headed by the distinguished Canadian industrial relations expert Mackenzie King, into the problem of industrial unrest. Some members of the commission staff immediately linked the prominence of Rockefeller interests in the Colorado Fuel and Iron strike to the proposed investigation.

Paul Kellogg brought the issue forcefully to the surface in a *Survey* editorial. Announcing the new Rockefeller investigation, Kellogg noted with approval both the high scientific standard of previous foundation investigations into social hygiene, disease, and "social evil" and the expertise and independence of Mackenzie King, "who has stood preeminently for the disinterested public in a succession of labor controversies." Kellogg criticized the work of the commission, which had "floundered badly, without clear-cut division of responsibility, and with great areas of the field before it practically untouched." McCarthy's ascension to be the research director in June "for the first time gave promise of coherence enough in the work to allow disinterested observers to make sure of its trend."[43] *The Survey* targeted the commission's failure to make the Colorado strike "a great laboratory exhibiting in masterful detail that industrial unrest which was prime subject matter for study" and its inability to avert a garment strike in New York the previous winter. Most of the editorial was directed at the new Rockefeller undertaking. Its limitations were less obvious than those of a public inquiry—no distraction of divergent viewpoints, no patronage assaults, and ample resources of time and money. The editorial did note that the Rockefeller inquiry "draws its funds from an interested source." Kellogg asserted, however, that the investigation had no connection to a particular strike and had hired a preeminent, disinterested expert. He justified the inquiry "upon the broad need felt by managers and men alike for a betterment of the complex industrial relations and reactions which both alike find unsatisfactory and wasteful."[44]

By the time the *Survey* editorial appeared, events were moving swiftly on several fronts. Before learning of the editorial, Walsh had directed McCarthy to begin preparations for hearings to examine the Rockefeller Foundation's proposed investigation. Citing public and expert criticism of previous Rockefeller inquiries and their refusal to cooperate with government agencies, "added to the Colorado situation," Walsh believed, "we may have the background to make a report to Congress recommending that the activities of this alleged Foundation be prohibited by law."[45]

Amidst the flurry of communications regarding the prospect of Rockefeller hearings, McCarthy received a visit in Madison from John Fitch, just returning from the West where he had shadowed the commission's hearings and written periodic reports for *The Survey*. Fitch launched into an agenda for research on labor organizations that undoubtedly reflected the assumptions of the *Survey* crowd. "He said that we ought to determine once for all whether the labor unions were good or not; . . . whether they were not more than little monopolies; whether they did not tend to level men down; whether the union was or was not an efficient machine; whether there was democracy in the rules of admission. He cited an instance where the evidence showed that it took $150 to get into one of these unions."[46] Such a perspective must have reinforced Walsh's view that some members of the reform community provided cover for the strident anti-unionism of employers like Rockefeller.

The intransigence of Rockefeller and his associates over opening the foundation's inquiry to public scrutiny and the continued meddling of Kellogg and the New York–based reformers prompted Walsh to respond with brutal frankness to Kellogg's editorial. "The editorial is cunning and dishonest. Though I sincerely regret it, I am forced to the conclusion that you were compelled to publish the same, at this particular time, by your patrons and masters, and that you are ashamed of it."[47]

Walsh's attack on the independence of Kellogg and *The Survey* precipitated a firestorm in the reform community. Kellogg insisted on publishing Walsh's more detailed critique of the *Survey* editorial in parallel columns with the editorial itself, and all related correspondence. Walsh attacked the presumed impartiality of Mackenzie King and the Rockefeller inquiry and responded to the criticisms of the commission's early months of investigation. He explained in detail how and why the commission had investigated the Colorado situation in the way it did. One of Walsh's associates, George P. West, who had been the principal investigator in Colorado, also replied to Kellogg's laudatory comments on previous Rockefeller-funded inquiries. "The difference is obvious between an inquiry in the field of the exact natural sciences and an inquiry in a field where the truth lies with one or the other of two conflicting social philosophies."[48]

The work of the commission, in the meantime, moved forward at an accelerating pace. Walsh began the long-awaited Colorado hearings in

Denver on 3 December, over the governor's objections. Those hearings produced ample evidence of direct involvement by Rockefeller in directing the company's response to the strike. At the same time, commission staffer Basil Manly reported to Walsh the preparations being made for what would now be far-reaching hearings in New York on the policies and methods of foundations and privately endowed reform organizations. The commission would examine not only the planned Rockefeller inquiry but the work of other charitable foundations, including Russell Sage, Carnegie, the National Civic Federation, and the Charity Organization Society. Manly reported that they would examine "what part the sources of their income play in the determination of their policies and methods and finally whether such self-perpetuating organizations must not necessarily be a menace. I think it can be shown that they inevitably take part in politics."[49] Manly also indicated that the hearings would consider the "centralization of industrial control and the labor policies of Big Business."

The New York hearings opened on 18 January and for the next month Frank Walsh elicited testimony that directly addressed the central themes that would find their way into the commission's final report (the "Manly Report"). Criticism and defense of the role of foundations as extensions of the corporations that spawned them was interwoven with personal testimony from survivors of the Ludlow massacre and leaders of the United Mine Workers of America in Colorado. John D. Rockefeller, Jr., held center stage for several days of cross-examination by Walsh. He was joined in turn by corporate magnates Andrew Carnegie (once again defending his role in the Homestead strike twenty-two years before), J. P. Morgan, Henry Ford, and George W. Perkins.[50]

During these hearings, Walsh spoke at an open forum in Public School No. 62 on the East Side and explained the connection he saw between an inquiry into "a labor war" and the great philanthropic foundations. He traced the development of work from the small shop to the great enterprise under the control of "absentee capital." He cited the growing industrial control over government in closed, company towns, exemplified by the "benevolent despotism" the New York directors of Colorado Fuel and Iron exercised over two Colorado counties where workers are "robbed of the rights of free men." Such denial of rights, he asserted, prostrates republican government from the county level to the election of a president. The source of industrial unrest has to do, he argued, "with men's relations to the natural wealth . . . men have a right to wrest a livelihood from nature." Here then was the connection to the great foundations generated by the income of corporations. Only labor produces wealth. "If property is so produced, under a democracy, who shall have the first say as to what becomes of it, but the man who produces it?" For Walsh, the path to solving the problem of industrial unrest was clear. "Industry must be democratized . . . and the man who toils is little better than the slave unless he has a voice in the conditions of labor."[51]

At the heart of Walsh's battles with Kellogg and the New York reformers, and his deepening disagreement over methods with Commons and McCarthy, lay a divergent analysis of the roots of the problems they had set out to investigate. For Walsh and those reformers closest to him, America remained a profoundly class-divided society in which the problems of democratic reform could only be addressed by a fundamental redistribution of power, "a voice in the conditions of labor." The Progressive reformers, for whom Commons, McCarthy, and Kellogg spoke, did not believe class divisions were endemic. They spoke for a "public" convinced that capital and labor could find a common interest. This process of class reconciliation would be facilitated by scientific inquiry, remedial legislation, and the proper administrative machinery for settling disputes, without significantly altering the existing distribution of power and wealth.

The New York hearings fueled the fires of conflict with Kellogg. George Creel published an article in *Pearson's Magazine* on "How 'Tainted' Money Taints," followed in succeeding months by Julian Leavitt's articles "The Menace of Benevolence" and "The Middlemen of Charity." When Creel called the *The Survey* "the voice of 'Monopolized Altruism'" and ridiculed Kellogg as the tool of Rockefeller interests, *The Survey*'s editorial columns once again erupted. Kellogg bitterly criticized Walsh and Creel for denying him the opportunity to rebut the charges in testimony before the commission. He reminded his readers of his committee's role in originating the public investigation into industrial unrest and its continuing "responsibility, as a piece of citizenship, to follow, interpret, and criticise that commission."[52]

Progressives and the Class Divide

The public drama of the New York hearings and the polarization of relations with Kellogg and *The Survey* signified a deeper, climactic crisis within the commission itself—a crisis rooted in fundamentally different conceptions of the commission, the sources of industrial unrest, and the role of Progressives in constructing remedies. The fiscal crisis the commission faced intensified divergent perceptions of the value of hearings.[53]

The crisis crystallized latent differences in perspective among the various Progressives associated with the commission. Those differences had manifested themselves in the early correspondence between Walsh and his closest associates, and in the different priority McCarthy and Walsh gave to what McCarthy consistently called "constructive work." The rapidly unfolding events—particularly the conflict in the coalfields of Colorado—sharpened and focused differences between the reform partisans that led to the breaking point in the early months of 1915. Despite some airing of disagreements in public, both sides reserved their most forthright expression of those differences for private correspondence. Publicly McCarthy and Commons spoke only of budgetary difficulties and alluded to mismanagement in the commission. For their part Walsh and his associates withheld their fire in the interest of holding together the majority of the commission through the balance of the hearings. In the end, the multiple final reports revealed the schisms within the commission in all their splendor, but the reports largely spoke past each other to what were now different audiences, the fragments of a coherent Progressive movement, no longer unanimous in the conviction that class conflict could be simply or permanently harmonized.

Speaking on behalf of those Progressives who had seen in the commission an opportunity to craft the machinery for class reconciliation, McCarthy also vented his personal frustration. "The aim of the Commission from the beginning has been to work out constructive programs." He outlined how he had expected the work to unfold. "We were to bring out some [research] bulletins which the Commission were to pass upon on all the great questions. Then, about April, we were to take all the data which we had, get a bill drafting department and draft up this material so that these bulletins and bills could go together." He had pursued this idea with the expectation of presenting "a great program" to the president "which all the progressives in America could get behind." He saw it as a "statesman-like, clear orderly program" that had the "strength of logic behind it." But this was something Walsh "has never understood." Walsh's pursuit of more hearings, he declared, will "leave us nothing for constructive work whatsoever."[54]

For his part Walsh had come to define a brand of progressivism that was distinctly at odds with that of Kellogg, McCarthy, and their reform allies. He had expected a greater flap after discharging McCarthy in early March. But it was only in a personal letter a few weeks later to his old ally and friend from St. Louis, William Marion Reedy, that he decided to "dump" the whole thing. Nowhere did he more clearly lay out his deep philosophical differences with the so-called constructive Progressives. Commons he noted was the only economist on the commission and a "fine, well-meaning man." He and McCarthy both were "heavily charged with the 'Wisconsin Idea,' which would seem, at least, in this work, to be not to do any investigating or make any recommendations, unless approved by so-called advisory committees of employers and workers." Walsh's ridicule of the scientific and professional pretensions of those subscribing to the "Idea" was relentless. They favor creating "what they call 'large constructive programs.'" "These consist of interminable 'bill-drafting'; the proposed measures containing legal machinery which would provide for countless employees, experts, and the like, 'of thorough scientific training',—the very thought of which should throw the legal profession into spasms of delight, and the proletariat into hopeless despair. While this is going on, fundamentals remain practically untouched."[55]

The researchers had expected the commission simply to adopt their "monographs" and publish them as the conclusions of the "final report." Walsh had something more in mind, and he noted that McCarthy and Commons were "well thought of by the philanthropic trust in New York, who have made more or less strenuous efforts to apply the methods of scientific philanthropy to the work" of the commission. He was bemused that his resistance to their plans had produced in these gentlemen "a state of irritation which would seem impossible for such cool and scientific beings." Walsh looked instead toward a final report that would have "the proper punch" and that would give "the real conditions of labor in the country and the true cause of industrial unrest."

In the final months of the commission's life, Walsh held the most dramatic and, in many ways, defining hearings of the investigation. In Washington during May, he called Rockefeller back to the stand. Armed now with correspondence uncovered by his investigators that showed Rockefeller's involvement in all phases of the strike and its conduct, Walsh set upon him with a vengeance not seen in previous testimony. He later admitted that he had "turned the young man inside out" to get at the truth and "left him without a single justification for anything that took place in Colorado."[56] Walsh's "rough" handling of Rockefeller generated a flood of publicity and, as he had hoped, focused attention on the responsibility of large corporations and their philanthropic arms for the industrial unrest that beset the country. Walsh had already been made the chief target by critics of the commission's meddling in industrial relations. Now a torrent of abuse poured forth from conservative and business critics. The *Iron Trade Review*, to give just one example, called his method "Walshing," which meant "to bully, to rage against 'capital' and 'plutocracy'; having the characteristics of a devil dancer, dervishkearney, a Haywood or a flubdubber; used to rock a fellow on the 'money' boat."[57]

Final Reports

With the public hearings concluded, Basil Manly, who now headed the pared-down commission staff, turned to producing the final report. When the "Manly Report" became available to commission members in July, the employer members and two public members, Commons and Harriman, roundly dissented from its findings and recommendations. Unable to reach consensus, the members finally in August issued a series of reports that reflected the deep splits within the commission. The fundamental divide lay between the official report written by Manly, reflecting Walsh's views, and supported by the three labor members, and the Commons report, signed by Harriman and, with some additional dissents, the three employer representatives.[58]

The Manly and Commons final reports, and the reaction of the reform community to them, further reveal the impact that deepening class conflict had on the commission and among Progressives. In the Manly report, according to the *New Republic*, Walsh "secured the kind of report which he wished." In his own supplemental statement, Walsh offered (in bold print) his central indictment: "We find the basic cause of industrial dissatisfaction to be low wages; or, stated in another way, the fact that the workers of the nation, through compulsory and oppressive methods, legal and illegal, are denied the full product of their toil."[59]

The commission's report (Manly's) made four fundamental points about the causes of industrial unrest and proposed recommendations for action regarding each. First, it argued that an unjust distribution of wealth, rooted in the growth of huge corporations, created vast poverty and undermined the ability of workers to defend their rights. Second, chronic unemployment and the "denial of an opportunity to earn a living" directly affected workers' incomes and security in a labor market dominated by monopolies. Third, the judicial system systematically denied workers' rights and aided employers in preventing their effective organization. Fourth, the denial of labor's right to organize in its own defense was the primary reason for unrest. The report recommended a steep, graduated tax on inheritance and the use of those monies for education and public works to relieve unemployment, the recovery of public control of all land and mineral rights "secured by fraud," new statutes and constitutional amendments to protect laborers' rights and personal liberties, and new legislation that would guarantee the right of labor to organize and bargain collectively without interference by employers.[60]

The Manly/Walsh recommendations looked ultimately to the political mobilization of labor on its own behalf and to a fundamental realignment of class power. They did not look to the administrative intervention of neutral experts or commissions as the primary avenue of redress. They placed little stock in mediation and conciliation; indeed Walsh dissented from Manly's modest recommendation for special mediation commissions, believing that the machinery of the Labor Department, if adequately supported, would be sufficient to the task.

The Commons Report offered a vastly different perspective. Short on analysis of the causes of industrial unrest and long on proposed remedies, Commons summarized the views of the expert investigators, many of them his own students, who would dominate the field of industrial relations in years to come. Drawing directly on his experience with the Wisconsin Industrial Commission, Commons proposed permanently instituted state and federal industrial commissions and advisory bodies for each, composed of management, labor, and public members. These commissions would set standards for wages, hours, and working conditions and mediate labor disputes on a voluntary basis. As Clarence Wunderlin has pointed out, this essentially voluntarist vision set limits to state administrative development while expressing great faith in the ability of skilled mediators to construct and maintain labor peace. Government would not be given a legislative mandate to regulate collective bargaining between private parties. But industrial commissions might facilitate dispute resolution and administer "laws on child labor, hours of labor, safety and health, workmen's compensation, sickness insurance and minimum wage." Only where industries failed to create orderly industrial relations through trade agreements might more direct state intervention be permitted. Again and again Commons stressed the impartial and deliberative nature of commissions. Only if industrial commissions are "removed from the heat of political controversy" could they "have the confidence of employers and employees." "The points of antagonism are enlarged and exaggerated when one side or the other, through practical politicians controls the offices. The points of harmony can only be discovered by investigation, and investigations must be cooperative between employers and unions, else neither side will have confidence in the results."[61] These views reflected the deepest convictions and the core values of the coalition of Progressive reformers who had first pushed for an investigatory Commission on Industrial Relations.

Reviewing the fruits of the commission's work, most Progressive publications found them wanting. The *New Republic* spoke for many when it declared that the "great task" set before the commission had been "to prepare the ground and point the way by which the democracy could accumulate the experience and the power for humanizing the conditions under which it works." While admiring Walsh's "honorable human passion" not only "to find the truth, but to spread it," the editors criticized the "almost mystical belief in the value of friction" which animated Walsh and his allies. "He was frankly on the side of the poor and the oppressed." Noting his emphasis on hearings at the expense of "expert investigation," the *New Republic* judged him to be an agitator. The final report sounds like "uncritical denunciation" because it offers only "a skeleton of evils instead of a tissue of realities." Failing to confront "haphazard opinion" with "scientific inquiry," Walsh could not "distinguish between what witnesses said and what investigators found." Even more detrimental to the fate of the commission, "he suggests no machinery for the future by which the clash of views in the industrial struggle can be fertilized by a steady stream of carefully ascertained facts."[62]

On the other hand, like many in the reform community, the *New Republic* described the Commons Report as "wise but unexciting . . . significant, even revolutionary, and yet humdrum." The editors found congenial the report's emphasis on impartiality, expert investigation, and administrative (rather than political) solutions. One of the primary virtues of Commons's vision of industrial relations was, in their view, the "constant cooperation of employers and employees" that the plan would engender. Once the employer recognized that he was dealing with "an impartial administrative body, representing no merely hostile interest . . . his former opposition oozes." This was, then, the quintessentially Progressive solution to reorchestrating class harmony and labor peace in an era of industrial unrest. "In short, the whole idea of labor legislation by means of administrative order, issued after thorough investigation by an impartial industrial commission, cooperating with representatives of all parties, rests upon the assumption that there is a certain basis of common interest between labor and capital."[63]

The labor movement, too, took a close look at the results of the commission's work but gave enthusiastic support to the report signed by Walsh and the labor commissioners, Lennon, O'Connell, and Garretson. But Walsh, more than any other commissioner, captured their imagination. Regarded initially "as the one unprejudiced and unaligned man on the Commission," he proved to be "heart and soul with labor . . . the greatest acquisition and force which has come to labor in a generation," according to the Colorado Federation of Labor.[64] To the accusation by Governor Carlson that Frank Walsh had spread "mendacious statements" regarding the situation in Colorado, UMWA columnist Mabel LaRue Germer wrote, "from [Carlson's] standpoint—yes. From the workers' standpoint—NO." She offered a perspective on "industrial unrest" at odds with that of Commons and the Progressive reformers: "Some of our smooth-tongued employers have fed us a soothing tonic all these years which they call 'Identity of Interests.' That mixture is now causing indigestion in the minds of wideawake workers, because we know the interest of the employer and that of the employe is not identical. If it were, why the industrial strife?"[65] To a representative of the labor press, Walsh denied that he was "a doctrinaire," nor, he noted pointedly, "a political economist." The inquiry had studied "life itself." And, he argued, "you cannot card-index the hopes, aspirations, happiness, miseries, laughter and tears of the human family." The case—the facts—were now in the hands of the jury—the people. The concentration of capital, the seizure of the resources of the country by a few to the detriment of "the rest of us" was clear. Convinced by the experience of the previous two years he believed that "the people have a growing sense of their power to overthrow this injustice over night if they but will do it so. When enough of us get the idea it may be done between days."[66]

In all of its final disagreement, the U.S. Commission on Industrial Relations revealed the profoundly disquieting fact that class division, the bane of Progressive reform, remained central to American life and not, at least for the time being, susceptible to administrative solution. Walsh had become either "a Jacobin" or "the heart and soul of labor" depending on one's vantage point.[67] The "causes of industrial unrest" had been identified in the public mind as never before and the complicity of capital arraigned, but no armistice in the "class war" seemed in sight.

Walsh and his allies proceeded to form their own "Committee on Industrial Relations" and to agitate and organize on behalf of the agenda put forward in the Manly report. The committee attracted to its executive board, in addition to the three labor members of the commission and Walsh and Manly, a group of reformers whose loyalties to labor were unquestionable.[68] It received strong financial backing from the United Mine Workers and in its public introduction sharply differentiated its appeal from those Progressives who might seek impartial mediation of class conflict. The committee announced that it would provide "a medium for the cooperation of the forces of organized labor and those citizens, who, though outside the labor movement, recognize in that movement the hope of democracy and realize the justice of its aims."[69]

By the early months of 1916 the war in Europe and the reelection campaign of Woodrow Wilson came to dominate the headlines and the attention of the reform community. The labor movement found itself in a rapidly changing environment that enhanced its bargaining position and invited its participation in a new national campaign to preserve democracy at home and abroad. But, shortly after the commission's final reports had been submitted to Congress, Basil Manly suggested to Frank Walsh ways in which the new climate of war might affect labor's program. He urged Walsh to use his 1915 Labor Day speech to make two points: "the necessity for labor organization as a basis for efficient industrial operation during war" and "the democratization of war preparations" or, more directly, "the rich should pay." Weaving together the themes of class war and European war, Manly suggested that "every union local should be made a voluntary military company and every union hall an armory. Organized on a volunteer basis militarism would be impossible." He believed that "a little agitation" on behalf of a "'Trade Union army' would do more to stop war talk than all the platitudes in the world." Finally, he noted, but urged Walsh not to mention it in his speech, that "there would be no Colorados or West Virginias with such a democratic army in existence."[70]

As the war in Europe drew closer, new alliances and new fissures developed in the ranks of Progressive reformers. The concept of "industrial democracy" acquired varied, often contradictory meanings as the magnetic pull of nationalism exerted greater force in American life. But before the Guns of August, before concerns over preparedness and war profiteers, before the Council on National Defense and George Creel's minutemen, the Progressive reform community had confronted the facts of a domestic war of classes, publicized by Frank Walsh through the hearings and reports of the U.S. Commission on Industrial Relations.[71] The effort to diagnose the causes of industrial unrest and prescribe remedies confronted Progressives with contradictions that threatened to undermine their movement, whose appeal had been premised so largely on the faith that class conflict could be eliminated and social divisions healed by a program of "constructive work" on behalf of a broadly shared public interest. Many Progressives, in the context of war, recast their faith in the healing powers of the public's interest around a nationalist program that pledged, among other things, to make the world safe for democracy. Other reformers, with close ties to labor, pushed a program of industrial democracy that sought to use the exigencies of war finally to grant labor a significant measure of control and recognition in the workplace and thereby address the problem of "industrial unrest," as they understood it.

Notes

1. See United States Commission on Industrial Relations, *Final Reports and Testimony*, 64th Cong., 1st sess., Senate Documents, 26 vols. (Washington, D.C.: Government Printing Office, 1916), vol. 1. For critical commentary, see "Industrial Conflict: Four Articles on the Reports of the Industrial Relations Commission," *New Republic* 4 (28 Aug. 1915): 89–92, and "Mr. Manly Takes Issue," ibid. (18 Sept. 1915): 183–84. The most useful treatments of the divisions within the USCIR are Leon Fink, "Expert Advice: Progressive Intellectuals and the Unraveling of Labor Reform, 1912–1915," in Leon Fink, Stephen T. Leonard, and Donald M. Reid, eds., *Intellectuals and Public Life: Between Radicalism and Reform* (Ithaca: Cornell University Press, 1996); Joseph A. McCartin, *Labor's Great War: The Struggle for Industrial Democracy and the Origins of Modern American Labor Relations, 1912–21* (Chapel Hill: University of North Carolina Press, 1998); and Graham Adams, *Age of Industrial Violence, 1910–1915: The Activities and Findings of the United States Commission on Industrial Relations* (New York: Columbia University Press, 1966); also Clarence Wunderlin, *Visions of a New Industrial Order: Social Science and Labor Theory in America's Progressive Era* (New York: Columbia University Press, 1992). For the formative influences on the USCIR, see Allen F. Davis, "The Campaign for the Industrial Relations Commission, 1911–1913," *Mid-America* 45 (Oct. 1963): 211–28.

2. Frank Walsh, "To Urge Recommendations on Congress," *United Mine Workers Journal*, 11 Nov. 1915, 1.

3. See Shelton Stromquist, *Reinventing a People: The Progressive Movement and the Class Question* (forthcoming). The networks of social reform organizations are documented in a variety of specialized studies: Irwin Yellowitz, *Labor and the Progressive Movement in New York State, 1897–1916* (Ithaca: Cornell University Press, 1965); Clarke Chambers, *Paul U. Kellogg and the Survey: Voices of Social Welfare and Social Justice* (Minneapolis: University of Minnesota Press, 1971); Robert H. Bremner, *From the Depths: The Discovery of Poverty in the United States* (New York: New York University Press, 1956); and Allen F. Davis, *Spearheads for Reform: The Social Settlements and the Progressive Movement, 1890–1914* (New York: Oxford University Press, 1967). On the intellectual allies of Progressive reform, see Robert Westbrook, *John Dewey and American Democracy* (Ithaca: Cornell University Press, 1991); and Andrew Feffer, *The Chicago Pragmatists and American Progressivism* (Ithaca: Cornell University Press, 1993).

4. Robert Wiebe was in one sense correct when he wrote that "the heart of progressivism was the ambition of the new middle class to fulfill its destiny through bureaucratic means" (*The Search for Order* [New York: Hill and Wang, 1967]). What he failed sufficiently to note was the profound moral and social dimension of the Progressive vision rooted in nineteenth-century Protestant and republican reform traditions.

5. The racialized boundaries of the Progressive vision are addressed in Rivka Lissak, *Pluralism and Progressives: Hull House and the New Immigrants, 1890–1919* (Chicago: University of Chicago Press, 1989); Ralph Luker, *The Social Gospel in Black and White: American Radical Reform, 1885–1912* (Chapel Hill: University of North Carolina Press, 1991); Elisabeth Lasch-Quinn, *Black Neighbors: Race and the Limits of Reform in the American Settlement House Movement, 1890–1945* (Chapel Hill: University of North Carolina Press, 1993); and George Fredrickson, *The Black Image in the White Mind* (New York: Harper and Row, 1971).

6. The existence of a "progressive movement" was called into question by Peter Filene, "An Obituary for the Progressive Movement," *American Quarterly* 22 (1970): 20–34. See also John Buenker, *Urban Liberalism and Progressive Reform* (New York: Scribner, 1973); and Daniel Rodgers, "In Search of Progressivism," *Reviews in American History*, Dec. 1982, 113–31. Also helpful, though emphasizing a different basis for the Progressive movement's ideological coherence, is Richard L. McCormick, "The Discovery That Business Corrupts Politics: A Reappraisal of the Origins of Progressivism," in Richard L. McCormick, *The Party Period and Public Policy* (New York: Oxford University Press, 1986), 311–56.

7. Davis, "Campaign for the Industrial Relations Commission"; "The Industrial Platform of the New Party," *The Survey*, 24 Aug. 1912, 668–70; Allen F. Davis, "The Social Workers and the Progressive Party, 1912–1916," *American Historical Review* 69 (Apr. 1964): 671–88; on the Bull Moose platform, see John A. Gable, *The Bull Moose Years: Theodore Roosevelt and the Progressive Party* (Port Washington, N.Y.: Kennikat Press, 1978), 77–110. Melanie Susan Gustafson, "Partisan Women: Gender, Politics, and the Progressive Party of 1912" (Ph.D. dissertation, New York University, 1993).

8. On the endemic character of class conflict in the Rocky Mountain West, see Melvyn Dubofsky, "The Origins of Western Working-Class Radicalism," in Daniel Leab, ed., *Labor History Reader* (Urbana: University of Illinois Press, 1985). On the developing pattern of labor conflict after the economic downturn of 1907, what was termed "the revolt of the laborers," see David Montgomery, *The Fall of the House of Labor* (New York: Cambridge University Press, 1987), 288–89, and his influential essay, "The 'New Unionism' and the Transformation of Workers' Consciousness in America, 1909–22," *Journal of Social History* 7 (Summer 1974): 509–29.

9. See Meredith Tax, *The Rising of the Women: Feminist Solidarity and Class Conflict, 1880–1917* (New York: Monthly Review Press, 1980); Annelise Orleck, *Common Sense and a Little Fire: Women and Working-Class Politics, 1900–1965* (Chapel Hill: University of North Carolina Press, 1995); Steve Fraser, *Labor Will Rule: Sidney Hillman and the Rise of American Labor* (New York: Free Press, 1991); Steve Golin, *The Fragile Bridge: Paterson Silk Strike, 1913* (Philadelphia: Temple University Press, 1988); Ardis Cameron, *Radicals of the Worst Sort: Laboring Women in Lawrence, Massachusetts, 1860–1912* (Urbana: University of Illinois Press, 1993). An unpublished study that examines the profile of "violent strikes" in this period is Daniel Swinarski, "Statistical Characteristics of Violent Strikes, 1908–1914," unpublished essay, University of Iowa, 1991.

10. Edward T. Devine, "Social Forces," *Charities and the Commons* 21 (3 Oct. 1908): 2.

11. Graham Taylor, "Class and Mass in Labor," *Charities and the Commons* 21 (3 Oct. 1908): 67–68.

12. John Graham Brooks, "Industrial Democracy: Trade Unions and Politics," *The Outlook* 85 (5 Jan. 1907): 29.

13. Paul Kellogg, "Conservation and Industrial War," *The Survey*, 30 Dec. 1911, 1412.

14. "Larger Bearings of the McNamara Case," *The Survey*, 30 Dec. 1911, 1413–29, esp. 1414, 1417, 1419–20.

15. The early campaign for an investigating commission is best covered in Davis, "Campaign for the Industrial Relations Commission."

16. "Petition to the President for a Federal Commission on Industrial Relations," *The Survey*, 30 Dec. 1911, 1430–31.

17. "Movement under Way for Industrial Commission," *The Survey*, 2 Mar. 1912, 1821.

18. Davis, "Campaign for the Industrial Relations Commission."

19. Ibid., 222–25; Florence Harriman, *From Pinafores to Politics* (New York: H. Holt & Co., 1923), 133; the nomination of the chairman is surrounded by conflicting accounts. See also John R. Commons, *Myself* (New York: Macmillan, 1934), 166–67; and L. A. Halbert to Frank Walsh, 13 June 1913, box 33, file 68 (hereafter cited as box/file), Frank Walsh Papers, New York Public Library, New York.

20. Dante Barton, "Frank P. Walsh: The Man Chosen by President Wilson to Lead the Commission on Industrial Relations," *Harper's Weekly* 58 (27 Sept. 1913): 24.

21. Graham Adams, Jr., "Francis Patrick Walsh," *Concise Dictionary of American Biography* (New York: Scribner, 1980), 691; George Creel, "Why Industrial War?" *Colliers'*, 18 Oct. 1913, 5–6; George Creel, *Rebel at Large* (New York: G. P. Putnam's Sons, 1947); and McCartin, *Labor's Great War*, 16–19.

22. Creel, "Why Industrial War?" 6.

23. L. A. Halbert to Frank Walsh, 13 June 1913, and Boyd Fisher to Frank Walsh, 27 June 1913; also FW to L. A. Halbert, 14 June 1913, all in 33/68, Walsh Papers.

24. Davis, "Campaign for the Industrial Relations Commission."

25. Frank Walsh to Edward J. Ward, 29 Apr. 1915, and Frank Walsh to William Marion Reedy, 17 Apr. 1915, in 33/39, Walsh Papers.

26. L. A. Halbert to Frank Walsh, 13 June 1913, and Frank Walsh to L. A. Halbert, 14 June 1913; Frank Walsh to Boyd Fisher, 24 June 1913, all in 33/68, Walsh Papers.

27. Frank Walsh to George Creel, 18 Aug. 1913, in 33/40, Walsh Papers. Creel's article based on his "interview" with Walsh appeared as "Why Industrial War?" in *Colliers'*.

28. Paul U. Kellogg, "The Government, the People and the Labor Problem," *American Review of Reviews*, Sept. 1913, 344–45; "The Constructive Work before the Industrial Relations Commission: A Symposium with Introduction by Paul Kellogg," *The Survey*, 2 Aug. 1913, 571–88, esp. 571.

29. Commons, *Myself*, 171–72.

30. See Adams, *Age of Industrial Violence*, 146–75; George P. West, *Report on the Colorado Strike* (Washington, D.C.: Government Printing Office, 1915); Montgomery, *Fall of the House of Labor*, 343–47. Other sources on Ludlow include Howard Gitelman, *The Legacy of the Ludlow Massacre* (Philadelphia: University of Pennsylvania Press, 1988); and Helen Z. Papanikolaos, *Buried Unsung: Louis Tikas and the Ludlow Massacre* (Salt Lake City: University of Utah Press, 1982).

31. Telegram, John R. Commons to Frank Walsh [n.d., presumably Nov. 1913], 33/60; Maurice Dower to Frank Walsh, 22 Dec. 1913, in 33/38; Frank Walsh to John R. Commons, 17 Jan. 1914, in 33/64, Walsh Papers. Testimony of Charles McCarthy, USCIR, *Final Reports and Testimony*, 1:377–90.

32. Frank Walsh to Jett Lauck, 10 Jan. 1913; Florence J. Harriman to Frank Walsh, 14 Jan. 1913, both in 33/64, Walsh Papers; Mark Perlman, *Labor Union Theories in America: Background and Development* (Evanston, Ill.: Row, Peterson, 1958), 284–85; USCIR, *Final Reports and Testimony*, vol. 1.

33. Testimony of Charles McCarthy, USCIR, *Final Reports and Testimony*, 1:377–80; see also Wunderlin, *Visions of a New Industrial Order*.

34. Clara R—— to Charles McCarthy, [ca. Mar. 1914]; Charles McCarthy to Frank

Walsh, 21 Apr. 1914, both in 6/2, Charles McCarthy Papers, State Historical Society of Wisconsin, Madison, Wis.

35. Charles McCarthy to Frank Walsh, 29 May 1913, 6/3, McCarthy Papers.

36. Frank Walsh to Charles McCarthy, 1, 2, 3, and 4 June 1913, 6/4, McCarthy Papers.

37. W. Jett Lauck to Charles McCarthy, 3 Oct. 1914, 7/3, McCarthy Papers.

38. Charles McCarthy to Thomas I. Parkinson, 19 June 1913, 6/4, McCarthy Papers.

39. Jeremiah Jenks, a distinguished economist, had codirected the U.S. Immigration Commission; Ben Lindsey was a reformer and Colorado juvenile court judge; and John Glenn was director of the Russell Sage Foundation.

40. "Memorandum—Legal Division and Violence, based on conference at New York, 6/18," [ca. June 1914], 6/5; Charles McCarthy to Frank Walsh, 28 Aug. 1914, 7/1, McCarthy Papers.

41. Frank Walsh to Charles McCarthy, 1 Sept. 1914, William Leiserson to Charles McCarthy, 4 and 14 Sept. 1914, 7/2, McCarthy Papers.

42. Previous scholarship has focused on the divisions within the commission without situating those divisions in the context of the wider ideological divisions among Progressives. See Adams, *Age of Industrial Violence;* Wunderlin, *Visions of a New Industrial Order;* Perlman, *Labor Union Theories in America;* and Leon Fink, "Expert Advice."

43. Paul Kellogg forwarded advance proofs of the *Survey* editorial to McCarthy with a brief explanation of his approach (Paul Kellogg to Charles McCarthy, 7 Oct. 1914, 7/4, McCarthy Papers); "Editorials," *The Survey,* 10 Oct. 1914, 54.

44. "Editorials," *The Survey,* 10 Oct. 1914, 53–55.

45. Frank Walsh to Charles McCarthy, 8 Oct. 1914, 7/4, McCarthy Papers.

46. Charles McCarthy to Frank Walsh, 8 Oct. 1914, 7/4, McCarthy Papers.

47. Frank Walsh to Paul Kellogg, 19 Oct. 1914, 33/39, Walsh Papers.

48. "Editorials," *The Survey,* 14 Nov. 1914, 175–81; George P. West, "Industrial Relations," *The Survey,* 12 Dec. 1914, 303–4.

49. *New York Times,* 26 Nov. 1914, 17:3, 3 Dec. 1914, 14:3; Basil M. Manly to Frank Walsh, 3 Dec. 1914, 33/38, Walsh Papers.

50. The New York hearings were extensively reported in the *New York Times.* See for instance, 21 Jan. 1915, 1:3; 26 Jan. 1915, 1:1; 31 Jan. 1915, 1:3; 6 Feb. 1915, 1:1; see also John A. Fitch, "The Absentee Ownership of Industry on the Stand in New York," *The Survey,* 30 Jan. 1915, 467–69; Fitch, "The Rockefeller Interests in Industry and Philanthropy," *The Survey,* 6 Feb. 1915, 477–80; Fitch, "Ludlow, Chrome, Homestead and Wall Street in the Melting Pot," *The Survey,* 13 Feb. 1915, 531–34.

51. "Great Foundations and the Industrial Unrest," *The Survey,* 23 Jan. 1915, 437–38.

52. George Creel, "How 'Tainted' Money Taints," *Pearson's Magazine* 33 (Mar. 1915): 289–97; Julian Leavitt, "The Menace of Benevolence," *Pearson's Magazine* 33 (Apr. 1915): 385–96; Leavitt, "The Middlemen of Charity," *Pearson's Magazine* 33 (May 1915): 581–88; "Letting George Do It," *The Survey,* 13 Feb. 1915, 541–42; see also exchange of letters, Paul Kellogg to Frank Walsh, 5 Feb. 1915; Frank Walsh to Paul Kellogg, 6 Feb. and 4 Mar. 1915, all in Walsh Papers.

53. The financial predicament of the commission is discussed in William Leiserson, "Memorandum of Meeting, Sunday, Feb. 28, 1915," 8/7, McCarthy Papers; for

McCarthy's own defense of his relations with Rockefeller, see Charles McCarthy to Frank Walsh, 15 Feb. 1915, 7/6, McCarthy Papers; for a discussion of the complex relationship between McCarthy and Rockefeller, see Fink, "Expert Advice," 203–9.

54. Charles McCarthy to Redmond S. Brennan, 1 Mar. 1915; Charles McCarthy to John Fitch, 1 Mar. 1915, both in 8/7, McCarthy Papers; John A. Fitch, "Field Investigations of the Industrial Relations Commission," *The Survey*, 27 Feb. 1915, 578–82.

55. Frank Walsh to William Marion Reedy, 17 Apr. 1915, Walsh Papers.

56. Frank Walsh to Dante Barton, 24 May 1915, Walsh Papers, quoted in Adams, *Age of Industrial Violence*, 171. Adams has a useful account of Walsh's interrogation of Rockefeller and the public's response (164–73).

57. Quoted in Perlman, *Labor Union Theories in America*, 290–91.

58. USCIR, *Final Reports and Testimony*, vol. 1. The best general accounts of the commission's final reports are Perlman, *Labor Union Theories in America*, and Adams, *Age of Industrial Violence*.

59. "Industrial Conflict," 89. "Supplemental Statement of Chairman Frank P. Walsh," USCIR, *Final Reports and Testimony*, 1:153.

60. USCIR, "Manly Report," *Final Reports and Testimony*, vol. 1; see also Perlman, *Labor Union Theories in America*, 292–93; Adams, *Age of Industrial Violence*, 216–17.

61. Commons Report, USCIR, *Final Reports and Testimony*, 1:186, 195.

62. "Industrial Conflict," 89–90.

63. *New Republic*, 28 Aug. 1915, 91–92. Not surprisingly, *The Survey* also continued its close coverage of the commission through a critical evaluation of its final reports; see John A. Fitch, "Probing the Causes of Industrial Unrest: A Series of Three Installments Reviewing the Reports Issued by the United States Commission on Industrial Relations," *The Survey*, 18 Dec. 1915, 317–33; 1 Jan. 1916, 395–402; and 8 Jan. 1916, 432–34.

64. "Report of President John McLennan, Colorado State Federation of Labor," *United Mine Workers Journal*, 30 Sept. 1915, 8.

65. Mabel LaRue Germer, "Governor of Colorado and Frank P. Walsh," *United Mine Workers Journal*, 2 Sept. 1915, 16.

66. "Undisputed Facts for All the People," *United Mine Workers Journal*, 30 Sept. 1915, 7.

67. "Who Is This Man Walsh?—Sketch of the Two-fisted Irishman of Missouri Who Has Been Catechizing Capitalists," *Current Opinion* 59 (Aug. 1915): 90–92.

68. Prominent members of the Committee on Industrial Relations included Frederic Howe, Cleveland reformer and immigration commissioner; Amos Pinchot, who had fought to wrest control of the Progressive party from its corporate patrons; Agnes Nestor of the WTUL; Helen Marot of the AFL; and John White of the United Mine Workers of America.

69. Frank Walsh to Austin Garretson, 2 Nov. 1915; Dante Barton to Frank Walsh, 11 and 12 Nov. 1915; Committee on Industrial Relations, introductory letter, n.d., all in 34, Walsh Papers. "Support Needed and Deserved," *United Mine Workers Journal*, 11 Nov. 1915, 4; "From Committee on Industrial Relations," *United Mine Workers Journal*, 25 Nov. 1915, 4. See also Adams, *Age of Industrial Violence*, 220–21.

70. Basil M. Manly to Frank Walsh, 24 Aug. 1914 [*sic*] [letter should have been dated 1915], 33/39, Walsh Papers.

71. The schisms within the Progressive movement induced by the war are discussed in David Kennedy, *Over Here: The First World War and American Society* (New York: Oxford University Press, 1980), and Eugene M. Tobin, *Organize or Perish, America's Independent Progressives, 1913–1933* (Westport, Conn.: Greenwood Press, 1986), 57–61, Adams, *Age of Industrial Violence,* 222–26. On the meanings of "industrial democracy," see Fraser, *Labor Will Rule,* 114–15, 124–27, 136–39; McCartin, *Labor's Great War;* and Milton Derber, "The Idea of Industrial Democracy in America, 1898–1915," *Labor History* 7 (Fall 1966): 259–86.

Chapter 5

The Workers' State

Municipal Policy, Class, and Taxes in the Early Depression

CECELIA F. BUCKI

IN RECENT YEARS, there has been much controversy over the implementation of public policy—over private versus public responsibility for social ills, over raising and spending of public funds, and ultimately over a definition of the public good. Such issues aren't new; they have been raised in American society before, often in the form of debates about taxes and public policy. This particular debate originated in the early 1930s. While stories about Hoover and Roosevelt are well known, little attention has been paid to the local level. Yet for the average working-class citizen, political decisions at the municipal level mattered more than those in the national capital, especially before New Deal programs got underway. Even those early New Deal programs were initially shaped by municipal and state politics.

This essay explores public opinion on the raising and allocation of government resources—taxing and spending—at the dawn of the liberal welfare state in the early 1930s. It finds that working people united around an expansive and inclusive idea of social welfare, drawing on long traditions of labor and ethnic mutualism. Ultimately, this impulse was thwarted by conservative forces within national, state, and local politics. Thus, while Lizabeth Cohen rightly celebrates the "culture of unity" of working people around the New Deal and the CIO in the 1930s, she neglects the fractious aspects of New Deal social policy. Alternately, others find the roots of the present-day backlash against liberalism among these same working people. But these studies often discount the ways in which the compromises embedded in New Deal politics exacerbated intraclass tensions.[1]

While historians have debated the nature of labor's relationship in the workplace, less attention has been paid to the class dimensions of other political decisions of this era, like the structure of emerging social-welfare laws.[2] The early years of the Great Depression, 1930 to 1933, provoked a debate over the definition of the public good, pitting formerly politically passive working people against local businessmen and traditional party elites over the issue of social spending. This debate revealed what working people thought about their role in the polity and what they demanded from their government. In the process, the controversy highlighted the multiple influences on the emerging New Deal, how working people entered politics, and what became of political alternatives in the mid-1930s.

Historians have called attention to the new character of politics in this volatile era, featuring a new American-born generation of ethnic workers who with their immigrant parents formed a new electorate. These first-time voters became the base for the New Deal Democratic party.[3] That this ethnic, working-class electorate would have distinctive ideas about social welfare should come as no surprise. A case study of Bridgeport, Connecticut, in the early 1930s will probe working people's vision of the emerging welfare state through analysis of municipal politics and policies, culminating in the electoral victory of the Bridgeport Socialist party in 1933. Bridgeport was a thriving industrial city specializing in the metal trades, a World War I war-boom town, and the site of some remarkable developments that embodied a radical trajectory of the labor movement in the United States, both economically and politically. The unique Bridgeport evolution from war-boom town to third-party city provides a fresh perspective on the more general national experience. At the same time, its social and economic contours typified many industrial cities from World War I to the 1930s. Bridgeport was different, but not exceptional. An analytic focus on one city allows an in-depth look at the social and economic changes that gave rise to patterns of urban politics that had profound influences on the nature of national politics in the interwar era.

~✐

Two major questions preoccupied cities across the United States in the early 1930s: first, who should pay the bill for the effects of the economic catastrophe, and second, who should control the social programs that were established. Welfare issues had undergone change in the late nineteenth and early twentieth centuries. From colonial times, town governments had cared for their poor. Since the Gilded Age, this aid had often been privatized and handled by "professional" charity agencies and social workers who labeled their charges "deserving" and "undeserving" poor. Nonetheless, the boundaries between public and private welfare remained porous. In the heady days of municipal reform in the early twentieth century, cities streamlined their growing relief programs by creating departments of public welfare, partly to fend off private charity organizations' accusations of corruption and incompetence. An uneasy working relationship developed, with a mix of public and private funding and administration. Both sectors continued to believe in local self-sufficiency, however, and neither contemplated the effects of extended unemployment on their limited system of social provision.[4]

As unemployment and deprivation spread in the United States from 1930 to the economic nadir of 1933, the public sphere raged with debate over the merits of private versus public remedies for unemployment. President Herbert Hoover believed that voluntarism and private relief sufficed for the temporarily displaced, and urged companies to adopt voluntary "Share-the-Work" programs. Local chambers of commerce launched "Buy Now" campaigns, encouraging increased consumption for the sake of economic recovery. Lawmakers at all levels debated the advisability of using public revenues for relief.

Industrialists by and large looked to the private marketplace and opposed groups that sought to place the burden of recovery squarely on their backs. The manufacturing sector attempted to solve the social welfare dilemma through a simple schema of "group responsibility" (i.e., businesses' responsibility to their own work forces) and "community responsibility" (i.e., local government's responsibility for the improvident or for the casual work force).[5]

"Group responsibility" was the term used by forward-looking employers who in the 1920s had pioneered "welfare capitalist" programs for their long-term employees. As scholars of "welfare capitalism" have observed, these initiatives were based on rigorous company control of eligibility and benefits. With the coming of the depression, major industrial employers argued they were responsible for their employees alone. In-house unemployment funds sprang up in firms that had experimented with welfare plans before and during the 1920s.[6]

General Electric Company (GE) was in the forefront of this initiative, just as it had been in 1920s "welfare capitalism." But the example of GE illustrates the limits of liberal corporatist thinking. Its unemployment insurance fund derived from a 1 percent deduction on workers' paychecks, matched by an equal contribution from the company. GE president Gerard Swope was adamant about the "joint and equal" contribution feature, steadfastly refusing to consider a plan funded by the company alone. In his famous speech, "The Stabilization of Industry," he urged employers to follow his lead on unemployment funds and other benefits, to head off a federal mandate. He also argued for cartelization by industry associations, with government oversight. Founded on the "associationalism" of Hoover's commerce department in the 1920s, such large-scale economic planning was echoed by other business-sponsored schemes like the U.S. Chamber of Commerce's Harriman Plan, though the others rarely included welfare plans.[7] Similarly, the chairman of the Connecticut State Emergency Committee on Unemployment, industrialist James W. Hook, who also sat on President Hoover's Emergency Committee for Employment (PECE), advised Connecticut companies to set up unemployment reserve funds; the alternative, he warned, was a compulsory public unemployment insurance fund "that will force upon industry a disproportionate amount of the load."[8] The crucial difference between Hook's proposal and a public unemployment fund was that, much like the GE plan, employers would be responsible only for their own workers and would control disbursements from this joint fund.

These industrialist programs were compatible with those of the Hoover administration. Hoover had resisted all calls for federal involvement in relief or economic planning in favor of voluntary effort and community responsibility. Neither of Hoover's two committees, the 1930 PECE or the 1931 President's Organization on Unemployment Relief (POUR), distributed any relief funds and both were only mandated to cooperate with industry, with POUR organizing a national advertising campaign designed to stimulate private charity. Senator Robert Wagner's legislative efforts on behalf of federal unemployment relief—government employment agencies, statistics-gathering, and modest employment stabilization plans via public works—made little headway in 1930–31. Moreover, Hoover, the Republicans, and the Democratic congressional leadership continued to stick to the weary principle of balanced budgets, refusing to consider emergency appropriations for relief or public works. This made unemployment relief a state and local responsibility.

~⌁

It is here that we may explore how Connecticut answered the crisis and how the debate gained local expression in Bridgeport. Connecticut was a strongly industrialized state, caught between the identities and major markets of its two metropolitan neighbors, New York City and Boston. To resolve this confused identity, Connecticut had fallen back on its Yankee farmer heritage, summed up in its slogan "The Land of Steady Habits." Yet by the 1920s, it was a largely immigrant state. A conservative Republican party, composed of a coalition of rural representatives (the state's malapportioned legislature gave immense power over the burgeoning cities to the dwindling rural towns) and corporate interests, ruled the state in the early twentieth century.

Bridgeport, a mixed-industry city of about 150,000, had used its locational advantage on Long Island Sound, close to New York City and the brass industry of the Naugatuck Valley, to establish itself as an important metal-working and machine-tool center by 1900. World War I had transformed it into the preeminent munitions center on the East Coast, flooding the city with skilled workers and sparking a great wave of labor unrest that captured national attention. While most of these strikes failed to create permanent organizations, the legacy of radical organizing had subtly transformed Bridgeport politics in the 1920s. The city remained open to alternative political voices, even if factories had become hostile places for unions. In a remarkable political twist in the early 1920s, the Bridgeport Republican party, having been repudiated by its business supporters in a wrangle over property taxes, attracted ethnic working-class support with antibusiness rhetoric. This more populist tack allowed the local GOP to retain control over city hall for much of the decade. Local business leaders, however, succeeded in winning state legislation taking taxes and budgeting out of the hands of elected city officials and placing them in the hands of a governor-appointed Board of Apportionment and Taxation.[9]

While a few states began to set up state unemployment relief projects and funds for unemployed workers and their families in 1930 and 1931, Connecticut believed in "pay-as-you-go" spending and balanced budgets; it did little to relieve cities and towns of the growing burden of their "community responsibility." A conference of Connecticut mayors meeting in Bridgeport in April 1932 urged the governor to call a special session of the legislature to pass measures to deal with the crisis of the cities, suggesting a gasoline sales tax to fund relief and measures to force banks to reduce interest and mortgage rates and to declare a moratorium on second mortgage payments. The governor refused. For its part, the Hoover administration was only slightly more responsive in June 1932 to a similar national meeting of mayors of large cities that urgently requested federal relief funds.[10]

Both the Connecticut State Unemployment Commission and the Manufacturers Association of Connecticut promoted city plans to care for those not covered by company plans: the "chronically unemployed," casual and transient workers, and "unemployables." Both groups lavished attention on the Waterbury Plan and the special Hartford work-relief project, which were privately run and not subject to control by public officials. Both of these plans were instructive examples of the power dynamics surrounding debates over the collection and distribution of relief funds. They relied on private money—in Waterbury, worker contributions matched by company contributions, and in Hartford, donations to the Community Chest—and were administered by private charity agencies. Money was solicited from both business and the public, and put in the hands of business leaders, bypassing local governments.[11]

Similarly, the Bridgeport Community Chest, an entity led by local corporate executives, attempted to control relief expenditures. But this charity had its limits. As the *Bridgeport Sunday Herald* columnist "M.J.R." noted, by 1932 the charitable drives of the Community Chest had reached too deeply into humble pockets: "You might canvass the men engaged on public works through the department of public welfare and discover that most of them contributed a year ago to the Community Chest. . . . Of course, the idea of the framers of the Community Chest was to lessen the burden of the wealthy by compelling the city employees and the factory help to contribute." It was time, he argued, for the "men and women of means to . . . subscribe the [needed] amount."[12]

M.J.R. had hit upon the crucial question. *Who* should pay for relief from the economic disaster? The private company plans extracted money from worker and company alike, reducing workers' take-home pay while giving companies who set up reserve funds a tax break. The charity drives also extracted money from rich and poor alike. Both company plans and charity drives kept relief funds and work-relief projects in private elite hands, not in public coffers or under democratic community management.

The history of voluntary charity agencies in the United States in the 1920s reveals a trend toward "broadening the base" of donations beyond the usual well-to-do donors. In 1913 Cleveland became the first city to experiment with financial federation of local charities and community fund drives. This development got a boost from the federal government's endorsement of War Chests during World War I, which coordinated community fund-raising for war-related services and relief. During the 1920s, Community Chests appeared in many cities and towns, led by major corporate donors and heads of private agencies who sought to make giving more efficient and effective by running one annual combined fund appeal. Community Chests developed workplace-based funding drives in the form of the payroll checkoff, reaching into the pockets of ordinary citizens. The Chest movement was not fully inclusive, as religious and ethnic charity organizations outside of the mainstream had to apply for funding. By the late 1920s the Chest movement nationally conceded that public expenditures from taxes and other revenues far exceeded the amount raised by private charity, and called for "teamwork" between public and private agencies. Nonetheless, many Community Chests and their corporate leaders insisted on overseeing the relief effort in the early 1930s, fearful of profligacy and corruption on the part of elected city officials.[13]

On the other hand, municipally run relief efforts, funded with tax dollars, were controlled by elected officials. But debates over tax policy reveal a similar trend in "broadening the base" in this same era. As the Manufacturers Association of Connecticut put it, "the tax base must be broadened. . . . Taxes should be at low rates designed to fall upon a large number of people."[14] This meant shifting taxes, which in Connecticut relied heavily on real estate and personal property, away from manufacturing and toward sales and other consumer taxes. Nationally, congressional debate raged over a national sales tax, which, as Senator George H. Moses (R-N.H.) succinctly explained, was "based upon the surest foundation for one's ability to pay—namely one's ability to buy, and he who buys most, pays most—as he should. Under such a tax the rich are soaked, and the poor do not escape."[15] Such thinking proved unpopular, as Socialist leader Norman Thomas quipped, "It's a wonder they don't put a tax on tickets to the breadline."[16] A coalition of Democrats and progressive Republicans responded to President Hoover's proposed Revenue Act of 1932 by substituting a more progressive tax plan—a steeply graduated income tax, higher estate, gift, and corporate-profits taxes, and a return to various excise taxes. However, the new federal revenue was not intended for relief but to make up for the fall in tax receipts due to the business decline. State and local governments remained in charge of relief efforts.[17]

City governments around the country were stretched to their limits in 1930 and 1931, with no federal or state relief funds in sight. As Senator Hiram Bingham (R-Conn.), the former Yale history professor, had argued in early congressional debate over relief:

If we take away from the localities concerned the need of providing for their own suffering, we do away with just that much incentive toward their taking part in local self-government. . . . It is an attack on the very self-respect of local communities. . . . it is upon the development of sturdy, self-reliant citizenry that this Republic must in the long run depend for its long life. If we build up a body of citizens who are always depending on the central Government we will make weak citizens rather than strong citizens.[18]

This elite definition of respectable citizenry was rejected by Bridgeport citizens who accepted their civic responsibilities and agreed to pay their fair share. They saw no contradiction in calling upon government for relief assistance.

The burden of relief crystallized the debate over private versus public needs and private versus public responsibility. The crisis in fiscal affairs directly influenced the municipal elections of 1931 and 1933, which will be analyzed below. Ironically, in the battle over municipal priorities that raged in 1931–33, Bridgeport business leaders moved to deprive Bridgeport's "sturdy, self-reliant citizenry" of democratic control over city finances precisely because those same citizens rejected a business-endorsed municipal solution in favor of the local Socialist party.

The antibusiness, pro-union legacy of the World War I years, which had been reinforced by municipal politics during the 1920s, drew strength from the economic catastrophe of the Great Depression. In 1920–21, the incumbent Republicans, seeking to gain the votes of working people in their tax fight against their erstwhile industrialist allies, had launched an extensive municipal work-relief program to combat postwar unemployment.[19] They earned the support of the still influential radical machinists, now in the independent Amalgamated Metal Workers of America. Socialist party (SP) activists, led by their perennial mayoral candidate, the diligent slate-roofer Jasper McLevy, took advantage of the controversies over taxes and the splits within business ranks (many small businessmen opposed the political machinations of the large industrial firms) to push their own critique of the patronage-run city and to stress their own solutions for the city's problems.[20]

Now in the deep depression of 1930, the city Board of Public Welfare instituted a large municipal work-relief program to alleviate unemployment, one of the first in the country, modeled after its successful post–World War I plan. (Indeed, the designer of that plan, Republican Angus Thorne, was still the public welfare superintendent.) By 1931, however, the city, like many others around the nation, had fallen hopelessly in debt. Incumbent city Democrats faced unpalatable choices, either a shrinking of public services, another round of municipal-bond-selling, or a tax increase.[21]

In the late 1920s, the Bridgeport Republican party, now back in the hands of industrial leaders, had again become the launching pad for manufacturers' intrusions into city affairs. In 1931, the local Republicans endorsed a businessman for mayor, who campaigned for fiscal austerity, a controlled budget, and lower property taxes. The incumbent Democrats had won few friends when they were forced to slash relief payments and cut city payrolls by shortening the school year. They were also hindered by financial scandals. The 1931 election attracted little interest among citizens until the Socialist party began campaigning.

The Bridgeport SP had survived the quiescent 1920s by digging deeply into ethnic communities (Jewish, German, Swedish, Polish, Finnish) and the craft unions where they represented a leadership stratum (carpenters, painters, machinists, typographers). The core of the party, then, consisted of unionized craft workers, who were linked by ethnicity to the semiskilled workers and small retailers who made up immigrant Bridgeport. Membership in the Workmen's Sick and Death Benefit Society, the Jewish Workmen's Circle, the Polish Mutual Benefit Society, ethnic lodges of mainstream fraternals like the Odd Fellows, along with singing societies and the like, tied SP members to the Bridgeport neighborhoods. Though they remained in the background, wives of SP activists shouldered the burden of facilitating many of the family-oriented activities like suppers, picnics, and, during campaign seasons, keeping the district storefronts open.

The Bridgeport SP revived the basic themes that it had expounded for the last decade, and added specific measures related to the depression. The party combined antimachine rhetoric with a working-class vision of what a well-run city should look like. For example, Socialists contrasted the incumbent Democrats' work-relief project of a new municipal golf course with their own proposals for new sewers, playgrounds, and street improvements in working-class neighborhoods. They campaigned on soapboxes on street corners and at factory-gate rallies, attracting large crowds of three hundred to six hundred. The SP contrasted the business agenda of the Republican party and the so-called Citizens' Emergency Committee on Employment, which called for cutting city payrolls and limiting relief expenditures, to the SP platform of "better[ing] the living conditions of the working man" by "sound and economical administration of the affairs of government" through "socialization and democratic administration of public utilities," the first step on the road to the socialist commonwealth. Bridgeport Socialists added their standard litany of state legislative proposals—old-age pensions, unemployment insurance, and minimum wage and maximum hours laws.[22] At the crux of this debate was the "service-ability of organized government" (the phrase is from Milwaukee's mayor, Socialist Daniel Hoan), which business groups and taxpayer revolts were assailing throughout the country.[23]

The "serviceability of organized government" was the key principle underlying the tension between those business interests who opposed state interference in the economy and those welfare-capitalist business leaders and the public who favored it. On the state and municipal front, the former wanted lowered government expenditures; the latter two wanted full-service government but fought over who should pay and how it should be run.[24] The Socialist Party of America, with a number of municipal governments at this time, challenged the notion that cities were spendthrift and that the best city was the one with the lowest tax rate. Hoan addressed the issue in his 1933 pamphlet, *Taxes and Tax Dodgers*, in which he claimed that "civilization may be judged by the amount of service that the people in a community demand, and what they can afford to pay for, and not by how low a tax rate they have." Contending that government service was cheaper than a comparable private service, he stated his solution: "not lower taxes, but fairer taxes." The SP favored steep income and inheritance taxes, and deplored the taxpayers' leagues who used "the bogey of 'high taxes' for no other purpose than to undermine public confidence in the serviceability of organized government, and to keep the tax burden falling on the poor instead of the rich."[25]

Jasper McLevy, Socialist mayoral candidate in Bridgeport in 1931, felt the tide turning in his favor. He declared to the press, "The solid fellow who earns a good wage and goes home to his family at night is with me."[26] This vision of the respectable worker informed the Bridgeport SP program. Productivist, honest, mutualistic, family-centered, male-defined—as sober-minded citizens these self-conscious workingmen saw their task as bringing fairness, honesty, and social justice to the community.

On Election Day 1931, the SP captured 35 percent of the city's vote, some three thousand votes behind the Democrats and well ahead of the Republicans. Sixty percent of the potential electorate had turned out, far more than ever in a municipal election and not that far behind the record 1928 presidential turnout. The SP elected three sheriffs, two selectmen, and a councilman, carpenter Fred Schwarzkopf from the working-class East Side Twelfth District, the largest single voting district in the city.

At this point Bridgeport's business community stepped in. The election results that had so inspired Socialist hopes also stimulated business leaders to develop plans to assume control of the city's budget. Business elites, clearly worried about the volatility of the Bridgeport citizenry, also distrusted the local Democrats and doubted the GOP's ability to win. So in early 1932, the Bridgeport Manufacturers' Association and the Chamber of Commerce created a new entity, the Committee of One Hundred on Municipal Affairs, to investigate city finances. Other groups soon joined them—the East End Business Men's Association, the West End Business Men's Association, and the Federated Council of Business Men, representing small merchants and real estate interests, and finally the Bridgeport Citizens and Taxpayers League (small businesses and homeowners)—all interested in cutting taxes. As the Federated Business Men's Council, which claimed to represent nine hundred small businesses, stated in a resolution to the city council, "There will be no business recovery until the government applies the pruning knife to government costs, and cuts deeply." They demanded a 25 percent cut in the tax rate.[27]

With city coffers nearly empty in late 1932 and a cold winter looming, the Democratic city administration moved to rein in expenditures through salary cutting and budget slashing, with the school system taking the brunt of the cuts. The Committee of One Hundred presented its own solution of an immediate 25 percent across-the-board cut in municipal wages and salaries. It also introduced a bill to the Connecticut General Assembly for a $1.6 million city bond authorization (this was needed since Bridgeport had already exceeded its statutory bonding limit). This was tied to a bold rider that transferred *all* power over taxes, finances, and municipal hiring, as well as disbursement of the bonding revenue, to the existing governor-appointed Board of Apportionment and Taxation (the 1925 legacy of the last business challenge to municipal budgeting). This, then, would finally accomplish business elites' goal of taking the city budget out of public hands.

The proposals of the Committee of One Hundred opened a heated public debate that pitted city officials against business, single teachers against married teachers, public employees against taxpayers, labor against business. The plan even divided the elite along gender lines. For example, the board of directors of the YWCA, made up of wives of the businessmen leading the Committee of One Hundred, protested the committee's plan to cut the costs of city court by eliminating juvenile court.[28]

"This thing of a cut is not local," observed Connecticut Federation of Labor secretary-treasurer John J. Egan, himself a Bridgeport resident. "It is engineered by the big bankers who have their eye wholly upon cutting the cost of government without considering other costs."[29] Neighborhoods opposed closing fire stations, and many citizens opposed shutting Bridgeport Normal School (the locally funded teacher-training school that operated as an adjunct to the city high school). Policemen, firemen, and teachers resisted the Democratic mayor's proposed flat 20 percent pay cuts, which had been voluntary under the present city charter, and proposed instead a sliding scale. Popular outrage over the Committee of One Hundred's budget and legislative proposals drew a deluge of letters to its key members, particularly utility company chiefs who were threatened with public boycotts.[30] Married teachers supported a proposed tenure-in-office bill in the general assembly, while young teachers, who would be laid off if married teachers stayed on the job, opposed that plan. Finally, the Reverend Paul F. Keating, pastor of the predominantly Irish St. Mary's Roman Catholic church, preached from the pulpit against the pay cuts for city workers. He reminded his congregation that Catholics—presumably a large percentage of city employees affected, and no doubt Irish as well—were both good citizens and taxpayers, and saved the city over $300,000 by supporting their own schools for over fifty-six hundred students.[31]

While some Common Council members pressed for more efficient tax collection, Socialist councilman Fred Schwarzkopf spoke in opposition to wage cuts and relief cuts. Instead, he advocated cuts in other operating expenditures, such as the water rates paid to the Bridgeport Hydraulic Company (run by one of the heads of the Committee of One Hundred). The question, according to Schwarzkopf, was not spending, but *how* to spend.[32]

Schwarzkopf, who had appealed to the class interests of his neighborhood for two years on the city council, enjoyed considerable support. He had joined a group of 450 angry East Side residents in opposition to a manufacturer who wanted to run freight along abandoned trolley tracks on neighborhood streets. He reminded the residents of deaths that had occurred along this street before the New Haven Railroad had been forced to elevate its tracks above street level. In yet another zoning hearing, Schwarzkopf led the opposition to a businessman's request to build fuel oil storage tanks on his East End property. The *Bridgeport Herald* noted disapprovingly that Schwarzkopf "spent too much time appealing to class prejudice and social standing, . . . [using] trick phrases of 'working men's rights' and 'protection of homes.'" But "his discourse," the paper conceded reluctantly, was what the neighborhood people wanted.[33]

Class interest was readily apparent in the Committee of One Hundred's plans for the city. Concerned that the city be placed in the right hands and have the right environment for doing business, local elites felt they were doing the best thing and justified their proposals to the Connecticut General Assembly with stories of city corruption and extravagance. Opposition to the Committee of One Hundred took the form of a broad coalition of Common Councilmen, taxpayers' groups, and Socialists, all united around the principle of Home Rule. However, the general assembly gave the committee virtually everything it wanted, including greater power to the Board of Apportionment.[34] With the operating budget and control over relief spending now safely in the hands of trusted businessmen and with bonding privileges extended, the Board of Apportionment breathed a sigh of relief and set taxes at the previous year's rate of 29.5 mills. The Committee of One Hundred gloated that "the administration of our financial affairs [is] vested in the group of public-spirited men in the Board of Apportionment and Taxation . . . free from political control which might limit the exercise of the power given to them."[35] According to the Socialists, however, this legislative move by businessmen "surrender[ed] the rights of the people to govern themselves by the Democratic methods our forefathers fought for."[36]

The next municipal campaign in 1933 reverberated with popular anger over the Committee of One Hundred's program. The GOP campaign slogan, "Pledged to Sound Government," mirrored its commitment to work with the Board of Apportionment and Taxation to reduce the city's expenses and tax rate, while incumbent Democrats weakly tried to identify with the new Roosevelt administration. A new Citizens and Taxpayers League ticket also entered the election contest, pledged to its earlier position of a 25 percent cut in the city budget.

The heated SP campaign stressed taxes, corruption, and potential bankruptcy. When asked what he would do in office, mayoral candidate McLevy responded that he would promptly do what the incumbent Democrats were *not* doing, that is, take advantage of new federal funds available under the first New Deal programs: "Employment is the most serious problem that is facing us. . . . To secure Federal funds would not only aid in employment but would help many types of merchants as well."[37] Here was a party unafraid of using the machinery of government, and now willing to appeal across class lines.

Exploiting small businessmen's outrage over the Committee of One Hundred, the SP campaigned on the principle of home rule and an end to corporate hegemony over city affairs. The Socialist appeal was so broad that McLevy was invited to speak at Slavic, Italian, Armenian, and Hungarian ethnic halls that had never been identifiably radical. Tensions within Democratic and Republican ethnic ranks over the previous months had led to feuding between party officials and some ethnic leaders, leading councilman Schwarzkopf to observe that "the foreign element in Bridge-port had been fooled too long by the false leaders among the old party politicians, especially by those leaders who play upon the nationality of those to whom they wish to appeal."[38] In a last-minute switch, Italian fra-ternal leader Luigi Richards, a longtime Republican, endorsed McLevy and his slate. Women Socialists taunted the Federation of Democratic Women activists, reminding Bridgeport women that the SP had supported women's suffrage long before the Democratic party had and that women had "equal rights" in the SP. A significant block of British machinists, at-tracted to the city in the 1920s by work in the metal trades, enthusiasti-cally joined the Bridgeport SP, calling it the equivalent of the British La-bour party in which they had previously been active. The SP brought in nationally prominent Socialist speakers, such as Frank Crosswaith, the African-American organizer for the International Ladies' Garment Work-ers Union, August Claessens of the Rand School, and finally Milwaukee mayor Daniel Hoan, who had been such a hit in Bridgeport in the 1932 presidential campaign along with Norman Thomas. "NRA strikes" by over three thousand Bridgeport garment, metal-trades, and trucking workers in the months leading up to the election added to the ferment in the city. The favorite SP leaflet was a sketch of a workingman in overalls exhort-ing voters: "Let's Go, Bridgeport, Vote Socialist!"[39]

The Socialists won the election, with over twenty-two thousand votes (mostly in a straight ballot vote for the whole SP slate) for a plurality of 48 percent. In a related ballot, Bridgeport voters made their will known on spending priorities, voting a resounding "Yes" to the ballot question, "Shall the Bridgeport Normal School be continued?" This in effect re-pudiated the budget-cutting decisions of the previous Democratic admin-istration. That election night, an estimated ten thousand people crowd-ed into downtown Bridgeport, accompanied by marching bands and contingents from several Italian fraternal societies, all acting, according to Bridgeport Unemployed Council organizer Michael Russo, "like a rev-olution had come here."[40]

The election in Bridgeport was a more than a protest vote against in-cumbents. It was a ringing endorsement of an alternative agenda. In their success in raising the issue of who pays for social services and who con-trols the public purse, the Socialists gave shape and direction to public protest against patronage politics and against the business-inspired expe-dient of cutting services and wages. At the same time, the Socialists had legitimized the grievances of working-class Bridgeport. As Russo, a local Communist Party critic of McLevy, remembered that election night: "it wasn't a protest vote, it was more than that. . . . This . . . proved that there was this process of becoming radicalized, and they turned to McLevy. . . . They *thought* he was a socialist."[41] The Connecticut Socialist paper, the *Commonwealth*, described the majority of Socialist votes as coming from the "conservative, small home-owning, factory working people who have tried the Democratic and Republican parties for years without protest, and found them wanting."[42]

A statistical examination of the votes reveals who voted Socialist (see tables 5.1 and 5.2).[43] While the Socialists in 1931 had not attracted large numbers of low-rent households (the Democrats seem to have retained most of these), the SP had the higher correlation to low-value homeowners. This correlation was even stronger in the 1933 election, while low-income renters now also turned to the Socialists. What is clear is that contemporary speculation about a "silk-stocking" protest vote for McLevy was wrong; the correlations between high-income indicators and the parties shows that those areas strongly voted Republican in 1931 and 1933. Indeed in 1933 those areas drifted a bit into the Democratic camp rather than cause the election of a Socialist. On the other hand, the foreign-stock vote, which divided equally between the Democrats and the SP in 1931, deserted the Democrats for the Socialists in 1933.[44] All indications are that, just as the *Commonwealth* had claimed, the foreign-stock, low-value homeowner, those voters vitally concerned with the well-being of the city budget and worried about taxes on their modest homes, voted Socialist to assure a fiscally wise administration responsive to the concerns of low-

Table 5.1. Correlations for 1931 and 1933 Mayoral Votes

	Socialist	Democrat	Republican
1931			
Foreign-stock	.28	.24	−.75*
Low-rent	.10	.37	−.65
Low home-value	.43	.13	−.77*
High-rent	−.42	−.16	.79*
High home-value	−.46	−.16	.84**
1933			
Foreign-stock	.61	−.42	−.67*
Low-rent	.39	−.15	−.73*
Low home-value	.53	−.31	−.72*
High-rent	−.55	.35	.67*
High home-value	−.53	.33	.66*

Source: Bridgeport Municipal Register, 1932 and 1934.
* = Pearson's *r* correlations significant at −.01.
** = significant at −.001.

Table 5.2. Relationship of Ethnic to Economic Variables, 1930

	Foreign-stock
High-value home	−.62
Medium-value home	−.24
High-rent household	−.84**
Medium-rent household	−.68*
Low-value home	.61
Low-rent household	.87**

Source: U.S. Census, 1930.
* = Pearson's *r* correlations significant at −.01.
** = significant at −.001.

income residents. These were the citizens who viewed big business tax agendas and corrupt political machines in the same light. At the same time, the fact that many ethnic organizations around the country had invested in municipal bonds may have led ethnic voters to be more aware of city finances.[45]

Nonetheless, after November 1933, the Socialists found that they lacked the political tools to implement their social reform program in the city. In his sober reflection on the political events of 1933, *Bridgeport Times-Star* journalist Alan Olmstead noted that the Socialists were elected to offices that had "little power." On the other hand, the "big business men," who had succeeded legislatively in wresting control of the city budget away from elected officials, "did not know what to do with the power they had."[46] The Committee of One Hundred had succeeded in ending popular control over city finances, and for the next three years the Socialist party would find itself locked in battle with big-business leaders in setting financial priorities. Political deadlock ensued.

When Bridgeport voters sent three Socialist senators and one Socialist representative to the Connecticut General Assembly the following year, the party took its agenda to the state capitol. There it fought for stronger labor legislation and proposed a state old-age pension plan and a state income tax to finance relief. This was in contrast to other regressive forms of taxation like sales taxes, favored by Democrats and Republicans. The fact remains that, overall, the New Deal increased the regressivity of the national tax system during the decade, as Mark Leff has shown.[47] Moreover, many states and cities had paralleled Connecticut in the early depression, relying on voluntarism and then placing public monies in the hands of private individuals to keep relief money out of the dangerous hands of "the machine."[48]

Bridgeport's case casts light on the many tax revolts in the early depression. David Beito, one of the few to focus on this phenomenon with his study of the most famous tax revolt in Chicago, asserts that widespread tax delinquency tapped a deep "anti-big-government" sentiment.[49] From his evidence, "anti-big-government" sentiment clearly motivated large real-estate interests, but not small property owners. My evidence indicates that while small property owners, working-class or middle-class, may have been moved by antimachine sentiment, this does not mean that they rejected an expanded government role, especially in this crisis era. Working-class citizens strongly supported cleaning out city hall for the benefit of the public good, but were unconvinced that turning over the reins of government to elite hands or to private relief inspectors promoted that public good. They insisted on electing their own publicly accountable representatives, whether Democrat, Republican, or Socialist.

In Bridgeport and elsewhere, electoral politics in the early 1930s was a cauldron of competing ideological agendas. The events in Bridgeport reveal that early depression-era politics at the grass roots had a class character beyond the occasional Roosevelt utterance on behalf of the "forgotten man." The Bridgeport SP successfully raised the related issues of who pays for social services, who controls the public purse, and which services to fund. The fact that Bridgeport voters had a number of electoral options for lowered taxes and still chose the SP meant that low-income taxpayers wanted responsible government, not less government, and were willing to pay for it if other sectors contributed their fair share. The Socialists gave shape and direction to public protest against patronage politics and against the business-inspired expedient of cutting service and wages. Moreover, their call for greater democracy and public accountability in city government touched a responsive chord with a citizenry disenchanted with the self-interested stance of local corporate leaders and their political minions.

The Bridgeport Socialist party, which enjoyed a remarkably long political life (it remained in power until 1957), consisted of skilled AFL workers from mostly "old" ethnic groups, whose political philosophy was the moderate "constructive" socialism of Victor Berger and the Progressive-Era Milwaukee Socialists.[50] It was not a "radical" party, by contemporary standards, but in its successful bid for political power it became a lightning rod for working-class grievances. In this instance, the electoral events in Bridgeport prefigured the brief successes of other third parties in 1934, such as the Commonwealth Builders in Washington State, the

Progressive party in Wisconsin, the Farmer-Labor party in Minnesota, even the failed California EPIC campaign of Upton Sinclair.[51] In the city of Bridgeport, the crisis in city government revealed a decline of both old parties and a realignment of political forces that brought to power a third party with an identifiable working-class constituency. This new political representation was part of the unraveling of links between the grassroots and traditional political elites and the validation of the social needs of a majority working class.

Labor historians have been disappointed in their search for a national Labor party effort, blaming the overwhelming popularity of FDR for co-opting labor into the Democratic party where it was prey to conservative impulses.[52] But the internal strife within the labor movement, the rivalry between the AFL and the emerging CIO, did much to weaken labor's influence as an independent political force. So too did the conservative assault on the New Deal later in the decade that made the Democratic party the only viable vehicle for labor's activities.

Nonetheless, labor historians have failed to appreciate the social-welfare claims that working people made in the early 1930s, whether through independent forces or through the Democratic party, as part of a working-class political challenge. For example, the pension and relief plans of Huey Long, Father Charles Coughlin, and Dr. Francis Townsend put tremendous pressure on the Roosevelt administration, which began drafting a Social Security bill. Meanwhile, social and labor reformers, along with fraternal organizations, pressed ahead with proposals for federal relief and old-age pensions, the most popular of which was the "Workers' Bill." The Workers Unemployment and Social Insurance Act, introduced in 1934 by Farmer-Labor congressman Ernest Lundeen, contrasted markedly with the president's Social Security Act in inclusiveness, comprehensiveness, and funding. It was endorsed by many national unions, locals, city and county governments and ethnic fraternal organizations.[53] While the Lundeen bill was overwhelmed in Congress by the administration's Social Security Act, the fact that working people chose the more comprehensive plan should alert us to popular consciousness of and preference for alternatives. Similarly, John L. Lewis's call for "democratiz[ing]" the American Red Cross by appointing union members to its board makes us aware of how unions and workers of the 1930s viewed private charity using other people's money in elite noblesse oblige.[54]

The limits of independent political party challenges, regardless of their internal weaknesses, can be seen in Bridgeport from the mid-1930s on.

In attempting to govern, the Bridgeport SP soon found that it had to accommodate to local business demands. The SP found itself thwarted at every turn by the opposition of organized parties, institutional frameworks (including New Deal agencies), and constitutional constraints. When federal relief money finally came to the state agency to be distributed to towns and cities, the State Emergency Relief Commission gave Bridgeport's funds, not to the elected Socialist administration but to a businessmen's board composed of Community Chest and Committee of One Hundred leaders, who then disbursed it carefully and parsimoniously to the city Department of Public Welfare.

The manner in which Bridgeporters dealt with many of the issues raised in the political sphere during the early 1930s, from simple political recognition to the complex processes of urban finance, reflected the ways in which working people conceived of themselves and their place in the public sphere. They demanded public control over such issues as unemployment and relief instead of private charity and elite decision making. They made public streets instead of private party clubrooms the spaces for political debate. They expanded democracy in both economic and political spheres. This was their vision of a government responsive to the needs of working people.

Notes

This essay was presented in earlier versions to the 1993 North American Labor History Conference, Detroit, and to the 1994 Annual Meeting of the Organization of American Historians, Atlanta. I would like to thank the commentators—Paula Baker, Mark Leff, Amy Bridges, and Bruce Nelson—for their helpful critiques. I would also like to thank the editors of this volume for their astute readings.

1. Lizabeth Cohen, *Making a New Deal: Industrial Workers in Chicago 1919–1939* (New York: Cambridge University Press, 1990); Thomas J. Sugrue, "Crabgrass-Roots Politics: Race, Rights, and the Reaction Against Liberalism in the Urban North," *Journal of American History* 82 (Sept. 1995): 551–78; Alan Brinkley, "The Problem of American Conservatism," *American Historical Review* 99 (Apr. 1994): 409–29; Michael Kazin, "The Grass-roots Right: New Histories of U.S. Conservatism in the Twentieth Century," *American Historical Review* 97 (Feb. 1992): 136–55; Theda Skocpol, "The Limits of the New Deal System and the Roots of Contemporary Welfare Dilemmas," in Margaret Weir, Ann Shola Orloff, and Theda Skocpol, eds., *The Politics of Social Policy in the United States* (Princeton: Princeton University Press, 1988), 293–311.

2. The debate has been whether federal labor laws were empowering or co-optive for the labor movement. The most recent argument in favor of the idea that New Deal labor laws were empowering to workers' movements is Melvyn Dubofsky, *The State and Labor in Modern America* (Chapel Hill: University of North Carolina Press, 1994). A representative work with the view of this era's labor laws as co-opting is Christo-

pher L. Tomlins, *The State and the Unions: Labor Relations, Law, and the Organized Labor Movement in America, 1880–1960* (New York: Cambridge University Press, 1985). David Montgomery presents the New Deal formula as having both empowering and limiting features ("American Workers and the New Deal Formula," in *Workers' Control in America: Studies in the History of Work, Technology, and Labor Struggles* [New York: Cambridge University Press, 1979], 153–80).

3. The classic statement on the rise of a new electorate is Samuel Lubell, *The Future of American Politics* (New York: Harper & Row, 1952), substantiated by statistical work done by Kristi Andersen, *The Creation of a Democratic Majority 1928–1936* (Chicago: University of Chicago Press, 1979), and Gerald H. Gamm, *The Making of New Deal Democrats: Voting Behavior and Realignment in Boston, 1920–1940* (Chicago: University of Chicago Press, 1989).

4. James T. Patterson, *America's Struggle against Poverty 1900–1985* (Cambridge, Mass.: Harvard University Press, 1986), chap. 2; Cecelia F. Bucki, "Poor Relief in Pittsburgh, 1830s–1880s" (M.A. paper, University of Pittsburgh, 1977); Michael B. Katz, *In the Shadow of the Poorhouse: A Social History of Welfare in America* (New York: Basic Books, 1986), chaps. 1–8. David Montgomery notes the extent to which the able-bodied unemployed were considered pariahs and often subjected to criminal prosecution in the late nineteenth century (*Citizen Worker: The Experience of Workers in the United States with Democracy and the Free Market during the Nineteenth Century* [New York: Cambridge University Press, 1993], 71–89).

5. These terms are taken from the definitive statement and policy recommendation of the Manufacturers Association of Connecticut, *Unemployment and Its Remedies* (Hartford: Manufacturers Association of Connecticut, 1933), 134–38. This document echoed recommendations from the New England Council and the National Association of Manufacturers.

6. For overviews of business activity in the employee welfare arena in this era, see Edward Berkowitz and Kim McQuaid, *Creating the Welfare State: The Political Economy of Twentieth-Century Reform*, 2d ed. (New York: Praeger Publishers, 1988), 1–34, 54–68; Stuart D. Brandes, *American Welfare Capitalism 1880–1940* (Chicago: University of Chicago Press, 1976); David Brody, "The Rise and Decline of Welfare Capitalism," in *Workers in Industrial America: Essays on the Twentieth Century Struggle* (New York: Oxford University Press, 1980), 48–81; Gerald Zahavi, *Workers, Managers, and Welfare Capitalism: The Shoeworkers and Tanners of Endicott Johnson, 1890–1950* (Urbana: University of Illinois Press, 1988).

7. Berkowitz and McQuaid, *Creating the Welfare State*, 92–95; Ronald W. Schatz, *The Electrical Workers: A History of Labor at General Electric and Westinghouse, 1923–60* (Urbana: University of Illinois Press, 1983), 53–61. The full text of Swope's address, as well as the plans and comments of others including the U.S. Chamber of Commerce, is in Charles A. Beard, ed., *America Faces the Future* (Boston: Houghton Mifflin, 1932), 160–73. Further information on business plans in the early depression is detailed in Cecelia F. Bucki, "The Pursuit of Political Power: Class, Ethnicity, and Municipal Politics in Interwar Bridgeport, 1915–1936" (Ph.D. dissertation, University of Pittsburgh, 1991), 340–53.

8. James W. Hook, "Industry's Obligation to the Unemployed," *Mechanical Engineering* 53 (Oct. 1931): 707–13; Hook, "The Unemployed—What Shall We Do with Them?—A Complete Plan of Unemployment Relief for the Future," Address, 2 Dec.

1931, American Society of Mechanical Engineers, New York, pamphlet, Misc. Publications on Unemployment, Mudd Library, Yale University, New Haven, Conn.

9. See Cecelia Bucki, "Dilution and Craft Tradition: Munitions Workers in Bridgeport, Connecticut, 1915–19" (in Herbert G. Gutman and Donald H. Bell, eds., *The New England Working Class and the New Labor History* [Urbana: University of Illinois Press, 1987], 137–56), for descriptions of the World War I strikes, and Bucki, "Pursuit of Political Power," chap. 1, for the World War I era and 1920s taxation and electoral battles.

10. "Conference of Mayors [Connecticut]," 15 Apr. 1932, typescript in box 380, file "Emergency Committee for Employment," Governor Cross Papers, RG 5, Connecticut State Archives, Hartford; "How the Cities Stand," *Survey* 68 (15 Apr. 1932): 71–75, 92; Mark I. Gelfand, *A Nation of Cities: The Federal Government and Urban America, 1933–1965* (New York: Oxford University Press, 1975), 35–37.

11. For additional Connecticut and Bridgeport evidence, see Bucki, "Pursuit of Political Power," chap. 5.

12. *Bridgeport Herald*, 13 Mar. 1932.

13. Roy Lubove, *The Professional Altruist: The Emergence of Social Work as a Career, 1880–1930* (Cambridge, Mass.: Harvard University Press, 1965), chap. 7; United Way of America, *People and Events: A History of the United Way* (Alexandria, Va.: United Way of America, 1977), 21–57; William J. Norton, *The Cooperative Movement in Social Work* (New York: Macmillan, 1927), 112–30, 154–72; Richard Carter, *The Gentle Legions: National Voluntary Health Organizations in America* (1961; reprint, New Brunswick, N.J.: Transaction Publishers, 1992), 279–80; Eleanor L. Brilliant, *The United Way: Dilemmas of Organized Charity* (New York: Columbia University Press, 1990), 18–26; Katz, *In the Shadow of the Poorhouse*, 156–57.

14. *Connecticut Industry* 10 (Jan. 1932): cover page; Bucki, "Pursuit of Political Power," 376–79.

15. George H. Moses, "Death—and Taxes," *Saturday Evening Post*, 27 June 1931, 97, as quoted in Jordan A. Schwarz, *The Interregnum of Despair: Hoover, Congress, and the Depression* (Urbana: University of Illinois Press, 1970), 110.

16. Schwarz, *Interregnum of Despair*, 127; Peter Fearon, *War, Prosperity and Depression: The U.S. Economy 1917–1945* (Lawrence: University Press of Kansas, 1987), 123–25.

17. For a national context for these tax debates, see Mark H. Leff, *The Limits of Symbolic Reform: The New Deal and Taxation, 1933–1939* (New York: Cambridge University Press, 1984), 16, 48–90; Schwarz, *Interregnum of Despair*, 106–41; Arthur M. Schlesinger, Jr., *The Age of Roosevelt: The Crisis of the Old Order, 1919–1933* (Boston: Houghton Mifflin Co., 1957), 252–55. Data on state and local expenditures are in U.S. Bureau of the Census, *Historical Statistics of the United States: Colonial Times to 1970*, bicentennial ed., 2 vols. (Washington, D.C.: Government Printing Office, 1976), 2:1127–30. Note that by the late 1920s states less often relied on personal income and corporate income taxes (James T. Patterson, *The New Deal and the States: Federalism in Transition* [Princeton: Princeton University Press, 1969], 3–25, 31).

18. *Congressional Record*, 12 May 1930, 8742, as quoted in James L. Sundquist, *Dynamics of the Party System: Alignment and Realignment of Political Parties in the United States*, rev. ed. (Washington, D.C.: Brookings Institution, 1983), 201–2.

19. Bucki, "Pursuit of Political Power," 113–17.

20. The Bridgeport SP had been reasonably successful in Progressive Era elector-

al politics, with machinist Fred Cederholm winning the East Side aldermanic seat in 1913. The Bridgeport SP always gathered a small but respectable municipal vote of 4 to 6 percent throughout the 1920s (Bucki, "Pursuit of Political Power," 37–70, 147–69).

21. Further details on the early depression's impact on Bridgeport, as well as the 1931 and 1933 campaigns, are in Bucki, "Pursuit of Political Power," chap. 5.

22. *Commonwealth* 8 (Dec. 1931): 1.

23. Daniel W. Hoan, *Taxes and Tax Dodgers* (Chicago: Socialist Party of America, 1933).

24. GE leader Gerard Swope, who, like other welfare-capitalist spokesmen such as Owen D. Young, Edward A. Filene, and Henry Dennison, had originally favored private corporate plans, now campaigned fully for government involvement in economic planning and a federal public-works program. The GE unemployment fund had run out of money by early 1932 (Sanford M. Jacoby, *Employing Bureaucracy: Managers, Unions, and the Transformation of Work in American Industry, 1900–1945* [New York: Columbia University Press, 1985], 207–23; Irving Bernstein, *The Lean Years: A History of the American Worker 1920–1933* [Boston: Houghton Mifflin Co., 1960], 289–90, 351).

25. Hoan, *Taxes and Tax Dodgers*, 3–4, 16.

26. *Sunday Herald*, 1 Nov. 1931.

27. *Black Rock Beacon*, 12 Feb., 29 July 1932; unidentified clip [1932], in "Committee of 100" clipping file, Bridgeport Public Library, Bridgeport, Conn. (hereafter BPL); *Bridgeport Post*, 30 Oct. 1932.

28. Board of Directors Minutes, 30 Jan. 1933, Minutes Books, Bridgeport YWCA Papers, BPL. The female-led YWCA had long championed the needs of lower-class women and children in the city, though usually with a sense of noblesse oblige. In the 1920s they sponsored a day-care center for children of immigrant mothers who had to work, and their International Institute targeted women in immigrant communities with English and Americanization classes.

29. *Bridgeport Post*, 15 Jan. 1933. Also see 7 Jan. 1933.

30. The utilities were still smarting from the sullied reputation they had received in the 1932 state election with the publicity surrounding maverick Albert Levitt's gubernatorial campaign. Levitt, in a series of campaign exposés of tax-dodging on the state and local level by various utilities, had succeeded in placing a spotlight on the corrupt influence of the utilities in state Republican politics and the Public Utilities Commission. Albert Levitt later summarized his accusations against Connecticut GOP boss J. Henry Roraback, chief of the Connecticut Light & Power Company, in "Who Owns Connecticut?" *Nation* 138 (2 May 1934): 504–7.

31. The budget and legislative debates are contained in: unidentified clippings, 14, 23, 27 Jan., 24 Feb., 25 Mar. 1933 (McLevy scrapbook, McLevy-Schwarzkopf Papers, BPL); Sanford Stoddard to Governor Cross, 18 Mar. 1933, and Sumner Simpson to Cross, 18 Mar. 1933, "City of Bridgeport" file, box 384, Governor Cross Papers; *Bridgeport Post*, 7 Jan. 1933 (BPL clipping file), 17, 19, 20, 25, 31 Jan., 6 Feb., 28 Mar. 1933 (McLevy scrapbook); *Bridgeport Times-Star*, 8, 22, 24 Feb. 1933 (McLevy scrapbook), 10 Mar. 1933; *Bridgeport Telegram*, 24 Jan., 7 Feb. 1933 (McLevy scrapbook); *Commonwealth* 10 (Apr. 1933): 4; Minutes, 7, 8, 10 Feb. 1933, Board of Apportionment Minute Books, Bridgeport City Archives.

32. Unidentified clipping, 24 Feb. 1933 (clipping scrapbook, McLevy-Schwarzkopf Papers); *Bridgeport Post*, 19 Jan. 1933; *Bridgeport Herald*, 20 Mar., 7 Aug. 1932; *Commonwealth* 10 (Feb. 1933): 1; Minutes, 2 Feb. 1932, Board of Apportionment Minute Books.

33. *Bridgeport Herald*, 12 Apr., 7 Aug. 1932.

34. Brief reports of actions on Bridgeport bills by General Assembly Committee on Cities and Boroughs are contained in Committee Hearings, 1933 General Assembly, Legislative Division, Connecticut State Library. The Committee on Cities and Boroughs approved all the Committee of One Hundred's proposals, while reporting unfavorably on most other approaches (*Bridgeport Post*, 1 Apr. 1933 [McLevy scrapbook]).

35. *Bridgeport Post*, 16 June 1933 (BPL clipping file).

36. *Bridgeport Times-Star*, 10 Mar., 30 Sept. 1933; *Bridgeport Post*, 1 Apr., 15 and 16 June 1933; *Commonwealth* 10 (Apr. 1933): 4. A total of $871,000 in 1933 city bonds were sold through a New York City bond syndicate (*New York Times*, 24 June 1933). No list of buyers of the city's bonds was published.

37. *Bridgeport Life*, 28 Oct. 1933, part 2, 1.

38. Speech to 1,000 attending the SP annual picnic, *Commonwealth* 10 (July 1933): 4.

39. Leaflet, 1933, reel 94, sect. G, Socialist Party of America Papers, microfilm ed. (Glen Rock, N.J.: Microfilming Corporation of America, 1975). The additional information about the 1933 campaign can be found in Bucki, "Pursuit of Political Power," 406–29.

40. Michael Russo interview, Cambridge, Mass., 28 Sept. 1983, tape in author's possession.

41. Ibid.

42. *Commonwealth* 8 (Nov. 1934): 1, 4.

43. An engaged electorate, larger than ever before, had spoken in Bridgeport. In 1933, the turnout of the *potential* electorate was 62 percent, an impressive response for any local election and the largest turnout to date in any municipal election. Indeed, it was close to the 67 percent that had turned out for the 1932 presidential election.

44. The calculations in tables 5.1 and 5.2 were performed with SPSS/PC+. The fact that there are only twelve cases in this analysis raises the unavoidable possibility of meaningless correlations except where noted as significant, but the statistical evidence is consistent with qualitative data. My thanks to Professors Peter Tuckel of Hunter College-CUNY and Kurt Schlichting of Fairfield University for sharing their expertise and pooling their data with mine. Note that these findings are consistent with the data presented by Bruce Stave, "The Great Depression and Urban Political Continuity: Bridgeport Chooses Socialism," in Stave, ed., *Socialism and the Cities* (Port Washington, N.Y.: Kennikat Press, 1975), 173–74, though my emphasis is different. Stave chose to focus on the conservative "continuity" that the Bridgeport SP was supposed to represent. Though he may have been closer to the mark on the later years of McLevy's reign (McLevy was mayor until 1957), the evidence I have examined does not support his contention about the early years. Some small and medium-sized businesses may have supported the SP in the early years, but the record shows that major industrialists fought the SP in its first term. See Bucki, "Pursuit of Political Power," chaps. 5 and 6.

45. For example, in Minneapolis, the Croatian Fraternal Union had urged its members to get involved in politics to protect their benefits (Peter Rachleff, "Class, Ethnicity, and the New Deal: The Croatian Fraternal Union in the 1930s," in Peter Kivisto, ed., *The Ethnic Enigma: The Salience of Ethnicity for European-origin Groups* [Philadelphia: Balch Institute Press, 1989], 93; also see the Rachleff essay in this volume).

46. Alan H. Olmstead, "The Wailing Wall," *Bridgeport Times-Star,* 30 Dec. 1933 (clipping in wooden scrapbook, McLevy-Schwarzkopf Papers).

47. Leff, *Limits of Symbolic Reform.*

48. Philadelphia in the early depression comes to mind here as another example (Bonnie R. Fox, "Unemployment Relief in Philadelphia, 1930–1932: A Study of the Depression's Impact on Voluntarism," *Pennsylvania Magazine of History and Biography* 93 [Jan. 1969]: 86–108). See also Rosemary Feurer, "The Nutpickers' Union, 1933–34: Crossing the Boundaries of Community and Workplace," 29 (on St. Louis), and Peter Rachleff, "Organizing 'Wall to Wall': The Independent Union of All Workers, 1933–37," 54–55 (on Austin, Minn.), both in Staughton Lynd, ed., *"We Are All Leaders": The Alternative Unionism of the Early 1930s* (Urbana: University of Illinois Press, 1996), for mention of community struggles with local private relief agencies.

49. David Beito, *Taxpayers in Revolt: Tax Resistance during the Great Depression* (Chapel Hill: University of North Carolina Press, 1989).

50. Attention to other aspects of the Bridgeport SP's membership, program, and limitations is in Bucki, "Pursuit of Political Power," 147–59 and chap. 5. On "constructive" socialism, see Sally M. Miller, *Victor Berger and the Promise of Constructive Socialism, 1910–1920* (Westport, Conn.: Greenwood Press, 1973).

51. See Robert S. McElvaine, *The Great Depression: America, 1929–1941* (New York: Times Books, 1993), 229–37, for a summary of these movements.

52. Cohen, *Making a New Deal,* has a benign view of Democratic party inclusion, while other historians have been more critical. See Mike Davis, "The Barren Marriage of American Labor and the Democratic Party," in Davis, *Prisoners of the American Dream: Politics and Economy in the History of the U.S. Working Class* (London: Verso, 1986), 52–101; Eric Leif Davin, "The Very Last Hurrah? The Defeat of the Labor Party Idea, 1934–36," in Lynd, ed., *"We Are All Leaders,"* 117–71; Bruce Nelson, "'Give Us Roosevelt': Workers and the New Deal Coalition," *History Today* 40 (Jan. 1990): 40–48. For the renewed influence of conservative ethnic elites in urban politics, see Cecelia F. Bucki, "Workers and Politics in the Immigrant City in the Early Twentieth-Century United States," *International Labor and Working-Class History* 48 (Fall 1995): 40–42.

53. The "Workers' Bill" was first drafted by the Communist-dominated Unemployed Councils in 1931, and then redrafted by social reformer Mary Van Kleeck. It provided for a federal system of benefits for involuntary unemployment due to a variety of causes, such as sickness, accident, maternity, or old age, with all categories of wage labor included. This inclusive, noncategorical plan, which treated all needs equally, was to be funded out of general revenues. In contrast, the eventual Social Security Act was funded from a separate flat tax, ruled out some categories of labor like domestic service and farm work (thus revealing its racial bias), and categorized the needy by cause, privileging only old age. In a *New York Post* poll in April 1935, comparing the administration's Wagner-Lewis bill, the Lundeen bill, and the Townsend bill, 87 percent of reader-respondents chose the Lundeen bill (Kenneth Casebeer, "The

Workers' Unemployment Insurance Bill: American Social Wage, Labor Organization, and Legal Ideology," in Christopher L. Tomlins and Andrew J. King, eds., *Labor Law in America: Historical and Critical Essays* [Baltimore: Johns Hopkins University Press, 1992], 231–59).

54. Lewis's speech to the 1939 CIO convention quoted in Foster Rhea Dulles, *The American Red Cross: A History* (New York: Harper & Bros., 1950), 303–4. See also Casebeer, "Workers' Unemployment Insurance Bill"; Linda Gordon, *Pitied but Not Entitled: Single Mothers and the History of Welfare* (New York: Free Press, 1994), 236–41; David Montgomery, "Labor and the Political Leadership of New Deal America," *International Review of Social History* 39 (Dec. 1994): 335–60.

Part 2

Class and Culture

Chapter 6

"Work That Body"

African-American Women, Work, and
Leisure in Atlanta and the New South

TERA W. HUNTER

THE EXPANSION OF capitalism at the turn of the twentieth century sub-
stantially transformed work and leisure everywhere in America. Increasing numbers of industrial workers enjoyed higher wages and more leisure
time; many nonindustrial workers, however, did not reap such benefits.
Domestic workers continued to work seven days a week and had little time
off for themselves. Alice Adams, a domestic worker in Atlanta in the 1910s,
recalled the difficulties of going out in the evenings while working long
hours every day. "I wanted time off," she stated. "Time off to visit my
friends and my friends to visit me, just like I was entertaining [my employer's] friends, I wanted to entertain my friends, and I wasn't satisfied until
I did." Though her husband reminded her that she was fortunate to have
nice employers, Adams persisted: "I say, that's not the thing, I wants time
off. And I got it."[1]

The study of working-class history has widened considerably in recent
decades, since the pioneering work of John R. Commons and his protégés,
to include considerations of the issues raised by Alice Adams. David Montgomery, Herbert Gutman, and other scholars in the 1960s began to broad-
en the field beyond earlier preoccupations with labor unions, to include
additional dimensions of working-class experiences both within and be-

yond the workplace. Labor history remains focused primarily on work; leisure has devolved to cultural historians. The limitations of such a bifurcation become readily apparent when one considers seminal scholarship like Lawrence Levine's *Black Culture and Black Consciousness: Afro-American Folk Thought from Slavery to Freedom* (1977). Levine shows us that racial and class consciousness were formulated in cultural practices outside workplaces as well as those within them. Following in the wake of books like Levine's, labor historians since the 1980s have increasingly devoted attention to recreation and leisure to reconstruct fuller pictures of working-class experiences.[2]

This essay contributes to this growing body of literature through an examination of the everyday lives of women like Alice Adams at work, at home, and in their leisure from the 1870s through the 1910s. In the urban South, African Americans and white southerners developed distinctive and competing ideas about work and leisure within a context marked by the vestiges of slavery and the codification of segregation. African-American women were at the heart of the contests that ensued as a result of these differences. While their work as domestics was considered marginal to the New South economy, it was in fact ubiquitous in southern cities and indispensable to the sustenance of white family livelihood and the perpetuation of racial inequalities. As African-American women struggled to balance the demands of wage work with the imperatives of non-wage work required for maintaining homes of their own, and the desire for personal growth and enrichment, they placed a high priority on autonomy and collective life and the creation of social spaces for respite and recreation. In the process, they helped to create a distinctive culture in their neighborhoods and communities. This essay analyzes controversies over the relationship between work and play that were particularly pronounced with regard to public dancing. Black vernacular dancing drew sharp criticism from middle-class Atlantans—black and white—reflecting broader anxieties about race, class, and sexuality in the Jim Crow South. Conflicts over the rules and expectations of public etiquette and social decorum attending the changes in the modernization of popular culture were especially conspicuous in Atlanta, the self-proclaimed model of the New South.

By the turn of the century, Atlanta was en route to becoming the metropolis that its urban boosters imagined. The city had traveled far from the antebellum period when it was a mere hamlet in the foothills of north

Georgia, to its soaring growth as a strategic transportation point for the Confederate Army during the Civil War, and to its continued rise as a regional center of commerce and industry over the next several decades. Ambitious young businessmen, journalists, and politicians had colluded since the 1880s to make Atlanta the model of the "New South." They promised to rescue the region from plantation slavery and one-crop agriculture, by diversifying economic development and harmonizing race relations. They accomplished the former by building cotton mills, rolling mills, and foundries, as well as manufacturing plants that produced a multitude of such consumer products as the world-renowned Coca-Cola, clothing, pianos, and furniture. They accomplished the latter by codifying a modern system of segregation to control interracial commerce, residency, and mobility in the interests of whites.[3]

The fortunes of African Americans in the city dovetailed with its overall development. The black population soared after the Civil War as slaves and ex-slaves migrated to find work and respite from the debilitating economic and social conditions of plantation life. As agriculture was reorganized, women who were single, divorced, or otherwise unattached to men proved particularly disposable to landowners. As a result, women far outnumbered men in the migration stream, and black women moved to cities like Atlanta in disproportionate numbers to find work to support themselves and to feed their families. By 1880 black women constituted 50 percent of the city's entire black work force.[4]

Black women migrants encountered something less than the freedom they had hoped to find in Atlanta. Despite a diverse and burgeoning economy, they were relegated to the bottom of the labor market in the worst paid and least desirable manual jobs. Barred from industries reserved for white or male workers, black women were primarily confined to domestic work from adolescence until disability or death. They labored as cooks, maids, and child-nurses in the homes of white employers, and as laundresses in their own homes, on behalf of white clients. Yet their paltry wages did not meet their most fundamental needs for food, shelter, and clothing. Black men were only slightly better off in some ways, and worse off in others. They found more diverse jobs open to them on the railroads, in city government, hotels, restaurants, and a variety of businesses that hired common labor. Though their wages were higher than women's, on average, they faced more frequent layoffs and firings in a capricious labor market.[5]

Black women found ways to reconcile the hardships of their occupational confinement in domestic labor. Married women and women with children often chose to do laundry work because it allowed them to juggle wage work with the responsibilities of household maintenance. Washerwomen picked up loads of dirty clothes from their patrons on Monday; washed, dried, and ironed throughout the week; and returned the finished garments on Saturday. This work yielded a day off and exempted workers from employer supervision. It also allowed them to care for children, perform other duties intermittently, and incorporate other family members into the work routine.[6] Laundry workers represented the largest single category of women in waged housework in Atlanta. According to the U.S. Census, by 1900 there were 4,817 laundresses as compared to 4,261 women in all other domestic jobs combined.[7]

Laundry work also provided the benefits of community, since it allowed women to work together within their neighborhoods. Women who washed in nearby streams or at common wells commiserated over shared struggles, swapped news and information, and ultimately created the networks of reciprocity that sustained them.[8] The value of this support system rose appreciably in crises caused by sickness, unemployment, disability, or death.

African-American domestic workers, such as cooks, maids, and child-nurses, who spent most of their time in white households sought to establish autonomy by insisting on living in their own homes. "They seem to think that it is something against their freedom if they sleep where they are employed," one employer explained. "Married or unmarried. They will rent a little house, perhaps a mile off, and pay $10 a month for it, and go there to sleep, when perhaps you would be willing to pay them just as much and give them a comfortable bed or cottage on your own place," he continued.[9] Black women recognized that the benefits of live-in service accrued mostly to employers. "Free" accommodations and food were usually meager and paled in comparison to the benefits of a separate life. Independent living arrangements distinguished domestic work in the South from the North where live-in service predominated until blacks began migrating there in large numbers between the 1910s and 1940s.[10]

Household workers pursued autonomy in other ways. They fought against the long hours and low wages that deprived them of a just standard of living. When employers refused to compromise or relent, the workers seized the initiative by quitting and seeking other employers. Though long hours and low wages were fairly uniform and changing jobs did not guarantee improvement, quitting gave workers some control over their labor. It also kept employers frustrated on their inability to keep the same workers permanently. Domestic workers also moved in and out of the labor force for temporary periods—frequently returning to the same employer after meeting whatever "emergency" prompted departure.[11] Movement from job to job was relatively easy because the demand for domestics was high and labor markets tight. Moreover, quitting did not require direct confrontation, for workers could simply not show up for work. This allowed household workers to maneuver creatively within the strictures of wage work, to balance competing demands on their time as mothers and wives.

Household laborers resorted to a number of age-old working-class survival strategies to increase resources and stretch their meager budgets. Women and children rummaged through the streets in search of recyclable goods in garbage pails of grocery stores, restaurants, fruit stands, and other merchants. Desperate washerwomen even gathered discarded cinders for fuel to heat water for the laundry. Women also recycled goods from the public domain for use, trade, or resale in the neighborhood or took them to local pawn shops in exchange for cash. Unable to take advantage of buying large quantities at volume discounts, they stretched their dollars by buying fresh foods and pantry items in small amounts, which at least had the benefit of preventing spoilage.[12]

Women's nonwage work at home was encumbered by the challenges of living in a city, which was still primitive. By the 1870s, such city services as water, gas lines, street paving, sewer connections, and fire protection were reserved largely for industries and wealthy white neighborhoods, reflecting the larger pattern of nascent segregation in the South. African Americans lived in the worst areas of the city on low-lying areas subject to floods and sewerage spills. Their one- to three-room shanties were constructed of cheap materials, badly ventilated, built on wood or brick piles for foundations, and lined alleys or unpaved and muddy streets with stagnant cesspools that met occupants at the front door. Common outdoor privies, wells, and street hydrants provided the only options for water and sanitation.[13]

Women negotiated the rugged conditions of urban life by pooling resources, mobilizing informal relationships in their neighborhoods. Their dense networks underpinned such formal institutions as mutual aid and benevolent associations, also called secret societies, extensive throughout the South after the Civil War, especially in cities. These associations paid benefits for sickness, death, and unemployment and offered outlets for education, socializing, trade association, and political organizing. They were at the center of institutions designed for urban survival, race advancement, and personal enrichment. Domestic laborers participated actively and visibly as leaders and members in the Daughters of Bethel, Daughters of Zion, Sisters of Friendship, and Sisters of Love. Elizabeth Russell and Mildred Fane, president and vice president of the Daughters of Bethlehem, were both washerwomen. The True Sisters of Honor elected Harriet Tolliver, a washerwoman, as vice president, and her daughter Keziah Wood as a member of the finance committee.[14]

Domestic workers demonstrated their commitment to these groups by taking leave from work to carry out organizational duties and obligations. The benefits of community occasionally outweighed the wages earned by cooking, cleaning, or washing for white employers. Organized mutuality also strengthened the workers' hand against employers, as one employer regretfully acknowledged: secret society membership "makes them perfectly independent and relieves them from all fear of being discharged, because when they are discharged they go right straight to some of these 'sisters.'"[15] Although the number of associations designated as labor groups were few, organizations that brought workers together for other purposes sometimes assumed trade union functions.[16] The domestic workers who shared their work experiences and frustrations with fellow members also drew up blacklists or boycotted recalcitrant employers. Such organizations transformed seemingly individual tactics, such as quitting or refusing to work for a particular employer, into collective power. Local and state candidates for political office such as George Brown, who ran for mayor in Atlanta in 1912, and Joseph M. Brown, of no relation, who ran for governor of Georgia in 1914, promised that if elected they would regulate or outlaw black secret societies for these reasons.[17]

By the turn of the century then, African Americans were linked to one another through kinship, friendship, and organizational affiliations across the city. As African-American women negotiated their livelihoods as wives, mothers, wage earners, fraternal members, and neighbors at work and at home, they sought to balance wage work with other ways of fulfilling social, material, and emotional needs. Their capacity to fulfill needs and desires faced constant challenges from bosses bent on keeping them subordinate and oppressed. White households were sites of conflict between workers and employers, not unlike more conventional workplaces. Relief or concessions could not be sustained without continuous struggle.[18]

Employers developed their own tactics to counter workers' resistance and maintain the upper hand. They implemented "insurance fees" or monetary advances against the future wages of newly hired domestics to discourage quitting. They imposed severe penalties and fines for petty lapses and infractions. Some employers coerced workers to buy discarded items, such as old clothing, deducting the prices from wages to keep workers in debt and minimize cash wages. Or, they simply refused to pay wages at all. Some organized "Housewives' Unions" to unite employers against workers. And when all else failed, employers resorted to the law, to extralegal vigilante violence exercised by the Ku Klux Klan, or to officially sanctioned brutality perpetrated by the police.[19]

The daily grind of the physical labor of wage housework and the constant battles with employers prompted black women to find other means of earning a living wherever opportunities arose. The first sign of any measurable change in black women's occupational distribution occurred between 1900 and 1910, when the proportion of black women in domestic work dropped from 92 to 84 percent. Black women were beginning to enter the sewing trades, commercial laundries, and small manufacturing jobs.[20] As an entertainment industry grew after the turn of the century, black women also found jobs in the "underworld" economy of gambling, bootlegging, and prostitution.[21] The boundary between work and play blurred for these women workers whose jobs involved excitement and danger. Still, few black women could escape domestic work, no matter how hard they tried; they sought instead to balance their pecuniary interests with other needs, offsetting the rigors of wage labor in their own world of popular amusements. But when they left behind the mops, brooms, wash tubs, kitchen stoves, and sinks at the end of the day, the women encountered other challenges. In the dynamic world of commercial entertainment lurked many of the same racial, class, and gender conflicts that permeated their work lives. The interconnections between their struggles at work and at play are revealing, especially in the pursuit of leisure in the dance halls on Atlanta's Decatur Street.

~

By the 1910s, African Americans enjoyed greater opportunities for nightlife in saloons, billiard rooms, restaurants, gambling dens, vaudeville, and motion picture houses. Most of these outlets were clustered on the infamous Decatur Street, the epicenter of the urban leisure milieu. Its resemblance to other seamy metropolitan districts sometimes conjured comparisons with Canal Street in New Orleans, the Bowery of New York City, the Champs Élysées of Paris, and Chinatown of San Francisco. On weekends, local residents and country transients flocked there in large numbers to dicker with street vendors or auctioneers amid the commingled smells of peanuts, tobacco, near beer, hot dogs, fried fish, horse manure, and cheap perfume. Secondhand clothing stores and a multitude of shoe stores attracted scores of astute consumers looking for snazzy outfits at bargain prices. Others brought items to exchange for cash in the pawnshops—the places where victims of larceny headed hot on the heels of thieves in hopes of reclaiming stolen property.[22]

The conspicuous presence of Chinese laundrymen, Jewish and Greek shopowners, Yankee spielers, Italian chorus men, and moonshine mountaineers rubbing shoulders with one another reinforced the street's reputation as the "melting pot of Dixie." Petty entrepreneurship among black women was also visible along Decatur Street—another avenue of escape for black women seeking nondomestic work. Ella Jackson and Nettie Penn, two black women who owned lunchrooms, shared the same block with Fred Ketchum's jewelry store, and Nathan Weitzman's barbershop. Similarly, Lina Richardson's lodging house sat a few doors away from Isaac Sinkovitz's pawnshop, Evan Williams's grocery store, and Lula Edwards's brothel. Decatur Street's "melting pot" meant more than the coexistence of ethnic businesses, however. It was one of the few places where different racial and ethnic groups mingled freely. Nonetheless, Decatur Street was best known as a "negro playground."[23]

African-American workers were especially devoted to the dance halls that were concentrated on Decatur street. Dancing was becoming popular throughout urban America in the 1910s as prejudices about the propriety of heterosexual socializing began to change. Previously, social dancing, as defined by polite society, required strict boundaries of patterned movements, disciplined gestures, and formal distance between acquaintances to minimize intimacy. In the pre–World War I era, however, dancing between strangers became more acceptable, and dance itself became more inventive and less rigid in style and bodily movement, encouraging lingering physical contact.[24] Black culture heavily influenced these changes; the syncreticism of African and European inflections in their music and their movements traveled back and forth through migrants and itinerant entertainers moving from country to town to city and from South to North, forming common ties with people of African descent across the nation. White Americans adopted some black dance styles witnessed in the cabarets where blacks performed for them and in black dance halls where they went "slumming."[25] Still, neither public dancing in general nor black vernacular dance in particular enjoyed universal acceptance.

As early as the 1870s and 1880s, the emergent black bourgeoisie and the white elite in Atlanta and other southern cities voiced strong objections to black dance and the social institutions that sustained it.[26] The drive to get rid of dance halls and other "dives" intensified at the peak of the

Progressive Era. Black and white ministers, politicians, and social purity reformers were prominent critics of such black dance halls. The opposition heated up in 1903 when the Atlanta City Council imposed an exorbitant tax on black dance halls in an effort to force them out of business. This effort failed as proprietors and patrons reconfigured makeshift spaces out of sight if necessary to circumvent regulation. The council moved to abolish these establishments altogether, blaming them for producing a "carnival of crime," but again failed to control devoted dancers who averted these and other attempts to regulate or prohibit dance halls.[27]

Black and white critics of dance halls articulated several arguments against them. The seamy reputation of Decatur Street in general and the close proximity of legal and illegal merriment tainted the reputation of dance halls in the minds of critics who associated them with crime and "vice." Some dance halls continued earlier traditions of sharing quarters with saloons, though most were makeshift rooms, usually located in basements—ergo the moniker "dives." The combination of gambling, alcoholic drinks, and excited bodies moving in time to the music intoxicated some, leading to misunderstandings that could occur in festive crowds on any occasion, as petty skirmishes sometimes ended in melees. Police records in Atlanta are replete with examples of lively partying gone awry, and fights that included women domestic workers were commonplace. Pinkie Chandler, for example, was injured by a beer glass thrown in her face by Helen Henry when she accidentally brushed up against Henry's partner while dancing. Delia Mitchell created trouble when she tried to squeeze onto an already crowded dance floor, only to be pushed aside by another woman. The action outside the dance halls could generate a theater of its own, as couples necked or said their farewells and youths gathered for the last brouhaha. Lighthearted fraternizing on the way home could turn sour as well, embroiling women in fights with each other or with men.[28]

Opponents also disapproved of the distinctive physicality of black vernacular dance, which challenged Euro-American conceptions of proper bodily carriage and etiquette. African-American dance emphasized the movement of body parts, often asymmetrically and independent of one another, whereas Euro-American dance demanded rigidity to mitigate sensuality. Black vernacular dance generally exploded outward from the hips; it was performed from a crouching position with the knees flexed and the body bent at the waist, which allowed a fluidity of movement in a propulsive rhythmic fashion. Facial gestures, clapping, shouting, and yelling of provocative phrases reinforced the kineticism.[29]

Middle-class observers discerned cultural differences that they inter-preted to fit ideas about black inferiority. Even some middle-class blacks saw black vernacular dance through the lens of dominant, pejorative as-sumptions. As Henry Hugh Proctor, the pastor of the First Congrega-tional church and a leading dance hall opponent, stated bluntly: "In the name of Anglo-Saxon civilization, remove these things that are ruining the character of our young men and stealing away the virtue of our young women."[30] Proctor, a product of the black elite, used choice words—Anglo-Saxon civilization, character, and virtue—which were loaded ra-cial constructions frequently invoked in the ideology of white suprema-cy.[31] Proctor reinforced what many whites believed, that "primitive" black expressive culture threatened Victorian notions of self-restraint.

While Proctor drew on narrow cultural standards, he recognized the sexual connotations evident in black working-class dance. The sultry set-tings, dimmed lights and prolonged musical renditions did invite intima-cy. The "slow drag," one of the most popular dances, was described by one observer this way: "couples would hang onto each other and just grind back and forth in one spot all night." The Itch was described as "a spasmodic placing of the hands all over the body in an agony of perfect rhythm." The Fish Tail put the emphasis on the rear end, as the name suggested; the "buttocks weave out, back, and up in a variety of figure eights." The names of other dances had erotic overtones also: the Grind, Mooche, Shimmy, Fanny Bump, Ballin' the Jack, and the Funky Butt. Skirt lifting, body ca-ressing, and thrusting pelvic movements were indecent in the eyes of moral reformers.[32]

Vernacular dance assumed these characteristics in large part from the inspiration of the music, reflecting the inseparability of music and dance in black culture. African-American music of the era was an engaging social practice where audiences and performers were expected to respond to one another orally and physically. Complex rhythmic patterns of voice and in-struments inspired mimicry of the emotions they evoked, using bodily movement such as foot stomping, hand clapping, and leaping around.[33]

The music enjoyed in the dance halls was varied and fluid, typically characterized as ragtime or "lowdown" blues, usually performed live. The blues, with its roots in the field hollers, work songs, and spirituals of the South, emerged toward the end of the nineteenth century and matured in the dance halls, rent parties, and vaudeville theaters, becoming more formalized in the 1910s and 1920s. In some venues, the blues were played by a pianist, a fiddler, or by one or more individuals "patting juba"—a practice dating back to slavery that involved clapping hands, snapping fingers, and patting limbs and armpits rhythmically, shouting and yelling as they moved.[34]

While the sight and sound of black music and dance suggested certain ideas to middle-class critics, black workers invested them with different kinds of meanings.[35] The blues and popular dance evoked positive affirmations of cultural memories and revisionings of postemancipation life. Like its ancestors, the blues inspired active movement rather than passive reception, and dance provided the mechanism for the audience to engage the performer in a ritual communal ceremony. Despite the connotations of its name, the blues was "good-time" music that diverted and drove away depression among a people whose everyday lives were filled with adversity. The blues served as "the call" and dance as the "response" in a symbiotic performance in which ecstatic bodily movements mocked the lyrics and instrumentation that signified pain and lamentation.[36]

This close link between the blues and dance troubled middle-class and religious people as African Americans renegotiated the relationship between sacred and secular culture. Secular culture assumed a larger significance to blacks facing the exigencies of a new urban, industrializing world. The tensions that resulted were most pronounced in the evolution of music and dance and their relationship to religion and the church. The shared pedigree of sacred and secular music and dance complicated matters for the pious, who drew a sharper line between shouting for the Lord and shouting for the Devil. The similarities in the ritual, cathartic, communal, and expressive purposes of secular and sacred music and dance threatened the province once occupied primarily by religion in African-American life. For middle-class Christians like Proctor, the close resemblance between raucous secular dancing and ecstatic religious worship made the former doubly objectionable. Small wonder that elite black religious denominations and individual churches consciously sought to divorce themselves from traditional styles of worship, preaching, and singing that were considered "heathen" or reminiscent of Africa and the plantation South.[37]

The masses of black worshipers continued to practice ecstatic religious expressions in spite of middle-class criticism. The sacred shout, as musical sound and bodily movement, was a variant of the "lowdown" blues that filled the airwaves of the nightclubs and dance halls.[38] Such black worshipers, however, objected less to vernacular dance and more to the fact that secular performances paid homage to the Devil rather than to the Holy Ghost. In other words, the social context and intentions of dance mattered more than the physical movements per se. In fact, members of the Sanctified church movement, the most fervent practitioners of the ring shout, eagerly embraced corporeality, which they validated as ultimate expressions of salvation.[39]

Reconciling worldly pleasure and spiritual reverence was not always as simple as choosing right over wrong, or God over the Devil, even for devout church people. In 1916, delegates at the annual Georgia Conference of the African Methodist Episcopal (AME) church railed against the evils of the card table, the theater, and the modern dance.[40] Yet those individuals who engaged in popular amusements on Saturday night were often among those who attended church on Sunday morning. Even as the gap between the sacred and the secular widened, the boundaries between these domains remained permeable and fluid. How else could one explain the pronouncements by the AME church and the simultaneous practices of its congregates in Atlanta openly embracing popular amusements even in their own sanctuaries? Henry McNeal Turner, himself an AME bishop, hosted vaudeville and minstrel shows in his well-regarded Tabernacle. Allen Temple AME sponsored Leon the Boy Magician, Ebenezer Baptist Church entertained Ulysses the Magician, and along with Olive Baptist Church and Phillips ME Church, they also showed nightly motion pictures. Even Proctor's church sponsored an annual secular music festival, though he clearly intended Negro jubilee and European classical music to provide a moral alternative to those "places in this city that tend to drag down the colored servant."[41]

Critics of public dance halls were especially harsh on black women domestic workers. The ubiquity of black, female servants on the urban landscape, in the minds of most whites, made them metonyms for the black race. The black bourgeoisie fully understood and resented this "guilt" by association. It dealt with this tendency by lamenting the shame that befell the entire race when workers failed to live up to the expectations of dutiful service. Dance halls were a menace, declared Proctor, because "the servant class tried to work all day and dance all night."[42] He warned employers that household laborers would perform poorly if they used their leisure unproductively—dancing instead of resting in preparation for the next day of work. The white newspaper agreed and called for a reform: "Let the dance halls and places of low resort for the negro give way to schools for the domestic training of the race—schools for cooking and housework." It continued, "instead of dancing and carousing the night away, he (and especially she) will learn to become proficient in the task [for which] he is employed."[43]

For their part, white employers echoed Proctor's sentiment; they opposed the violation of what they considered their rightful claim to restrict black women's exertions to manual work. They also objected to black domestic workers' dancing because they feared that the dance halls bred social contagions that would infect their homes. Some child-nurses were accused of sneaking into the "dives" with white children during the day, exposing the little ones to immorality and vice. The discourse of scientific racism bolstered fears of racial and sexual pollution. According to one clergyman: "The servants of the white people of the city were enticed into [dance halls] and corrupted by them. So the white people of the city were also affected by their presence."[44] Here again, the close affiliation between music and dance implicated both cultural expressions. The seductions of black music proved difficult to contain, even in this era of racial segregation. Dancing embodied the music and became the means by which abstract, fleeting sounds were extended and articulated kinesthetically. The sexual connotations of black dance exacerbated anxieties about women's behavior. The black and white middle classes believed that dancing encouraged sexual promiscuity among black women, who would then pollute white households. The combination of the racial threat and the sexual fears of black bodies contaminating white bodies heightened the anxieties of late Victorian middle classes, all the more so given the interracial conviviality on Decatur Street.

Ironically, aspects of middle-class criticism had something in common with the meaning conferred by the working class itself. Though working-class people did not have a voice in public discourse, as it was circulated through the media and civic proceedings, they made their views known through their actions. Both sides understood that dancing interfered with wage work, though they viewed it from antithetical perspectives. The elite saw dancing as a hindrance to a chaste, disciplined, and submissive labor force. Workers saw it as a respite from the drudgery of toil and an important aspect of personal independence. Blacks could reclaim their bodies from appropriation as instruments of physical toil and redirect their energies toward other diversions.[45]

More than this, black dance embodied a resistance to the confinement of the body in wage work. The transformation of physical gestures in black dance from slavery to freedom constituted rejection of wage work as the only outlet for physical exertion. Ex-slaves thus abandoned references and gestures mimicking labor routines in their dances that they had practiced during slavery (such as "pitchin hay" or "shuckin' corn") as urban freedom enabled a living standard beyond the needs of subsistence.[46] Increased levels of consumption, new forms of entertainment, and greater personal gratification were vital to working-class livelihoods and an essential component of an emergent modern ethos. In the world of urban poverty and segregation, where enjoyments were limited, the affirmation of life embodied in dancing captivated working-class women and men and offered moments of symbolic and physical restoration of their subjugated bodies for joy, pleasure, and self-delight.

Further evidence of black women workers' pursuit of alternatives to wage work can be detected in their dress. Domestic workers wore uniforms to work or other plain outfits that signified poverty and social subordinance. But when they left work behind, they shed the sartorial symbols of servility for clothes that reflected respectability and self-worth. As Alice Adams remarked: "I would always go to work neat and clean. But my dress up clothes, I didn't wear 'em to work. Because when I went out I wanted to change and I wanted to look different."[47] For Adams, demarcating the line between work and play was an important part of claiming personal dignity. Changing clothes was a clear way to draw that line.

The emphasis on dress provided another line of assault for critics of women in dance halls. The proclivities African Americans were presumed to have for stylish dress, conspicuous consumption, and personal adornment were seen as immoral. As Anthony Binga, a black minister from Virginia and critic of dancing and other urban "vices," complained: "The fashionable dress, which is too thin and scantily cut to sleep in—even in a tropical clime—is worn through the cold night air to and from this [dance] room, where the temperature is sometimes in the nineties." He concluded: "the child of vanity will scarcely allow wrapping to touch her body for fear of disarranging her toilette."[48]

Though women's fashion was increasingly less modest and restrictive, Binga overstated the case. Some extant photographs of dance-hall dress indicate appropriation of middle-class taste, though African-American workers had their own aesthetic standards and put their own twist on fashion instead of blindly adopting mainstream forms. The men donned hats, vests, jackets, and trousers held up by suspenders. The women wore flat top or wide-brimmed hats, full length skirts that hugged the hips and flared out at the bottom, blouses with pouter pigeon bodices and sleeves that were puffed near the shoulders and fitted around the forearms.[49] The women gave careful attention to their dress style, from their hairdos down to their underwear. The disclosure of pretty petticoats made of fine linen and crocheted edges became a part of such dances as the Funky Butt. Moreover, the emphasis and glorification of body parts, such as the buttocks, subverted dominant standards of beauty. Black women were caricatured as grotesque and ugly in popular representations in the dominant culture. But in dance halls, black beauty could be highlighted and celebrated. Anthropologist Zora Neale Hurston summed up one alternative criterion of good looks in a colorphobic society: "even if she were as black as the hinges of hell the question was 'Can she jook?'"[50]

The literal stripping of the outward symbols of servility helped to reinforce the importance of dance as an activity used to recover from the exploitation of wage labor. It is also important to note that the connotation of "work" in black culture was complex. The title of this article, "Work That Body," is a play on these multiple meanings. Work not only meant physical labor, it also meant dancing. The phrase "work that body" is a variation of a common refrain shouted on the dance floor to praise and encourage the talents of dancers and musicians. In addition, it meant engaging in sex.[51] Dancing enabled an escape from wage work, even as dance itself was considered work—of a different order. The ethics of drive, achievement, and perseverance took on a different meaning when removed from the context of wage relations. Dancers put a high value on mastery of technique and style and competed with one another in jest and formal contests in which "working hard" became the criterion of a good performance. The proof was found in the zeal and agility of body movements or in the perspiration that seeped through one's clothes. James P. Johnson, a pianist, suggested another way: "I saw many actually wear right through a pair of shoes in one night. They danced hard."[52]

The value placed on dancing as hard work resonated in particular with African-American women workers in a society in which the highest valorization of womanhood was largely defined by abstinence from work. The ideal woman avoided wage work, for the obligations of motherhood and comforts of home. Leola B. Wilson (aka Coot Grant) remembered her childhood in Birmingham, Alabama, at the turn of the century. Her aspirations to become an entertainer were nourished by her furtive glimpses through a peephole she drilled in a wall of her father's honky-tonk in order to observe adult entertainment. Wilson's recollections years later demonstrate how black women could reconstruct notions of womanhood through dance. "I remember a tall, powerful woman who worked in the mills pulling coke from a furnace—a man's job," she added. "It was Sue, and she loved men. When Sue arrived at my father's honky tonk, people would yell: 'Here come Big Sue! Do the Funky Butt, Baby!' As soon as she got high and happy, that's what she'd do, pulling up her skirts and grinding her rear end like an alligator crawling up a bank."[53] Sue worked hard, like a man, during the day, but at night she shed her industrial pants and worked hard as a woman in a setting in which femininity was appreciated for its compatibility with work—of several different orders.

Working-class women found respite in commercialized establishments on Decatur Street, especially in dance halls where they could make their bodies their own. They danced for fun and recreation, above all. They used dance to heal, commune, and transcend, momentarily, their daily travails. Dance was an affirmation of their racial heritage, reinforcement of shared cultural values, and a means of reenacting community. It also enabled the construction of positive self-identities in a society that measured them against standards of womanhood that they could not or would not meet.

Dancing became transgressive in light of the criticisms and actions of middle-class reformers intent on exorcizing it from the public realm. The mere sight of African Americans, especially domestic workers, deriving pleasure and expressing symbolic liberation in dance halls by posing alternative meanings of bodily exertion was unsettling.[54] The distinctive features of black dance seemed threatening to whites who expected deference from African Americans and who were increasingly wary of signs and symbols of their independence. Unlike other commercialized recreation, such as the new amusement parks, where one encountered replicas of industrial life in the mechanized, standardized forms of play, dance halls still allowed for a great deal of creativity, imagination, improvisation, and, thereby, change.[55] Dance halls contained a strong element of impulsiveness and unpredictability, as dancers and musicians inspired one another to enact infinite permutations of gestures and utterances. Some social purity reformers tried to mitigate these tendencies by introducing tame, patterned movements to counteract the forms of free expression that were difficult to suppress when dancers were left to their own devices.[56]

Yet despite the tirades of incensed critics, dancing probably did have the effect of renewal and recovery, even if on the workers' own terms. It reinvigorated them for the next day of work and enabled them to persevere. It was one among many elements that helped to maintain social stability by providing an outlet for workers to release their tensions, to purge their bodies of their travails on the dance floor. Dancing hard, like laboring hard, was consistent with the work ethic of capitalism. African Americans' assertion of this expressive practice replicated dimensions of the social order around them.

Much was at stake for the black middle class in this struggle over vernacular dance. The controversy occurred as a modern black bourgeoisie asserted its claim to define progress and lead the race. The black elite sought to impose its own values and standards on the masses, to obliterate plebeian cultural expressions that, in its view, reinforced racial degradation. While the black elite asserted its paternalism through the language of morality, "civilization," law and order, and the Protestant work ethic, the white elite exercised rhetorical and repressive authority through state power. White southerners had even more at stake in controlling black leisure and dancing as they sought greater control over black labor power. White fears of the bodily excesses perceived in dance were rooted in racial and class-coded constructions of bodily carriage, in their own obsessions with sex, and in their anxieties about interracial coupling. The racial paranoia was further nurtured by the context in which much of the dancing occurred, in the subterranean world of the red light district on Decatur Street, "the melting pot of Dixie," where urban dwellers crossed over the color line more freely than elsewhere in the city. White fears were contradictory, however; the very Anglo-Saxon values used to measure "racial" fitness were themselves undergoing change. Victorianism was losing its luster; white middle-class people felt shackled by their own inhibitions and began adopting the very same behaviors (such as passion, rough sport, and visceral amusements) that they so derisively associated with the "lower orders."[57]

African-American women demonstrated through their resilient public dancing, as they had in their work and community activities, that they valued autonomy and collectivity. They made efforts to carve out space for self, family, and community within the constraints of their confinement to poorly paid jobs at the bottom of the wage labor hierarchy. For laundry workers, the realms of wage labor, family, and community overlapped; they could find pleasure in the social dimensions of their labor. For domestics like Alice Adams, who worked full-time in white workplaces, however, it became even more important to find avenues of escape totally removed from the workplace. Yet no matter what their occupation, black women could not escape the inevitable tensions produced by race, class, and sexuality in the Jim Crow South—on or off the job.

Notes

1. Alice Adams, interview by Bernard E. West, 20 Nov. 1979, tape recording, Living Atlanta Collection, Atlanta History Center, Atlanta, Ga. (hereafter cited as AHC).

2. Roy Rosenzweig, *Eight Hours for What We Will: Workers and Leisure in an Industrial City, 1870–1920* (Cambridge: Cambridge University Press, 1983); Kathy Peiss, *Cheap Amusements: Working Women and Leisure in Turn-of-the-Century New York* (Philadelphia: Temple University Press, 1986); Robin D. G. Kelley, *Race Rebels: Culture, Politics, and the Black Working Class* (New York: Free Press, 1994); Earl Lewis, *In Their Own Interests: Race, Class, and Power in Twentieth-Century Norfolk, Virginia* (Berkeley: University of California Press, 1991); Joe William Trotter, Jr., *Coal, Class, and Color: Blacks in Southern West Virginia, 1915–32* (Urbana: University of Illinois Press, 1990); Lizabeth Cohen, *Making a New Deal: Industrial Workers in Chicago, 1919–1939* (Cambridge: Cambridge University Press, 1990); Jacquelyn Dowd Hall et al., *Like a Family: The Making of a Southern Cotton Mill World* (Chapel Hill: University of North Carolina Press, 1987); Gary R. Mormino and George E. Pozzetta, *The Immigrant World of Ybor City: Italians and Their Latin Neighbors in Tampa, 1885–1985* (Urbana: University of Illinois Press, 1988); Alexander Saxton, *The Rise and Fall of the White Republic: Class, Politics and Mass Culture in Nineteenth Century America* (London: Verso, 1990); David R. Roediger, *The Wages of Whiteness: Race and the Making of the American Working Class* (London: Verso, 1991); Christine Stansell, *City of Women: Sex and Class in New York, 1789–1860* (1986; reprint, Urbana: University of Illinois Press, 1987).

3. Howard N. Rabinowitz, *Race Relations in the Urban South, 1865–1890* (New York: Oxford University Press, 1978); John Dittmer, *Black Georgia in the Progressive Era, 1900–1920* (Urbana: University of Illinois Press, 1977); James Michael Russell, *Atlanta, 1847–1890: City Building in the Old South and the New* (Baton Rouge: Louisiana University Press, 1988).

4. Jacqueline Jones, *Labor of Love, Labor of Sorrow: Black Women, Work, and the Family from Slavery to the Present* (New York: Basic Books, 1985). Tera W. Hunter, *To 'Joy My Freedom: Southern Black Women's Lives and Labors after the Civil War* (Cambridge, Mass.: Harvard University Press, 1997); Jerry Thornberry, "The Development of Black Atlanta, 1865–1885" (Ph.D. dissertation, University of Maryland, 1977); Rabinowitz, *Race Relations in the Urban South;* U.S. Department of the Interior, *Statistics of the Population of the U.S. at the Tenth Census* (Washington, D.C.: Government Printing Office, 1883), 1:862.

5. Jacqueline Jones, *Labor of Love;* Hunter, *To 'Joy My Freedom;* David M. Katzman, *Seven Days a Week: Women and Domestic Service in Industrializing America* (1978; reprint, Urbana: University of Illinois Press, 1981); Rabinowitz, *Race Relations in the Urban South.*

6. On laundry work see Sarah Hill, "Bea, the Washerwoman," Federal Writer's Project Papers, Southern Historical Collection, University of North Carolina, Chapel Hill (hereinafter cited as SHC); Jasper Battle, "Wash Day in Slavery," in George P. Rawick, ed., *The American Slave: A Composite Autobiography* (Westport, Conn.: Greenwood Press, 1972–78), vol. 2, pt. 1, 70; Katzman, *Seven Days a Week,* 72, 82, 124; Daniel Sutherland, *Americans and Their Servants: Domestic Service in the United States from 1800–1920* (Baton Rouge: Louisiana University Press, 1981), 92; Faye E. Dudden, *Serving Women: Household Service in Nineteenth Century America* (Middletown, Conn.: Wesleyan University Press, 1983), 224–25; and Patricia E. Malcolmson, *English Laundresses: A Social History, 1850–1930* (Urbana: University of Illinois Press, 1986), 11–43.

7. U.S. Department of Commerce and Labor, Bureau of the Census. *Special Reports: Occupations at the Twelfth Census* (Washington, D.C.: Government Printing Office, 1904), 486–89.

"Work That Body" 171

8. For an example of a communal laundry location see *Atlanta Constitution*, 20 July 1881.

9. Testimony of Albert C. Danner, U.S. Senate Committee on Education and Labor, *Report upon the Relations between Labor and Capital* (Washington, D.C.: Government Printing Office, 1885), 105 (hereafter cited as *Labor and Capital*).

10. See Katzman, *Seven Days a Week*; Elizabeth Clark-Lewis, *Living In Living Out: African American Domestics in Washington, D.C.* (Washington, D.C.: Smithsonian Institution, 1994); Hunter, *To 'Joy My Freedom*.

11. For examples of the role and impact of quitting see *Atlanta Daily Intelligencer*, 25 Oct. 1865; Myrta Lockett Avary, *Dixie after the War: An Exposition of Social Conditions Existing in the South during the Twelve Years Succeeding the Fall of Richmond* (Boston: Doubleday, 1906; reprint, 1937), 192; entries for 17 June through 2 Dec. 1866, Samuel P. Richards Diary, AHC; entries for May 1865, Ella Gertrude Clanton Thomas Journal, Duke University Archives, Durham, N.C. (hereinafter cited as DU); Emma J. S. Prescott, "Reminiscences of the War," 49–55, AHC.

12. See for example, *Atlanta Journal of Labor*, 14 May 1915; and *American Missionary* 13 (Apr. 1869): 75; Ruth Reed, *The Negro Women of Gainesville, Georgia* (Athens: University of Georgia, 1921), 31.

13. James M. Russell, "Politics, Municipal Services, and the Working Class in Atlanta, 1865 to 1890," *Georgia Historical Quarterly* 66 (Winter 1982): 467–91; Thornberry, "Development of Black Atlanta"; Dana F. White, "The Black Sides of Atlanta: A Geography of Expansion and Containment, 1970–1870," *Atlanta Historical Journal* 26 (Summer-Fall 1982–83): 199–225; W. E. B. Du Bois, "The Problem of Housing the Negro: V. The Southern City Negro of the Lower Class," *Southern Workman* 20 (Dec. 1901): 688–93; Rabinowitz, *Race Relations in the Urban South*; and C. Vann Woodward, *Origins of the New South, 1877–1913* (Baton Rouge: Louisiana State University Press, 1951), 355.

14. U.S. Department of Treasury, Register of Signatures of Depositors in the Branches of the Freedmen's Savings and Trust Company, Atlanta Branch, 1870–74. The Freedmen's bank records provide information on individual mutual aid groups and listings of officers. For more information on these organizations see: W. E. B. Du Bois, ed., *Efforts for Social Betterment among Negro Americans* (Atlanta: Atlanta University, 1909); Evelyn Brooks Higginbotham, *Righteous Discontent: The Women's Movement in the Black Baptist Church, 1880–1920* (Cambridge, Mass.: Harvard University Press, 1992); Armstead Robinson, "'Plans Dat Come from God': Institution Building and the Emergence of Black Leadership in Reconstruction Memphis," in Orville Vernon Burton and Robert C. McMath, Jr., eds., *Toward a New South? Studies in Post–Civil War Southern Communities* (Westport, Conn.: Greenwood Press, 1979); Elsa Barkley Brown, "Womanist Consciousness: Maggie Lena Walker and the Independent Order of Saint Luke," *Signs* 14 (Spring 1989): 610–33; Peter J. Rachleff, *Black Labor in the South: Richmond, Virginia, 1865–1890* (Philadelphia: Temple University Press, 1984); Kathleen C. Berkeley, "'Colored Ladies Also Contributed': Black Women's Activities from Benevolence to Social Welfare, 1866–1896," in Walter J. Fraser et al., eds., *The Web of Southern Social Relations: Women, Family, and Education* (Athens: University of Georgia Press, 1985); Anne Firor Scott, "Most Visible of All: Black Women's Voluntary Associations," *Journal of Southern History* 56 (Feb. 1990): 3–22.

15. Testimony of Mrs. Ward, in *Labor and Capital*, 344. See also, Ma [Margaret Cronly] to darling Rob [Cronly], 29 June 1881, Cronly Family Papers, DU.

16. *Atlanta Constitution*, 31 Mar. 1910; Reed, *Negro Women of Gainesville*, 46. Canadian and other working-class mutual aid organizations carried out similar functions. See Varpu Lindström-Best, *Defiant Sisters: A Social History of Finnish Immigrant Women in Canada* (Toronto: Multicultural History Society of Ontario, 1988), 56–60; and E. P. Thompson, *The Making of the English Working Class* (New York: Pantheon, 1966), 418–29.

17. See 1914 campaign literature, Joseph M. Brown Papers, Atlanta History Center. On George Brown see *Atlanta Constitution*, 8–29 Sept. 1912. For a fuller discussion of these events see Hunter, *To 'Joy My Freedom*.

18. See David Montgomery, *Workers' Control: Studies in the History of Work, Technology, and Labor Struggles* (Cambridge: Cambridge University Press, 1980).

19. See for example, Elizabeth Kytle, *Willie Mae* (New York: Knopf, 1958), 116; Meta Morris Grimball to J. Berkeley Grimball, 18 Dec. 1865, Grimball Family Papers, SHC; "Account of Ann Crawle," 1884, Edwin Edmunds Papers, SHC; Valeria Burroughs Commonplace Book, 1865, SHC; *Atlanta Constitution*, 8 Oct. 1914. On Ku Klux Klan violence see, for example, testimony of Alfred Richardson, in *Testimony taken by the Joint Select Committee to Inquire into the Condition of Affairs in the Late Insurrectionary States*, 42d Cong., 2d sess., House Report 22, pt. 6 (Washington, D.C.: Government Printing Office, 1872), 1:12, 18.

20. W. E. B. Du Bois, ed., *The Negro American Artisan* (Atlanta: Atlanta University Press, 1912), 46; U.S. Department of Commerce and Labor, Bureau of the Census, *Special Reports: Occupations Twelfth Census* (Washington, D.C.: Government Printing Office, 1904), 486–89; U.S. Department of Commerce and Labor, Bureau of the Census, *Thirteenth Census: Population, Occupations* (Washington, D.C.: Government Printing Office, 1914), 536–37.

21. For black prostitutes and bootleg operators see *Atlanta Constitution*, 15 May and 18 June 1900, 30 Nov. 1902; *Atlanta Journal*, 12 Apr. and 12 Aug. 1901; *Atlanta Independent*, 22 Sept. 1906; "Condition of the Negro in Various Cities," *Bulletin of the Department of Labor* 2 (May 1897): 257–359. Gretchen Maclachlan, "Women's Work: Atlanta's Industrialization and Urbanization, 1879–1929" (Ph.D. dissertation, Emory University, 1992), 203–25; "Reports of the Martha Home," 1913–15, in Christian Council Papers, Men and Religion Forward Movement, AHC; Minute Book, 1908–18, Neighborhood Union Papers, Robert W. Woodruff Library, Clark Atlanta University, Atlanta, Ga.

22. *Journal Magazine*, 18 May 1913, in Franklin Garrett, *Atlanta and Environs: A Chronicle of Its People and Events*, 3 vols. (Athens: University of Georgia, 1969), 2:607–9.

23. Ibid.; and Atlanta City Directory, 1910.

24. Lewis A. Erenberg, *Steppin' Out: New York Nightlife and the Transformation of American Culture, 1890–1930* (Westport, Conn.: Greenwood Press, 1981), 20, 150–55.

25. Katrina Hazzard-Gordon, *Jookin': The Rise of Social Dance Formations in African American Culture* (Philadelphia: Temple University Press, 1990), 63–94; Zora Neale Hurston, "Characteristics of the Negro," in Nancy Cunard, ed., *Negro Anthology* (1934; New York: Negro Universities Press, 1969), 29–30.

26. Rabinowitz, *Race Relations in the Urban South*, 243–46.

27. Atlanta City Council Minutes, 6 Apr. 1903, 20:19, AHC; *Atlanta Constitution*, 13 July 1903; and *Atlanta Journal*, 28 May 1903.

28. For stories of police arrests of women and men for crime related to dance halls see *Atlanta Constitution*, 23 June 1900, 7 May 1904, 9 Mar. 1905; *Atlanta Journal*, 19 and 23 June, 12 Sept. 1900. See comments by Henry Hugh Proctor and Monroe N. Work in W. E. B. Du Bois, ed., *Some Notes on Negro Crime* (Atlanta: Atlanta University, 1904), 50–51.

29. Hazzard-Gordon, *Jookin'*, 15–20, 83–84; Marshall Stearns and Jean Stearns, *Jazz Dance: The Story of American Vernacular Dance* (New York: Macmillan, 1968).

30. *Atlanta Constitution*, 7 July 1903.

31. For a cogent analysis of the racial implications of the discourse of "civilization" at the turn of the century see Gail Bederman, *Manliness and Civilization: A Cultural History of Gender and Race in the United States, 1880–1917* (Chicago: University of Chicago Press, 1995).

32. Stearns and Stearns, *Jazz Dance*, 1–12, 21, 24, 27; William H. Jones, *Recreation and Amusement among Negroes in Washington, D.C.: A Sociological Analysis of the Negro in an Urban Environment* (Westport, Conn.: Negro Universities Press, 1970), 121–23.

33. Sterling Stuckey, *Slave Culture: Nationalist Thought and the Foundations of Black America* (New York: Oxford University Press, 1987), 57–59; Lawrence Levine, *Black Culture and Black Consciousness: Afro-American Folk Thought from Slavery to Freedom* (New York: Oxford University Press, 1977), 16, 203; Susan McClary, *Feminine Endings: Music, Gender, and Sexuality* (Minneapolis: University of Minnesota Press, 1991), 8–25, 54–57, 153.

34. *Atlanta Constitution*, 6 Aug. 1900, 13 July 1902; Paul Oliver, *Blues Fell This Morning: Meaning in the Blues* (Cambridge: Cambridge University Press, 1960), 1–11; Levine, *Black Culture and Black Consciousness*, 221–39; Leroi Jones, *The Blues People: Negro Music in White America* (New York: William Morrow and Company, 1963), 50–94; Roger D. Abrahams, *Singing the Master: The Emergence of African American Culture in the Plantation South* (New York: Pantheon Books, 1992), 94–95.

35. On the importance of the sight of music and dance performed see Richard Leppert, *Music and Image: Domesticity, Ideology, and Socio-Cultural Formation in Eighteenth-Century England* (Cambridge: Cambridge University Press, 1988), chap. 5; and Leppert, *The Sight of Sound: Music, Representations, and the History of the Body* (Berkeley: University of California Press, 1993).

36. Albert Murray, *Stomping the Blues* (New York: McGraw Hill, 1976); Larry Neal, "The Ethos of the Blues," *Black Scholar* 3 (1972), reprinted in Michael Spencer, ed., *Sacred Music of the Secular City* (Durham, N.C.: Duke University Press, 1992); Paul Oliver, *Songsters and Saints: Vocal Traditions on Race Records* (Cambridge: Cambridge University Press, 1984), 18–46; Levine, *Black Culture and Black Consciousness*.

37. Levine, *Black Culture and Black Consciousness*, 136–297; Murray, *Stomping the Blues*, 21–42; William H. Jones, *Recreation and Amusement*, 65–66; Higginbotham, *Righteous Discontent*, 44, 199–200.

38. See *Atlanta Constitution*, 10 Nov. 1908, 13 and 14 Aug. 1910. A group of white Holy Rollers were arrested on similar charges. See *Atlanta Constitution*, 13 Oct. 1910.

39. Jerma Jackson, "Testifying at the Cross: Thomas Andrew Dorsey, Sister Rosetta Tharpe, and the Politics of African-American Sacred and Secular Music" (Ph.D. dissertation, Rutgers University, 1995), 60–61.

40. Dittmer, *Black Georgia*, 53.

41. *Atlanta Constitution*, 29 and 15 June 1913, 4 July 1914. For advertisements and news stories of church events see *Atlanta Independent*, 1903–10.

42. *Atlanta Constitution*, 3 July 1903. Employers of domestics and other workers in the North also complained about "Blue Monday," the trouble getting workers to perform their duties after a weekend of festivities. See Peiss, *Cheap Amusements*, 34.

43. *Atlanta Constitution*, 21 and 19 Feb. 1905.

44. *Atlanta Constitution*, 20 Feb. 1905; and *Atlanta Journal*, 10 Jan. 1900.

45. See Paul Gilroy, "One Nation under a Groove: The Cultural Politics of 'Race' and Racism in Britain," in David Theo Goldberg, ed., *Anatomy of Race* (Minneapolis: University of Minnesota Press, 1990), 74.

46. Hazzard-Gordon, *Jookin'*, 87.

47. Alice Adams interview, AHC.

48. Anthony Binga, *Binga's Address on Several Occasions: Should Church Members be Disciplined for Attending Balls or Theaters* [Printed by Vote of the General Association of Virginia, ca. 1900], 9, Schomburg Center for Black Culture, New York Public Library, New York.

49. *Atlanta Constitution*, 6 Aug. 1900, 5; 13 July 1902, sect. iv, 1. For a range of dress during the period see Patricia K. Hunt, "Clothing as an Expression of African-American Women in Georgia, 1880–1915," *Georgia Historical Quarterly* 76 (Summer 1992): 459–71. Also see Peiss, *Cheap Amusements*, 57–65.

50. Hurston, "Characteristics of the Negro," 30. This is not to romanticize notions of beauty among African Americans. By this time, ads for skin whiteners and hair straighteners were appearing regularly in black newspapers. Hurston makes the point that black women were disparaged in some black folklore and songs, some of which were probably sung in jook joints.

51. See Oliver, *Blues Fell This Morning*, 108–11; Levine, *Black Culture and Black Consciousness*, 243; Paul Gilroy, *"There Ain't No Black in the Union Jack": The Cultural Politics of Race and Nation* (1987; reprint, Chicago: University of Chicago Press, 1991), 203.

52. Stearns and Stearns, *Jazz Dance*, 24.

53. Ibid.

54. See John Fiske, *Understanding Popular Culture* (Boston: Unwin Hyman, 1989), 49–95.

55. See John Kasson, *Amusing the Million: Coney Island at the Turn of the Century* (New York: Hill and Wang, 1972).

56. Irene and Vernon Castle were among the most famous dance instructors who tried to introduce tamed versions of vernacular dance. See Vernon Castle and Irene Castle, *Modern Dancing* (New York: Harper and Bros., 1914); Peiss, *Cheap Amusements*, 103, 187.

57. Bederman, *Manliness and Civilization*, 10–15.

Chapter 7

Mobilizing Community

Migrant Workers and the Politics of Labor Mobility
in the North American West, 1900–1920

GUNTHER PECK

To NEWLY ARRIVED Greek immigrant Harry Mantos, the North American West was less a particular fixed place than a process of constant movement. Like a well-polished ball in a pinball machine, Mantos rapidly bounced from job to job between 1906 and 1909. He began 1907 laying railroad track near Salt Lake City, Utah, then took a water-main construction job in Twin Falls, Idaho, and later a position loading mail for the Union Pacific Railroad Company in Green River, Wyoming, before securing a position as a copper mucker in Bingham, Utah, that summer. The next year brought more movement. In the spring, Mantos left Utah for a bootblack job in Omaha, Nebraska, returned to Green River to be a track laborer, and eventually traveled to Deadwood, South Dakota, to make cans. He returned to Bingham again in the winter of 1908 and remained there until the summer of 1909, when he and three hundred Greek coworkers went on strike for a pay increase. Two months later, he left Utah without a job and moved to Seattle, Washington, to make boats.[1]

To many contemporary observers during the Progressive Era, the constant mobility of men like Mantos typified the footloose tendencies of the nation's burgeoning population of unskilled, migrant workers. Nativist intellectuals attributed their seeming rootlessness and social anomie to cultural and moral weakness, while more liberal academicians looked to structural economic causes. Yet both groups argued that transient immigrants were culturally debased figures, whose mobility signaled the absence of familial or community ties. Transiency had emasculated and atomized Mantos and his fellow "birds of passage," depriving them of the domestic and communal bonds that defined middle-class manhood and respectability.[2]

Although historians have rejected many of the assumptions that defined middle-class perceptions of worker transience in 1910, they have left unexamined the assumption that transience culturally impoverished immigrant workers. Labor historians have been no exception to this pattern, despite their exploration of immigrant agency and power in their work lives. Like most social historians, they have focused on the lives of persistent workers, the men and women who built communities in one place and resisted or accommodated capitalist change in fixed locales and spaces. When transient workers have been subjects of historical inquiry, they are too often described in dubious terms, as members of an "underclass" or a "culture of poverty."[3] Such studies have affirmed a commonly held notion that community is by definition a local construct, tied to particular neighborhoods and fixed residency. Because migrant workers did not stay in one place very long, the reasoning follows, they failed to develop strong attachments to local communities or their institutions.[4]

But Harry Mantos and his immigrant compatriots were not, in fact, culturally impoverished by mobility. Quite unseen to middle-class observers and many subsequent historians were seemingly invisible communal and familial connections that enabled men like Harry Mantos to "bounce" between numerous jobs each employment season. Although the mobility of Mantos and his cohorts transformed and scattered the traditional locus of family and community ties, these connections remained more crucial than ever to the experience and survival of immigrant "birds of passage." The mobility of Mantos expressed not so much the collapse of kinship and community ties as their durability, flexibility, and geographic expansion in North America.[5]

Rather than presuming migrant workers had no community, we need to investigate the political impact their mobility had on the creation of numerous immigrant communities.[6] Transience did indeed pose daunting challenges to building community institutions. Where, after all, would immigrant workers locate community when they occupied not one but numerous locales in the space of a single year? Which organizations would express community solidarities when local experience varied so dramatically for "stable" immigrant businessmen and "floating" industrial workers? Establishing who belonged to a community on the local level was only one dimension of the problem. Integrating people's diverse local experiences into larger imagined visions of community was another. How, in more abstract terms, would imagined communities—the class, the ethnic group, the race, the nation—be linked to immigrants' divergent local experiences?

Answering these questions requires examining, in the first half of the essay, the footprints of men like Harry Mantos across the North American West and the specific contours of their transient communities. Because of their mobility, sojourners like Mantos lived in relative isolation from their many employers and an organized working class in North America. But their communities did not develop in a social vacuum. I shed light on the relational and political nature of transient workers' communities in the second half of the essay by focusing on their contentious relations with an emerging middle class of residentially persistent immigrant businessmen.[7] Throughout the essay, I place the stories of men like Harry Mantos in a comparative context, examining the politics of labor mobility within three specific "communities" of immigrants in the North American West: Italian track workers in the Canadian Rockies and the Italian businessmen in Montreal who directed their movement out west; Greek miners and track workers working in Utah, Nevada, Idaho, Colorado, and Wyoming and Greek businessmen in Salt Lake City, Utah; and Mexican agricultural and industrial workers scattered throughout the midwestern United States and Mexican-American elites in El Paso, Texas. These particular groups of migrant workers and the immigrant elites who sought to control them were not the most conspicuous or necessarily typical in the North American West, but they highlight the varied sites and kinds of political conflict that transience fomented between 1900 and 1920.

Tracking the footprints of men like Harry Mantos has been a challenging endeavor since they left few written records of their travels, suggesting one reason they have remained on the margins of historical scholarship. The surviving evidence indicates that the proportion of Greek, Italian, and Mexican immigrant workers traveling to make a living was extremely high.[8] Of sixty-five Greek workers living in Bingham in the fall of 1907, for example, just 3 percent remained when federal census counters arrived in 1910. Employment records of Italian workers on the Canadian Pacific Railway Company likewise indicate that a vast majority of them stayed on the job less than one year before moving. The small percentage of Greek and Italian workers who did remain in one locale longer were often better connected to their transient friends and relatives than to each other. Greek immigrant Isidore Kambouris, for example, provided lodgings and help to scores of friends and relatives during his five years in Bingham, Utah, including his nephew, Haralambos, who found work as a copper mucker for a few months in 1914.[9] Just as much as Haralambos, Isidore constructed his community around scattered and transient friends and family.

Yet despite such help during his travels, community initially seemed a distant abstraction to Haralambos. Consider the anguished poem he wrote to himself in 1914, after wandering between small industrial towns for months without work.

> Those of us in strange lands far from our parents
> We are like lonely birds in a winter dawn.
> It would be a great happiness to all of us
> If we could once more see our beloved country . . .
> Fate did not keep her exiled children.
> Countrymen, friends, relatives, if you want to be joyful,
> Don't leave our sweet country.

When Kambouris finally secured work as a track laborer, he grew even more depressed. As he recalled in his journal, "I studied three choices: first to kill myself, to be fired, or to make money." Kambouris chose the last option, but "the work was unbearable." His alienation confirms the notion that mobility could indeed have a corrosive impact on the transient immigrant's self-esteem and identity.[10]

Yet to freeze the picture at the moment of Kambouris's greatest despair obscures the most remarkable aspect of his life story. Within a year of contemplating suicide, Kambouris had become a booster for the Greek community of Utah, writing comedies and tragedies for church functions and fraternal organizations throughout the region. Kambouris would in fact never return to his "sweet country" of Greece, despite several opportunities to go. To understand his dramatic relocation, one must consider first the power of imagined communities in organizing his experience in North America. Even in the depths of despair, his warnings to imagined cohorts affirmed an intimate connection to transient compatriots and expressed a vision of community that proved vital to his new duties as the playwright for Utah's Greek community. Equally important, one must consider the networks of kin and adopted kin that village and fraternal societies organized among the region's migrant Greeks. Alienation and despair were indeed powerful aspects of sojourning for Kambouris; but so too were the bonds between young men that sojourning created and that sustained both powerful experiences of community and compelling visions of imagined community.[11]

Greek immigrants' most extensive fraternal organizations were village societies that embraced networks of family members and friends scattered throughout North America. Two of the most prominent in Utah were the village associations of Megara and Stomi. These organizations provided members with insurance and helped channel information between fellow villagers in Utah and Greece, often raising money for community improvements in both locations. A few weeks before Greek Orthodox Christmas in 1907, for example, Salt Lake City's Greek newspaper *O Ergatis* (The worker) published a list of thirty-two men from Stomi who had donated $256 for "the building of a new church in Stomi, Parnassus." All donors were also miners and residents of Bingham Canyon. By gathering money in Bingham to build a church in Greece, members of the Stomi village society expressed solidarities in two places, fusing divergent local experiences on both sides of the Atlantic into one community organization.[12]

Yet the geographic range of Greek village societies extended beyond the confines of two fixed neighborhoods in Greece and Utah, as the wide dispersion of the Megara village society in North America suggests. Of the twenty-eight Megariotes, as they were known, who arrived in New York on the transatlantic steamer SS *La Gascagne* on 22 March 1907, eighteen were bound for small mining camps in Utah, the other ten for Chicago, New York, Cleveland, and St. Louis. Together they comprised a mini-diaspora in North America. Like any community located in one place, Megariotes frequently disciplined wayward members. When Petros Georgakis embezzled $87 from the society's coffers in Bingham in 1907, he could not easily escape the long reach of his mobile compatriots. The day after his theft was discovered, fellow Megariotes in Utah expelled Georgakis from the organization, declaring "he was no longer considered a compatriot." They also pursued him to Chicago, where two Chicago-based Megariotes administered a more direct punishment. Village societies may have expressed loyalties to one place, but they transformed the old world village community in the process, enforcing community standards in towns scattered across North America.[13]

Community for transient Greeks was not created merely out of imported village loyalties, however well-organized across space they may have been. Greek workers like Harry Mantos also created communities rooted in new work routines. For Greek track workers in the West, the work gang was a crucial site of both exploitation and community formation, one in which common laborers exercised limited forms of control over the pace of work and the boundaries of the work gang itself. American foremen who attempted to define these boundaries risked driving workers to rebellion. In 1908, *O Ergatis* reported that four Greek track workers had beaten their American supervisor with "sticks and rocks" after he fired a member of their work gang.[14] Such militancy was not uncommon on Greek work gangs throughout the West and led many labor agencies and railroad firms to stop hiring them. According to one prominent labor agent in Texas in 1926, "I used to ship Greeks. . . . When one would fire one the whole bunch would quit."[15]

The solidarities of such work gangs also manifested themselves in the domestic arrangements that immigrants adopted in their temporary living quarters. Angelo Georgedes, a coal miner from Carbon County, Utah, recalled the patterns of domestic work among his co-workers in 1912: "Greek fellows working in the mine . . . probably 8, 12, 15 of them would live together. And they would take regular turns, some to clean the house and some to cook. . . . One day one would fix the breakfast, or fix the lunches the night before. . . . See we didn't have no cook."[16] Divisions of household labor among these transient men were remarkably fluid and adaptable to the mobility of both single and married men, who rotated all domestic work while laboring in one particular location.[17] By sharing domestic work and holding all residential leases in partnership, transient Greeks minimized the financial risks that would be incurred as household heads while maximizing their ability to leave at a moment's notice.[18] In so doing, they expanded the circumference of domestic ties to include a much larger group of transient workers throughout the industrial West.

The cultural center of the transient Greek's community was the coffeehouse, an institution that sprang up wherever a few dozen Greeks were temporarily employed in the West. As the central meeting place for transient men like Harry Mantos, coffeehouses expressed both traditional and new aspects of the communities they created in North America. On the one hand, coffeehouses reaffirmed ties to Greek culture as immigrants reconnected with village and family relations and watched the Karaghiozi, a puppet show, in which the "slyly stupid Greek always got the better of the supposedly crafty Turk."[19] Coffeehouses also cemented new communities, serving as the place where Greek workers discussed regional work conditions and opportunities in North America. Distinctions between new and traditional communities often blurred in this context. In the coaltowns of Price and Helper, Utah, for example, traditional religious holidays assumed a new look in the local coffeehouse. The bar's stash included ouzo and other alcoholic comforts as well as religious vestments for the transient cleric or lay person who performed rituals on feast days, name days, and religious holidays and at funerals.[20]

Like transient Greeks, Italian sojourners similarly relied on family connections, kinship networks, and village ties to build transient communities. Italian laborer Antonio Sicari informed Canadian government investigators that he had migrated from Italy in the spring of 1904 with "twenty of my fellow villagers," all of whom found work together in the same gang. Most work gangs were constructed from such local loyalties. Foreman Pompei Bianco, for example, allowed only fellow villagers from Somite Cheta into his 104-member work gang during the winter of 1903.[21] All summer long, Bianco and his men worked with fellow villagers, maintaining close ties to one place in Italy even as they traversed the Canadian Rockies laying railroad track. Here the "local" boundaries of the work gang incorporated both traditional and new experiences.

One reason Canadian Pacific Railway (CPR) work gangs helped preserve traditional village boundaries was that Italian workers rarely quit their jobs or "bounced" between three to four jobs each work season. Such immobility between jobs derived from the tight control exercised by padrone Antonio Cordasco, who hired and fired all of the CPR's Italian employees and demanded tributes from them for each trip to and from British Columbia. Italian workers were also constrained from quitting by the same family relations that fomented their sojourning. Unlike Greek sojourners, who were mostly young and single, Italians were predominantly married fathers seeking to make money for their dependents in Italy. Quitting what were "steady" seasonal jobs on the CPR would have eliminated vital income for their families and compromised their ability to return to Italy in the off-season. However onerous the work of laying railroad track or paying Cordasco's tributes may have been, positions on the CPR were prized precisely because the pay was steady and ties to local village communities were preserved.[22]

Geography, family relations, and the padrone system thus combined to restrict Italian workers' mobility and shape the context of community formation. But Italian track workers continued creating transient communities. For most, the boxcar constituted a surrogate home, however cramped and unpleasant. Like Greek transients, Italians shared all domestic chores, taking turns cooking and washing clothes. Although Italian track workers did not possess coffeehouses in their boxcars, they succeeded in creating their own forms of recreation. Games of chance in the evenings were popular, as were occasional dances provided with help from traveling Italian minstrels, who made their living performing for track gangs of many nationalities throughout the Canadian West each work season.

Traveling minstrels evoked the same nostalgic longing for community that inspired Haralambos Kambouris's poetry. When track worker Cesidio Simboli's work gang heard the distant sound of the familiar organ approaching along the railroad tracks one hot afternoon, "the picks and shovels were set aside," as all listened intently to their countryman play and sing. Fulvio, the local labor agent, demanded that the organ grinder immediately stop playing. The musician initially ignored him and continued his spirited performance, but when Fulvio punched him in the face a minor rebellion erupted. "The outraged gang surged forward like a solid, fearful phalanx," recalled Simboli, and Fulvio was soon begging for mercy after being "dragged left and right," punched, kicked, and cursed by the enraged workers.[23] This conflict was in part a struggle over the terms of labor—when and for how long Italian track workers would remain on the job. Behind this issue, however, was the larger question of who controlled social life on the move, Italian workers or their labor agents. Fulvio may have believed he possessed the power of a "slave driver," as one worker put it, but his control was permanently undone by the strength of Italian workers' communal ties.

For Mexican track workers and sugar beet workers migrating through El Paso, Texas, between 1905 and 1920, village loyalties were every bit as important to defining community as they were for Greek and Italian workers. Most Mexicans worked in the United States only during the summer before returning to their families in villages scattered throughout northern and central Mexico. These migration strategies helped create what Sarah Deutsch has called a "regional community," one whose boundaries remained linked to particular towns but which flourished across vast spaces of the southwestern and midwestern United States.[24] Out on the tracks, Mexicans encountered a great variety of Mexican settlements, many of them transient and temporary but communities nonetheless. The regional community of the Mexican worker was defined not only by his original village but by the connections he crafted while sojourning.

As was the case with Italian and Greek workers, community formation reflected patterns of geography and family relations. The vast majority of Mexican immigrants were young, single men with fewer dependents relying upon their paychecks. Family and relatives lived only one or two days away by train, in northern Mexico. Consequently, single male immigrants could easily return home before, during, and after the work season. The number of Mexicans who "jumped" their railroad jobs in the early twentieth century was staggering. Labor agent G. A. Hoff, of the L. H. Manning labor agency, told sociologist Paul Taylor in 1928 that "46 or 47 percent of our shipments on the average desert us." On return trips in the fall the percentage of Mexican workers jumping grew even higher. Labor agent Ben Williams of Chicago estimated that "about 60 percent of the Mexicans shipped south leave the job after working a day or so." For labor agent William Clark, of the Holmes Supply Company in El Paso, the percentage of desertions reached two-thirds. "Recently we shipped six hundred men for a two hundred man gang around Dawson, Arizona," stated Clark, explaining that "they all leave for cotton. The Mexicans know the locations of the towns."[25]

But if Mexican solos could more easily "jump" their jobs than Italians on the CPR, they were by no means atomized by such mobility. Mexican kin connections, rooted in family relations and new patterns of domestic work, enabled solos to find better work in North America.[26] The mutualism that informed how one group of Mexican workers organized their nonwaged work was very much on the minds of this migrant: "I did not know how to cook when I came here, but I have learned so that now I can cook better than a woman. We six men all buy our groceries and keep them in a separate box. We all use the same kitchen and the same bedrooms."[27] These domestic arrangements tended to enhance Mexican workers' mobility but proved impermanent. Indeed, when one of the six track workers tried to formalize their new domestic routine by buying food wholesale, his partners balked. As the Mexican recalled to Paul Taylor, "They are irregular in their buying and do not want a large supply because they want to be free to leave at a moment's notice."[28] Sharing housework chores built networks that facilitated workers' mobility, but did not transform the gendered meanings of housework itself.

Like Greek and Italian workers, Mexican solos also used folk music to extend and cement ties among transient workers. Lyrics to Mexican folk songs did not celebrate transience as something emancipatory but more often lamented, like Kambouris's poems, the difficulties it created. Disenchantment suffused the popular ballad "El Enganchado" (the contract laborer) that Paul Taylor transcribed in 1926: "I came under contract from Morelia, To earn dollars was my dream, I bought shoes and I bought a hat, and even put on trousers. . . . Now I'm overwhelmed. I am a shoemaker by trade, but here they say I am a camel, and good only for the pick and shovel." But if such lyrics expressed the disappointments with life and work in North America, they also embodied a culture that was mutualistic rather than impoverished. Such lyrics were not sung in isolation but in small gatherings that affirmed a shared outlook and collective vision. The collective voice that Mexican workers used to describe their lives confirmed as much. "We the laborers live here like birds of the air," stated one track worker to Taylor in 1928. "When the work closes down, we are away to any place we can hear of steady work." For Mexican track worker Jesus Garza, the experience of mobility created bonds that literally superseded the power of traditional family ties. "My pal was a Mexican and we cared for each other more than brothers," recalled Garza. "When one didn't have money the other did and we helped each other in everything."[29]

The mutualism of Mexican solos' culture found expression not only in folk songs and village societies but in mutual aid organizations throughout the regions they traveled. As Emilio Zamora and Zaragosa Vargas have shown in Texas and Detroit respectively, *mutualista* organizations organized Mexican workers to improve their material circumstances with health benefits and insurance and defend their political interests in the United States and Mexico.[30] Although local chapters of the "Benito Juarez" society in Laredo, Texas, and Indiana Harbor, Indiana, comprised many long-term residents of these Mexican communities, they were adapted to the needs of their transient working-class compatriots. Membership dues were quite low and transient members were encouraged to transfer their standing to another local chapter or to a "sister" organization when they moved on to a new sojourning community.[31] Like the Greek coffeehouse, Mexican mutual aid societies sprang up in even the smallest and most temporary of Mexican settlements. One researcher of Mexican settlements commented in 1926 that "It is rare to find a city with fifty or more Mexicans that does not have a Mexican society."[32]

The specific contours of community varied for Italian, Greek, and Mexican workers. Italian workers moved and worked on CPR rails to preserve connections to their wives and families in Italian villages. Mexican workers likewise maintained close ties to their home villages by returning there in the off-season, but as single men they moved frequently between jobs in North America. Greek workers, for their part, also bounced between numerous jobs as single men, but did not return to Greece each off-season. Although a majority of Greek industrial workers eventually returned to Europe, their mobility was confined to a larger region in North America.[33] In each case, kinship ties and village identities provided important starting points for how immigrants created and sustained community. But they were only starting points. In their boxcars, coffeehouses, and work gangs, immigrant workers built connections that expanded and transcended immediate village loyalties and family relations. The experience of transience created bonds of "kinship" that were themselves mobile and geographically expansive.

Such was not the case for middle-class immigrants living in more established ethnic neighborhoods in El Paso, Salt Lake City, and Montreal. Here immigrant businessmen sought to define and control the forms of ethnic community by founding institutions closely tied to the urban neighborhoods where they acquired power. Other businessmen profited from the mobility of their compatriots, however, and tried to create imagined communities that preserved their control over workers' transience. Workers were ostensibly welcome to join all such elite-inspired institutions but only if they were also "stable" and "respectable." To understand how transient workers responded to such efforts, let us examine the dialogues between mobile and persistent immigrants that shaped the contours of their class, ethnic, racial, and national communities.[34]

On 23 January 1904, two thousand Italian sojourners marched in a military-style parade down the streets of Montreal chanting "Viva Edouardo VII, Viva le Canada, Viva Antonio Cordasco, Viva le Canadian Pacific Railway!" At the end of the procession, Italian workers watched as their labor contractor Antonio Cordasco was crowned "King of the Laborers" by his foremen while managers for the CPR watched nearby.[35] With his coronation, Cordasco sought first to persuade doubting company officials that he still controlled Italian workers. Only one month earlier six Italian laborers had successfully sued the CPR for the reimbursement of job fees paid to Cordasco the previous fall, an ominous development for CPR managers.[36] Cordasco also hoped the pageantry and sheer size of his coronation would persuade doubting immigrant workers of his benevolence and virtue. Here, for the first time in North America, was their own king, a man whom workers had ostensibly brought to power. Wherever Italian workers traveled, Cordasco would remain their point of connection to an Italian nationalist community in both North America and Italy.

Cordasco possessed many rivals to his throne, however, chief among them Italian labor agent Alberto Dini and the Italian Immigration Aid Society of Montreal, of which Dini was vice president. Founded in 1902, the Immigration Aid Society proposed to eliminate sojourning among Italian immigrants by settling them on vast tracts of public land in the Canadian Northwest. Stabilizing this vast migratory population on landed plots would solve the "problem" of how to represent sojourning Italians in two ways. First, as agriculturalists they would be members of persistent and therefore respectable Italian communities in North America. And second, they would no longer need Cordasco's "protection."[37]

Dini and his supporters in the aid society also considered themselves to be the most legitimate nationalist representatives of Italians in Canada. Indeed, in December 1903 all members of the aid society began wearing uniforms replete with the symbols and insignias of the Italian monarchy. Perhaps more significant, over three-fourths of the society's annual budget came directly from the Italian monarchy itself under the direction of Count Mazza, a nobleman given the title of "Honorary President" of the society. They were thus horrified and perhaps jealous of Cordasco's preemptive coronation three months after their uniforms arrived.[38]

Yet if Cordasco won the competition to embody Italian nationhood, he unwittingly highlighted the tenuousness of his symbol of imagined community to the majority of transient Italians. His attempt to acquire legitimacy by briefly mobilizing two thousand sojourners backfired badly. No sooner had Cordasco officially made himself "king of the laborers" than Italian sojourners began expressing contempt for his seeming generosity. When Cordasco provided several kegs of beer to his "loyal" subjects after the parade, Italian workers ceremoniously dumped it in the streets. Such hostility expressed these workers' collective frustrations at having had to pay for Cordasco's banquet, an exaction that nonetheless preserved their coveted jobs on the CPR.[39]

Cordasco quickly realized the potential dangers of having thousands of his Italian subjects concentrated in one locale and sought to ship his rebellious workers out of town. But this prescription ran afoul of a late spring thaw in 1904, as hundreds more of his "sojourning" subjects filled the streets of Montreal, waiting for the work season to begin. Tensions between Cordasco and sojourning workers erupted dramatically in June when hundreds of Italian track laborers descended on his office, demanding work or the complete refund of all job fees. When Cordasco refused and threatened violence, the workers complained to Canadian government officials about Cordasco's broken promises and coercive methods. Their testimony proved devastating to Cordasco's career, as he lost his position at the CPR and was subsequently sued by fifteen angry foremen and workers, each of them demanding a refund of their job fees and compensatory damages. Instead of stability, Cordasco's coronation fomented oppositions that discredited his claim to being the legitimate representative of sojourning Italians.[40]

Cordasco's failure did not lead to Dini's subsequent success as a community leader. To the contrary, opposition to Cordasco had a crippling effect on the leadership claims of many elite Italians in Montreal, as Dini was himself sued by three transient workers for having failed to fulfill his promises a few months later. Such activity reflected the success of sojourning Italians in expanding control over their communities. So did the dramatic expansion of sojourning settlements in the Canadian Northwest. In the spring of 1904, fully 87 percent of all Canada-bound Italians listed Montreal as their final destination, a reflection of the strength of Cordasco's power to control the family relations, mobility, and boundaries of the sojourning community. All sojourners passed through Montreal and paid Cordasco tribute as they went. In 1907, by contrast, just 7 percent of Canada-bound Italians listed Montreal as their final destination. Italian sojourners more fully controlled the contours of community formation, founding temporary settlements throughout the Canadian Northwest without the interference of persistent elites.[41]

In the spring of 1905, Mexican labor agent and former policeman Roman Gonzalez seemed ready to lay claim to being "king" of the Mexican solos. Gonzalez was one of the most prominent Mexican Americans in El Paso, Texas, the first Hispanic policeman in the city's history in 1901 and the second to own his own labor agency in 1905. As the enforcer of the city's vagrancy laws between 1901 and 1905 in Chihuahuita, El Paso's Mexican barrio, Gonzalez wielded tremendous authority over his compatriots. With the power to deport any "vagrant," he literally defined the boundaries of community in El Paso.[42]

Like Cordasco, Gonzalez parlayed his economic and political power into cultural authority. He did so not as a spokesman of Mexican nationalism but by Americanizing and whitening himself. Becoming a United States citizen gave him very real powers as a policeman, but it did not connote whiteness, particularly on the United States/Mexican border where Asian immigrants continually tried to evade immigration authorities by dressing as successful Mexican-American businessmen. Rather, Gonzalez sought to whiten his status by claiming European and therefore white ancestry, renouncing his loyalty in 1901 to the king of Spain rather than Mexico's Porfirio Díaz. Although Gonzalez was in fact formerly a Mexican citizen, born in Chihuahua, he hoped to ascend a racial hierarchy above his Mexican "Indian" charges in Chihuahuita.[43]

But Gonzalez never became a powerful community leader to Mexican workers or transcended the somewhat narrow confines of Chihuahuita. To understand why we need to consider more carefully what Gonzalez's whiteness and citizenship meant to transient Mexicans. Most Mexican solos remained nonwhite in the eyes of Americans and were oppressed by a legal system that frequently denied them even basic privileges. As Mexican contract laborer Juan Castillo put it in 1928, "there is a law for the Americans but none for the Mexicans." Many Mexicans expressed contempt for the pretensions of Mexican elites like Gonzalez. "Many Mexicans don't speak the language their mothers taught them," went the lyrics of one popular folk song, "and go about saying they are Spanish and denying their country's flag. . . . Some are darker than chapote (black tar) but they pretend to be Saxon; They go about powdered to the back of the neck and wear skirts for trousers." The cultural authority that Gonzalez sought as a white cop proved elusive. Indeed, to many Mexican solos attempts to whiten oneself with "Spanish" blood only emasculated the would-be Mexican leader, as whiteness was equated with feminine powders on the "back of the neck."[44]

A key reason Gonzalez's claims to whiteness did not produce cultural authority was that his power was predicated on the continuing exclusion of Mexican workers from white ranks. This tension took shape in his portrayal of the racial character of his compatriots to Americans. "There is work in plenty for Mexican laborers on the railroad," Gonzalez told the *El Paso Times* in 1905, "but the Mexicans can't stand the cold. They are weak." Such generalizations about the character of his compatriots legitimated the racial distance he sought to broker as a white Spanish-speaking United States citizen. Gonzalez's limited mastery of the laws of the United States and of its racial hierarchies provided little protection and perhaps even less comfort to Mexican migrants. His citizenship status likewise created little credibility, especially after the Mexican revolution began in 1910. For all sides in this conflict, hostility to the United States was a fundamental tenet of emergent Mexican nationalism. Advocating United States citizenship to acquire power over Mexican communities turned out to be a contradiction in terms.[45]

In 1915, Gonzalez attempted to rectify some of the damage his citizenship switch had caused, when he filed proceedings in civil court to change his original naturalization papers. He declared his identification with Spain had been the result of "error and inadvertence of the clerk at the said court" and that he had been "at all times prior to his admission to citizenship of the United States . . . a citizen of Mexico." At the peak of the Mexican revolution, Gonzalez deemed whiteness less important than a patriotic Mexican heritage to establishing power among his compatriots. Though he amended the public record, the revolution was too advanced and his career too checkered for him to become a representative of national community to transient Mexicans.[46]

~✦

Like Gonzalez, Greek businessmen in Utah had ambivalent relations with their transient compatriots. On the one hand, they sought to legitimate their authority over men like Harry Mantos by claiming to be leaders of ethnic community; on the other, they tried to maintain a certain distance between themselves and transient workers whose culture and community compromised the status they sought in the eyes of assimilated white Americans. These tensions were apparent in the efforts of two Greek businessmen, Andrew Pappas and Nicholas Stathakos, to build a Greek Orthodox church in Salt Lake City. They did so by founding an American corporation entitled "The Greek Community of Utah," an organization officially open to all Greek immigrants but whose bylaws effectively excluded the transient. All potential members had to make "a written application stating the acceptance of all the articles of the by-laws," a requirement impossible for illiterate Greek migrants. Maintaining membership was also difficult. Members who missed their dues three months in a row were expelled from the community, a restriction that effectively excluded all seasonal railroad workers. Finally, voting privileges—keys to influencing the choice of trustees—were further limited to members who had been in good standing for at least a year. Membership and power in the official Greek community of Utah were reserved for persistent and literate Greeks. Indeed, every member of the board of trustees was a businessman and long-term resident of Salt Lake City.[47]

Conflicts between the official Greek community of Utah and sojourning workers became manifest on traditional Greek holidays and festivals. In Salt Lake City, home of Utah's leading Greek business leaders, Greek Orthodox Christmas was an occasion for demonstrating the civility and respectability of their settled community. In 1908, the *Ergatis* reported that Christmas culminated with a service at the Orthodox church, which had been "decorated properly with flags and candles." Most noteworthy, however, was the presence of "many distinguished Americans," including lawyers, judges, and journalists, who "were greatly impressed."[48] Among transient Greeks, by contrast, no such civility or refinements were observed. In 1908, the *Ergatis* reported that Christmas in the coal town of Sunnyside, Utah, began with "shotgun blasts in the air," followed by a parade and a service at the local Greek coffeehouse. But "the thing which aroused the excitement of the Italian, American, and Austrian workers," according to the American reporter, "was the fact that a man wearing Cretan clothes started dancing. All were soon drunk and all began dancing with the Greeks together."[49] Three years later, Greek Christmas in Bingham, Utah, became another occasion for working-class celebration. The event "struck terror into the hearts of the peaceful citizens of Bingham," and began with explosions of "a dozen sticks of giant powder," followed by more gunshots and fireworks in Bingham's coffeehouses.[50] Both persistent and transient Greeks possessed audiences larger than their own immediate ethnic community in these celebrations. While middle-class Greeks postured as "Americanized" to Utah's political leaders, Greek workers recast their religious celebrations within the culturally heterodox world of the region's transient and largely immigrant working class.

But not all Greek businessmen located ethnicity within Salt Lake City and the official community's boundaries. For a time, labor agent Leon Skliris successfully bridged the gap between persistent and transient by mobilizing both groups around a nonpartisan vision of Greek nationhood. In 1905, he founded the Kanaris Society, an organization whose "only target is to contribute to the raising of money for the national Navy." "The Kanaris Society," Skliris stated, "doesn't claim to represent the public opinion of Greeks in Utah." Ostensibly above partisan divisions, the Kanaris Society was also not confined to one neighborhood nor organized around restrictive membership requirements. Instead, it appealed to the central institution of transient Greeks' community, the coffeehouse. A Kanaris party held at a coffeehouse in Bingham in 1908, for example, featured bazoukia music, Karaghiozi shows, beer, lamb, special commemorative buttons, and "electric lights." Such efforts were quite successful, raising hundreds of dollars for the Greek navy. By linking Greek nationalism to truly popular forms of working-class celebration in coffeehouses, Skliris succeeded where Cordasco had failed in forging a notion of national community that united his transient compatriots.[51]

But Skliris also worked, like Gonzalez, to make the nationalist culture and community of Greek workers more respectable to middle-class American audiences. He did so paradoxically by convincing patriotic Greeks to become naturalized United States citizens. "I always try to persuade Greeks to realize that it is for their own good to become American citizens," Skliris stated in 1907. By changing their citizenship, his compatriots would not stop being Greek but rather would empower themselves to take advantage of opportunities in their new nation. Newspaper editor Panayiotis Siouris, a champion of Skliris's citizenship drive, explained that

Greeks "should seem assimilated to Americans, while keeping their patriotic flame alive hidden in their breast." In calling for his fellow Greeks to adopt this dualist national identity, Skliris in effect rationalized his own career path as the best way to create stable community in the United States. By persuading enough Greeks to honor the wisdom of his career choices, he might better function as their representative leader. "This is the most progressive country in the world," Skliris insisted, "and every smart Greek can help the progress of this country. Those who are not of this disposition, we don't want here." By harmonizing both national identities into one vision of democracy and progress, Skliris tried to improve the perceived character of sojourning Greeks without hindering their mobility or settling them on agricultural lands. Workers' mobility, after all, was very profitable to Skliris, who charged transient workers fees for every new job acquired at mines and railroads scattered throughout the region.[52]

Although hundreds of sojourners donated money to the Kanaris Society, very few heeded Skliris's call to become United States citizens. Skliris boasted to an American reporter that "within a few weeks, about six hundred Greeks will apply for citizenship." Only fifty in fact did so, nearly all of them educated businessmen from Salt Lake City. In 1908, just two out of fifteen hundred Greek copper miners in Bingham Canyon petitioned for citizenship. More transient workers became members of the official Greek community of Utah and joined the Orthodox church in Salt Lake City, but even by 1915 less than 10 percent of all Greeks in Utah were members. With the exception of the Kanaris Society, none of the institutions founded by persistent Greeks before 1915 represented more than a small fraction of transient Greeks.[53]

Yet as their celebrations suggested, transient Greeks did adopt notions of American community along working-class lines that sharply conflicted with "respectable" visions of ethnic and national community. In the summer of 1912, over one thousand Greeks in Bingham Canyon joined the local American-led labor union, a chapter of the Socialist Western Federation of Miners, and promptly voted to strike the Utah Copper Company for union recognition and the immediate dismissal of Skliris and all other immigrant "padrones" as company labor agents. When Nicholas Stathakos, vice president of the Greek community of Utah, and newly hired Orthodox priest Vasilios Lambrides attempted to calm strikers at an outdoor meeting a few days into the strike, they were booed off the podium. Stathakos, Pappas, and Skliris then claimed to American newspapers that Greek workers "do not understand the significance of a union

and are ignorant of such American customs." A striker named George
Gatzouros penned an angry reply, denouncing "all those self-posed leaders of the Greeks once and for all" and warning them "to desist from
making themselves prominent or misleading the public regarding the
strike . . . or we will be compelled to show them up."[54]

The power of such Greek communities was reflected not only in their
defiance of "self-posed leaders" but also in the geographic pattern of their
resistance during the 1912 strike. Like Italians in Montreal, transient
Greeks marshaled their collective strength in one place by building breast-
works, stockpiling guns, and leading the multi-ethnic and militant strike
movement in Bingham Canyon. But they also spread themselves across a
much larger region. Two weeks into the strike, seven hundred Greek sojourners walked off their jobs in the mining camp of Ely, Nevada, for union
recognition and the abolition of padrone hiring systems in all companies
owned by the Utah Copper Company. Support for these Nevada strikers
poured in from transient Greeks throughout the region, many of them
sending their favorite guns to relatives and "kin" in both Ely and Bingham for battle against Skliris. Greek sojourners thus made it difficult for
Skliris to hide from their vigorous protest. Their pressure succeeded in
compelling the Utah Copper Company to fire him as their labor agent.
Now it was Skliris's turn to become transient, fleeing the region for Mexico, legend has it, where he perhaps hoped to reinvent himself as a spokesman for Mexican nationalism. The mobility Skliris had sought to control
had indeed been turned against him with a vengeance.[55]

The creation and institutionalization of community—always a contested
process—was particularly contentious among immigrant workers and
immigrant elites in the North American West during the early twentieth
century. Neither the working class nor the ethnic group possessed self-
evident boundaries when "local" experiences varied so dramatically among
immigrants. Ethnic groups and classes were geographically dispersed by
transience and internally divided over questions that mobility raised.
Immigrant elites remained ambivalent about the merits of sojourning and
how best to represent immigrant community. Some, such as officers of the
Greek Community of Utah and the Italian Immigration Aid Society,
sought to contain sojourning and restrict ethnic community to one place—
the Holy Trinity Church or the countryside of the Canadian plains. Others, such as labor agents Cordasco and Skliris, profited from workers'

mobility and instead attempted to invent forms of imagined community that transcended fixed locales.

Immigrant workers were also divided by their transience. Although Greek workers succeeded in turning mobility to their advantage at the strike's outset in 1912, they were ironically defeated by Greek strikebreakers imported into Bingham by Gus Paulos, one of Skliris's former lieutenants. These transient Greeks were no strangers to the political meanings of mobility, for many were in flight from the draft in Greece that had been instituted during the Balkan wars.[56] Yet their recognition of mobility's political features did not create a coherent strategy of resistance as a class of unskilled immigrants in North America. The celebrated ingenuity of Mexican solos in creating communities was likewise collective and mutualistic, but built few working-class organizations on the move, a fact that has plagued the United Farm Workers of America in recent decades. Italian workers in turn only accidentally discovered how to control their mobility in the spring of 1904. Indeed, the circumstances of Italian workers' mobilization—a late thaw—highlight the contingency of their resistance to immigrant elites and corporate bosses.

And yet while transient workers rarely founded enduring working-class institutions in one place, they succeeded in creating vibrant working-class communities. They were built, out of necessity, across local, regional, and national boundaries rather than within a single place or neighborhood. Village societies and less formal kin networks functioned to bring coherence to an otherwise atomized life. In their boxcars, coffeehouses, and shantytowns, immigrant workers constructed mutualistic ties and communal bonds quite distinct from the ethnic institutions founded by middle-class immigrants. The fraternal bonds incorporated ties of village and family connections, but expanded the boundaries of kinship to include wider circles of transient workers. Such bonds and the informal organizations they stimulated could at times function as surrogate unions, providing communal contexts to discuss working conditions and workers' grievances. Village societies and fraternal networks did not so much compete with established labor unions as fill needs created by organized labor's neglect of transient immigrants from their ranks.[57]

Transient workers' communities transformed how immigrant elites defined ethnic community in diverse ways. Italian workers momentarily pooled their numbers and influence in one fixed place, changing how and where Italian community would be represented in Canada. Mexicans resisted their elites by remaining relentlessly mobile and beyond the reach

of any residential community's boundaries. Greeks combined both strategies and resisted their "would-be leaders" simultaneously in fixed locales
and on the move through a larger region, using both fight and flight to
their advantage. In each case, immigrant workers left their imprint on the
ethnic institutions that survived the first "generation" of immigration to
North America.

Struggles between elite and working-class immigrants over the boundaries of ethnic and national community were hardly unique to transient
immigrants in the North American West. Like their counterparts in the
immigrant neighborhoods of New York, Boston, and Philadelphia, immigrant elites in El Paso, Montreal, and Salt Lake City attempted with some
success to muffle an emerging working-class culture among their compatriots. But the remarkable transience of immigrant workers vastly complicated the process by which ethnic elites gained and maintained power.
Because traditional institutions and sites of power—the church, the local
fraternal club, the neighborhood itself—rarely reached transient men like
Harry Mantos, immigrant leaders struggled to find ways to represent and
control immigrant community among sojourners. Mexican, Greek, and
Italian sojourners, by contrast, were remarkably adept in creating their
own transient communities. Mobility did not leave them impoverished or
make them truly radical, as organizers for the Industrial Workers of the
World hoped and claimed. But immigrant workers succeeded in subvert-
ing their leaders' quest for "respectability" and power. Although middle-
class Greeks, Italians, and Mexicans would determine, among second-
generation immigrants, the form and content of ethnic community, they
never persuaded first-generation sojourners of the virtue of their community prescriptions. Rather, most sojourners like Harry Mantos simply
continued moving, finding new industrial jobs in towns like Trinidad,
Colorado, before returning home to their families in Greece, Italy, and
Mexico.

The political impact of transient workers' communities remains vital
not simply to third- and fourth-generation ethnic Americans who contem-
plate the meaning and origins of their identity but also to migrant workers today, who continue to build communities capable of mobilization in
one place and across a broader region. As recent debates over free trade
suggest, labor mobility remains a deeply politicized aspect of working-class
experience. While the mobility of capital has been celebrated and protected by the recent "free" trade agreements, the mobility of labor remains
restricted and segmented. As in the North American West at the turn of
the twentieth century, however, transient and persistent workers will con-

tinue trying to use labor mobility to their advantage. Their success will depend on their ability to build regional movements that make fighting in one place and mobility complementary tactics in controlling the shape of their communities, both local and imagined.

Notes

1. Harry Mantos interview by Louis Cononelos, 9 Dec. 1974, Greek Oral History Collection, Marriott Library, University of Utah, Salt Lake City.

2. On nativist explanations of mobility among unskilled immigrant workers, see Edward Alsworth Ross, *The Old World in the New: The Significance of Past and Present Immigration to the American People* (New York: Century Co., 1914), 95–119; and Carleton Parker, *The Casual Laborer and Other Essays* (New York: Harcourt, Brace and Howe, 1920). For liberal analyses of the "problem" of labor mobility, see William Leiserson, *Adjusting Immigrant and Industry* (New York: Harper, 1924), 28–48; and Sumner Schlicter, *The Turnover of Factory Labor* (New York: D. Appleton, 1919).

3. On historical investigations of an "underclass," see Jacqueline Jones, *The Dispossessed: America's Underclass from the Civil War to the Present* (New York: Basic, 1992); Michael Katz, ed., *The "Underclass" Debate: Views from History* (Princeton: Princeton University Press, 1993). On studies of transience that emphasize its impoverishing impact, see Melvyn Dubofsky, *We Shall Be All: A History of the Industrial Workers of the World*, 2d ed. (Urbana: University of Illinois Press, 1988); and Peter Way, *Common Labour: Workers and the Digging of North American Canals, 1780–1860* (Cambridge: Cambridge University Press, 1993).

4. Dubofsky, *We Shall Be All*, 5; Way, *Common Labour*, 168. For exceptions, see Donna Rae Gabaccia, *Militants and Migrants: Rural Sicilians Become American Workers* (New Brunswick, N.J.: Rutgers University Press, 1988); Sarah Deutsch, *No Separate Refuge: Culture, Class, and Gender on an Anglo-Hispanic Frontier in the American Southwest, 1880–1940* (New York: Oxford University Press, 1987); and David Montejano, *Anglos and Mexicans in the Making of Texas, 1836–1986* (Austin: University of Texas Press, 1986).

5. On the power of kinship ties in shaping chain migrations, see John Bodnar, *The Transplanted: A History of Immigrants in Urban America* (Bloomington: Indiana University Press, 1985), 68; Charles Tilly, "Transplanted Networks," in Virginia Yans-McLaughlin, ed., *Immigration Reconsidered: History, Sociology, and Politics* (New York: Oxford University Press, 1990), 79–95; and Gabaccia, *Militants and Migrants*, 76–90.

6. On the political struggles inspired by labor mobility, see Michael Piore, *Birds of Passage: Migrant Labor and Industrial Societies* (New York: Cambridge University Press, 1979); Lucie Cheng and Edna Bonacich, eds., *Labor Immigration under Capitalism: Asian Workers in the United States before World War II* (Berkeley: University of California Press, 1984); Alejandro Portes and Robert Bach, *Latin Journey: A Longitudinal Study of Cuban and Mexican Immigrants in the United States* (Berkeley: University of California Press, 1985); Patricia Cooper, *Once a Cigar Maker: Men, Women, and Work Culture in American Cigar Factories* (Urbana: University of Illinois Press, 1987), 75–93. On the theoretical importance of space and mobility to social history, see David Harvey, *The*

Urbanization of Capital: Studies in the History and Theory of Capitalist Urbanization (Baltimore: Johns Hopkins University Press, 1985), 33–35, 415–17; Iain Chambers, *Migrancy, Culture, Identity* (London: Routledge, 1994).

7. I have chosen to focus on intra-ethnic class relations not because immigrant workers were unaffected by the actions and motives of their many employers but because sojourning workers' consciousness of class often emerged most conspicuously out of political conflicts within immigrant communities.

8. Estimating precisely the length and degree of workers' persistence is a difficult task given the absence of city directories or residential maps in the rural contexts in which most migrants worked.

9. *O Ergatis*, 28 Sept. 1907, 1; Bureau of the Census, Thirteenth Census of the United States, manuscript census, Population Schedules, Salt Lake County, Utah, 1910; Bruno Ramirez, "Brief Encounters: Italian Immigrant Workers and the CPR, 1900–1930," *Labour/Le Travail* 17 (Spring 1986): 9–27; Haralambos Kambouris, "Pages of My Life and Various Poems," translated from Greek by Helen Papanikolas, American West Center, Marriott Library, University of Utah, Salt Lake City.

10. Haralambos Kambouris, "Pages of My Life and Various Poems," 28 Dec. 1914.

11. Ibid., 1915–49. For examinations of the "rough culture" that immigrant workers created on the move, see Peter Way, "Evil Humors and Ardent Spirits: The Rough Culture of Canal Construction Laborers," *Journal of American History* 79 (Mar. 1993): 1397–1428.

12. *O Ergatis*, 28 Sept. 1907, 2; 21 Dec. 1907, 5; my translation.

13. Passenger lists, ship manifests at the Port of New York, 22 Mar. 1907, microfilm #849, National Archives, Washington, D.C.; *O Ergatis*, 12 Oct. 1907, 3. On the transplantation of local communities to North American urban neighborhoods, see Franc Sturino, *Forging the Chain: A Case Study of Italian Migration in North America, 1880–1930* (Toronto: University of Toronto Press, 1990), 195–96; John Briggs, *An Italian Passage* (New Haven: Yale University Press, 1979); Albert Camarillo, *Chicanos in a Changing Society: From Mexican Pueblos to American Barrios in Santa Barbara and Southern California, 1848–1930* (Cambridge, Mass.: Harvard University Press, 1979).

14. *O Ergatis*, 18 Apr. 1908, 2.

15. Paul Taylor interview with Mr. Kennedy, S.W. & A. Labor Agency, San Antonio, Tex., Interviews with Labor Contractors, Field Notes 26–31, BANC-MSS-74/187C, Paul Taylor Papers, Bancroft Library, University of California-Berkeley, Berkeley, Calif. Personal names in the Taylor Papers are cited as they appear there, sometimes without accents.

16. Angelo Georgedes, *The Oral History of Angelo Georgedes* (Madison: State Historical Society of Wisconsin, 1973), 8.

17. Although all-male camps of transient Greek workers could not literally reproduce themselves, they were actively engaged in the cultural work of building communities, albeit highly mobile ones. For a debate on whether such all-male camps were indeed "communities," see John Mack Faragher, "Americans, Mexicans, Metis: A Community Approach to the Comparative Study of North American Frontiers," in William Cronon, George Miles, and Jay Gitlin, eds., *Under an Open Sky: Rethinking America's Western Past* (New York: W. W. Norton, 1992), 95.

18. Some 86 percent of all Greek workers in Bingham, Utah, for example, held their residential leases in partnership in 1910. See Gunther Peck, "Reinventing Free La-

bor: Immigrant Padrones and Contract Laborers in North America, 1880–1920," (Ph.D. dissertation, Yale University, 1995), 321. Figures were compiled from a one-in-ten random sampling of all residents of Bingham, Utah in the Thirteenth Federal Census, Salt Lake County, Utah.

19. Helen Papanikolas, "Toil and Rage in a New Land: The Greek Immigrants of Utah," *Utah Historical Quarterly* 38 (Spring 1970): 118–19.

20. Paul Borovilos interview by Helen Papanikolas, Apr. 1970, Greek Oral History Collection. For debates on the Greek coffeehouse as an institution expressing ethnic or working-class identities, see Dan Georgakas, "Greek Americans," and Charles Moskos, "Georgakas on Greek Americans: A Response," *Journal of Hellenic Diaspora*, 14 (Spring 1987): 5–54, 63–72.

21. Testimony of Antonio Sicari, *The Royal Commission Appointed to Inquire into the Immigration of Italian Labourers to Montreal and the Alleged Fraudulent Practices of Employment Agents* (Ottawa: S. E. Dawson, 1905), 36, 29.

22. On Cordasco's career, see Robert Harney, "Montreal's King of Italian Labour: A Case Study of Padronism," *Labour/Le Travail* 4 (1979): 53–79; Gunther Peck, "Reinventing Free Labor: Immigrant Padrones and Contract Laborers in North America, 1885–1925," *Journal of American History* 83 (Dec. 1996): 848–71. Over two-thirds of all Canada-bound Italians entering North America through New York in March 1901 were married, compared to just one quarter of all Utah-bound Greeks in 1912 (ship manifest lists, Port of New York, Mar. 1901, Mar. 1912, National Archives). On the reluctance of Italians to quit on the CPR, see *Royal Commission*, 52. On the seasonal nature of their work, see Bruno Ramirez, "Brief Encounters: Italian Immigrant Workers and the CPR, 1900–1930," *Labour/Le Travail* 17 (Spring 1986): 9–27.

23. Cesidio Simboli, "When the Boss Went Too Far," *World Outlook* (Oct. 1917) in Wayne Moquin, ed., with Charles Van Doren, *A Documentary History of the Italian Americans* (New York: Praeger, 1974), 147.

24. Deutsch, *No Separate Refuge*, 35, 40–41. On Mexican communities in the Midwest, see Dennis Nodin Valdes, *Al Norte: Agricultural Workers in the Great Lakes Region, 1917–1970* (Austin: University of Texas Press, 1991).

25. G. H. Hoff interview by Paul Taylor, 1928, Field Notes 46–556, BANC-MSS-74/187c, Paul Taylor Papers; Ben Williams interview, ibid.; William Clark interview by Taylor, 1928, Field Notes 98–103, ibid.

26. On the theoretical importance of unpaid labor to conceptions of community and class, see Jeanne Boydston's "To Earn Her Daily Bread: Housework and Antebellum Working-Class Subsistence," *Radical History Review* 35 (Apr. 1986): 7–25. See also Boydston, *Home and Work: Housework, Wages, and the Ideology of Labor in the Early Republic* (Oxford: Oxford University Press, 1990); Eileen Boris and Cythnia Daniels, eds., *Homework: Historical and Contemporary Perspectives on Paid Labor at Home* (Urbana: University of Illinois Press, 1989); Judith Coffin, *The Politics of Women's Work: The Paris Garment Trades, 1750–1915* (Princeton: Princeton University Press, 1996).

27. Paul Taylor, *Mexican Labor in the United States* (Berkeley: University of California Press, 1932), 184.

28. Ibid.

29. Ibid., vii, 257, 275; Jesus Garza interview by Manuel Gamio, 1928, in Manuel Gamio, ed., *The Mexican Immigrant: His Life Story* (Chicago: University of Chicago Press, 1931), 18.

30. Zaragosa Vargas, *Proletarians of the North: A History of Mexican Industrial Workers in Detroit and the Midwest* (Berkeley: University of California Press, 1993), 149–55; Emilio Zamora, *The World of the Mexican Worker in Texas* (College Station: Texas A & M University Press, 1993), 86–109; Jeffrey Marcos Garcilazo, "Traqueros: Mexican Railroad Workers in the United States, 1870–1930" (Ph.D. dissertation, University of California at Santa Barbara, 1995).

31. Zamora, *World of the Mexican Worker in Texas*, 72, 104; "Mexicans in Indiana Harbor," 11 Oct. 1926, Field Notes, George L. Edson, in "Interviews with Labor Contractors," BANC-MSS-74/187C, Paul Taylor Papers.

32. Report by Luis Recinos, Manuel Gamio Papers, Bancroft Library, University of California-Berkeley, Berkeley, Calif., cited in Zamora, *World of the Mexican Worker in Texas*, 93.

33. Return migration was quite high among Italians, Greeks, and Mexicans, though the length of their individual sojourns varied. Though precise percentages of return migration are hard to calculate given the difficulty of tracking individual immigrants through successive migrations, Thomas Archdeacon has estimated that 46 percent of all Italians and 54 percent of all Greeks remigrated to their homelands. See Archdeacon, *Becoming American: An Ethnic History* (New York: Free Press, 1983), 139.

34. On distinctions between local and imagined communities, see Benedict Anderson, *Imagined Communities: Reflections on the Origin and Spread of Nationalism* (London: Verso Editions, 1983). On the role of class relations in shaping the formation of ethnicity, see James R. Barrett, *Work and Community in the Jungle: Chicago's Packinghouse Workers, 1894–1922* (Urbana: University of Illinois Press, 1987); David Emmons, *The Butte Irish: Class and Ethnicity in an American Mining Town, 1875–1925* (Urbana: University of Illinois Press, 1989); Dirk Hoerder, ed., *"Struggle a Hard Battle": Essays on Working-Class Immigrants* (DeKalb: Northern Illinois University Press, 1986); Kevin Kenny, *Making Sense of the Molly Maguires* (New York: Oxford University Press, 1998); Kerby Miller, "Class, Culture, and Immigrant Group Identity in the United States: The Case Study of Irish-American Identity," in Yans-McLaughlin, ed., *Immigration Reconsidered*, 96–129.

35. *Royal Commission*, 167. For those who missed his coronation, Cordasco displayed his crown in a glass case in his labor agency office. See Harney, "Montreal's King of Italian Labour," 58.

36. See "Vacha vrs. The Canadian Pacific Railway," case 1067, 15 Jan. 1904, Records of the Superior Court of Montreal, Canadian National Archives, Montreal Branch.

37. *Constitution of the Immigration Aid Society for Canada in Montreal* (Montreal, 1902), articles 15, 16, and 42, Canadian National Archives, Ottawa; *First Annual Report of the Italian Immigration Aid Society for Canada* (Montreal, 1904), 3, ibid.

38. *First Annual Report of the Italian Immigration Aid Society*, 4; *Constitution*, 19.

39. Testimony of Pompei Bianco, *Royal Commission*, 163.

40. See the damaging testimony of three transient workers, Giovanni Morillo, Michelle Cilla, and Vincenzo Sciano in *Royal Commission*, 32, 37, 67; see the court cases of thirteen Italian workers and foremen against Cordasco in the fall of 1904 (all in Records of the Superior Court of Montreal): "Giuseppe d'Abramo v. A. Cordasco," case 2787; "Pietro Bazzani v. A. Cordasco," case 1359; "Michelle Cilla v. A. Cordasco," case 2575; "Fillip D'Allesandro v. A. Cordasco," case 2357; "Alfredo Folco v. A. Cordasco," case 2223; "Nicola Fondino v. A. Cordasco," case 3127; "Giuseppe Mignel-

la v. A. Cordasco," case 503; "Benvenuto Missiti v. A. Cordasco," case 1420; "Salvatore Molla v. A. Cordasco," case 2135; "Donato Olivastro v. A. Cordasco," case 2198; "Domenico Poliseno v. A. Cordasco," case 572; "Giuseppe Teolo v. A. Cordasco," case 990; and "Michelle Tisi v. A. Cordasco," case 2513.

41. Affidavits by Sacco Luigi and Antonio Lamore, 2 May 1904, Toronto, and by Brugno Serafino and Luigi Turturani, 26 May 1904, Toronto, RG 33/99, Canadian National Archives, Ottawa; passenger manifest lists, Port of New York, Mar. 1901, Mar. 1907, National Archives, Washington, D.C.

42. El Paso City Council, minutes, 23 May 1901, 181, Southwest Collection, El Paso Public Library, El Paso, Tex.; *El Paso City Directory*, 1905, ibid.

43. Naturalization Records, El Paso County, Tex., microfilm # 48, case file #3488, 5 Mar. 1900, El Paso County Courthouse, El Paso, Tex.; Marcus Braun to Honorable Frank Sargent, Commissioner General of Immigration, 12 Feb. 1907, Exhibit J, file 52320/1, box 95, Records of the Department of Immigration and Naturalization, National Archives, Washington, D.C. On similar racial negotiations among Polish and Jewish leaders, see Matthew Jacobson, *Special Sorrows: The Diasporic Imagination of Irish, Polish, and Jewish Immigrants in the United States* (Cambridge, Mass.: Harvard University Press, 1995). Among the Irish, see David Roediger, *The Wages of Whiteness: Race and the Making of an American Working Class* (London: Verso, 1991); and Noel Ignatiev, *How the Irish Became White* (Oxford: Oxford University Press, 1995). On Mexicans, see Neil Foley, *The White Scourge: Mexicans, Blacks, and Poor Whites in Texas Cotton Culture* (Berkeley: University of California Press, 1997). On the dilemmas of ethnic elites more generally, see John Higham, ed., *Ethnic Leadership in America* (Baltimore: Johns Hopkins University Press, 1979); and Victor R. Greene, *American Immigrant Leaders, 1800–1910: Marginality and Identity* (Baltimore: Johns Hopkins University Press, 1987).

44. Juan Castillo interview by Taylor, Field Notes 284–454, BANC-MSS-74/187c, Paul Taylor Papers; "El Enganchado," in Taylor, *Mexican Labor in the United States*, vii.

45. *El Paso Times*, 6 Feb. 1907, 5. On the role of anti-American sentiment in Mexican nationalism, see Alan Knight, *The Mexican Revolution: Porfirians, Liberals, and Peasants*, vols. 1 and 2 (Cambridge: Cambridge University Press, 1987); and John M. Hart, *Revolutionary Mexico: The Coming and Process of the Mexican Revolution* (Berkeley: University of California Press, 1987). By the late 1920s, United States citizenship had become a path to power for the founders of the League of United Latin American Citizens (LULAC) and other Mexican elites. See Zamora, *World of the Mexican Worker in Texas*, 88–90.

46. "Ex parte v. R. G. Gonzalez," 22 Sept. 1915, District Civil Court Records, El Paso County, case 3488, El Paso County Courthouse, El Paso, Tex.

47. *By-Laws of the Greek Community of Utah* (Salt Lake City, 1905), articles 3, 4, 12, and 25, State Archives of Utah, Salt Lake City, Utah.

48. *O Ergatis*, 11 Jan. 1908, 4.

49. *O Ergatis*, 18 Jan. 1908, 5.

50. *Salt Lake Tribune*, 10 Jan. 1911, 3.

51. *O Ergatis*, 26 Oct. 1907, 1; 28 Sept. 1907, 1.

52. *Salt Lake Evening Telegram*, 10 Dec. 1907, 1; *O Ergatis*, 14 Dec. 1907, 3; ibid., 16 Nov. 1907, 1; ibid., 14 Dec. 1907, 3.

53. U.S. Naturalization Records, 9 Aug. 1905–1 Sept. 1906, Third District Court, Salt Lake County, State Archives of Utah; Minutes of the Greek Community of Utah, 1910, Holy Trinity Greek Orthodox Church, Salt Lake City, Utah.

54. On the 1912 strike, see Helen Papanikolas, "Toil and Rage in a New Land: The Greek Immigrants of Utah," *Utah Historical Quarterly* 38 (Spring 1970): 100–204. On the race, ethnic, and class relations that the strike dramatized, see Gunther Peck, "Padrones and Protest: 'Old' Radicals and 'New' Immigrants in Bingham, Utah, 1905–1912," *Western Historical Quarterly* 24 (May 1993): 157–78; *Salt Lake Evening Telegram*, 30 Sept. 1912, 12; *Salt Lake Evening Telegram*, 2 Oct. 1912, 9.

55. *Ogden Evening Standard*, 2 Oct. 1912, 1; *Salt Lake Tribune*, 2 Oct. 1912, 1; George Lamb interview by Helen Papanikolas, 3 Sept. 1972, Greek Oral History Collection.

56. Peck, "Padrones and Protest," 176.

57. On the overall exclusion of Mexicans from organized labor, see Zamora, *World of the Mexican Worker in Texas*, 66. On tensions between Italian and Greek immigrants and American-born union radicals, see Peck, "Padrones and Protest"; and Phil Mellinger, "How the IWW Lost Its Western Heartland: Western Labor History Revisited," *Western Historical Quarterly* 27 (Autumn 1996): 303–26. On the AFL's larger racism toward unskilled immigrants from Europe, see Gwendolyn Mink, *Old Labor and New Immigrants in American Political Development: Union, Party, and State, 1875–1920* (Ithaca: Cornell University Press, 1986). On tensions between transient workers and persistent unionists within one ethnic group, see Emmons, *Butte Irish*.

Chapter 8

Popular Narrative and Working-Class Identity

Alexander Irvine's Early Twentieth-Century
Literary Adventures

KATHRYN J. OBERDECK

THIS ESSAY EXAMINES the early literary career of Alexander Irvine—a socialist minister who achieved some success as a writer for the popular periodical press in the early twentieth century. It focuses on how Irvine's literary self-portraits changed over time as he used the field of popular literature as a laboratory of class identity. Through this process, Irvine proves a useful guide to the ambiguous languages through which various writers tried to make sense of contemporary class divisions and of the ethnic, race, and gender divisions with which they intersected. Irvine's literary trajectory illuminates this cultural encounter with class difference in three important ways.

First, Irvine learned to frame his representations of class in the language of new periodicals that fostered literary conventions friendly to explorations of class difference and shaped the way such differences were conceived. These magazines popularized what I call an "evolutionary vernacular" that cast class differences in terms of distinctions between "civilized" lifestyles and more vigorous but brutal virtues that prevailed in the "social pit." Often this language expressed a sense of cultural superiority that encouraged Progressives' efforts to "manage" groups they perceived as living beyond the racial, ethnic, or class boundaries of "civilization." But the same language could facilitate explorations of the ambiguities of working-class identity.

A second instructive feature of Irvine's literary experiments lies in his deployment of an especially scintillating device for such exploration: investigative disguise. Shortly after he began his literary career, Irvine traveled south to the coal mines, turpentine camps, and stockades of Alabama. Affecting the dress and manner of a recently arrived immigrant laborer, he befriended immigrants and African Americans who had contracted as peons. He worked these experiences into journalism and fiction that illuminated his own process of working-class self-construction and also elucidated broader trends in the representation of class. In particular, Irvine's southern experimentation with a working-class perspective highlighted the ways that distinctions of race and ethnicity figured into his construction of a proletarian identity.

In his later narratives, Irvine substituted ethnic solidarity for the brutal vitality that marked working-class identity in other renditions of the evolutionary vernacular. This change constitutes a third aspect of his early literary career that illuminates wider cultural trends. It links Irvine's narrative explorations of class identity to a wider shift in early twentieth-century American intellectual life. This shift revised nineteenth-century social conceptions that pictured distinctions of class and race in terms of hierarchically ranked inequalities determined by the mechanics of evolution. It gave rise to a more pluralistic vision of varied cultures from which people seek value and meaning. This development is frequently associated with the work of professional intellectuals who came increasingly to emphasize community as the key to social life. Irvine reached a similar conclusion, but he arrived there through a more direct engagement with the class politics of working-class identity than many intellectuals undertook. His literary experiments suggest how the politics of class—as it intersected discourses of race, ethnicity, and gender and found expression in popular literature—contributed to such broader cultural transformations.[1]

By identifying Irvine's autobiographical literature as a crucible of class identity, this study contributes to recent scholarship that recognizes popular narrative as a cultural practice that generated contested vocabularies of class, gender, ethnicity and race.[2] This approach to narrative has been informed in part by poststructuralist perspectives that locate the meanings of class in cultural maneuvers and linguistic systems. Historians who embrace such perspectives sometimes position themselves in opposition to those who insist on finding "objective" sources of class position within the structures of social and material relations.[3] However, recent studies of popular narrative and identity suggest more nuanced approaches to this dilemma. In *City of Dreadful Delight*, for example, Judith Walkowitz analyses diverse class narratives of sexual danger in late Victorian London in terms of "historically situated authorial consciousness" as well as the way narratives themselves produce identity.[4] Similarly, my discussion of Irvine's literary adventures situates the narrative production of class identity in specific political and social conflicts. It also draws on the approach to working-class subjectivity developed by Regenia Gagnier, who emphasizes not only how cultural practices like narrative produced identities but also how nineteenth-century British working-class autobiographers transformed prevailing vocabularies of class.[5] By showing how Irvine's autobiographical self-representations changed as he wrestled simultaneously with popular narrative formulae and practical social divisions, I aim to illuminate how his literary experiments shifted the terms in which class identity was construed.

In the process, this essay also suggests new perspectives on the relation between popular literature and class politics in the United States. Cultural historians such as Christopher Wilson and Matthew Schneirov have discussed the robust, Darwinian tropes that prevailed in the popular periodicals where Irvine cut his literary teeth.[6] Ambiguities in Irvine's deployment of the "evolutionary vernacular" suggest that these terms of class difference lent themselves to alternative interpretations that have remained relatively unexplored. In Irvine's narratives, the evolutionary vernacular provoked an extended interrogation of the intersections of working-class identity with divisions of race, ethnicity, and gender. Meanwhile, his political trajectory connected his literary explorations of class to trade unionist and socialist debates that he engaged throughout the United States. His literary career thus provides one way of studying a juncture that labor historian Leon Fink has identified as central to the definition of "working-class culture" at the turn of the century: the intersection between working-class politics and commercial culture. It also suggests how innovations in the meaning of class worked out at this juncture contributed to cultural changes usually associated with intellectual history.[7]

Jack London as Model: The Socialist Bildungsroman *and the Evolutionary Vernacular*

In 1906, when he began his literary career, Irvine was an embattled minister in New Haven, Connecticut. His journey toward this particular crisis had already moved him to ponder the cultural meaning of class in some

depth. Born in 1863 to a Protestant cobbler and his Catholic wife in the
Ulster town of Antrim, Irvine remained illiterate throughout his youth.
After an evangelical conversion experience in the 1870s, however, he became impatient to explore a wider world of self-improving possibilities.
Early jobs as chauffeur and coal miner left little time for education. But
after Irvine joined the Royal Marines in 1881, he learned to read and write,
toured the Holy Lands dear to his evangelical heart, and prepared himself for a life of missionary service. In 1888, he abandoned the navy to
pursue this mission in the United States. Evangelical institutions like the
New York City Missionary and Tract Society eagerly exploited his self-
improving zeal. However, Irvine also discovered alternatives to the message of cultural uplift and pious work he preached to working-class audiences. In New York City he encountered early Social Gospelers eager to
redefine evangelical individualism in terms of ideals of economic justice.
In Omaha, the fading Knights of Labor and local Populists taught him
their philosophies of collective self-help. These lessons prepared Irvine
for more direct alliances with New Haven trade unionists, who taught him
to identify the cultivated accomplishments of professors, clergymen, and
middle-class parishioners as "so-called culture," to which he opposed an
alternative, collective vision of working-class culture.

Irvine had trouble finding an audience to sustain this vision. Craft union
exclusions of immigrant and women workers belied the democratic cultural vision the labor movement had helped him to forge, while New
Haven churches resented his efforts to expand their social boundaries. In
1903, he turned to socialism as the most promising expression of his cultural politics, but this only alienated craft unionists and churches the more.
Irvine was therefore ready to learn new methods for popularizing his views
on culture and class when, in January of 1906, he crossed paths with a
writer well equipped to teach him. In his capacity as state secretary of the
Socialist party, Irvine engaged Jack London for a lecture held at Yale
University's Woolsey Hall.[8]

London offered a model of socialist publicity that spoke to Irvine's socialist ideals while suggesting revisions in his self-presentation. London's
fiery speech, "Revolution," generated widespread shock by describing
growing numbers of socialists poised for a cataclysmic class upheaval.[9] But
his most enduring influence on Irvine came through the autobiographical remarks he aimed at Yale students whom he was trying to recruit to
the Intercollegiate Socialist Society. London presented his life story in the
form of a socialist *Bildungsroman*—a story of youthful aspiration followed
by cruel disillusionment, culminating in an adult resolution that in his case

was marked by vital political associations.[10] He began by describing his childhood in terms that expressed the perspective of someone at the base of the hierarchies Irvine had been learning to question. "I had no outlook," London quipped, "but what you might call an uplook. . . . Above me towered the colossal edifice of society; and I thought that up there were beautiful clothes; men wore boiled shirts and women were beautifully gowned. . . . I felt also that up there I would find things of the spirit, clean and noble living and deeds and ideals."[11] In the next phase of London's narrative, such visions were wiped out by the rigors of body-breaking labor. He descended into what he described as "charnel houses of civilization," where one saw "the men who had been worked out by society, the men who sold their muscles." The bitter agonies of this "abyss" sparked his determination to become a merchant of brain rather than muscle. London spoke of how the "parlor floor" of society then admitted him, revealing a deadening materialism where he had imagined sweetness and light. Among the institutions on this plane of society, only the university struck him as being "clean and noble" enough to approximate his ideals. But it was not sufficiently "alive." London ended his *Bildungsroman* by recommending socialism to reinvigorate intellectual institutions with a healthy respect for robust working-class virtues.[12]

In addition to the personal narrative that London presented at Yale, the strenuous language in which he delivered it decisively shaped Irvine's literary development. London had established himself as an author by writing virile tales in an evolutionary vernacular for the inexpensive mass magazines that were proliferating in a literary market previously dominated by genteel monthlies such as *Harper's* and the *Atlantic. Munsey's, McClure's* and *Cosmopolitan* pioneered the new periodical form in the 1890s; by the turn of the century *Ainslee's, Metropolitan,* and others joined them. Trained in metropolitan journalism, advertising, and commerce, the editors of these new journals disdained the "literary" style that the genteel monthlies favored.[13] A melding of Spencerian vocabulary with hierarchically arranged racial categories came to characterize many explorations of the "submerged" and the "exotic" they offered.[14] As he followed London into popular authorship, Irvine adopted this evolutionary vernacular to enhance his literary popularity. Crafting it into narratives of emerging class consciousness, he highlighted its significance as a mode of exploring the era's most acute cultural distinctions.

London's Yale *Bildungsroman* also illustrated ambiguities within the popular evolutionary style that would be crucial to the ways Irvine adapted this style to his own narrative purposes. By using terms such as "sordidness" and "wretchedness" to portray his early proletarian experiences and describing "charnel houses of civilization" where he found "inefficients" consigned by social Darwinism to the wastes of human progress, London reproduced a conventional hierarchy that ranked what he called the "parlor" level of middle-class society "above" the rigors of working-class existence. London had long subscribed to this social vision. From the 1890s he had embraced socialism less as a humanitarian creed than as a historical necessity bearing out racist social-Darwinian beliefs that he never entirely abandoned. However, during his lecture tour he diluted these beliefs with an enthusiasm for "THE PEOPLE" that was reflected in the denouement he fashioned for his *Bildungsroman*. This aspect of London's story played to a popular fascination with a "vitality" associated with "lower" classes, "exotic" cultures, and nature in the "raw." Such appreciation for the vigor of working-class culture appealed to Irvine's imagination even though he found London's Darwinian racial categories perplexing.[15]

Soon after London's New Haven appearance, Irvine began a series of adventures in authorship that revealed the force of London's example. In January 1907, *Appleton's Magazine* published Irvine's first commercial story, "Two Social Pariahs," which showed how much he had learned from his mentor.[16] Drawn from Irvine's experiences on the Bowery in the 1890s, "Two Social Pariahs" recounts a tale told by a former lawyer whose career crumbled after he defended Jim Farren, the local degenerate in a Connecticut town. In Irvine's representation of the trial, the lawyer attributes Farren's notorious violence to his status as an outcast from society. In twenty-eight years, the lawyer explains, "the prisoner never had the touch of a kindly hand nor the sound of a tender word from a human soul. . . . Jim Farren is what this community made him by neglect."[17] This description of Farren closely parallels London's 1906 novel *White Fang*, which recounts the career of a dog born to the bestial laws of "EAT OR BE EATEN" but adopted into the world of men who set new laws for him by their behavior—laws of violent struggle through cruelty or laws of affectionate loyalty through kindness.[18] Similarly, Irvine limned Farren as the creature of a social abyss that reduced men to muscled boors. The lawyer insists that Farren could nevertheless respond to human kindness: Farren risked his life for the town sheriff, who showed him compassion. Such behavior, the attorney claims, proves that Farren is not the "insensate brute . . . rotten to the very core" that the prosecutor describes. He wins his point and Farren gets two years rather than the maximum penalty of thirty years for stealing six shoats. But the story ends with the lawyer joining Farren as a "social pariah."[19]

"Two Social Pariahs" was an auspicious beginning for Irvine's career in commercial storytelling. On the strength of this success, *Appleton's* offered him a new literary assignment—an undercover investigation of peonage in the lumber and turpentine camps of Alabama—that provided further opportunities to borrow from London's techniques. Irvine's adventures in investigative disguise demonstrate how the evolutionary vernacular served as a laboratory of class identity where he could forge the terms of his own socialist *Bildungsroman*.

"*My Life in Peonage*" *and* From the Bottom Up: *Alexander Irvine Makes a Working-Class Self*

"My Life in Peonage" appeared as a series of three articles in *Appleton's* during the summer of 1907. These articles vividly described the conditions in the camps of the Jackson Lumber Company of Lockhardt, Alabama, whose officials had recently been prosecuted under federal antipeonage statutes. The trials exposed the customary violence of this system of forced labor, which was prevalent not only in the turpentine and lumber industries Irvine visited but also on railways and farms in the South.[20] In his opening piece, "The Situation as I Found It," Irvine described his methods for investigating these practices: "Arranged in a beard, a pair of overalls, and with a bright yellow bundle in my hand I went in quest of the facts. If slavery existed, the best way to find it was by being a slave— a wage slave."[21] This kind of adventure was both a journey into a world of oppressed peons and an exercise in the widespread practice of journalistic investigation aimed at elucidating class difference.

Dressed up as a peon, Irvine joined a diverse group of investigators who crossed class and ethnic lines in industrial America and reported their experiences. He had been preceded into Alabama's peonage camps during the summer by a Mary Grace Quackenbos, a lawyer specializing in the concerns of East Side immigrants.[22] And Irvine himself had tried undercover investigation before: in the 1890s, he had masqueraded as a laborer to tour Bowery drinking establishments as part of Rev. Charles Parkhurst's crusade against police corruption.[23] Cross-class investigators served many other purposes besides the journalistic, moral, and juridical ambitions that Irvine, Parkhurst, and Quackenbos pursued. Middle-class consumers probed the work environments where the goods they bought were produced. Housing reformers photographed "how the other half lives" to terrify middle-class audiences into tenement reform. Factory detectives sought the secrets of labor organization and working-class culture. Social

scientists made academic careers out of ethnographic research on workers and "tramps." Authors flouted the canons of genteel literature to convey the hopes and miseries nursed by people who lived beyond the social
and geographical precincts of the middle-class readership. Together, these
investigators made working-class impersonation a remarkably versatile
genre.[24]

Especially when planning to narrate their experiences in prose, such
investigators usually exchanged their customary selves for dramatically
assumed identities. In adopting his "overalls and a bright yellow bundle,"
Irvine again followed Jack London's example. In his 1903 exposé of the
East End of London, *The People of the Abyss*, London described his experiences in a slum "filled with a new and different race of people," which he
entered by donning "a pair of stout though well-worn trousers, a frayed
jacket with one remaining button, a pair of brogans which had plainly seen
service where coal was shoveled, a thin leather belt, and a very dirty cloth
cap." Such disguises equipped investigators to "blend in" and to "experience" the feelings of those who inhabited the social realms they visited.[25]
They used competing languages to portray such experiences. While London and Irvine leaned toward the evolutionary vernacular, other writers
preferred more aesthetic styles, and academic and governmental investigators tended toward clinical depictions of disease and disorderliness
among the poor. But these languages often overlapped, especially in their
representation of working-class life as a distinctive social, cultural, and
moral realm.

Usually this realm ranked below the "civilization" with which disguised
investigators identified themselves and their readers. But the practice of
investigative disguise could be as ambiguous in this regard as the evolutionary vernacular sometimes used to convey its discoveries. Here again
Jack London was a model. In *The People of the Abyss*, London oscillated
between expressions of distance and sympathy toward the laboring poor
of the East End. Describing his transformation through disguise and his
periodic retreats to the comforts of baths and bed linen, he emphasized
his own familiarity with soft gray suits, light comfortable shoes, cleanliness, and white sheets. But he also addressed his readers as soft people
whose remoteness from the slums fed a self-serving ignorance of miseries that produced their "civilization."[26] Irvine's investigative pieces would
betray similar cultural equivocations.

The working-class disguise that Alexander Irvine adopted for his peonage articles encouraged him to enact wage labor as a rugged struggle
amidst abysmal conditions. Describing the labor he undertook as an un-

dercover peon, Irvine explained: "I courted the danger points. I went where conditions were savage, where life was cheaper than lumber, where the physically fit survived. I came under the lash of a driver's tongue several times, but escaped the more painful experience of a peon. There were very good reasons for my escape. I looked like a man who when struck on one cheek turns the other fellow's. Besides, I could do more work than was required of me, and do it very well."[27] While Irvine emphasized the robust vigor of his own working-class persona, he described the peons he met as vitiated by the regimen that turpentine bosses administered according to "the law of beak and fang and claw—the law of forest and jungle."[28] Moreover, though he was "unkempt in appearance, and with a yellow bundle in my hand," Irvine claimed, his disguise could not completely camouflage the intimacy with refined culture that separated him from other peons. These qualities did not interfere with the stupendous vitality that characterized his impersonation of a "brother workingman," but they made it difficult for him "to find things in common" with laborers who savored profanity, smutty stories, and heavy drink. The narrative momentum of "My Life in Peonage" developed out of Irvine's growing passion to pit his vigor against the boss's brutality, a passion disappointed when the boss "tackled a weaker man." Here, Irvine followed London in offering a managerial solution for the plight of poor workers. Formulated by bosses and "superior" workingmen, such solutions proposed a reformed "civilization" in which the mass of laborers—those who had not self-consciously dressed for their parts—would have little cultural stake.[29]

Yet "My Life in Peonage" also betrayed Irvine's ambivalence about such visions of "civilization" and hinted at preferences for proletarian solidarity. Irvine described with special respect the sensibilities his fellow peons derived from communities defined by ethnicity, nationality, or race. He admired the "bright young Russian Jew," Herman Orminsky, "who having successfully eluded the terrors of Kishenev and the 'black hundred'" was virtually enslaved in Alabama. Irvine empathized with doubts about American "civilization" that Orminsky derived from this comparison.[30] He also appreciated the occasional Hungarian melody that entertained the white workers' boxcar dormitory. But his greatest sympathy seemed reserved for the segregated African-American laborers, whose somber spirituals contributed a gravity and sweetness to peons' leisure moments. Even the black workers' card games seemed to Irvine charged with an "intense excitement" he found woefully absent among the inebriated revelers in his berth. He decided that "the most interesting place in the camp was the negro car."[31]

In his peonage articles—and afterward, as he reworked these experiments in proletarian self-representation into an autobiographical *Bildungsroman* of his own—Irvine followed such sympathies into complex negotiations of the ethnic and racial differences that bedeviled the evolutionary vernacular he had learned from Jack London.[32] In "My Life in Peonage" this negotiation took the form of repeated mockery of racial and ethnic hierarchies to which bosses and laborers subscribed. Indulging the epithets used by his lumber-camp peers, Irvine noted that it was "amusing to hear the men who were held in the woods by fear talk of the 'nigger's' inferiority, in the face of the fact that the 'nigger' was doing the best work in the camp." He observed that immigrants won little status through such hierarchical gambits, since "there was a small class of Southern lumber jacks who talked of these 'superior' men as 'dagos' and 'sheenies.'" Ultimately, he attributed such slurs to the degrading influence of the peonage system itself. His final article told the story of Arthur Buckley, an Italian-American tenement youth turned peon, whose "experience in the South as a slave at the wheel of labor gave him not the slightest hint of class consciousness." Instead, peonage's strongest effect on Buckley was "a race consciousness that at times is as bitter as anything found in Alabama." As Irvine explained: "They called him a 'Dago.' He in turn calls the black man a 'nigger.' They told him to keep his place—the place of an inferior—of a slave. That is exactly what he learned to say of the colored man. Some bitter experiences that have left no bitterness, and a legacy of hatred, are the net results of his journey into that region where things are raw—where life means only labor and where labor and life are cheap."[33] Irvine believed that such racial and ethnic denigration derived from the brutal regime that reduced the peons to the status of craven cowards. If laborers could shed their "crouching subservience" for the virile class consciousness he enacted, he implied, their ethnic and racial jealousies would dissolve into class solidarity.[34]

But Irvine's literary career involved repeated reevaluations of the relations between class, race, and ethnicity. In later efforts to express what his southern adventures had meant personally, he began to portray ethnic culture as a catalyst for class solidarity, rather than an obstacle to class consciousness. His peonage investigations encouraged this tendency by provoking him to enact ethnic sensibilities of his own. At first Irvine drew on his Irish origins to fashion an ethnic identity for the edification of New York labor agents. According to his *Appleton's* account, he quickly changed to a Finnish character when he learned that the agents considered Irishmen too intractable for southern labor. Thereafter, Irvine continued to feature ethnic identity as a crucial dimension of the proletarian self he was constructing. In the process, he also negotiated the meaning of racial division for narratives of ethnicized working-class life. Irvine's literary career fascinates in part because of the way he imported lessons from American class conflict into a literary market that was itself shaped by anxieties over the meaning of ethnicity and race.[35]

Two years after his peonage articles appeared, Irvine produced an autobiography in which these intersecting social differences took on intriguing and ominous new contours. Titled *From the Bottom Up*, the autobiography signaled Irvine's arrival as a spokesman for working-class culture in the arena of periodical literature. It was commissioned for Doubleday-Page's house journal, the *World's Work*, which Walter Hines Page was trying to make into a popular, progressive periodical. Irvine's articles for Page seethed with the virile evolutionary vernacular he had practiced for *Appleton's*.[36] The autobiography demonstrated that his investigative experiments in proletarian self-assertion had fostered a personal socialist *Bildungsroman*.

In both serial and book form, *From the Bottom Up* traced Irvine's life in images that clearly echoed London's Yale *Bildungsroman*. Irvine described a childhood among hungry people who struggled for existence amidst limited resources. This struggle inhibited all ambitions toward refinement— as his mother's alcoholism and his father's beatings attested. Then a glorious sunset and the lines of a hymn inspired an adolescent conversion that aroused him to an "upward look." Irvine portrayed this new perspective in images redolent of London's picture of the "parlor" level of society. His spiritual epiphany provoked him to see that he was "in rags and dirty" and prompted exertions at cleanliness, grooming, and Bible study. Outfitted as a stableboy at a landed estate, he found fuel for his new aspirations in an improved wardrobe and glimpses of the "inner world of beautiful things" his employers enjoyed. He resolved to find a way into the "world of beauty for God's good people," to seek "a life where people had time to think, and to live a clean, normal, human life."[37]

But before finding a path out of "shameful" ignorance, the youth of *From the Bottom Up* descended into an industrial abyss. The coalpits of Scotland convinced him that wage labor was incompatible with his religious program of self-improvement. The Scottish mines that Irvine recounted contained "a writhing, squirming mass of blackened humanity struggling for a mere physical existence." Such language paralleled the evolutionary idiom Jack London had used to portray the charnel houses of civilization that had terrified him into "brain work." In Scotland, Irvine recalled, "the desire to learn to read and write returned to me with renewed intensity" and led him out of the pits into the Royal Marines.[38]

In recounting his military training, Irvine again alternated between elevating influences and more vigorous adventures. With his attention focused initially on the classroom, Irvine recalled, "it took a good deal of forcing to interest me in the handling of guns, bayonets, and swinging of clubs, vaulting of horses, and other gymnasium exercises." A drill sergeant determined to alter Irvine's ambitions by means of a thrashing in the gymnasium boxing ring. Duly stunned, Irvine bargained with a barrack-room mate for boxing lessons and hastened back to the gymnasium to repay his first assailant. Drawing on the experiments in ethnic identity he had begun in his peonage articles, Irvine's account of the match produced a virile Celtic rendition of the Londonesque evolutionary vernacular: "There is something fiendish in the Celtic nature, some beast in the blood, which, when aroused, is exceedingly helpful in matters of this kind. . . . There was a positive viciousness in my attack. . . . it was the first time I had ever felt the beast in my blood, and I turned him loose. . . . inside of thirty seconds, I had stretched my instructor on his back at my feet, and in absolute joyfulness and ecstasy of my soul, I yelled at the top of my voice: 'Hurry up, ye blindtherin' spalpeen, till I knock yez down again!'" Irvine represented this episode as a lapse in his efforts to shed the marks of his humble origins—his ignorance and Irish brogue—in order to become a more effective evangelist. Still, in the account of his military service, the vitality of the boxing match repeatedly resurfaced to rebuke overrefined emissaries of cultivation such as the fellow Bible students who held in contempt his "red-blooded and jubilant" Irish nature.[39]

Irvine next shifted his story to industrial America, where he encountered anew the opposition between effete gentility and robust proletarianism. He began as a Bowery missionary by making the rounds of lodging houses and saloons armed with a Bible and a contempt for the "pale, haggard" people there. But he soon changed his view. Irvine's account of the change both demonstrated his ability to contend with the raw forces of a Londonesque "social abyss" and illuminated his struggles with the cultural ambiguities of the evolutionary vernacular. As Irvine recalled, he focused his first missionary efforts on a Bowery lodging-house bouncer named Gar. Gar was "the toughest specimen of a man I ever saw. . . . There was a challenge in him which I at once accepted. . . . It was an intimation that he was master—that missionaries were somewhat feeble-minded and had to do with weak people. . . . I outlined a plan of campaign the major part of which was the capture of this primordial man."[40] In order to "capture" his "primordial man," Irvine explained, he had to survive "nauseating" visits to cheap restaurants and saloons and witness vicious attacks on bunk-house denizens without betraying disgust. Clearly, to win this man's allegiance was, in Irvine's Londonesque terms, to bridge the gulf between civilizing improvement and the more virile energies of the social pit. But there remained some question as to what his success implied. From the perspective of his missionary employers, Gar's conversion demonstrated the superiority of Christian "gentleness and love" over the lower-class "brutality." Within the narrative of Irvine's *Bildungsroman*, however, Gar's transformation attracted Bowery converts who pushed Irvine further away from his early program of individual "improvement." From this perspective, Irvine's success with Gar lay in the class solidarity that followed from his own enactment of proletarian vitality.[41]

The fruits of this interpretive shift appear in Irvine's final chapter on his Bowery experiences. Here the proletarian circle to whom Gar introduced him offered a new perspective on missionary work. "After some years' experience in missions and mission churches," Irvine explained, "I would find it very hard if I were a workingman living in a tenement not to be antagonistic to them; for, in large measure, such work is done on the assumption that people are poor and degraded through laxity in morals . . . social salvation is out of the question." To the new "political economy" his converts taught him, Irvine recalled, he soon added a new theology gleaned from street politics on the East Side. "The East Side has a soul," he discovered, "but it is not an ecclesiastical soul! It is a soul that is alive—so much alive to the interest of the people that many times I felt ashamed of myself when I listened to the socialistic orators on the street corners. . . . The soul of the East Side expressed itself in the Yiddish press . . . and in the spoken word of the propagandist whose ideal . . . made him a flame of living fire." Irvine recalled the thrill of repudiating orthodox religious beliefs in order to say to himself, "Soul, if this multitude is doomed to hell, be brave; gird up your loins and go with them!"[42]

As he described his missions in the Midwest and New Haven, Irvine recounted how this enthusiasm for lively working-class camaraderie developed into the mature socialism that served as the culmination of his *Bildungsroman* narrative. He continued to flirt with what Jack London called society's "parlor floor" in these passages. In Omaha in the mid-1890s, Irvine parlayed his association with New York's middle-class charity and vice crusades into an alliance with midwestern progressives who provided him with a paying congregation. Later in the decade, Irvine's work for the New Haven YMCA offered intimacy with Congregational notables who were national leaders in progressive religious thought. But the call of proletarian solidarities prevailed. While preaching to Omaha's bourgeoisie, Irvine lived in a squatters' camp along the Missouri River, which provided abundant material for the tales of combative virility he wove into his proletarian self-presentation. Such experiences prepared him for the epiphany of trade union alliance and then socialist belief in New Haven.[43] Socialism combined the virtues idealized in evangelical self-improvement with proletarian vitality and solidarity. "As I looked around . . . at the churches and the university," Irvine wrote of his new faith, "I could find nothing equal to the social passion of the socialists—it was a religion with them. True, they were limited in their expression of that passion, but they were live coals, all of them, and I was more at home in their meetings than in the churches."[44] Jack London's visit to Yale capped Irvine's tale of spiritual homecoming by revealing how he could give expression to socialist passion by borrowing the tools of the popular press.

In the final chapters of the autobiography, however, Irvine suggested misgivings about this culmination of his journey. These chapters portrayed his work at New York's Church of the Ascension, his recently purchased rural home on the Hudson, and his Christian socialist beliefs. From 1907 to 1910, Irvine ran a forum on social issues at the Ascension church, drawing large audiences from varied class backgrounds and political persuasions.[45] In his autobiography he welcomed this opportunity to foster "a new attitude toward society as well as a change of the heart." But he also complained that his socialist message found its warmest welcome among the church's richest members, while the poorest sneered at socialism as "dividing up" and complained about the preponderance of Jews among the radicals. "The average laboring man is incapable of such conference," he explained, "for . . . it is only when he becomes a Socialist that he becomes an intelligent advocate of anything." Yet developments on his farm suggested that socialist convictions did not unfailingly produce the amalgam of virtue and vitality on which Irvine now staked his hopes. Though Irvine exulted that "Socialists are the only people who seem to have the Bible idea of work," those he invited to spend a summer camping on his land were more visionary than vigorous when it came to manual labor. "In a community where the communers have to chop the fire-wood," he philosophized, "canned salmon is a good standby."[46] Culinary solutions notwithstanding, the tension between socialist ideals and working-class vigor posed a fundamental challenge to the integrity of Irvine's proletarian persona. This was a difficulty common to *Bildungsroman* narratives: how to blend the protagonist's adult identity into a wider community full of ongoing conflicts and new disappointments.

The chapter of *From the Bottom Up* devoted to Irvine's peonage investigation identified race as a central touchstone for such conflicts. Like Irvine's peonage articles, this chapter opened with a costume change that promised glimpses of a proletarian viewpoint. Then Irvine recounted experiences left out of his *Appleton's* pieces, including a train journey to his first job in the South as a miner's helper, for the Tennessee Coal and Iron Company (TCI) near Bessemer, Alabama. Here the sympathy with African-American workers in "My Life in Peonage" gave way to a truculent haggling over the application of Jim Crow. Irvine recounted how, as the "leader" of a contingent of European laborers herded into a Virginia railroad car marked "colored," he rose to inquire of a black porter whether Virginia had a law on "the separation of the races." The porter grinned in response, "Dere sho' is boss—but you ain't no races. You is jest Dagoes, ain't you?" Placed on a second Jim Crow car in Georgia, Irvine tried again "to solve my race problem" by inquiring about segregation laws. This time the porter answered by silently changing the car's "Colored" sign to "White." The camp where Irvine and his fellow laborers debarked brought his "race problem" into further relief. Lodged in unfinished buildings on a hill "where the blacks lived," pressed into labor that rendered black and white alike "in color and condition," the laborers from the North quickly reached the lowest standing Irvine could imagine. Rather than using a cross-racial ideal of class solidarity to rebuke immigrants who claimed superiority over black workers, Irvine now acquiesced in the view that equality with black laborers represented the meanest condition to which white workers could fall.[47]

Of course, the "race problem" Irvine located on the railroad cars of his autobiography was not his alone. It shared in interconnected social and literary distinctions that were symptomatic of the ways that race and class intersected in the United States at the turn of the century. Significantly, the mines on which Irvine focused the southern scenes of *From the Bottom Up* witnessed a dramatic triumph of racial division over class solidarity in the years he visited and wrote about them. From the 1870s on, the Greenback-Labor movement, the Knights of Labor, and the United Mine Workers (UMW) had each defied the rising tide of racial segregation to form organizations articulating the shared economic grievances of black and white workers. Anti-union forces in the Birmingham mining region combated these initiatives by fanning fears of "social equality"—that is, of interracial unions promoting integrated social interactions in which blacks might exert baleful "moral" influences on whites, especially white women. These efforts succeeded in all but eradicating the UMW from Alabama in 1908. Though, as Daniel Letwin observes, "social equality" was only one weapon in the anti-union arsenal, it was an especially powerful one in a period when the progress of Jim Crow had already advanced to a crescendo of terror over the supposed moral dangers of race mixing. Irvine's autobiographical silence about the crumbling interracial culture of the UMW and his suggestion that equality of industrial conditions fostered a frightening equality of social standing among black and white workers were surely also products of this pervasive racial dread.[48]

These developments in race relations found further expression in debates over the changing literary fashions that had shaped Irvine's writing career. As Kenneth Warren has pointed out, in an era that saw the social and legal institutionalization of racial segregation, it is intriguing that literary criticism adopted the imagery of railway trains—highly visible sites of racial separation—to discuss the dangers of expanding the frontiers of literary discourse too far. Warren focuses on Henry James's equation of the changing literary market with train travel in the era of Jim Crow. James pictured the new periodical press for which London and Irvine wrote as a "ponderously long" train that can only begin its journey with every seat occupied and therefore resorts to mannequins when there are not enough passengers. As Warren observes, James associated these "dummies" with a proliferation of criticism that was "fatal as an infectious disease," polluting the sensitive organism of literature through "bad company" that caused it to lose heart. Such language, Warren suggests, echoed many defenses (and pale critiques) of Jim Crow legislation by focusing on "the fear of suffering harmful effects from forced association with unworthy others." In this context, the analogy between letters and trains made literary culture the equivalent of a segregated conveyance. Rejecting even the ambiguous proletarian vitality that writers like Irvine and London injected into literary narratives of social difference, James tried to redefine true literature as a safe haven from the specter of "social equality" in the popular press.[49]

Irvine's Jim Crow car scenes betrayed similar fantasies of retreat. Of course, by transposing his own prejudices into the popular cultural idiom he had learned from Jack London, Irvine demonstrated an affinity for the "bad company" James could never bring himself to characterize fully in print. But in doing so, he adopted a popular vernacular associated with the Darwinian racism London never entirely abandoned. In some respects this was but a more visceral variation of James's genteel squeamishness about his literary intercourse. However, as Irvine continued to revise his self-representation in response to new political experiences, he rethought the relations between class, ethnicity, and race he was weaving into his life story. His revisions reveal intriguing links connecting the literary formulas he had mastered to popularize his working-class allegiances, the political conflicts he continued to engage, and intellectual shifts in the meaning of culture itself.

The Magyar *and* My Lady of the Chimney Corner: *Ethnic Community and the Meaning of Class*

In the years following the publication of his autobiography, Irvine weathered a series of personal and political struggles that moved him to change the terms in which he had cast his life story. First, both feminist activism and changes in his own domestic relations challenged Irvine to rethink his assumptions about masculinity and femininity. Previously, he had drawn fairly conventional distinctions between a public realm where men addressed "the great social problems of the community" and a private realm in which women organized domestic life. These divisions were common in the labor and socialist circles that had shaped his cultural politics.[50] By 1909, however, "New Women" of diverse class and political backgrounds were redrawing gender lines in politics, social policy, consumer behavior, and popular culture, among other arenas. Irvine was in the thick of such challenges as he directed social forums at the Church of the Ascension and immersed himself in the culture of New York City socialism. Socialist women had established a national network of women's branches that pressed the party to institute a Women's National Committee in 1908, and reverberations of this insurgency became apparent in Irvine's public oratory. His Ascension sermons called for equal pay for equal work and attacked the "bourgeois" assumption that women's sole sphere of agency was the home.[51] Private tragedy sharpened these feminist issues for Irvine. His wife Maude had long suffered under a heavy load of domestic responsibility. She managed a large household beset by scarce funds and the ostracism her husband's crusades entailed. In 1910 something snapped, and Maude repeatedly tried to murder her two youngest sons. Bewildered and despairing, Irvine sent his wife to a mental asylum and began to address more consciously in literature the roles of wife- and motherhood he had long taken for granted in life.[52]

As he reassessed gender politics, Irvine became engaged in a controversy over the meaning of socialism that also had intersecting personal and public facets. Events at the Church of the Ascension in 1910 shattered the contradictory socialist sensibility Irvine had expressed in *From the Bottom Up*. In June, the church's wealthy vestry ousted him in order to escape taunting headlines that embarrassed them on Wall Street. Many socialists were unsurprised. André Tridon editorialized in the *New York Call* that Irvine's employers had justly fired him for failing to represent their views. Tridon added that, liberated from the position of "paid retainer of wealthy men and women," Irvine now had a chance "to regain his self-respect."[53] The party's prize publicist and candidate Eugene Debs soon provided a vehicle for Irvine's rehabilitation by recommending that the minister assume some of the far-flung speaking engagements that Debs could no longer pursue.[54] From the summer of 1910, Irvine stirred audiences across the nation as he promoted the most popular socialist weekly in the United States, the *Appeal to Reason*. Widespread enthusiasm for his speeches won Irvine another party job as campaign manager for socialist candidate Job Harriman in the 1911 Los Angeles mayoral race. This position placed Irvine in the thick of a socialist schism that amplified his own political ambivalences.

Association with Harriman linked Irvine to the party's "constructivists," whose program of gradual social evolution and working-class education resembled evangelical uplift. But when his campaign work catapulted him into the party's National Executive Committee in 1912, Irvine developed a fond respect for "revolutionist" Bill Haywood, the constructivists' bitterest foe. Haywood, leader of the syndicalist Industrial Workers of the World, rejected political and educational programs in favor of militant class conflict founded on workplace solidarities. Haywood was also the sole voice raising questions of Negro rights at the Socialist party's 1912 national convention, which Irvine attended. Haywood's relative militancy on racial equality may have been particularly appealing to Irvine, who by this time was reevaluating the racial lines he had drawn in his autobiography. The bitter controversy between Haywood and his detractors anguished Irvine to the point that he abandoned active political engagement to rethink the values and solidarities on which he had staked his adult, socialist identity.[55]

Irvine eventually fashioned his most popular literary work, *My Lady of the Chimney Corner,* out of this process of personal and political reorientation. In this 1913 memoir of his childhood in Ulster, he managed to reconcile the competing programs of socialism he had encountered. He did this by tracing constructivist and revolutionary socialism back to lively characters he remembered from childhood. This device of locating adult convictions in childhood influences produced a sentimentally popular version of the *Bildungsroman* motif that worked well for Irvine. By the time of his death in 1941, *My Lady* had appeared in ten editions in the United States and fifty in Britain. Irvine also used its characters to produce other salable stories and books over the three decades after it appeared. But while *My Lady* affectingly identified Irvine's adult beliefs with his parents' plebeian wisdom, the urge to make this identification derived from his struggle to comprehend his life in the midst of the intersecting politics of class, race, and gender in early twentieth-century America. To see how this struggle produced *My Lady*, it is helpful to examine briefly the less successful novel Irvine produced two years before—*The Magyar: A Story of the Social Revolution.*

Written during Irvine's first year with the *Appeal to Reason, The Magyar* bore the marks of the struggles he was confronting. Its patently autobiographical main character is a minister named Stephen Ruden. At the beginning of the book, Ruden alienates his elite Connecticut congregation by embracing socialism in a public lecture. In addition to expressing political sensibilities, however, the novel also examines their domestic consequences. The book's early chapters focus on an ongoing quarrel between Ruden and his wife Madeline, who disdains her husband's "nearness to the heart of the great unwashed," complains that his conscience robs their children, worries that Ruden carries the blood of "a foreign proletariat," and pleads for more social intercourse with "people who succeed—people who are dominant." Ruden's socialist lecture brings this battle to a crisis. Convinced that Ruden's open avowal of socialism will place him beyond the pale of respectability, Madeline departs for an opulent plantation where her school-friend Mabel presides in the splendor Ruden has rejected. This break shifts the action to the South, where for most of the novel Ruden and Madeline separately adopt a series of assumed identities in search of their authentic selves.[56]

In order to follow Madeline south, Ruden dons a working-class disguise and contracts to write magazine articles on labor conditions. In the process, he enacts Irvine's reassessment of the lines of class, ethnicity, and race he had crossed in his own undercover travels. Again race provides an especially delicate touchstone for working-class identity. Ruden alternately adopts the invidious racial distinctions that permeated turn-of-the-century social thought and attacks the inhumanity of racist practice. *The Magyar* recapitulates the railroad car scenes in *From the Bottom Up*, with their complicity in Jim Crow. It also includes several Londonesque flourishes of a "Saxon" vitality with which Ruden defends helpless black men from the brutality of prison officials and peonage bosses. At the same time, the novel celebrates traits it identifies as peculiarly African-American. The black laborers Ruden encounters sing about liberty in a heavenly home, providing a "spiritual wind up" appreciated by all workers. And, when he questions a socialist in Montgomery on the practice of maintaining segregated party locals in the city, Ruden learns that white men can't keep up with the eager activism of their African-American comrades.[57]

Here, Irvine called upon long-established traditions that defined white working-class identity and politics through ambiguous preoccupations with African-American culture. Many of Irvine's black characters speak in the cadences of the nineteenth-century blackface minstrel show that had provided the most visible institutionalization of these traditions. Historians of this legacy differ in their estimations of the degree to which racist ridicule overpowered the cross-racial sympathies implied in the minstrel show.[58] Irvine's autobiographical gloss on minstrel traditions suggests how fused these two moments in the legacy of proletarian appropriations of black culture had become by the 1910s. His political associations during the years he worked on *The Magyar* may well have augmented these confused cultural politics of race. He was deepening his alliances with socialists in New York City and throughout the country in a period when they were renegotiating their own ambiguous relation to the racial plight of African-American workers. In 1910 and 1911, the leadership of Local New York was pressed to address the concerns of African-American workers in their midst; they eventually responded by briefly employing a black party organizer.[59] Meanwhile, national Socialist party conventions of 1908–12 saw a series of debates about acceptance of the resolution condemning immigration restrictions based on national or racial grounds that had been passed at the 1907 International Socialist Congress at Stuttgart. American socialist positions on the Stuttgart resolution ranged from London's Darwinian racism to a minority position insisting on racial equality.[60] The *Appeal to Reason*, where Irvine was most active during this period, was itself a study in socialist divisions over race. Its pages featured socialist calls for racial equality, but its founder, Julius Wayland, predicted that socialism would produce a voluntary segregation based on the preferences of black and white workers for "their own communities."[61]

Such appeals to community, which often cloaked racism in a beguiling appreciation for cultural particularities, proved to be central to the personal revision of proletarian selfhood that Irvine effected in *The Magyar*. The novel is primarily concerned with a journey of self-discovery that helps Ruden locate the origins of his socialist faith in an ethnic identity modeled on the romanticized African-American culture Irvine had first celebrated in his peonage articles. Ruden begins this personal quest while he is waiting at the Magyar Slovensky Hotel in New York to be transported south as a peon. Here he befriends Franz, a Hungarian youth whose native tongue sounds vaguely familiar, "like the sounds of a life [Ruden] had lived before." Franz is a model of working-class self-respect who carries his certificates as a journeyman butcher and defies any deviation from his contract. Ruden's efforts to defend Franz in the wake of this defiance land the minister in a penitentiary and then a stockade. During these episodes Ruden meets convicts whose stories lead him to a southern mill town with an admirably interracial working-class community that revolves around Zapolya, a Hungarian immigrant who turns out to be Ruden's long-lost father. Through the educated Zapolya, Ruden's ethnic heritage bequeaths the mixture of class loyalty and cultural accomplishment that Irvine struggled to reconcile in his own socialist creed.[62]

While Ruden is discovering the ethnic roots of his proletarian sympathies, Madeline also assumes disguises that carry her across social lines to address some of Irvine's quandaries about gender politics. At first she is pampered at Wetumpka Mansion, the Alabama plantation owned by Congressman Llewellyn Oglethorpe. Oglethorpe goes to great expense to show her off at a Christmas ball, where she wins the admiration of the governor. Both men promise further extravagances, along with access to political power, in return for Madeline's complicity in adultery and social injustice. Madeline learns from this adventure a new respect for Stephen Ruden's class loyalties and socialist ideals. Rejecting pompous display for a working-class identity, Madeline gains admission to the circle of proletarian solidarity that Ruden's ethnic traditions represent. She, too, finds Zapolya, and through him a dedication to socialism and reunion with Ruden. Irvine uses this reconciliation to claim peculiar domestic virtues for the working-class culture that *The Magyar* dramatized in ethnic terms. Abandoned by Madeline, Ruden had fallen in love with a religious protégé, Ethel Ainsworth, who had long since renounced her privileged background to embrace his Christian socialist vision. Ethel enjoys her own adventure in disguise as a peonage investigator and legal counsel for the Justice Department, modeled on the real-life Mary Grace Quackenbos. Such an independent New Woman brings to *The Magyar* Irvine's recent acknowledgment of feminist challenges to his own long-held assumptions about gender. In the end, though, Irvine reasserts conventional domestic propriety, albeit in socialist terms. Stephen and Madeline stay married, not in order to comply with bourgeois gender prescriptions but out of their

KATHRYN J. OBERDECK

allegiance to socialism. Since the appearance of sexual impropriety might harm the socialist movement, they reunite in "service and the joy of comradeship."[63]

Though not very successful as a novel, *The Magyar* does illuminate the construction of working-class identity in early twentieth-century America. Unable to sell it to a commercial press, Irvine resorted to an *Appeal to Reason* advertisement to raise money for its publication. He attributed this difficulty to the novel's politics, but *The Magyar* is also stylistically at odds with itself: it careens from Londonesque flights of strenuous masculinity to maudlin dialect sketches of dying peons, from poignantly realist depictions of everyday working-class life to the romantic platitudes of emotionally overcharged protagonists.[64] If some of Irvine's stylistic devices served him ill, however, his use of the artifice of disguise still poignantly testifies to the larger significance of this device as a way of probing the investigator's own identity. Even where investigators focused on what they had learned about the communities they visited, the lines of class and ethnic difference they drew by means of costume, language, and description told much about how their investigations helped to define their own social location. Irvine's case amplified this subjective dimension of investigative disguise. His successive investigative narratives continuously redefined what working-class origins and socialist politics meant personally. *The Magyar* was an important milestone on this journey. By imagining, through Ruden's character, that proletarian compassion and socialist faith derive from ethnic traditions and portend revised domestic relations, Irvine transformed his experiments in investigative disguise into a narrative of self-discovery tailored to some of his current political dilemmas. *The Magyar's* triteness rendered this amalgam of selfhood and politics a largely personal achievement, but Irvine soon reformulated it more successfully in what became his most popular work, *My Lady of the Chimney Corner.*

My Lady of the Chimney Corner is primarily a tribute to Irvine's mother Anna. She provides the main voice for the book's folksy morals, which address various contradictions within Irvine's adult ethic of socialist solidarity. On one hand, she combines Irish wit and class pride into a response to the feminism Irvine had encountered among socialists. True to *The Magyar's* resolution, Anna is a domestic angel on the hearth. But she is also a capable spokeswoman for working-class solidarity. She is Madeline Ruden and Ethel Ainsworth. Anna unambiguously renounces all of the snobbery that Madeline exhibited at the beginning of the earlier book, but she retains Madeline's fierce protection of her domestic circle. She uses some of Ethel's skills to defend this circle against condescending intruders. When a genteel Methodist tract distributor gives young Alexander a moralizing lecture on private property to discourage his penchant for raiding local cherry trees, for example, Anna delivers a sharp rebuke to the well-meaning evangelist. She points out that the good Methodist would not dream of lecturing the son of a local gentleman. Anna admonishes, "because we've no choice ye come down here like a petty sessions-magistrate and make my bhoy feel like a thief because he goes like a crow an' picks a wild cherry or a sloe that would rot on a tree." This logic prompts her husband to compare Anna favorably to a notorious contemporary barrister. The compliment reinforces Irvine's portrayal of Anna as wielding within the domestic circle the skills New Women were claiming as public rights.[65]

Not only a vision of domesticity revised, Anna's chimney corner is also the site of an ethnic camaraderie that expressed Irvine's effort to resolve the political dilemmas he faced as he wrote *My Lady*. To encourage this fellowship, Anna maintains a stage-Irish banter that serves to sustain the debate between educational uplift and workerist solidarity that had torn Irvine's socialist faith. Anna carries on this debate with a cynical stonebreaker named Willie Withero, the Irvine family's closest friend. Their arguments recast the socialist battle between gradualism and revolution into delightful voices from Irvine's earliest Antrim education. Both Anna and Willie measure human worth in terms that certify the dignity of their own impoverished community against the disregard shown them by local "quality." They differ over strategies for fostering that dignity. Anna favors patient and persistent education in an outlook of hopeful change. Her methods—Irish fairy stories, Bible verses, and commercial story papers—look much like those Alexander Irvine adopted in adulthood. Withero, Haywood-like, derives his ideals from manual labor: he sums up his personal creed as "A good day's stone breakin's my prayer." While *My Lady* ultimately indicates a preference for Anna's way, the common bonds of Irish identity permit the avowal of both strategies.[66]

My Lady of the Chimney Corner's vision of these ethnic bonds offered a much rosier picture of Irvine's early experiences than he had provided in *From the Bottom Up*. But it still bore the marks of the experiments in self-narration Irvine had made since launching himself into print. Through these experiments he had found his own substitute for the naturalist social pit he had originally borrowed from Jack London's narrative examples. Where the social pit had been, Irvine now put the ethnic community, whose combined social and personal meaning he had concocted as he sought his own identity in the genre of investigative disguise. The motif of a *Bildungs-*

roman leading from poverty through self-improving aspirations, disillusionment, and finally a mature collective consciousness remained. But now the ethnic community's comradely wisdom constituted the collective sensibility to which the erring striver must return, after learning that what looked like more sophisticated creeds, including evolutionary racism, are not what they seem. This shift constituted a culmination of Irvine's narrative quest for proletarian identity and an important transformation of the evolutionary vernacular many of his narratives had employed.[67]

The continued appeal of what Irvine called his "Irish books" attests to a broader intellectual turn that links his narrative efforts with more familiar early twentieth-century American intellectual products.[68] Irvine composed his memories of Irish camaraderie just as prominent thinkers were theorizing about community in ways that have received much more attention in the annals of intellectual and cultural history. Philosophers such as William James and John Dewey envisaged a democratic community forged out of the pragmatic test of a plurality of ideas. Social settlement workers and social scientists tried to foster the neighborhood bonds—or, in the more scientific parlance, primary groups—they saw as the foundations of healthy communities. Iconoclastic young ethnologists, inspired by the cultural relativism they learned from Franz Boas, set out to comprehend the logic and meaning of cultures that Darwinian schemes had classed as "backward" or "primitive." In the 1920s, the investigators of culture in "Middletown" decried the disintegration of a gemeinschaft that dissolved into the giant forces of mass industry and communication.[69] In all these versions, American intellectuals of the Progressive Era and beyond focused on community as a social construct that could resolve tensions between cultural improvement and cultural differentiation that bedeviled an increasingly outworn tension between gentility and the social pit. In this respect, Irvine's succession of shifting personal narratives helps to illuminate further a broad intellectual trajectory that led from questions about cultural hierarchy and Darwinian struggle to questions about the sustenance of community. His simultaneous engagement in class politics, popular literature, and proletarian self-representation reminds us to look beyond the conventional precincts of intellectual history to the intersecting public spheres of popular culture and class conflict to account for important cultural shifts in twentieth-century thought. As Irvine's process of self-definition suggests, these were crucial sites not only for the production of working-class narrative but also for changing conceptions of class distinction and ethnic difference that have shaped our own cultural debates, from wars over cultural relativism to the dilemmas posed by identity politics.

Notes

The author would like to thank the editors of this volume, the Social History Group at the University of Illinois at Urbana-Champaign, and Jacqueline Dirks and William Munro for comments on previous versions of this paper, and Andrew Nolan for research assistant support.

1. On Progressive thinkers concerned about class conflict see Dorothy Ross, *The Origins of American Social Science* (Cambridge: Cambridge University Press, 1991); James Kloppenberg, *Uncertain Victory: Social Democracy and Progressivism in European and American Thought, 1870–1920* (New York: Oxford University Press, 1986); and Mark Pittenger, *American Socialists and Evolutionary Thought, 1870–1920* (Madison: University of Wisconsin Press, 1993).

2. See Patrick Joyce, *Democratic Subjects: The Self and the Social in Nineteenth-Century England* (Cambridge: Cambridge University Press, 1994); Judith Walkowitz, *City of Dreadful Delight: Narratives of Sexual Danger in Late-Victorian London* (Chicago: University of Chicago Press, 1992); Regenia Gagnier, *Subjectivities: The History of Self-Representation in Britain, 1832–1920* (Oxford: Oxford University Press, 1991); Carolyn Steedman, *The Radical Soldier's Tale: John Pearman, 1819–1908* (London: Routledge, 1988); Regina Kunzel, "Pulp Fictions and Problem Girls: Reading and Rewriting Single Pregnancy in the Postwar United States," *American Historical Review* 100 (Dec. 1995): 1465–87; Sean McCann, "A Roughneck Reaching for Higher Things: The Vagaries of Pulp Populism," *Radical History Review* 61 (Winter 1995): 4–34; Ann Fabian, "Making a Commodity Out of Truth: Speculations on the Career of Bernarr Macfadden," *American Literary History* 5 (Spring 1993): 51–76; Mari Jo Buhle and Paul Buhle, "The New Labor History at the Cultural Crossroads," *Journal of American History* 75 (June 1988): 151–57.

3. See Joyce, *Democratic Subjects*; Joan Wallach Scott, "The Evidence of Experience," *Critical Inquiry* 17 (Summer 1991): 773–97; Scott, "On Language, Gender and Working-Class History," *International Labor and Working-Class History* 31 (Spring 1987): 1–13; Christine Stansell, "A Response to Joan Scott," *International Labor and Working-Class History* 31 (Spring 1987): 24–29; and Bryan Palmer, *Descent into Discourse: The Reification of Language and the Writing of Social History* (Philadelphia: Temple University Press, 1990).

4. Walkowitz, *City of Dreadful Delight*, esp. 7–9; see also Kunzel, "Pulp Fictions and Problem Girls," and David Mayfield and Susan Thorne, "Social History and Its Discontents: Gareth Stedman Jones and the Politics of Language," *Social History* 17 (May 1992): 219–33.

5. Gagnier, *Subjectivities*, 8–10.

6. Christopher P. Wilson, *The Labor of Words: Literary Professionalism in the Progressive Era* (Athens: University of Georgia Press, 1985); Matthew Schneirov, *The Dream of a New Social Order: Popular Magazines in America 1893–1914* (New York: Columbia University Press, 1994).

7. Leon Fink, "Looking Backward: Reflections on Workers' Culture and Certain Conceptual Dilemmas within Labor History," in J. Carroll Moody and Alice Kessler-Harris, eds., *Perspectives of American Labor History: The Problems of Synthesis* (DeKalb:

226   KATHRYN J. OBERDECK

Northern Illinois University Press, 1990), 19–20; Leon Fink, "Relocating the Vital Center," *Journal of American History* 75 (June 1988): 158.

8. Alexander Irvine, *From the Bottom Up: The Life Story of Alexander Irvine* (New York: Doubleday, Page & Co., 1910) (cited hereafter as *FBU*); Kathryn Oberdeck, "Labor's Vicar and the Variety Show: Popular Religion, Popular Theatre, and Cultural Class Conflict in Turn-of-the-Century America" (Ph.D. dissertation, Yale University, 1991), forthcoming from Johns Hopkins University Press under the working title *The Evangelist and the Impresario: Religion, Entertainment, and Cultural Politics in America, 1884–1914.*

9. Joan London, *Jack London and His Times* (New York: Doubleday, Doran & Co., 1939); Philip S. Foner, "Jack London: American Rebel," introduction to Foner, ed., *Jack London: American Rebel* (New York: Citadel Press, 1947), 3–130; Joan Hedrick, *Solitary Comrade: Jack London and His Work* (Chapel Hill: University of North Carolina Press, 1982). Mark E. Zamen, *Standing Room Only: Jack London's Controversial Career as a Public Speaker* (New York: P. Lang, 1990).

10. *Jack London at Yale*, ed. State Secretary of the Socialist Party of Connecticut (New Haven: Socialist Party of Connecticut, 1906), 15–16; Todd Kontje, *Private Lives in the Public Sphere: The German Bildungsroman as Metafiction* (University Park: Pennsylvania State University Press, 1992) and *The German Bildungsroman: History of a National Genre* (Columbia, S.C.: Camden House, 1993); and Franco Moretti, *The Way of the World: The Bildungsroman in European Culture* (London: Verso, 1987).

11. *Jack London at Yale*, 15–16.

12. Ibid.

13. Amy Kaplan, *The Social Construction of American Realism* (Chicago: University of Chicago Press, 1988), 18–19; Wilson, *Labor of Words*, chaps. 2 and 4; Schneirov, *Dream of a New Social Order*, chap. 4.

14. Frank Luther Mott, *A History of American Magazines* (Cambridge, Mass.: Harvard University Press, 1957), 48–50, 483–93, 590–602; Richard Lingeman, *Theodore Dreiser: At the Gates of the City, 1871–1907* (New York: G. P. Putnam's Sons, 1986), 193; Wilson, *Labor of Words*, chaps. 2 and 4; Schneirov, *Dream of a New Social Order*. To emulate the new periodicals, *Harper's* and the *Atlantic* also published work like London's.

15. Jack London, *John Barleycorn* in *Novels and Social Writings* (1913; New York: Viking Press, 1982), 1065–66; Carolyn Johnston, *Jack London—An American Radical?* (Westport, Conn.: Greenwood Press, 1984), 45, 51–53; Joan London, *Jack London*, 125–36, 166–67.

16. D. Appleton Co. to Alexander Irvine, 24 Oct. 1906, Scrapbook, Irvine Collection, which I used while the collection was in the possession of Anna Irvine Buck; it is now at Huntington Library, San Marino, Calif.

17. Alexander Irvine, "Two Social Pariahs," *Appleton's Magazine* 10 (Jan. 1907), 118–21.

18. Jack London, *White Fang* (New York, 1906).

19. Irvine, "Two Social Pariahs."

20. United States Dept. of Justice, *Report on Peonage* (Washington, D.C.: Government Printing Office, 1906); Pete Daniel, *The Shadow of Slavery: Peonage in the South, 1901–1969* (Urbana: University of Illinois Press, 1972); Jonathan Wiener, *Social Origins of the New South: Alabama 1860–1885* (Baton Rouge: Louisiana State University

Press, 1978); William Cohen, *At Freedom's Edge: Black Mobility and the Southern White Quest for Racial Control* (Baton Rouge: Louisiana University Press, 1991).

21. Alexander Irvine, "My Life in Peonage: The Situation as I Found It," *Appleton's Magazine* 9 (June 1907): 643.

22. Dept. of Justice, *Report*, 20–21; Daniel, *Shadow*, 83–84.

23. Irvine, *FBU*, 148.

24. See Jacqueline Dirks, "Righteous Goods: Women's Production, Reform Publicity, and the National Consumers' League, 1890–1920" (Ph.D. dissertation, Yale University, 1996), chap. 4; Toby Higbie, "Crossing Boundaries: Tramp Ethnographers and Narratives of Class in Progressive Era America," *Social Science History* 21 (Winter 1997): 559–92; Alan Trachtenberg, "Experiments in Another Country: Stephen Crane's City Sketches," in E. J. Sundquist, ed., *American Realism: New Essays* (Baltimore: Johns Hopkins University Press, 1982), 138–54; Mark Pittenger, "A World of Difference: Constructing the 'Underclass' in Progressive America," *American Quarterly* 49 (Mar. 1997): 26–65; Jacob Riis, *How the Other Half Lives* (New York: C. Scribner's Sons, 1890); Mrs. John and Marie Van Vorst, *The Woman Who Toils* (New York: Doubleday, Page, 1903); Whiting Williams, *What's on the Workers' Mind, by One Who Put on Overalls to Find Out* (New York: C. Scribner's Sons, 1920). These are examples of a vast contemporary literature of social exploration.

25. Jack London, *The People of the Abyss* (reprint, New York: L. Hill Books, 1995), 7, 10, 12. London emulated Stephen Crane, "An Experiment in Misery" in Joseph Katz, ed., *The Portable Stephen Crane* (Middlesex: Viking Press, 1969). See also Gagnier, *Subjectivities*, 118ff.; Peter Keating, ed., *Into Unknown England, 1866–1913* (Manchester: Manchester University Press, 1976); and Micaela di Leonardo, "Foreword," to London, *People of the Abyss*.

26. London, *People of the Abyss*, 12–13, 75–77, 136–37; See also Jack London, "South of the Slot," in Foner, ed., *Jack London*, 258–72.

27. Irvine, "My Life in Peonage: The Situation," 643–44.

28. Ibid., 647.

29. Alexander Irvine, "My Life in Peonage: A Week with the 'Bull of the Woods,'" *Appleton's Magazine* 10 (July 1907): 3–15, quotes from 5, 10, 12.

30. Irvine, "My Life in Peonage: The Situation," 649–50.

31. Irvine, "My Life in Peonage: A Week," 9, 12, 13.

32. For London's racism see his letters to Cloudsley Johns, Jack London, *The Letters of Jack London*, ed. Earle Labor, Robert C. Leitz III, and I. Milo Shepard, 3 vols. (Stanford, Calif.: Stanford University Press, 1988), 1:81–93. For his cross-racial sympathies, see "The Chinago" (1909), "Mauki" (1909), and "The Mexican" (1911), in Jack London, *Novels and Stories* (New York: Viking Press, 1982), 834–48, 868–82, 920–44.

33. Irvine, "My Life in Peonage: A Week," 9; Alexander Irvine, "My Life in Peonage: The Kidnapping of 'Punk,'" *Appleton's Magazine* 10 (Aug. 1907): 197.

34. Irvine thus anticipated the cross-racial organizing among timber workers led in 1913 by the IWW-affiliated Brotherhood of Timber Workers, on which there is a considerable literature; see most recently David Roediger, "Gaining a Hearing for Black-White Unity: Covington Hall and the Complexities of Race, Gender and Class," in *Towards the Abolition of Whiteness* (London: Verso, 1994), 127–80.

35. Kenneth W. Warren, *Black and White Strangers: Race and American Literary Realism* (Chicago: University of Chicago Press, 1993).

36. Isaac F. Marcosson, *Adventures in Interviewing* (New York: Dodd, Mead and Co., 1931), chap. 2; Wilson, *Labor of Words*, 54–55; *World's Work* 18 (July 1909): cover; Alexander Irvine, *A Fighting Parson* (Boston: Little, Brown & Co., 1930), 94.

37. Alexander Irvine, "From the Bottom Up: Boyhood in Ireland," *World's Work* 18 (July 1909): 11790, 11793–97; *FBU*, 11–14, 15–21.

38. Irvine, "From the Bottom Up: Boyhood," 11797–98; Irvine, *FBU*, 18–23.

39. Irvine, "From the Bottom Up: Training for the British Navy," "From the Bottom Up: Life on Board a British Man-of-War," "From the Bottom Up: The Gordon Relief Expedition," *World's Work* 18.4, 5, 6 (Aug., Sept., Oct., 1909): 11948–12029, 12033–37; 12126–27; Irvine, *FBU*, 24–51.

40. Irvine, *FBU*, 106.

41. Irvine, "From the Bottom Up: The Battered Hulks of the Bowery," *World's Work* 19 (Dec. 1909): 12365–68; Irvine, *FBU*, 105–9.

42. Irvine, *FBU*, 156–59.

43. Ibid., chaps. 13, 14, 16, 17.

44. Ibid., 234; *New Haven Union*, 15 Oct. 1903, 2; 23 May 1904, 1; 27 Oct. 1904, 5; Oberdeck, "Labor's Vicar," chap. 5.

45. Oberdeck, "Labor's Vicar," chap. 7; Madge Jenison, "The Church and Social Unrest," *Outlook* 79 (May 1908).

46. Irvine, *FBU*, chaps. 21, 22.

47. Ibid., 256–58, 265.

48. See Paul B. Worthman, "Black Workers and Labor Unions in Birmingham, Alabama, 1897–1904," *Labor History* 10 (Summer 1969): 375–407; Daniel Letwin, "Interracial Unionism, Gender and 'Social Equality' in the Alabama Coalfields, 1878–1908," *Journal of Southern History* 61 (Aug. 1995): 519–54; Herbert Gutman, "The Negro and the United Mine Workers of America," in *Work Culture and Society in Industrializing America* (New York: Knopf, 1976), 121–208; on Jim Crow see C. Vann Woodward, *The Strange Career of Jim Crow* (New York: Oxford University Press, 1955); Joel Williamson, *The Crucible of Race* (New York: Oxford University Press, 1984), chap. 7.

49. Warren, *Black and White Strangers*, 106–8.

50. Kathryn J. Oberdeck, "Religion, Culture, and the Politics of Class: Alexander Irvine's Mission to Turn-of-the-Century New Haven," *American Quarterly* 47 (June 1995): 236–79; Kathryn J. Oberdeck, "'Not Pink Teas': The Seattle Working-Class Women's Movement, 1905–1918," *Labor History* 32 (Spring 1991): 193–230; Joseph Cohen, "Socialist Sociology," *International Socialist Review* 9 (May 1909): 875; Mari Jo Buhle, *Women and American Socialism, 1870–1920* (Urbana: University of Illinois Press, 1983).

51. Buhle, *Women and American Socialism*, chaps. 3–7; Meredith Tax, *The Rising of the Women: Feminist Solidarity and Class Conflict, 1880–1917* (New York: Monthly Review Press, 1980), chaps. 6–7; Nancy Cott, *The Grounding of Modern Feminism* (New Haven: Yale University Press, 1987), chap. 1; Alexander Irvine, "Equal Pay for Equal Work: Address delivered . . . at Church of the Ascension . . . May 16, 1908"; "Women and the Bourgeois Mind: Address Delivered . . . At Church of the Ascension . . . March 20th, 1910," both in Irvine Collection.

52. Irvine, *Fighting Parson*, 89–96; Irvine fictionalized the disaster in an unpublished manuscript, "Little Pilgrims of the Dawn," Irvine Collection.

53. Irvine, *Fighting Parson*, 85; "Can Socialism and Christianity be Reconciled?" (review of Irvine, *FBU*, quoting *Call* criticism), *Current Literature* 49 (Aug. 1910): 176–78.

54. Eugene V. Debs to George D. Brewer, 26 June and 7 July 1910, in J. R. Constantine, ed., *Letters of Eugene V. Debs*, 3 vols. (Urbana: University of Illinois Press, 1990), 1:364–66.

55. *Appeal to Reason*, 17 Sept. 1910, 1; 12 Nov. 1910, 1; 11 Mar. 1911, 4; *California Social Democrat*, 2 Sept. 1911, 5; *Citizen*, 28 July 1911, 2; 13 Oct. 1911, 3; 20 Oct. 1911, 8; Alexander Irvine, *Revolution in Los Angeles* (Los Angeles: Citizen Print Shop, 1912). Irvine's ambivalence about factional fights appears in his *California Social Democrat* column from April through June 1912; see also Ira Kipnis, *The American Socialist Movement, 1897–1912* (New York: Columbia University Press, 1952), 370–420; James Weinstein, *The Decline of Socialism in America, 1912–1925* (New Brunswick: Rutgers University Press, 1984), chap. 1; Nick Salvatore, *Eugene V. Debs: Citizen and Socialist* (Urbana: University of Illinois Press, 1982), 251–67. For competing perspectives on race in the Socialist party see Kipnis, 130–33; Weinstein, 66–67; Roediger, *Towards the Abolition*, 143–44; and Philip Foner, *American Socialism and Black Americans* (Westport, Conn.: Greenwood Press, 1977), 94–127, 182–253.

56. Alexander Irvine, *The Magyar: A Story of the Social Revolution* (Girard, Kans.: Socialist Publishing Co., 1911), 1–42.

57. Ibid., 58, 71, 104, 191, 198.

58. Eric Lott, *Love and Theft: Blackface Minstrelsy and the American Working Class* (New York: Oxford University Press, 1993); David Roediger, *The Wages of Whiteness: Race and the Making of the American Working Class* (London: Verso, 1991), chaps. 5 and 6.

59. Foner, *American Socialism and Black Americans*, 207–18.

60. Ibid., 145–46; Weinstein, *Decline of Socialism*, 65–67.

61. Foner, *American Socialism and Black Americans*, 108; John Graham, ed., *"Yours for the Revolution": The Appeal to Reason, 1895–1922* (Lincoln: University of Nebraska Press, 1990), 52–53.

62. Irvine, *Magyar*, 55–57, 61–81, 214–28.

63. Ibid., 124–34, 240–77.

64. *Appeal to Reason*, 11 Mar. 1911, 2.

65. Alexander Irvine, *My Lady of the Chimney Corner* (London: Ernest Benn, 1931), 83–88.

66. Ibid., 82, 88, 148, 177.

67. Space constraints prevent the detailed analyses of Irvine's narratives, especially *My Lady*, that would be required to develop this transformation and its cultural context more fully.

68. Alexander Irvine to Anna Irvine Buck, n.d., Irvine Collection.

69. Ross, *Origins of American Social Science*, esp. chaps. 7–10; Robert Westbrook, *John Dewey and American Democracy* (Ithaca: Cornell University Press, 1991), esp. 346, 366; Pittenger, *American Socialists*, chap. 11; George W. Stocking, Jr., *Race, Culture and Evolution: Essays in the History of Anthropology* (New York: Free Press, 1968) and "The Ethnographic Sensibility of the 1920s and the Dualism of the Anthropological Tradition," in *The Ethnographer's Magic and Other Essays in the History of Anthropology* (Madison: University of Wisconsin Press, 1992); Robert Lynd and Helen Lynd, *Middletown* (New York: Harcourt, Brace and Co., 1929).

Chapter 9

Making a Church Home

African-American Migrants, Religion,
and Working-Class Activism

KIMBERLEY L. PHILLIPS

SARA BROOKS MIGRATED to Cleveland in 1940, found work, and joined
a church. Membership in this new spiritual community anchored her faith
and empowered her to engage in purposeful action in her home, community, and workplace. Brooks concluded that while her marriage "didn't turn
out," and persistent poverty in Alabama had forced her to leave her children with her parents for long periods of time as she searched for work,
her faith "gave me the strength and [it] gave me the mind to go on." She
eventually migrated north and reunited with her children; she found steady
work, regularly stood up to abusive employers, and bought a home of her
own. Using an enduring biblical image, she measured these gains in Cleveland against her constant struggle for a living in Jim Crow Alabama: "I
saw all those peach trees [in Alabama], and they were hanging just so ful-
la fruit. They were so pretty, and I don't know why, but I didn't get a chance
to get any of it." She concluded her moving narrative, *You May Plow Here*,
with an affirmation of the faith that had pushed her from the South: "So
thank goodness I'm able to thank the Lord that He brought me through
all this up until now."[1]

The braiding of faith and personal agency in Sara Brooks's account is
evident in other African-American migrants' linking of religion and sec-

ular activism.[2] These narratives suggest the range of blacks' religious experiences following migration, as well as the ways in which church participation amplified the prophetic meaning of migration and called them to act on their own behalf. Brooks juxtaposed her ability to work, buy a home, and reunite her family in the North with her inability to lay claims to the fruits of her labor—symbolized by the ripe peaches on the tree—in a segregated South. In doing so, she revealed the porous boundaries between her sacred and secular life; she demonstrated how religiosity continued to have meaning even after migration, displaying a black working-class identity rooted in northern church communities with deep religious values that provided support for individual and collective struggle.

As migrants settled in Cleveland between 1915 and 1940, the number of its African-American churches rose from fourteen to hundreds. These new churches that emerged simply to accommodate the tens of thousands of African Americans arriving from the South included the older black Protestant denominations of Baptists and Methodists and the newer, rapidly expanding Holiness and Pentecostal denominations. Competition was brisk, as communicants moved freely and often from one church to another. Though such movement reflected efforts to find more comfortable locations for religious expressions, other issues also fueled the departures and the proliferation of new churches. African-American church building occurred as congregations questioned the efficacy of churches within the larger, secular society. Indeed, the linkage that Brooks made between religion and secular activism was open for contestation. Even as churches remained central to the everyday experiences in black Cleveland, African Americans themselves debated the proper role of the church in the urban, industrial United States.

Black working-class migrants' answer to this question was informed by their denominational sensibilities, identities as southerners, and their needs as working people. Bertha Cowan articulated what many working-class migrants felt when they first arrived in Cleveland: finding a "church home" where she would be comfortable was as urgent as finding work.[3] Embedded in this assertion was the enduring belief held by many African Americans that churches were of their own making and, therefore, should be responsive to their spiritual and secular (described as worldly) needs. As Robin Kelley has reminded us about black sacred life in the Jim Crow South: "The Church was more than an institution. In addition to providing fellowship, laying the foundation for a sense of community, and offering help to those in need, churches were first and foremost places of reflection and *spiritual empowerment* [his emphasis]."[4] Even as African

Americans' sacred cosmology might have shifted as the result of their growing literacy, the essential role of religion as the site for sacred empowerment and political organization remained.[5]

Many of the new studies of African Americans in northern cities during the era of the Great Migration have offered too brief analyses of the role churches played in migrants' sacred and secular lives. Because of this cursory glance, most have not significantly departed from older work that argued that the connections African Americans made between their religious life and secular activism weakened in the northern context.[6] According to this argument, going north may have been animated by sacred sensibilities, but once migrants crossed the Ohio River, religion ceased to fuel personal or collective agency. Paradoxically, the long migration between 1915 and 1950 led to an explosion in the number of churches, but not in the number of black church participants. Some historians have explained this puzzle by noting that in the first half of the 1920s, membership in the larger Baptist and African Methodist churches in northern cities grew as migrants transferred their earlier affiliation with churches in the South. Overall, church participation appeared to have declined. At the same time that some blacks abandoned the older denominations, others joined the newer denominations that practiced ecstatic worship. The general impoverishment of black communities and the rise of a secular culture eroded blacks' participation and financial support for their churches. The rapid growth of small, nondenominational churches with poor members further weakened the centrality of black churches.[7] As a result, scholars have concluded, churches and ministers remained part of urban life but, with few exceptions, not at its center.[8]

Recent studies on black life in the early twentieth-century South, however, have reminded us not to define black sacred life merely in institutional terms, or as an extension of any one minister. Evelyn Brooks Higginbotham has paid particular attention to church spaces in the South, arguing that black churches in the last years of the nineteenth century and the first decades of the twentieth took on a public character within the framework of Jim Crow, "afford[ing] African Americans an interstitial space in which to critique and contest white America's racial domination." Thus the black church did not function as "the embodiment of ministerial authority or of any individual's private interests and pronouncements, but as the social space for discussion of public concerns. During the late nineteenth and early twentieth centuries, the church came to represent a deliberative arena, whose character derived from the collective nature of the church itself, namely, as a body of many diverse members, and from race-conscious feelings of nationalism."[9] Even in the southern context, however, numerous tensions emerged over the role of churches in shaping blacks' activism. New denominations provided more immediate spiritual experiences and drew members away from the older denominations.[10]

As one of the primary destinations for black migrants leaving the Deep South between 1915 and 1950, Cleveland provides ample opportunity to understand southern migrants' struggles to build churches, shape worship practices, and retain the connections between their spiritual and secular lives. Even as migrants debated the role of churches in their lives, churches—as institutions and places of worship—could at once sustain or undermine secular activism. While some ministers and congregations eschewed black working-class needs, religious values and beliefs infused black workers' activism in their communities and workplaces. Rather than viewing the proliferation of churches as an indication of fragmentation in the community that eventually thwarted blacks' efforts to shape their lives in the urban setting, this essay examines working-class migrants' efforts to build churches and their insistence that these churches reinforce self-activity and provide resources for their activism.

Longtime black residents boasted that Cleveland had the largest native-born black population in Ohio before 1900. The dramatic influx of southerners over the next half-century elevated its status as one of the most popular destinations for the more than one million migrants seeking homes in the urban Midwest. Between 1910 and 1930, the black population exploded from 8,500 to over 71,000, which propelled the city into second place behind Detroit for the largest growth in the black population. By the start of World War II, the population exceeded 84,000, over half of whom were migrants from Alabama, with the remainder coming from other states in the Deep South.[11] The steady influx of migrants continually rejuvenated the southernness of black Cleveland, and by the eve of World War II, the black population had a distinctly southern character, evident in its churches, street life, and leisure activities.[12]

Over these four decades, the African-American population overflowed its small enclave, soon occupying a significant portion of the eastside neighborhoods in an increasingly segregated city. By the last third of the nineteenth century, the majority of the city's small black population shared neighborhoods with a predominantly eastern European immigrant mix clustered around the Haymarket district. With the rapid influx of migrants after 1915, however, black neighborhoods expanded northward into the Central Area and to the south into the Woodland Area. The intense concentration of African Americans in neighborhoods that once had been inhabited by immigrants was a dramatic change from the first decade of the twentieth century. As migration continued through the interwar years, blacks lived in every ward in these two areas, with 60 percent clustered between East Fifty-fifth Street and Euclid Avenue. By 1945, new migrants and longtime residents claimed neighborhoods abandoned by immigrants who moved to outlying suburbs. Within this context of growing segregation, African Americans made distinctions based on region and class in their private and public associations.[13]

At the start of the Great Migration in 1915, longtime black working- and middle-class residents had differing interpretations of the impact newcomers from the South made on the community.[14] While they applauded blacks' greater access to industrial jobs brought about by the war, leaders openly worried that the new migrants from the Deep South might incite violence as they sought jobs and settled into immigrant neighborhoods. When attacks against blacks rose and informal (but often forceful) segregation increased after 1916, many of the longtime residents correlated the changes with the Deep South origins of the migrants.[15] Alarmed by riots occurring in other midwestern cities, some leaders responded by turning their attention to changing the behavior of the migrants. Harry C. Smith, editor of the *Cleveland Gazette*, urged the local branch of the National Association for the Advancement of Colored People (NAACP) "to go to the various plants in the city and talk to the newcomers from the South and tell them how to conduct themselves in public places so as to help and not hurt *our* people of *this* community."[16] Some felt outnumbered by what they saw as a "backward" population "who are proving so harmful to all our people of this community."[17] An editorial in the *Cleveland Gazette* suggested that one white man's declaration that "down south they make the niggers ride in the back end of streetcars and they ought to do the same here" might happen. The *Gazette* warned "If the loud-mouthed Negro here is not soon curbed, we may wake up some fine day and find this true here." Migrants were regularly criticized for the impropriety of their public behavior in the streets, workplaces, and leisure settings.[18]

In these anecdotes, leaders used the threat of rising segregation to chastise blacks' public behavior. Experience had taught longtime residents that they had to be vigilant in their efforts to prevent segregation. Their right to challenge their exclusion from public life, however, rested on behavior that was above reproach. The numerous editorials in the *Gazette* decrying migrants' public behavior revealed black elites' anxiety that the sheer volume of recent migrants with connections to the Deep South would threaten their social relations with whites. In the black press, on shop floors, and in the social welfare agencies, black leaders preached respectable behavior as an antidote to antiblack sentiments. Black elites conceded that the "the rising tide of segregation" could not be causally linked to either the arrival of migrants or their behavior, but their pronouncements nonetheless carried the marked distrust of Deep South traditions held by many longtime residents.[19]

Though migration tapered off somewhat after World War I, longtime residents continued to point out the cultural and behavioral differences between themselves and the new arrivals. These tensions remained in the postwar years as African Americans continued to stress the regional differences—interpreted as historical differences—between the migrants and the longtime residents. George Myers, the most influential African American in the local Republican party, articulated this tendency in a letter to Yale historian James Rhodes: "Many of the Negroes are of the lowest and shiftless class from when [*sic*] they came. We here 'to the manor born,' so to speak, are doing all we can to assimilute [*sic*] them. Our greatest task is to get them to see themselves from a northern, instead of a southern standpoint and leave their old condition and customs back in the South. Speaking in the vernacular—to quit being a southern darkey."[20] Elmer Thompson, the son of migrants, considered such distinctions too sharply drawn: "You see with me, it was just a case of one coming sooner than the other. We were all trying to get away from the cotton fields."[21]

As they had done for nearly a century prior to the influx of so many migrants, black churches sought to mediate the community's debates and provide a range of resources. Since the early part of the nineteenth century, most African Americans in Cleveland worshiped in either the all-black Methodist or Baptist churches, with much smaller populations belonging to Catholic, Congregational, or Episcopal churches. By 1910, fourteen churches served the eighty-five hundred African-American residents.[22] Many of these churches prided themselves on their educated pastors and well-organized memberships, as well as the gentility that both represented. In addition, ownership of church property indicated their financial and denominational stability.[23] While the black middle class and elite did not belong to any one church or denomination, membership patterns were nonetheless discernible. Many in this small population attended either Mt. Zion Congregational Church or St. Andrew's Episcopal Church.[24] More recently arrived middle-class blacks tended to affiliate with either St. James A.M.E. Church, Shiloh Baptist Church, or Antioch Baptist Church. Over the course of the 1920s, the middle and professional classes came to dominate the leadership roles in the older and larger A.M.E. and Baptist churches.

As migrants arrived, they first turned to the churches in their neighborhoods, adding to these congregations and strengthening their financial base. With much larger congregations, many churches had or were able to purchase or build new buildings. Both Triedstone Baptist Church and Friendship Baptist Church, for example, struggled after their formation at the turn of the century. By World War I, each had grown enough to buy larger churches.[25] By the mid-1920s, the membership at Antioch Baptist Church had grown from 500 to 1,400 and Shiloh Baptist gained over 3,000 new members, increasing its congregation to over 5,000. With larger memberships, both purchased bigger churches from departing white congregations.[26] Others followed this pattern. Many of these structures had been built at the turn of the century and had a neo-medieval architecture, which at once distinguished the established congregations from the growing number of storefront churches. Though each congregation would re-create the physical space to meet its needs, each congregation was nonetheless aware that the new location of their church carried implications of prestige and legitimacy.[27]

Dramatic expansion in church activities followed the explosion in church membership. Members of St. John A.M.E. saw the arrival of the migrants as a "new burden." Some churches responded by creating new organizations designed to address the needs of the migrants. Women frequently took the lead in these efforts, drawing upon a dense network of private societies and professional ties. Hazel Mountain, a prominent teacher and secretary of the statewide Ohio Federation for Uplift among Colored People, organized black women in the city who were associated with social welfare work. Within these efforts sponsored by the churches, women displayed a keen awareness of the limited resources available from other private organizations. Black women showed genuine concern about children traveling alone, and young women and men who were ill and dying, bereft of family. Various women's clubs in the churches formed the Helping Hand Charity Club in the summer of 1917 to raise money for migrants without adequate food or shelter.[28]

After the war, the larger black churches continued to provide resources to meet the religious, social, and economic needs of the community, but the tone of these efforts changed, revealing class divisions. Most of the large churches held a variety of evening and weekend classes to provide migrants with instructions on upright living habits, such as proper hygiene and the use of cutlery. Occasionally churches offered health care for pregnant and nursing women, inoculations for children, and visits with dentists. While migrants with little money for such services eagerly stood in long lines, they frequently received sharp critiques of their poverty as demonstrations of their backwardness because of their race and regional origins. There was, as several historians have persuasively argued, a conservative and racist shape to the rhetoric of racial uplift. The emphasis on thrift and cleanliness, for example, was not simply an attempt to inculcate values of self-help but rather an admonition designed to counter a widely shared perception of the "negative practices and behavior" of blacks.[29]

However much the tone in some congregations shifted toward a negative assessment of the new arrivals, for many migrants, particularly for live-in domestic workers, church activities became the one opportunity to mingle in the community. Many women sent children off to Sunday schools and received a much-needed reprieve from child care. On any Sunday afternoon throughout the decade, black Clevelanders could attend concerts and lecture series at Antioch Baptist Church or debates at St. John A.M.E. Church. In 1927, St. James A.M.E. Church, one of the churches with a significant population of longtime and middle-class congregations, became known as a center for cultural debate through its weekly literary forums. Young black men and women like William Murdock went to hear W. E. B. Du Bois, George C. Schuyler, Walter White, Mary McLeod Bethune, and Carter G. Woodson, among other prominent speakers. These programs proved so popular that other churches quickly copied them.[30]

The cultural activities at these churches continued the historic role of black churches as social places. In Cleveland, custom not law barred blacks from public spaces. Black clubs and organizations had little, if any, access to spaces owned or frequented by whites; the few amusement parks and dance halls that did admit blacks did so in a segregated manner. Though the social welfare agencies expanded their activities to accommodate the growing black population, they soon replicated the patterns of segregation mushrooming throughout the city. Increasingly, therefore, the larger black churches provided space for secular activities, sponsored by a variety of clubs and fraternal organizations such as the Knights of Pythias.[31] The differing resources that the older and larger churches provided strengthened their role as critical institutions.

Many migrants first joined the older churches that downplayed the expressive worship more prevalent in the rural and smaller urban churches in the South. Since the turn of the century, however, the churches in Cleveland had eradicated highly expressive worship styles. Even though his parents had just arrived in Cleveland from the South in 1906, Elmer

Thompson had witnessed their rapid adaptation to the more subdued worship practices by the end of the decade. The Thompson family was one of a few migrant families during these years, which might have hastened their adaptation. Thompson vividly remembered his more recently migrated grandmother's ecstatic responses to the preaching each Sunday. "Before we went to church, my sister would ask, 'You're not going to shout today, are you?'" Thompson recognized both the class and regional distinctions increasingly evident in church membership; shouting had been discouraged. Migrants like Thompson's grandmother sparked renewed efforts to diminish overly expressive behavior during church services. "That was the difference in the black churches. The more education the people had, the less noise you heard out of them."[32] By the early 1920s, many of the church leaders in the older denominations with educated ministers pondered just how to make their services less emotional.[33]

In a series of articles in the *Gazette* after World War I, Reverend William A. Byrd scolded migrants, proclaiming that "the decorum of the Colored churches should be improved. The wild outbursts of frantic emotionalism should be discouraged." Instead, he urged "the sane presentation of the truth in a dignified" manner. Byrd contemptuously complained that migration forced educated members to suffer the boorishness of the uneducated migrants and their ministers. "The Colored youth of the North receives the same training in thought, language, rhetoric, reasoning and speech that other youths receive. But the greater portion of these youths on the Sabbath day must listen to the ramblings and disconnected discourses, loud and boisterous ravings, ancient emotionalism and cant in addition to the murder of almost every principle of the English language."[34] In the face of such behavior, Byrd advocated middle-class values of racial uplift, where decorum, intellect, and the influence of an educated ministry would prevail.[35] Such denunciations of migrants' styles of worship led them to create new churches more tolerant of ecstatic worship, reasoning, as Reverend Frank Smith did, that middle-class ministers and their congregations felt "the Lord didn't need to hear all that shouting."[36]

Reverend Frank A. Smith arrived in Cleveland from Monticello, Georgia, just after the turn of the century. Although a child at the time, Smith recalled that his parents, along with other migrants from the small town, "were told that they could get employment here in Cleveland." Smith's family immediately began attending Cory Methodist Church, one of the oldest African-American Methodist churches in the city, but they soon became dissatisfied with the services. Joined by seven other migrant families from their town and other areas nearby, the Smith family held prayer meetings. Smith clearly remembered that "they were strangers here and they didn't like the other churches. They wanted a church where they could worship according to the way they had been used to [in Georgia]." The migrants formed Lane Memorial C.M.E. Church on 13 June 1902, first meeting in a church building purchased from a white congregation. After a large parade down the streets of the Central Area, in 1918, the black congregants settled permanently in a church previously owned by Christian Scientists.[37]

Years after Lane Memorial's founding, Reverend Smith recalled how important it had been for migrants to reject the subdued demeanor of the A.M.E. churches in Cleveland. "Some of the folks had become sort of sophisticated," recalled Smith, "and didn't have the 'Amens' that they were used to." More troubling, the migrants felt that longtime church members "didn't want the southern people up here. So it was a mutual situation. They didn't want us, and we didn't want them." The sentiments of the first members struck a responsive chord as other migrants from the South joined the church, swelling the membership into the hundreds by the next decade. For the next several decades, Lane Memorial (later Metropolitan) continued to attract hundreds of migrants because its longtime membership still practiced "familiar styles" of worship.[38]

Similarly, thirty-seven members of the Mt. Haven Baptist Church, dissatisfied with the moderate preaching in the city's churches, left the congregation as a group and organized Second Emmanuel in 1916. The church first settled in a storefront, but members soon acquired the money to purchase a building after a series of rallies to raise the necessary funds. By 1923, the church had six hundred members and a Sunday school.[39] Further examples of a church splintering over styles of worship occurred at about the same time in the Triedstone Baptist Church. In the mid-1920s, the Alabama Club and the minister at the Triedstone began to disagree. By 1926, these disgruntled members—most of them older migrants— formed Mt. Carmel Baptist Church. This congregation soon merged with members of St. Paul Baptist, which had formed out of unhappy members at Shiloh, and together they formed Mt. Hermon Baptist Church.[40] Several years later, another group of migrants at Triedstone left over intradenominational differences over worship practices. In 1931, forty members left Triedstone and organized the New Light Baptist Church; they changed their name to Olivet Baptist Church in 1933.[41]

Many of these new congregations did not have the resources to move quickly out of storefronts, theaters, and homes, but criticisms of the location of many of these new churches did not inhibit their growth. Marie Crawford helped organize one such storefront church in 1916. The first services took place in a white church until "those good white Christians got tired of us." The services were then held over a nightclub on East Fifty-fifth Street. Crawford recalled: "I tell my people in the church never get so proud to think we weren't a storefront. We were up over a storefront. The [nightclub] people that church people called wicked, they welcomed us and treated us better than those dear Christians did."[42]

Similarly, building a church rather than purchasing one remained elusive for many congregations. A small prayer group of mostly poor migrants from the South found that though they had the land, building Union Baptist Church could be a slow endeavor. Estimating that they needed fifty thousand bricks, they left a sign on the property pleading with passersby to "throw a brick over the fence" to hasten the process.[43]

Even in the face of such difficulties, African Americans' church affiliation and participation increased in relation to the greatly expanded population. Between 1920 and 1930, the Federated Churches of Cleveland reported that the number of black churches had grown from 54 to 132, with 60 percent of black Clevelanders affiliated. As in the early part of the century, over half the membership belonged to large churches that the congregations had either built or bought. While independent storefronts had made up just a fraction of the community's churches prior to 1920, by 1930 a majority of the churches were storefronts organized by recent migrants. Many of these the congregants could be identified as working class. Most often, these newer denominations were more associated with the working class than the middle class.[44] Some of these churches either folded not long after their formation or moved frequently, though the city's directories reveal that many attracted members and eventually purchased or built churches. C. Eric Lincoln documented this process in other cities with large populations of black migrants: "If [the migrants] did not feel comfortable in the large established churches, they helped to create smaller ones by first meeting in homes, then renting storefronts, and later purchasing their own church edifices."[45]

For many migrants, their worship practices either represented continuities with their southern past or an effort to acculturate into the northern setting. That many migrants shifted into or later organized churches that deliberately sought to retain southern-style ecstatic worship after they had first joined the already established churches signaled a desire to reaffirm their traditions. While many migrant churches slowly adopted more formal styles of worship, the influx of new migrants sustained the shouts, hollers, and fainting as each group helped to reaffirm their roots in the sacred traditions of the rural South. As Lawrence Levine has aptly noted: "Negro acculturation has been a complex process of shifting emphases and reaffirmations: of permitting certain new traits to permeate but of simultaneously re-emphasizing specific traditional loyalties and characteristics."[46] As we have seen, not all migrants left the older churches, choosing instead to participate in the more subdued and formal styles of northern worship. Some migrants, who had left these churches for new ones, occasionally returned to older churches as they identified as northerners or claimed middle-class social status. This pattern was most evident amongst the children of migrants who were either too young to remember the South or had been born in the North.[47]

Scattered but consistent evidence shows that longtime working-class black church members felt marginal in their churches as well. Increased differentiation along class and professional lines amongst longtime residents occurred simultaneous to migrants' church building. Geraldine Daniel's family had belonged to Shiloh since its creation in the 1850s. By the 1920s, rumors of the minister's contempt for congregants who worked as common laborers circulated through the church. Both Daniel and her older sister worked for the minister and both felt that he "barely acknowledged our help." Daniel, like other members of Shiloh, left for churches that they believed better met their needs. The Daniels' departure was precipitated by the minister's behavior, not a desire to break with her family's long ties to the church. Her grandmother, too, left the church when the minister accused her of stealing coal. Daniel joined Liberty Hill Baptist Church—formed by working-class migrants from Alabama—where she stayed a member for some time.[48]

Migrants' affiliation with a church continued a pattern developed in the rural South where churches provided spiritual sustenance, social contact, and most of the entertainment. For young women in particular, rural churches offered one of the few opportunities to meet young men under the watchful gaze of parents.[49] In Cleveland, migrants continued these patterns, with the added pleasure that churches were in their own neighborhoods and ministers held services each week. While many initially attended the established churches in their neighborhoods, they often found that they were marginal to the activities of those congregations. Elizabeth Clark-Lewis noted in her study of black migration to Washington, D.C., that black migrants in the city churches "felt relegated to the periphery of activity."[50] Black migrants to Cleveland found that churches helped them adjust to the city by providing contact with those already established. But these new urban dwellers also intended to make the city their own and many moved to become active and not passive participants in churches. In the larger churches middle-class congregants typically held the most prominent positions; working-class migrants found it especially difficult to become leaders of deacons', trustees', and mothers' boards.[51]

Though hampered by obligations of work and family, many black congregants nonetheless participated in church activities throughout the week in various committees and choir rehearsals. As churches increased their membership they tended to increase the number of organizations, not the size of the older committees. Such patterns demonstrate church members' desire to actively participate. Even small churches had Sunday schools and boards to assist the pastor. Often, these committees, trustee boards, missionary societies, and choirs were established along lines of gender, age, and length of membership.[52] In the larger churches, a variety of clubs emerged to meet social demands. By the early 1940s, the overwhelmingly southern congregation of St. Timothy Missionary Baptist Church formed over forty committees, including deacons' and trustees' boards, a mothers' board, six choirs, three usher boards, a pastor's aid club, a Sunday school, and a layman's league. They also formed six state clubs for members from Alabama, West Virginia, Tennessee, Georgia, Kentucky, and North Carolina. In its literature, the church affirmed its commitment to broad-based participation: "The Church where everybody is somebody."[53]

Church membership grew fastest in the Pentecostal, Holiness, Apostolic (originally Ethiopian), and nondenominational Sanctified churches, so much so that by the late 1930s these churches predominated. These new denominations, formed at the end of the nineteenth century, emphasized personally received faith. Unlike the older denominations, each emphasized ecstatic worship.[54] The shift toward these churches occurred *after* blacks migrated first to the urban South and then the urban North. Dissatisfied with the increasingly staid Baptist and Methodist practices, migrants in Cleveland formed the first churches in these denominations in the state. Located in former stores, taverns, and theaters, these churches settled in the heart of the Central Avenue area in the midst of the migrant population. Many of these churches literally appeared in the wake of migrants' arrivals, rather than through the conversion of longtime residents. Others emerged out of the numerous revivals now common in the city, with itinerant ministers from the South holding tent meetings that featured lively music and highly emotional, ecstatic worship punctuated by chants, shouts, weeping, and dancing. Large crowds attended these nightly meetings that frequently continued for several weeks.[55] The frequency of these revivals did not go unnoticed. An article in the *Cleveland Gazette* bemoaned "that corner 'preaching,' yelling, shouting, monkey-shines, comedian business, etc., etc. Stop it!"[56]

The worship in these new churches appealed to migrants' religious behavior in the South, particularly the rural areas regardless of denomination. Unlike the older denominations in Cleveland, members of the Sanctified churches were expected to actively participate in services. By testifying their faith (or struggles with faith) and initiating songs, participants could demonstrate their conversion and salvation. Ministers who delivered sermons in quasi-metrical units, thumped lecterns, and stomped their feet, reinforced their congregations' permission to continue in their own vocalizations.[57] As one ethnomusicologist has suggested, the weekly testifying in Black Holiness and Pentecostal churches provided members with "confirmation, protection, and sustenance." Within their various services and prayer meetings, African-American "worshipers have long sung, spoken, and enacted the positive and therapeutic involvement of God in their lives, thereby intensifying their individual faith and their community strength as they endure the ways of the world."[58] More to the point, some aspects of these worship practices continued African traditions rarely seen in northern churches. The rhythmic patting of the body, for instance, replaced the drum commonly used in African worship. Jon Spencer has noted that the body, like the drum, acted "as a sacred instrument possessing supernatural power that enables it to summon the gods into ritual communion with the people."[59]

African Americans' growing preference for a capella gospel music escalated the tensions over ecstatic worship in many congregations. Before the arrival of migrants, African-American worshipers in the older churches typically sang classical Protestant hymns and anthems. In the Episcopalian, Congregational, and Presbyterian churches, members insisted on regular performances of European-influenced Protestant hymns and not traditional African-American sacred music. In the mainline Methodist and Baptist congregations, some members who had graduated from Fisk University had organized jubilee choirs that sang European-influenced spirituals. The growing presence of a professional elite with a northern college education enhanced the trend toward highly trained choirs, music directors, and hymnals rather than improvisation, congregational participation, and ministers.[60]

In sharp contrast, in the Holiness, Pentecostal, and the smaller Baptist and Methodist missions, southern black rural and working-class sacred music flourished. Noble Sissle, whose father, Reverend George A. Sissle, was pastor of Cory Methodist Episcopal Church in 1906, recalled the infectious music: "I used to get a great thrill when my father or some member of the congregation would lead us in hymn, reading off the lyrics ahead of us. Then everyone would join in and every foot would keep time, and soon the whole church would be swaying in rhythm or patting their hands and feet. Whenever I sing a rhythm song—even today—I still pat my foot in the same way."[61] Though more traditional, these jubilee spirituals, Baptist lining hymns, shape-note hymns, and Watts hymns still did not match the highly spirited rhythms and instrumentations in the Holiness and Pentecostal churches with their tambourines, hand clapping, and ecstatic singing and vocalizations. Though describing a Holiness church in Chicago, Langston Hughes had just left Cleveland and could have similarly characterized worship in the latter city: "I was entranced by their stepped-up rhythms, tambourines, hand-clapping, and uninhibited dynamics. The music of these less formal Negro churches early took hold of me, moved me, and thrilled me."[62]

African-American workers who arrived from Alabama brought with them an experience with gospel quartets. Abundant oral testimony and more conventional evidence confirms that the work camps around Birmingham, Bessemer, and other areas of Jefferson County were the seedbed for gospel quartet singing. As thousands of workers arrived, they carried a range of sacred and secular music practices rooted in African and Anglo-American traditions.[63] While these quartets were most influenced by jubilee quartets from Fisk and Tuskegee, black sacred music from rural areas equally shaped early gospel quartets. One historian has noted that by the turn of the century, while "black quartet singing existed at every level of black culture," it was particularly prevalent amongst black workers who tended to belong to smaller Baptist churches or the emerging Holiness and Pentecostal churches. Equally important, many of these singers were Baptists and sought to offer more spirited singing than their congregations allowed; their music and performances, however, were more refined than the ecstatic singing in the Holiness and Pentecostal churches. Now in the context of the camps of the mills and mines, gospel quartets performed and perfected their styles. As they began to perform for local churches, they adapted their style to accommodate enthusiastic responses to the music. In these early performances, quartets were influenced by their audiences, creating a folk style that allowed rhythmic movements, vocal embellishments, and greater vocal ranges common in churches and not universities.[64] Known for their tight harmonies, these quartets mesmerized listeners through great skill and meticulous control. Though quartet singing allowed for call-and-response, an emphasis on close harmony meant that few could tell the voices apart.[65]

Much credit has been given to Thomas Dorsey's inarguably prominent role in shaping hard gospel in the early 1930s. Yet local and traveling quartets and the quickly emerging gospel quartets of the 1910s and 1920s did the hard work of making gospel popular and acceptable through their close harmony, dignity, and personal testimony. As Lawrence Levine has concluded, gospel music in style and presentation returned to "black church music the sounds and structure of the folk spirituals, work songs, and nineteenth-century cries and hollers; [gospel singers and composers] borrowed freely from the ragtime, blues and jazz of the secular black world."[66] In a single program, quartets like the Dunham Jubilee Singers answered the ironic songs of despair in the secular blues with the sacred songs of hope. Their song "Your Mama's Baby Child" depicted a son gone wild once he moved to Cleveland, but the group's "Lord Don't Pass Me By" contained the hope and faith of migration, like the hope for heaven, as a continuing possibility.[67] On a more personal level, these gospel hymns—rendered in highly ecstatic styles—armed performers and listeners with spiritual strength and the promise of redemption.

Beyond spiritual sustenance, gospel music in both its textual and performance strategies advanced more secular goals for individuals and their community. Hardly as otherworldly as some have claimed, gospel's emphasis on personal agency often depicted a militant Jesus Christ who scorned segregationists. In performances and in their identifications as gospel quartet singers, black men and women presented themselves as competent and skilled. African-American men presented images of elegance, challenging the now dominant image of them as dangerous. Only a minority of quartet singers were black women, but they took on male voices as tenors, basses, and baritones, tweaking the more narrow definitions of ladylike behavior advanced by middle-class black women. Most important, the sacred quartet singing that continued outside Sunday morning rituals—and outside middle-class churches—advanced a working-class congregational autonomy.

With their financial stability significantly weakened by the Great Depression, many ministers found their stand against gospel crumbling in the face of competition from other congregations that had embraced such music. While gospel choirs and soloists became increasingly prominent, gospel quartets remained outside Sunday morning worship. Instead, they typically performed in afternoon and evening services. Others led the midweek prayer services, held special programs to raise money for church buildings, or celebrated ministers' and congregations' anniversaries. Quartet singers appreciated the autonomy that such divisions provided. Though now considered part of the church services, quartet singers could push the boundaries of decorum when they performed outside church rituals. As many quartets focused on gospel songs, members typically began their programs with testimonials of their salvation from sin and their faith "in Jesus." Gospel quartet singing provided men and women the opportunity simultaneously to preach and to entertain. Arthur Turner put it simply: by singing gospel he "could lead a Christian life."[68]

As many migrants sought to expand their participation in their congregations, black women searched for access to leadership roles, finding opportunities in the nondenominational Sanctified churches. Within the Holiness and Pentecostal churches, black women formed the majority of the membership and often had control over the finances of their congregations. But just as the A.M.E. and Baptist churches had prohibitions against female ministers, these new denominations limited women's roles as pastors.[69] Instead, women called to minister established their own Spiritualist congregations that blended Protestant and Catholic rituals. In 1931, Addie M. Battle organized the Mt. Zion Holy Trinity Spiritual Church after a vision instructed her to leave her church and become a "prophet for the Lord." Although she did not envision herself as a female Father Divine or Daddy Grace, she did see herself as one of "God's chosen prophets endowed with the same power and privileges as St. John or Paul, the Apostle." Not tied to any denomination, her church blended theology and worship practices found in Catholic and Pentecostal churches. Dressed in white, she held her services in the kitchen.[70]

Along with an eclectic theology, Battle offered her largely female congregation a model for resistance in their lives as workers and family members. Communal prayers often focused on retaining dignity in the face of dismissive employers. In response to one member's plea for advice to halt the abuse she regularly received from an employer, Battle urged her to simultaneously "be careful on your job and keep your determination." Offering what was commonly called "motherwit"—a mixture of secular and spiritual wisdom—Battle demonstrated that black ecstatic worship was more than emotional outbursts and otherworldly exhortations. Services like hers enabled women and men to speak openly and collectively about their daily experiences as workers, migrants, and spiritual people. Her advice, in turn, specifically addressed these concerns, while affirming the individual's right to act on her own behalf.[71]

Battle and other women ministers provided particular guidance for women for their private lives. Battle offered consultations, spiritual advice, and comfort from the "many worldly problems involving love, money, and marital difficulties." She only required "faith from those seeking her help, plus the proper amount of finance," typically $2, to supplement her income. Battle urged wives to leave adulterous husbands and encouraged single women to socialize with male members of the church. The female pastor for the Jesus Only Church of God received no special salary, only donations from her working-class members, who attended services in her home. The largely female congregation of the Jesus Only Church of God had an elaborate list of prohibitions, including "adultery, fornication, lying and joking, back-biting, whoremongering, smoking, drinking, chewing tobacco, dipping snuff, dancing in public, wearing lipstick, earrings, beads, or short skirts."[72] Since female ministers advanced (and modeled) female independence and leadership, the insistence on restrained female public behavior suggests differences from the patterns of moral policing found in middle-class churches. Here, working-class blacks may have placed limitations on their own behavior, rather than simply accepting those handed down by the black middle class.[73]

As African Americans debated how they worshiped, they also pondered what role churches would play in their secular relations with the dominant white society. As in other northern cities, many of the older churches in Cleveland saw themselves as centers of worship and dispensers of critical resources. As churches underwent transformations in their membership, the leadership cadre of the city changed as well. While ministers remained prominent in the community, politics and the professions provided new opportunities for educated men and women. If, or how, a church participated in the political and economic life of the city increasingly depended on the personal qualities and ambitions of a minister, or the demands of the congregation. Though some elites were either supportive or ambivalent toward Booker T. Washington's ideas, for example, on the whole black Clevelanders proudly earned the reputation as vocal and sharp critics of the accommodationist. Still, from the pulpit in the large, traditional Protestant churches, black ministers continued to advocate a work ethic framed by belief in self-help, diligence, thrift, and capitalism. Few ministers openly critiqued employers or their policies that typically excluded or limited black workers' access to higher paying jobs.[74]

Black ministers may have muted or eliminated their open critiques of impediments to blacks' employment in the city not because of direct pressure from employers but rather because of the growing importance of black professionals within the city's social welfare system. Though some congregations solicited and received contributions from white employers to build or purchase churches, black ministers did not receive salaries or

advice form white business elites. Wealthy whites channeled their philanthropy through a highly organized system in the city that designated secular, not spiritual, organizations for funds. Within black churches, there
arose a growing population of black middle-class men and women whose
personal ties and professional expertise were intimately tied to white philanthropy. This indirect but nonetheless important link between black
churches and white employers is evident in William O'Conner's role as
mediator between a white business elite and the black community. O'Conner headed the Negro Welfare League (renamed the Cleveland Urban
League after World War I), whose main purpose was to "adjust" black
workers to industrial employment. Its funds were provided by, and its
executive board was made up of, white business owners and managers
committed to the open shop. O'Conner provided employment in the
Urban League and recommendations for other blacks in search of white-
collar work. In addition, black migrants in search of industrial employment first had to register with his Urban League. With such complicated
connections between black professionals and white employers, it became
common for the former, not black ministers, to hurl invectives at unions
and blacks who participated in workplace struggles. If churches provided
the space for community members to speak to each other, a professional
black class with interests rooted in the white business community had
increasing sway with their congregations. In this context, then, ministers'
silence about the needs of black workers served the interests of white
employers, but many black professionals had some interest as well.[75]

Even as ministers and elites sought to inculcate values that downplayed
unions, they nonetheless had to contend with black workers' self-organi-
zation around workplace concerns. Since the late nineteenth century, the
small population of black union members witnessed an erosion in their
right to participate in unions. Few black leaders condemned the growing
pattern of segregation in white unions' activities in the city, and many of
these leaders openly voiced anti-union sentiments. Yet black workers did
not readily capitulate. In 1910, St. John A.M.E., the first and largest African Methodist church in the city, hosted a convention that assembled at
the church and launched a large parade featuring various bands from
A.M.E. churches around the state. Cleveland musicians, who had organized a separate black union after a long dispute with white musicians,
refused to march with the unorganized groups. The middle-class leadership of St. John offered no support to its union members, later chastising
them in a church newsletter that labor issues had no place in the church.[76]
In the aftermath of black workers' highly visible participation in the long

1919 steel strike in Cleveland, community leaders and ministers used church meetings to warn black workers that association with labor agitators would cost them jobs in the only place where employment was still available.[77]

Similarly, while few middle-class blacks in Cleveland had much patience with Marcus Garvey and the Universal Negro Improvement Association (UNIA), Cleveland's black working class quickly joined. Unimpeded by middle class interference, the organization attracted thousands of men and women who labored as domestic workers and common laborers. In the first half of the 1920s, Garvey visited the city frequently and spoke at various churches. By the latter part of the decade, the Cleveland UNIA local had its own building complete with a chapel. Meetings tended to resemble the services of the nondenominational churches and more emotional New Light Baptists. Most black ministers denounced Garvey, but some became UNIA members and attended the meetings along with their congregation.[78]

As black workers waged a dual battle to gain access to employment and to labor unions throughout the 1920s, they challenged the pulpit to speak to their interests as laborers. In response to the pervasive racism in workplaces and union halls, black workers sought a modicum of control over their working lives through the formation of biracial unions and community-based labor associations. Few ministers publicly supported these endeavors; many in the largest and most prominent churches joined Urban League officials in denouncing workplace activism. Most often, ministers remained silent bystanders in such struggles. In spite of the ambivalent stances of ministers, black working-class members turned to their congregations for support. During the black waiters' and hotel workers' efforts to organize in 1929, for example, secular organizations within black churches, such as the caterers' clubs at Cory Methodist Church, provided strikers with support.[79]

While few ministers spoke out against employers' tactics, some, like prominent Antioch Baptist Church minister Reverend Wade McKinney, spoke in favor of black workers' organizing efforts. Antioch's ability to attract and retain migrants had much to do with McKinney's charismatic leadership. Like his new congregants, McKinney came from rural Alabama. Though his well-crafted sermons appealed to an educated black middle class, he also insisted that the church must be responsive to the economic needs of a struggling black working class. Unlike many of his peers, he did not, for example, make the causal link between blacks' personal behavior and their dire economic position in the city. Rather, in his weekly sermons and numerous editorials in the local black newspaper, McKinney offered a sharp critique of an economic system that demanded blacks' subordination, making it impossible for them to find work or create stable homes for their families. As many ministers denounced blacks' participation in protests at the start of the Great Depression (particularly those sponsored by the Communist Party), McKinney endorsed "courage and conflict" in secular life as exemplified by a "militant Christ."[80]

Throughout the 1930s, church-based clubs provided a location for black workers to organize support and financial assistance for the boycott and the unionization efforts of the Future Outlook League (FOL). Created in 1935 to launch a "Don't Buy Where You Can't Work" campaign, the FOL shifted its efforts toward organizing black workers in community-based unions. The FOL filled a vacuum left by the weakened local branch of the NAACP and the diminished clout of black Republican politicians. While the overwhelming majority of prominent ministers criticized the league, FOL members nonetheless drew on the associational base of churches to organize support. Like the UNIA, the ecstatic, charismatic style of worship shaped FOL meetings. Prayers, gospel music, and the call-and-response patterns of black preaching were common features. By the start of World War II, nearly all of the ministers with identifiable working-class congregations were either members of the FOL or publicly endorsed the league. Many allowed FOL meetings to take place in their churches and they offered financial support.[81]

Just how African-American workers linked organizing efforts with home and community organizations remains an important question. As this essay suggests, historians analyzing African-American communities in the wake of migration may have too narrowly conceived the links between black religiosity and working-class activism. The rapid church building and the shift toward more ecstatic worship may have been motivated as much by the debate about the role of churches in black folks' secular lives as by a desire to reestablish familiar styles of worship. Even as ministers may have endorsed the NAACP or decried racial discrimination in public spaces, most lent little support to blacks' workplace activism. Despite the imbalance in ministers' secular leadership, African Americans did not abandon churches or their religious beliefs to engage in labor activism. Indeed, values deeply rooted in Afro-Christianity that stressed self-determination, social responsibility, and accountability to the community gave many permission to participate in new forms of activism informed by religiosity. Rather than leaving their churches, black workers often drew on the resources of their congregations and goaded their ministers to respond to their needs. Such cross-fertilization could, at times, galvanize reluctant ministers and congregations to act.

The separate churches that working-class migrants created along class and regional lines reveal that shared neighborhoods and skin color did not make for a cohesive community. Class and gender, along with regional origin, time of migration, and ties to a regional culture, made community building a constantly negotiated process. The numerous churches working-class migrants created in the years between World War I and the start of World War II revealed a variety of efforts to shape their own lives. Most noticeably, this energetic religiosity attested to their desire to craft church spaces in their own image where they could meet regularly and hear ministers address their concerns as working-class southern migrants. These churches provided more than services for migrants' spirits and homes; in many instances, black churches and the religiosity they encouraged served as a catalyst for workplace organizing.

Notes

I want to thank Eric Arnesen, James R. Barrett, Kenneth Clark, Julie Greene, Bruce Laurie, and Patricia Miles Ashford for their comments and suggestions.

1. Sara Brooks, *You May Plow Here: The Narrative of Sara Brooks* (New York: Simon and Schuster, 1983), 221–22.

2. Personal interviews with Gus Joiner, 1 Nov. 1989, and Flowree Robinson, 29 Nov. 1989.

3. Interview with Bertha Cowan, St. James A.M.E. Oral History Project, 16 Jan. 1987, Western Reserve Historical Society (hereafter WRHS).

4. Robin D. G. Kelley, *Race Rebels: Culture, Politics, and the Black Working Class* (New York: Free Press, 1994), 42.

5. Lawrence Levine has asserted that since the late nineteenth century, African Americans' literacy "inevitably dilutes the predominance of the oral tradition and just as inevitably produces important shifts in the *Weltanschauung* of the group. Thus although it happened neither suddenly nor completely, the sacred world view so central to black slaves was to be shattered in the twentieth century" (*Black Culture and Black Consciousness: Afro-American Folk Thought from Slavery to Freedom* [New York: Oxford University Press, 1977], 158). Levine's argument has turned on African Americans' loss of oral tradition as a way of knowing the world. Some scholars have started to question this claim, instead focusing on emotion as a form of knowledge. See Peter D. Goldsmith, *When I Rise Cryin' Holy: African-American Denominationalism on the Georgia Coast* (New York: AMS Press, 1989), 57–58; Elsa Barkley Brown, "Negotiating and Transforming the Public Sphere: African American Political Life in the Transition from Slavery to Freedom," *Public Culture* 7 (1994): 107–46; Kelley, *Race Rebels*, 43. Kelley has asserted that divine intervention has remained a critical component of the African-American cosmos.

6. The older literature includes: St. Clair Drake, *Churches and Voluntary Associations in the Chicago Negro Community*, WPA Report (Chicago, 1940); Louise Venable Kennedy, *The Negro Peasant Turns Cityward: Effects of Recent Migrations to Northern Centers* (New York: Columbia University Press, 1930), 202–6; Benjamin Elijah Mays and Joseph William Nicholson, *The Negro's Church* (New York: Institute of Social and Religious Research, 1933); Arthur H. Fauset, *Black Gods of the Metropolis: Negro Religious Cults of the Urban North* (Philadelphia: University of Pennsylvania Press, 1944). Newer work includes some focus on black religious institutions; see: Allen R. Ballard, *One More Day's Journey: The Making of Black Philadelphia* (Philadelphia: Institute for the Study of Human Issues, 1984); Joe William Trotter, Jr., *Black Milwaukee: The Making of an Industrial Proletariat, 1915–45* (Urbana: University of Illinois Press, 1985); Peter Gottlieb, *Making Their Own Way: Southern Blacks' Migration to Pittsburgh* (Urbana: University of Illinois Press, 1987); James R. Grossman, *Land of Hope: Chicago, Black Southerners, and the Great Migration* (Chicago: University of Chicago Press, 1989); Carole Marks, *Farewell—We're Good and Gone: The Great Black Migration* (Bloomington: Indiana University Press, 1989); Joe William Trotter, Jr., and Peter Gottlieb, eds., *The Great Migration in Historical Perspective: New Dimensions of Race, Class, and Gender* (Bloomington: Indiana University Press, 1991); Robert Gregg, *Sparks from the Anvil of Oppression: Philadelphia's African American Methodists and Southern Migrants, 1890–1940* (Philadelphia: Temple University Press, 1994).

7. Gayraud S. Wilmore, *Black Religion and Black Radicalism: An Interpretation of the Religious History of Afro-American People*, 2d ed. (New York: Orbis Books, 1983), 152. For a more nuanced explanation, see C. Eric Lincoln and Lawrence H. Mamiya, *The Black Church in the African American Experience* (Durham, N.C.: Duke University Press, 1990).

8. W. E. B. Du Bois noted that by the turn of the century, African-American ministers were no longer preeminent in black communities and had become merely prominent. See W. E. B. Du Bois, *Souls of Black Folk* (1903; reprint, New York: Penguin Books, 1995), 190–92; William E. Montgomery, *Under Their Own Vine and Fig Tree: The African-American Church in the South, 1865–1900* (Baton Rouge: Louisiana State University Press, 1993), 307–32.

9. Elsa Barkley Brown and Gregg D. Kimball, "Mapping the Terrain of Black Richmond," in Kenneth W. Goings and Raymond A. Mohl, eds., *The New African American Urban History* (Thousand Oaks, Calif.: Sage Publications, 1996), 66–115; Earl Lewis, *In Their Own Interests: Race, Class, and Power in Twentieth Century Norfolk, Virginia* (Berkeley: University of California Press, 1991); Kelly, *Race Rebels*, 40–43; Evelyn Brooks Higginbotham, *Righteous Discontent: The Women's Movement in the Black Baptist Church, 1880–1920* (Cambridge, Mass.: Harvard University Press, 1993), 10.

10. For examples of these debates, see Montgomery, *Under Their Own Vine and Fig Tree*, 267–75.

11. United States Department of Commerce, *Negroes in the United States 1920–1932* (Washington, D.C.: Government Printing Office, 1935), 55; Kenneth Kusmer, *A Ghetto Takes Shape: Black Cleveland, 1870–1930* (Urbana: University of Illinois Press, 1976), 157–58; Gene B. Petersen, Laure M. Sharp, and Thomas F. Drury, *Southern Newcomers to Northern Cities: Work and Social Adjustment in Cleveland* (New York: Praeger, 1977), 1–12.

12. For an elaboration of this process, see Kimberley L. Phillips, *AlabamaNorth: African-American Migrants, Community, and Working-Class Activism in Cleveland, 1915–1945* (Urbana: University of Illinois Press, forthcoming).

13. Edward Miggins and Mary Morgenthaler, "The Ethnic Mosaic: The Settlement of Cleveland by the New Immigrants and Migrants," in Thomas F. Campbell and Edward M. Miggens, eds., *The Birth of Modern Cleveland* (Cleveland: Western Reserve Historical Society, 1988), 129.

14. Charles W. Chesnutt, "The Negro in Cleveland," *Clevelander* 5 (Nov. 1930): 3. Longtime residents' ambivalence about the arrival of migrants was not unique to Cleveland. For other examples, see Allan H. Spear, *Black Chicago: The Making of a Ghetto* (Chicago: University of Chicago Press, 1967), 168; Gottlieb, *Making Their Own Way*, 183–210; Marks, *Farewell—We're Good and Gone*, 160.

15. *Cleveland Gazette*, 30 July 1919.

16. Ibid., 20 Jan. 1917. After the report of violence at a local park, Smith urged blacks to "purchase a U.S. Army riot gun and plenty of ammunition for it and keep it in your home" (2 Aug. 1919). Efforts to inculcate proper behavior, however, were the norm.

17. Ibid., 19 May and 14 July 1917; personal interview with Reverend Frank A. Smith, 8 Aug. 1991. I am indebted to Patricia Miles Ashford for arranging for and participating in this interview.

18. *Cleveland Gazette*, 20 Jan. 1917 and 1 Mar. 1919.

19. For patterns of segregation and antiblack violence in Cleveland, see Kusmer, *Ghetto Takes Shape*, 53–65, 174–89. For conditions elsewhere, see Kenneth K. Gaines, *Uplifting the Race: Black Leadership, Politics, and Culture in the Twentieth Century* (Chapel Hill: University of North Carolina Press, 1996), 53.

20. Letter from George Myers to James Rhodes, 21 Feb. 1921, in John A. Garraty, ed., *The Barber and the Historian: the Correspondence of George A. Myers and James Ford Rhodes, 1910–1923* (Columbus: Ohio Historical Society, 1956), 124.

21. Thomas F. Campbell, interview with Elmer Thompson, Cleveland Heritage Foundation, Feb. 1981, Cleveland Public Library, Cleveland, Ohio.

22. Kusmer, *Ghetto Takes Shape*, 92–93, 207–9; Russell H. Davis, *Black Americans in Cleveland: From George Peake to Carl B. Stokes, 1796–1969* (Washington, D.C.: Association for the Study of Negro Life and History, 1972), 254–60; *The Baptist Answer in 1924–25: Being the 95th Annual Report of the Cleveland Baptist Association* (Cleveland, 1925); on African American Catholics, see Dorothy Ann Blatnica, *At the Altar of Their God: African American Catholics in Cleveland, 1922–1961* (New York: Garland, 1995). For an important overview of the growth and development of African-American religious institutions, see Lincoln and Mamiya, *Black Church in the African American Experience*; on the A.M.E. churches, see Clarence E. Walker, *A Rock in a Weary Land: The African Methodist Episcopal Church during the Civil War and Reconstruction* (Baton Rouge: Louisiana State University Press, 1982); Gregg, *Sparks from the Anvil of Oppression*.

23. Mays and Nicholson, *Negro's Church*; Lincoln and Mamiya, *Black Church in the African American Experience*; Foster Armstrong, Richard Klein, Cara Armstrong, *A Guide to Cleveland's Sacred Landmarks* (Kent, Ohio: Kent State University Press, 1992), 110–41.

24. Kusmer, *Ghetto Takes Shape*, 94.

25. Davis, *Black Americans in Cleveland*, 187–89. For an insightful and innovative discussion of the influence of built-space on African Americans' identities, see Brown and Kimball, "Mapping the Terrain of Black Richmond."

26. *Chicago Defender*, 24 May 1919; Armstrong, Klein, and Armstrong, *Guide to Cleveland's Sacred Landmarks*, 110–42.

27. *Chicago Defender,* 12 and 24 Feb. 1917; Lincoln and Mamiya, *Black Church in the African American Experience,* 121; Davis, *Black Americans in Cleveland,* 256–59; personal interview with Reverend Frank A. Smith. My interpretation of church architecture in Cleveland, generally, owes much to Jeanne Kilde, "Spiritual Armories: A Social and Architectural History of the Neo-Medieval Auditorium Church in the U.S., 1869–1910" (Ph.D. dissertation, University of Minnesota, 1991).

28. *Cleveland Gazette,* 14 July and 11 Aug. 1917.

29. Higginbotham, *Righteous Discontent,* 187; for a lengthy discussion of these perceptions, see Gaines, *Uplifting the Race,* 67–99.

30. Davis, *Black Americans in Cleveland,* 255–59; Chicago *Defender,* 17 May 1919; personal interview with Willa Davenport Thomas, 1 Dec. 1989; and Gwen Gregory Johnson, 16 Dec. 1991; interview with William Murdock, 19 Sept. 1986, St. James A.M.E. Oral History Project, WRHS.

31. For the development of segregated social welfare agencies and working-class black responses, see Adrienne Jones, *Jane Edna Hunter: A Case Study of Black Leadership, 1910–1959* (New York: Carlson, 1990); Kusmer, *Ghetto Takes Shape,* 149–51, 258–59.

32. Interview with Elmer Thompson; George Myers, "Religious Unity Is Presently Needed," *Cleveland Advocate,* 26 June 1915.

33. Personal interview with Reverend Frank A. Smith; Reverend Frank A. Smith, *A Pilgrimage in Faith: The History of Lane Metropolitan Christian Methodist Episcopal Church, 1902–1984,* pamphlet (Cleveland: n.p., 1984), 1.

34. *Cleveland Gazette,* 20 Jan. 1918.

35. For a discussion of these attitudes, see Gaines, *Uplifting the Race,* 88–93; and Higginbotham, *Righteous Discontent,* 42–47.

36. Personal interview with Reverend Frank A. Smith.

37. Ibid.; Smith, *Pilgrimage in Faith,* 1; Armstrong, Klein, and Armstrong, *Guide to Cleveland's Sacred Landmarks,* 122–23.

38. Personal interview with Reverend Frank A. Smith.

39. Ohio Church Survey Records, 1940, Ohio Works Progress Administration, box 1, Ohio Historical Society, Columbus, Ohio (hereafter OHS).

40. James E. Blackwell, "Black Storefront Churches in Cleveland: A Comparative Study of Five Negro Store Front Churches in Cleveland" (M.A. thesis, Western Reserve University, 1949), 23–24; Davis, *Black Americans in Cleveland,* 297.

41. Davis, *Black Americans in Cleveland,* 297; Lincoln and Mamiya, *Black Church in the African American Experience,* 22–23.

42. Interview with Marie Crawford, 20 Oct. 1986, St. James A.M.E. Oral History Project, WRHS.

43. Photograph, n.d., *Cleveland Press* Archives, Cleveland State University, Cleveland, Ohio.

44. *Cleveland Plain Dealer,* 22 Sept. 1930; Davis, *Black Americans in Cleveland,* 254.

45. Lincoln and Mamiya, *Black Church in the African American Experience,* 117.

46. Levine, *Black Culture and Black Consciousness,* 189.

47. Many of the men and women interviewed for the St. James A.M.E. Church oral history project self-consciously identified themselves and their church as middle-class. In other instances, the interviewees noted that the neighborhood surrounding the church was generally perceived as a middle-class neighborhood.

48. Interview with Geraldine Daniel, St. James A.M.E. Oral History Project, 28 Oct. 1986.

49. Interview with Bertha Cowan; Elizabeth Clark-Lewis, *Living In, Living Out: African American Domestics in Washington, D. C., 1910–1940* (Washington, D.C.: Smithsonian Institution Press, 1994), 34–38.

50. Clark-Lewis, *Living In, Living Out*, 87.

51. Ohio Church Survey Records, WPA, box 6, folder 116, OHS; Kusmer, *Ghetto Takes Shape*, 96.

52. Ohio Church Survey Records, WPA, box 6, folders 116 and 121, 1940, OHS.

53. "History, St. Timothy Missionary Baptist Church, 1940–1979," unprocessed collection of Reverend John T. Weeden, WRHS.

54. Hans Baer, *The Black Spiritual Movement: A Religious Response to Racism* (Knoxville: University of Tennessee Press, 1984); Iain MacRobert, *The Black Roots and White Racism of Early Pentecostalism in the USA* (New York: St. Martin's, 1988); Goldsmith, *When I Rise Cryin' Holy*, 69–190; James S. Tinney, "William J. Seymour: Father of Modern-Day Pentecostalism," in Randall K. Burkett and Richard Newman, eds., *Black Apostles: Afro-American Clergy Confront the Twentieth Century* (Boston: G. K. Hall & Company, 1978), 213–25. For a case study of Chicago's black Pentecostal churches, see Drake, *Churches and Voluntary Associations*, 298–305.

55. *Cleveland Call and Post*, 30 June 1934; Blackwell, "Black Storefront Churches in Cleveland," 23–24; Goldsmith, *When I Rise Cryin' Holy*, 69–190.

56. *Cleveland Gazette*, 21 July 1917.

57. Goldsmith, *When I Rise Cryin' Holy*, 95.

58. Jon Michael Spencer, "The Ritual of Testifying in the Black Church," in Pamela R. Frese, ed., *Celebrations of Identity: Multiple Voices in American Ritual Performance* (Westport, Conn.: Greenwood Press, 1993), 72.

59. Jon Michael Spencer, "The Rythms of Black Folks," in Alonzo Johnson and Paul Jersild, eds., *Ain't Gonna Lay My 'Ligion Down": African American Religion in the South* (Columbia: University of South Carolina Press, 1996), 39.

60. Michael W. Harris, *The Rise of Gospel Blues: The Music of Thomas Andrew Dorsey in the Urban Church* (New York: Oxford University Press, 1994); Kerrill Leslie Rubman, "From Jubilee to Gospel in Black Male Quartet Singing" (Ph.D. dissertation, University of North Carolina, Chapel Hill, 1980), 17–46.

61. Robert Kimball and William Bolcolm, *Reminiscing with Sissle and Blake* (New York: Viking Press, 1973), 26.

62. Quoted in Levine, *Black Culture and Black Consciousness*, 180.

63. Kip Lornell, *"Happy in the Service of the Lord": Afro-American Gospel Quartets in Memphis* (Urbana: University of Illinois Press, 1988), 11–17; Horace Clarence Boyer, *How Sweet the Sound: The Golden Age of Gospel* (Washington, D.C.: Elliott & Clark, 1995), 29–35.

64. On the widespread participation in male quartet singing, see James Weldon Johnson and J. Rosamond Johnson, *The Books of American Negro Spirituals* (New York: Viking Press, 1940), 35–36; and Rubman, "From Jubilee to Gospel," 34–35. On male quartet singing in work camps, see Lornell, *"Happy in the Service of the Lord,"* 19; Boyer, *How Sweet the Sound*, 32–33; and personal interview with Arthur Turner, 23 May 1996.

65. Personal interview with Arthur Turner; Lornell, *"Happy in the Service of the Lord,"* 22.

66. Levine, *Black Culture and Black Consciousness*, 186.

67. Personal interview with Arthur Turner.

68. Ibid.

69. Lincoln and Mamiya, *Black Church in the African American Experience*, 228. On black women and black churches, see ibid., 274–308; Higginbotham, *Righteous Discontent*; and Cheryl Townsend Gilkes, "'Together and in Harness': Women's Traditions in the Sanctified Church," *Signs* 10 (Summer 1985): 696–99.

70. Blackwell, "Black Storefront Churches in Cleveland," 72.

71. Ibid.; Jacqueline D. Carr-Hamilton, "Motherwit in Southern Religions: A Womanist Perspective," in Johnson and Jersild, *"Ain't Gonna Lay My 'Ligion Down,"* 72.

72. Blackwell, "Black Storefront Churches in Cleveland," 72–75, 83–89, 114.

73. Kelley has made a similar point. See *Race Rebels*, 40.

74. Kusmer, *Ghetto Takes Shape*, 113–15, 131–37, 142–43.

75. For an elaboration of these points, see Phillips, *AlabamaNorth*.

76. "The Reminder," May 1910, Bertha Blue Papers, WRHS. For the erosion in blacks' participation in unions, see Kusmer, *Ghetto Takes Shape*, 73–75; Frank U. Quillin, *The Color Line in Ohio: A History of Race Prejudice in a Typical Northern State* (Ann Arbor: George Wehr, 1913), 155–56; David Gerber, *Black Ohio and the Color Line, 1860–1915* (Urbana: University of Illinois Press, 1976); Phillips, *AlabamaNorth*, chap. 3.

77. Garrity, *Barber and the Historian*, 123.

78. "Bureau of Investigation Reports," 14 May 1920, in Robert Hill, ed., *The Marcus Garvey and Universal Negro Improvement Association Papers*, vol. 2: *27 August 1919–31 August 1920* (Berkeley: University of California Press, 1983), 340–44; *Cleveland Gazette*, 21 Jan. 1922; Randall K. Burkett, *Black Redemption: Clergymen Speak for the Garvey Movement* (Philadelphia: Temple University Press, 1978); Randall K. Burkett, *Garveyism as a Religious Movement: The Institutionalization of a Black Civil Religion* (Metuchen, N.J.: Scarecrow Press, 1978).

79. Interview with Elmer Thompson; for an overview of the strike, see Phillips, *AlabamaNorth*, chap. 3.

80. For an example of Reverend McKinney's perspective, see sermon delivered in late 1938 for "The Wings over Jordan" radio address, Reverend Wade McKinney Papers, WRHS; on overall attitudes of ministers, personal interview with Reverend Frank A. Smith.

81. For an extensive discussion of the Future Outlook League, see Phillips, *AlabamaNorth*, chap. 6. For a comparison with other black boycott efforts between 1929 and 1945, see August Meier and Elliot Rudwick, "The Origins of Nonviolent Direct Action in Afro-American Protest: A Note on Historical Discontinuities," in *Along the Color Line: Explorations in the Black Experience* (Urbana: University of Illinois Press, 1976), 307–404. For a different interpretation of the Future Outlook League, see Christopher G. Wye, "Merchants of Tomorrow: The Other Side of the 'Don't Spend Your Money Where You Can't Work' Movement," *Ohio History* 93 (Fall 1985).

Part 3

*Labor Activism and
Workers' Organizations*

Chapter 10

"To Sit among Men"

Skill, Gender, and Craft Unionism in the
Early American Federation of Labor

ILEEN A. DEVAULT

IN THE MIDDLE OF February 1889, ninety tailors in Omaha, Nebraska, went on strike. Initially they demanded restoration of a 10 percent wage cut. This wage demand did not continue to stand alone though. As "The Striking Tailors" declared in a letter to the local newspaper, "When the bosses only pay our bill of price . . . and give us the privilege to sit among men and make our work, we are satisfied."[1] What did it mean to the Omaha strikers "to sit among men and make [their] work" and why did this become an issue of the strike? Answering these questions leads us to confront issues of skill and gender—and the conflation of the two—in the craft unions of the early American Federation of Labor. This in turn provides insight into the sources of AFL union strength and into the problematic relationships among female and male workers and unionists.

Recent works of women's labor history have illuminated the lives and experiences of women workers by focusing on individual industries and locations.[2] In so doing scholars have provided a corrective to the sometimes sweeping generalizations made by earlier analysts of the relationships among men and women workers and unions. These authors have enlarged upon the insights of the "new labor history" of the past two decades, arguing that union experiences must be understood in the context of the social communities in which they were embedded. They have simultaneously attempted to avoid the universalizing characteristics of earlier feminist scholarship. In these recent works the actions of workers take on characteristics specific to the patterns of race, ethnicity, religion, and industrial development found in different circumstances. These works have therefore demonstrated the contingent nature of gender definitions: working-class men and women worked out the meanings and significance of manhood and womanhood in their specific communities. Awareness of this contingency makes us more able to deal with and account for racial and ethnic differences among women (and men) as well as helping us to better understand the specific development of individual industries and communities.

My goal in this essay is to move beyond this emphasis on contingency and explore the social construction of gender at two simultaneous levels.[3] On one hand, I examine below the ways in which national craft unions attempted to construct gendered definitions of both skill and union membership. On the other hand, their attempts to do this were complicated by the gendered experiences of particular groups of workers in specific locations. Leaders of the early AFL unions found that mediating these different constructions of gender allowed them to unite their male membership in an effective manner. An ongoing dialogue of words and actions among national union leaders, union activists, and rank-and-file union members resulted. This essay attempts to disentangle and analyze one stream of this dialogue.

The AFL would emerge from the depression of the 1890s as the leading workers' organization in the United States. Samuel Gompers and others in the AFL later argued that one of the critical factors allowing the young federation to survive the depression had been their careful adherence to the defining principle of craft unionism: organizing workers along lines of occupational skill, or "craft."[4] Workers who possessed crucial skills in any given industry retained a level of power against their employers because they could not be easily replaced during strikes. Furthermore, though Gompers and his colleagues would have vociferously denied that their craft unionism ignored women workers, they would have agreed that "manliness" was a defining feature of craft unions.

While this reliance on "manliness" can be heard superficially in unions' frequent calls upon the "manly" behavior of their members, its effects can be seen most clearly, and ironically, in cross-gender strikes, strikes that involved both male and female workers. Such strikes often required workers to spell out—for themselves as much as for the public—their understanding of the bounds of solidarity. Just who would be included and who would be excluded? Virtually all cross-gender strikes in the early years of the AFL craft unions sooner or later required workers to figure out just who belonged to their specific craft or skill group and who did not. As Selig Perlman and Philip Taft pointed out decades ago, "Solidarity . . . was thus a solidarity with a quickly diminishing potency as one passed from the craft group—which looks upon the jobs in the craft as its common property for which it is ready to fight long and bitterly—to the widening concentric circles of the related crafts, the industry, the American Federation of Labor, and the world labor movement."[5]

This potential solidarity of craft and the rocky road to its achievement on both the local and the national levels are the subjects of this essay. During the AFL's formative years, from the mid-1880s up to the start of the nationwide depression in late 1893, we can observe the ways in which gender was in fact an intrinsic part of its member unions' definitions of skill and of craft, and therefore of unionism itself. These definitions operated simultaneously on several levels. On a local level, workers in cross-gender workplaces faced gendered definitions of skill and craft every day without necessarily remarking upon them. In strike situations, however, that which ordinarily went unremarked could be accentuated. Strikes forced workers to act upon their notions of solidarity—and therefore of craft and of union membership.[6]

Strikes monitored by the national unions belonging to the AFL also demonstrate the sometimes tenuous nature of what it meant to workers to belong to national organizations. In their attempts to respond to and control members' often-precipitous actions, the national craft unions promulgated their own definitions of what constituted skill and manly behavior. The union as a whole would be strengthened when national union leaders' definitions coincided with local union members' definitions. Similarly, the national unions might gain strength if their members simply *thought* that they shared a gendered craft identity with their union brothers around the country.

For the AFL as a whole, gender might very well play the same unifying role. Almost completely amorphous in 1887, by the onset of the depression late in the summer of 1893 the model of "responsible" craft unionism promulgated by the AFL's leading unions had been constructed into a pattern built around behaviors defined as "manly." We will see that in those industries relying on the labor of both men and women, workers' definitions of "skill" itself were linked to gender-specific activities and expectations. For the nation's thousands of women workers the "skilled craft unionism" of the AFL might as well have been called "skilled crafts-*men's* unionism." With the rise of the AFL, women increasingly found themselves defined out of the nation's union movement. The craft union model constructed in these years thus left a legacy of exclusion that re-verberated into the twentieth century.[7]

This essay begins by examining several strikes in the custom tailoring trade as a way to explore the construction of the American Federation of Labor as a gendered union movement in the years leading up to the 1890s depression. Custom tailoring, its strikes, and its union are then compared to three other cross-gender industries during the same time period: cigars, textiles, and shoes. The differences and similarities seen across both indus-tries and geographical locations allow us to begin to think about gendered definitions of craft and skill and how these concepts operated throughout the early years and unions of the AFL.

The Journeyman Tailors' Union of America (JTUA), established in 1883, voted in 1887 to join the recently formed AFL. The Tailors' Union serves as a model of early AFL craft unionism for several reasons. Made up of workers in the custom tailoring trade, the union sought to control entrance into the trade as well as wage levels. A complex set of membership dues established a financial basis for the payment of strike benefits, though the union's executive board had to approve local strikes before benefits would be paid.[8] During the early years of its AFL membership, the Tailors' Union remained a loyal member of the federation, with the two organizations sharing the services of John B. Lennon, the Denver tailor who served as Tailors' Union general secretary from 1887 to 1910 and as AFL treasurer from 1888 to 1917.[9] Through this connection the Tailors' Union enjoyed a close working relationship with activists in other AFL unions.[10] The Tailors' Union thus provides a particularly appropriate example of the construction of the AFL as a gendered union movement in the late nine-teenth century.

The national officers of the Tailors' Union repeatedly and officially urged members to accept women as full and equal union members.[11] At the union's 1891 convention Lennon discussed the role of women in the union. Chastising those locals that failed to provide women with the same benefits and protection as men, Lennon argued that "Women are in the trade and they are in to stay." The proper response to this situation, he continued, was to strive to attain equal pay for women and men. If every union member worked to improve women's condition, Lennon promised them "the respect of all mankind, and greater power to elevate the condition of all custom tailors."[12]

Such rhetoric aside, in strike after strike of Tailors' Union members, both the question of equal wages for women and also the question of whether women were in fact qualified for membership in the union was up for grabs. Lennon and others did not call for equal status for *all* women; instead, they attempted to define membership in the union—and in "the trade"—so narrowly as to effectively exclude many, if not most, women performing tailoring tasks.

Custom tailors saw themselves as participants in a trade as highly skilled as any. However, they acknowledged a crucial difference between their trade and many others. As one tailor put it, "Tailoring is entirely different to many other skilled trades, in this respect, that the work is easily portable. . . . Tailors . . . can take their work under their arms and sit down almost anywhere and make it."[13]

This portability of the tailor's work stood at the heart of one of the union's primary goals: to abolish home work and replace it with "free back shops" provided by the employer.[14] While gaining such shops became a central goal of the Tailors' Union, members insisted that working in these shops was *not* in and of itself a defining characteristic of their skills. A series of painful struggles resulted that involved not only the place of work but also the tailor's role within his family and women's role within the union.

The Omaha strike of 1889 illustrates some of the difficulties raised by the home work issue for the Tailors' Union. In mid-February five of the firms belonging to Omaha's Merchant Tailors' Exchange announced a wage reduction of 10 percent. The subsequent strike of ninety tailors, including three women, thus began with a demand for the restoration of the earlier wage schedule, or "price list" in tailors' jargon.[15] In addition, leaders of the Omaha union insisted that all work be done in shops rather than in the homes of the tailors.[16] In doing so, the Omaha leaders followed the spirit of a resolution passed at the Tailors' Union 1887 convention that called for "the gradual substitution [for 'having the work done in our homes'] of the system of workshops provided by the employers of trades."[17]

While all the Omaha tailors supported the restoration of wages, some found the attack on home work unacceptable. Those union members who worked in their own homes with the assistance of members of their family and others left the Tailors' Union local when it raised this issue and formed a rival union.[18] Members of the new union proceeded to return to work for the members of the Merchant Tailors' Exchange. In the ensuing rhetorical battle, JTUA members called the rival union's adherents "scabs" and explicitly evoked their own manhood in contrast. At the beginning of the strike's fifth week, the Omaha newspaper published a letter from "The Striking Tailors" which reiterated the strikers' demands: that the shops of the exchange stop utilizing scab labor and that employers establish workshops in which they could "sit among men and make [their] work."

Thï Mc/chant Tailors' Exchange responded scathingly: "Now, men of the union, will you be truthful enough to state to the much-abused public how you find it degrading to sit among the so-called scabs! As a matter of fact, they are composed of good ex-union men—some of them that were such as late as two weeks ago; and, as a matter of truth, have you not . . . had your walking committee call on all so-called scabs and beseech them to join your union, which would, at once, transform them into men and first-class tailors, regardless of merit! So much for your pride."[19] The scorn of the Merchant Tailors' Exchange helped neither it nor the now-divided union. Though the Omaha tailors eventually won their strike, for the next two and a half years the "men and brothers" of the original union would have to deal with the "cutthroats and pirates" of a "scab union."[20]

When they affiliated with the JTUA, Omaha tailors joined an organization that understood the complexities of the home work issue for tailors but also took a firm stance in favor of free back shops. The columns of the union's journal, the *Tailor*, were filled with admonitions against home work[21] and calls for the establishment of back shops. Back shops, ran the usual argument, would enable union members to control working conditions; they would be able to tell exactly how much was being produced, who was producing it, and how much they were being paid. This would help minimize the effects of seasonal unemployment, allow tailors to enforce an eight-hour day, and in general further the cause of unionization.[22]

In addition to the pragmatic organizational implications of home work, however, the issue also had an emotional side. As one union member put it, "The sacred and endearing associations that cluster around the word home, are prostituted to the basest purposes when the workman is forced to convert his home into a workshop."[23] Back shops would make tailors' homes more pleasant and raise the moral standards of their families.[24] Home work, on the other hand, "begins the destruction of what makes life worth living, a happy home. . . . Every consideration is subordinated to this work; the meals of the family, cleanlik5ss, care of the babies, schooling of the children, loving intercourse between husband and wife, recreation, home comfort and all that sweetens existence."[25]

Despite such reverberating emotional appeals tailors continued to work at home. Sometimes, as in Omaha, they resisted attempts by their unions to change the system. It was not that union members really wanted "to make a factory of their houses."[26] Rather, as one union author pointed out, "They have their wives and daughters working with them. They can take all the hours God gives them, and make the whole family do the chores for them by running to and from the stores. So you can plainly see what you have to contend with in doing away with the home work. It is almost traditional with some of our members, and they know right well that it will never be changed while asking the employers for what our members themselves don't want."[27] Though rarely addressed directly, it was this partially acknowledged production by wives and daughters that lay at the root of rank-and-file tailors' general reluctance to take the actions necessary to put a stop to home work. As the Omaha union had learned, threatening this source of additional income could provoke strong responses.

While the home work issue raised questions about the role of members of tailors' families, the union always framed the issue in terms of the location of work rather than of the participants in that work. Officially, the union had already resolved the issue of wives' role in the union, if not exactly their place in the tailoring trade. In November 1890, the Springfield, Missouri, local posed a question to the general executive board of the national union. The local had passed a resolution stating that all tailors' helpers should join the union. Now, however, they were puzzled over whether the resolution covered tailors' wives as well. The executive board ruled "that unless the wife devotes her entire time to working as a helper she should not be compelled to join; that is, in case the wife does her own housework and helps her husband in her spare time, she should not be compelled to join the union."[28] For wives whose tailor husbands worked at home, then, the line between helpmate and helper would have been blurry and difficult to cross.[29]

The issue of the role of "helpers" in the tailoring trade (and in the Tailors' Union) involved questions of both the use of wives as helpers for home workers and the use of unrelated women as helpers in other settings. In the spring of 1887, the Tailors' Union local in Knoxville, Tennessee, found itself dealing with the complexities of the intersection between the two. At the time it was reported that roughly one-fourth of the union's members worked at home, while the rest worked in employers' back shops. As the local union secretary reported, "Some of the men employed women help, the men working home had help from their wives, one in particular had a jour[neyman] help with his wife. Some of the bosses employed female help in their back shops . . . but with the exception of one shop (F. I. Callan) not to an extent to hurt the interest of the jours." At this point, Callan began to expand his business and hire additional women. The union, arguing that employing lower-paid women was equivalent to "having work made under the bill," demanded that Callan fire all but one of his women workers. Callan refused, pointing out that "he had as much right to work a woman for profit as the jour, and if the union expected him to discharge his women he would consider the necessity of doing so when they, his jours, first set him the example." The union held a special meeting at which it decided that its members would "give up their female help" and stop working at home, demanding that all bosses provide back shops. A union committee gave Callan one week to comply with the union's demands. As they had in Omaha, responses of Knoxville union members varied. Some home workers refused to begin working in back shops and were expelled from the local. Other men working for Callan "discharged their women at the specified time only to see them transfer their services to Mr. Callan in accordance, it was then seen, with a pre-arranged plan." An apparently successful strike ensued, and, a year later, Callan was "running his trade without woman help."[30]

The Knoxville story highlights several important aspects of the "helper" issue. Home workers used wives (and daughters) as helpers without paying them in any formal sense. These family members helped the home-working tailor complete more work and therefore earn more money. Alternatively, some individual journeymen employed unrelated helpers. The journeyman then paid these helpers out of the money he received from his employer.[31] In effect, the individual journeyman acted as a subcontractor.

If the difference between casual assistance by tailors' wives and the more regular employment by tailors of female helpers was difficult to discern, the line between female helpers and "tailoresses" was equally so. The role of women in the trade and in the union became an increasingly controversial topic in the late 1880s and early 1890s as the clothing trade underwent continual changes. The problem, explained a Denver tailor in 1887, was not women per se. Women working under what he called the "piece master system" often did not realize that they were taking work away from men. On the other hand, skilled women should be admitted to the union, he argued: "If a woman can make a coat, pants or vest to the satisfaction of the employer and the customer, for what reason is she not entitled to the same amount of pay for the same amount of work? . . . I would never fear the woman who gets as much as I do for the same amount of work as myself, but it is the woman who is unable to get the same pay who is an injury to the tailors."[32]

The complexities of the issue of equal pay can be seen in an 1890 strike in Columbus, Ohio.[33] In mid-April of that year, members of Tailors' Union Local 27, acting with the approval of the national union, struck against thirteen shops belonging to the Columbus Merchant Tailors' Exchange. The union had presented a new wage bill to the exchange shops, requesting a wage increase for those union members working on pants and vests—a segment of the trade made up of women. The strikers reportedly included eighty men and thirty-four women, or almost all of the 130 union members in Columbus.[34]

The union's public appeals for support continually portrayed the women as helpless and at the mercy of men. The members of the Merchant Tailors' Exchange were the "bad" men, unfairly forcing honest and hardworking women into prostitution. On the other hand, the male members of Local 27 were the self-styled "good" men who provided vigorous material support for the women—in fact, "waging a bitter war" on their behalf. The picture of feminine vulnerability painted by the union officials is belied somewhat even by their description of the strike. The men "having worked and associated with these women in the shops for many years," did not *initiate* the movement for improvement of the women's wages. Rather, the women themselves "agitate[d] the movement of joining the Union, and finding that there was no opposition to the movement by our organization, . . . they requested the Union to admit them as members." The union's appeal presents Local 27 as the agent of the "forcible" strike action, but it also provides information that allows us to suspect that the women were themselves capable of taking "forcible" action.[35] Though we do not directly hear their voices, these do not seem to be passive, dependent women. After all, the women themselves had sought out union membership in order to support their demands for better wages.

Despite the unity of male and female workers the Columbus strike ultimately failed.[36] While Tailors' Union secretary Lennon praised the strike to the national union as "one of the most just and honorable ever engaged in by any union in America,"[37] the JTUA's varied experiences with the Columbus "tailoresses" did not leave the union with an untroubled position on the question of women's union membership and their wages. Even while the national union officially supported tailoresses' claims for wages equal to those of tailors, the failure of the Columbus strike exposed the difficulty in realizing such a goal. Soon after the Columbus defeat, the Nashville local petitioned the national union's executive board for support in its demand that women receive "the bill in full." The executive board advised the local "to act with caution, and send the Board fuller information as to the number of members that might become involved."[38] Theoretically enthusiastic about equal pay for women and men, the Tailors' Union leadership was also pragmatic. It was not going to encourage its locals to embark on a series of long, expensive—and probably unsuccessful—strikes.

In these various local conflicts the Tailors' Union worked out three possible roles for women, both in the tailoring trade itself and within the national union. As "tailoresses," co-workers with skills equivalent to those of many journeymen tailors, women were welcomed into the union as (almost) equal members. This welcome stemmed from an uneasy mix of an acknowledgement of their status as wage earners and a fear of their competition as low-waged workers. As "helpers" women were also to be allowed into the union on a par with male apprentices. This admittance of women arose from male tailors' concerns that conditions smacking of "sweating" cheapened the trade as a whole, risking their skills and livelihoods. Finally, as wives and daughters of journeymen tailors, women were expected to benefit passively from the union status of the male members of their family, even while contributing actively to the male-earned family income. While the Tailors' Union attempted on a national level to regulate each group in various ways, the exact moment at which a wife became a helper and a helper became a full-fledged tailoress would be worked out by the local unions.

All three of the women's roles in custom tailoring revolved around the tailor himself. The union believed that it was the male tailor who possessed the skills necessary for satisfactorily creating men's clothing. John Lennon could thus argue that limiting the number of female helpers allowed a union tailor "deprives him of work that should be *made by him*, but is now made by persons who have really no skill as tailors."[39] The union tailor had such a high level of skill, in other words, that his very supervision of the work process would itself ensure that that skill was embodied in the clothing produced. It was that ability to be the very personification of skill that supplied much of the force behind the "manly virtue" represented by the Tailors' Union as a craft union. Even when they acknowledged women as tailoresses, male co-workers viewed women's skills as limited, leaving them "at the mercy of their greedy employers" and in need of male union protection.[40]

The Tailors' Union recognized that it needed "to bring the extreme localities of this vast Continent together so that when a union is assailed in California, the members of our craft in the remotest part of the Continent will feel its affects."[41] One crucial way of doing this was to call upon a common sense of "manhood." At the same time, exact definitions of manhood would grow out of different local experiences. The national union called on the commonalities among those experiences to build a sense of solidarity—a sense of literal *brother*hood. Union membership would instill a sense of "sitting among men," of sharing certain skills and attitudes, across the entire nation.

The Tailors' Union was confronted with trade-specific issues in its efforts to define manhood in ways that would knit the union together rather than tear it apart. Yet its attempts to do this were echoed in other trades in which AFL-affiliated craft unions operated. The most direct parallels to the Tailors' Union appear in the cross-gender strikes under the direction of the Cigar Makers' International Union (CMIU). The leaders of these two national unions were close colleagues and friends and they and their industries defined similar roles for women workers.

In the 1880s and 1890s cigarmakers, like tailors, faced an industry that used women simultaneously in those segments of the industry dominated by home work (called tenement house work by the CMIU) and in the sectors of the industry increasingly reliant on new machines and an increased subdivision of the labor process. As in the Tailors' Union, the cigarmakers' attempts to negotiate these issues confronted them with combined issues of skill and gender.

Eileen Boris has demonstrated how the Cigar Makers' Union ultimately rejected a legislative strategy for dealing with the problem of tenement house work in the late 1870s and early 1880s. Under the leadership of Adolph Strasser and Samuel Gompers, the Cigar Makers' Union turned to an economic strategy premised on basic trade union principles. Similar to the Tailors' strategy on home work, the CMIU ruled that "Locals with any tenement house workers . . . were forbidden to maintain such workers in good standing as long as they labored at home." Boris contends that "Such a stand committed the CMIU against organizing the less skilled."[42] By defining tenement house cigarmakers as inherently less skilled than shop workers, the union denied the legitimacy of the contributions of family members—both wives and children—to production.

While similar to the Tailors' Union, the Cigar Makers' Union differed in a key way. Though tailors' employers certainly colluded with their workers in allowing home work that they knew probably incorporated the labor of family members, home work in the men's custom clothing industry formally acknowledged only the male tailor as a wage earner. The tailor himself often made the decision to participate in home work. In tenement house cigarmaking, the employer determined both the site of production and the identities of the producers. Cigar manufacturers would buy or lease a tenement and rent its apartments to chosen families who then would make cigars in order to pay their rent. Employers expected all members of the family to participate in cigar production. While manufacturers assumed that husbands would head the "cigarmaking teams," they retained the right to inspect work performed in the tenements.[43] By so doing they ensured that women working under this system would see themselves as employees. As a result, women and men working under the tenement house system continued to strike throughout the later 1880s and 1890s, despite a lack of support from the Cigar Makers' Union.[44] The CMIU both continued to decline opportunities to bring tenement house workers into its ranks and renewed efforts to abolish the tenement house system entirely.

While the Cigar Makers' Union fought against tenement cigarmaking, it also found itself faced with increased subdivision of the labor process in factory production. The activities enshrined as "skilled" by the union produced the entire cigar from prepared tobacco leaf.[45] As some factories began to use molds to form the tobacco into the basic cigar shape, the Cigar Makers' Union insisted that such cigars were inferior to hand-made ones. Union leaders phrased this denial in terms of the machines themselves rather than the gender of those machines' operators. Nonetheless, the fact that women made up many of the mold operators contributed to the union's opinion of the new cigars' quality.

The union responded to changes in the labor process by making certain concessions to factories producing molded cigars. In Davenport, Iowa, in 1886, for example, the union granted use of the CMIU label under special conditions to a cigar factory utilizing molds. The local allowed the factory to pay $1 less per thousand cigars than was paid by other local union-label factories, "considering his system of manufacturing (bunch making and rolling separated)."[46] The union only slowly tried to enroll all the workers in the factory, however. In 1888 the union embarked on an unsuccessful strike to force the factory's packers to join the union. The factory workers, however, both male and female, had a relatively tenuous relationship with the union. The fragility of the bonds among the factory's workers and between those workers and other members of the union in Davenport contributed to the ultimate failure of the strike. By pursuing a strategy of selectively granting use of the union label for factories using molds and therefore making exceptions to their usual rules governing both labels and membership, the union in effect created a second-class category of members. The union allowed some women working in specific factories and performing mechanized tasks into its ranks, but it did so by making exceptions rather than by changing its general rules.

Like the Tailors' Union, the Cigar Makers' Union therefore attempted to bring in some women. Also like the tailors, cigarmakers began by accepting the sexual division of labor within their industry. The Cigar Makers' Union seemed to have a broad definition of membership; its leaders urged all those involved in making cigars to join. Increasingly the issue facing the union became a question of a slightly different definition: just what constituted a cigar? Were the 5-cent molded "stogies" really equivalent to cigars? Should their makers be organized into the union? Ultimately the CMIU officially admitted stogie makers, many of them women operating various machines, but how actively it did this remained unclear even to many in the labor movement of the time. In the late 1890s, Gompers wanted to set up a separate national union for stogie makers. The Cigar Makers' Union president had to argue with his former union brother that his union already admitted stogie makers into membership.[47]

The Cigar Makers' Union had no such controversies over organizing workers in the highly mechanized cigarette industry. These workers—mostly women—were never even considered for membership by the CMIU. After all, in their eyes, the mechanically produced cigarette could never compete successfully with the well-rolled cigar for the loyalty of American customers. The skilled male cigar roller embodied the very definition of the CMIU's membership, even as his role in the economy declined. As Patricia Cooper has put it, "Women were not part of a community of insiders not only because they posed an economic threat, but also because they were women."[48] As long as "skilled" and "male" remained apparently indivisible, adherence to craft union principles continued to make sense for the Cigar Makers' Union.

The Tailors' and Cigar Makers' Unions thus faced very similar gender issues. However, strikes in markedly different industries suggest that other craft unions developed their own variations on the intersecting definitions of skill, manhood, and union membership. Workers in the textile and shoemaking industries, for example, confronted a very different set of cross-gender issues, issues that the industries' craft unions resolved by invoking a similar image of "manly" skill. Though the construction of

gendered unionism in these industries took different forms than in tailoring or cigarmaking, the end result was a similar sense of unionism as a
constituent element of manly behavior—and vice versa.

In sectors of the textile industry relying on mulespinning technology,
a strict sexual division of labor on the shop floor meant that gendering the
labor movement could be accomplished through a narrow definition of
"the craft" and its skills. While tailors and cigarmakers grappled with similar sets of issues, mulespinners believed that they only had to follow occupational lines in order to preserve the economic strength of their (male)
unions.

Mulespinning technology involved the use of large, heavy spinning
machines that required considerable manual strength in drawing out the
cotton threads. In this unmechanized process, mulespinners wielded considerable control over both the thickness and the quality of the threads
spun.[49] After mulespinning the yarn was worked into a final product. While
mulespinners comprised only a small portion of the workers in any textile mill, their position at the beginning of the production process gave
them crucial power. In Fall River, Massachusetts, this economic advantage led mulespinners to unionize in the late 1850s. This union, and its
successor the National Cotton Mule Spinners' Association (NCMSA),
drew upon the common ethnic heritage of the area's mulespinners, who
were mostly skilled immigrants from Lancashire, England, into the
1880s.[50] While the NCMSA switched its organizational affiliation back
and forth between the Knights of Labor and the AFL during the 1880s
and 1890s, throughout its history the union retained its craft identity. As
the name of the union suggests, the mulespinners drew their lines of
membership very narrowly. The strict sexual division of labor in cotton
spinning ensured that defining membership along occupational lines per-
petuated an all-male union.

In the late 1880s and 1890s strains began to appear in this strategy for
the Mule Spinners' Association. The limits of the strategy can be seen in
a strike sponsored by the Fall River–based union. Early in December 1890,
mulespinners at the thread mills of Kearney, New Jersey, walked off their
jobs, demanding the reinstatement of a fired co-worker and the discharge
of the mill's superintendent. The mulespinners (making up only 5 percent
of the mill's total workforce) convinced the rest of the men employed in
the mills (about 31 percent of the workforce) to follow their lead the next
day. The combined walkout of approximately 750 male workers led to the
closure of the mills, thereby throwing some 1,600 female employees out
of work.[51]

In the ensuing four-month-long strike the mulespinners' view of their less-skilled co-workers (female and male) never wavered, though the actions of the other workers varied considerably. The mulespinners' male "helpers" would be assisted by the union, including the payment of strike wages.[52] As for the female workers in the mill, one spinner explained that they had attempted to help them organize two years earlier: "He said that now they would make no effort at organizing the other employees, but would depend entirely on themselves."[53] While the mulespinners remained true to this sentiment, they were not above using the unorganized women workers in their appeals to public sympathy. This was particularly true when the AFL's executive committee declared a nationwide boycott of the mill's products. The boycott call in February 1891 claimed that "The men struck work and have now been out gallantly, heroically fighting for their own and labor's rights, to organize, to maintain their manhood, to protest against injustice and wrong."[54] Though the AFL's boycott was officially only on behalf of the organized male mulespinners, the superintendent's abusive treatment of the women workers was used repeatedly as the most prominent example of the "system of tyranny and persecution" at the thread mills.[55]

For their part, women workers began to organize almost immediately upon the start of the strike. Meetings of women workers drew up lists of demands, formed committees, helped organize benefits, and solicited donations.[56] Throughout the mulespinners' strike, and with the mulespinners' union's approval, women workers alternately walked off their jobs in support of the strikers and returned to work later for a few days' pay, only to repeat the cycle once again.[57] Apparently strongly in sympathy with the striking mulespinners, their solidaristic tendencies repeatedly clashed with their economic interests.

Meanwhile the mulespinners continued to refuse to take any financial responsibility for their female co-workers. While the male spinners consistently spoke of their sympathy with the unorganized women, they remained just that in the spinners' eyes: unorganized and women. Relations between the two groups reached their nadir in early January when representatives of the Mule Spinners' Association publicly asked other labor organizations to contribute only to the mulespinners and their male helpers in the future. The union's spokesman stated that the women "had given up their organization, and had not the courage to sustain it."[58] Despite the bad feelings created by this statement, women workers offered to walk off their jobs in support of the mulespinners several more times before the strike finally ended in mid-April 1891.[59]

Ultimately the tenuous relationship between the organized mulespinners and the women workers in the mill played into the hands of the company. Despite the spinners' belief in the necessity of their skills, and their skills alone, even the occasional employment of the women workers allowed the company to bring in strikebreakers and operate successfully. The eventual settlement of the strike stipulated that the mulespinners could not return to work in a body, only as individual applicants for jobs.[60]

The Kearney strike illustrates the simultaneous strengths and weaknesses of the Mule Spinners' Association's reliance on narrow occupational unionism. Though the Kearney spinners may have retained their "manhood," doing so through unionism became increasingly difficult for mulespinners in the following years. The spinners' participation in the perpetuation of a sexual division of labor originally instituted by management was itself a factor in the union's eventual downfall. Though the union was successful in its demands for high wages and a level of workers' control in the 1870s and 1880s, its strength played a role in fueling managers' constant search for a satisfactory replacement for mulespinning technology. As new mills were built outside of the Northeast in the late nineteenth and early twentieth centuries, owners and managers chose to use virtually any technology other than that of mulespinning. Though often requiring massive investments in machinery, the technologies chosen by southern and western mills provided major savings for capitalists when cheaper women workers—rejected for membership by the militant mulespinners' union—could be hired to run the new machines.[61] The National Cotton Mule Spinners' Association thereby ultimately preserved its craft, its union, and its male identification completely out of existence.

Just as changing technological realities in the textile industry operated to undermine the mulespinners' craft union strategy, similar changes threatened union power in the shoe industry. In her book on the nineteenth-century New England shoe industry Mary Blewett describes how the AFL's contribution to shoeworkers' unionism, the Boot and Shoe Workers' International Union (BSWIU), developed out of the long traditions of the Knights of St. Crispin, the Knights of Labor, and the Lasters' Protective Union.[62] Out of these ingredients Massachusetts shoe and boot workers fashioned a complex strategy in which they organized workers largely along separate occupational lines, but then coordinated the activities of the various unions. Ideally, this meant that all occupations and all skill levels as well as both women and men would address their own particular issues while still uniting to fight employer resistance. Skilled male lasters, cutters, and bottomers could and did acknowledge the skills of female stitchers, and all of these gendered groups of skilled workers operated in their unions in coordination with each other and with less-skilled co-workers, both male and female. Blewett describes in great detail how this strategy both did and did not work successfully for the shoeworkers of Essex County, Massachusetts. Looking at the experiences of shoeworkers' strikes in the late 1880s and 1890s and beyond Massachusetts makes this picture even more complex.

Initially, coordination of male and female shoeworkers' actions derived from the mutual acknowledgment of workers' skills. By the 1880s, however, mechanization had made major inroads into shoeworkers' skills.[63] While the shoeworkers of eastern Massachusetts might still call on traditions of cross-gender craft cooperation to hold together their union strategy, shoeworkers elsewhere worked in shops without these older traditions both within and outside the workshop. In this context, cross-gender unionism in other areas of the country had a rocky road ahead of it. Facing continued mechanization of various parts of shoe production, in the early 1890s the AFL's newly formed Boot and Shoe Workers' Union might turn to a more explicitly male-identified form of craft unionism.

In February 1892, seventy male lasters in the ladies' shoes bottoming department of a large Chicago factory went on strike against a wage decrease and the introduction of a new machine that the strikers argued would further reduce their wages. After two weeks, the lasters compromised and settled with the firm. Upon their return to work, they found seven strikebreakers still at work in the department. The lasters walked out once again. After the working day ended, all of the firm's male employees met to decide how to respond to the day's events. "After considerable discussion," the assembled workers voted to go to work the next day at the usual hour, but then to "walk out to a man" at 9:00 A.M.[64]

The following morning almost the entire male workforce of the factory walked out. The workers set up committees to hear grievances and then unanimously passed a resolution demanding the settlement of all of them. The strikers stressed the reasonableness and restraint of the lasters and other men in calling for arbitration of the original wage dispute. Furthermore, they pointed out that the striking lasters had "behaved like gentlemen, keeping away from the factory, making no threats and molesting nobody in any way, manner, or form, and sustaining their dignity by appeals to their fellow-workmen against the violence of any kind."[65]

That evening about two hundred of the factory's female employees, all of whom had remained at their jobs that day, met with the male strikers' chairman, who described the situation to the women and encouraged them to join the strike, assuring them that "their grievances would also be presented to the firm for adjustment. No man would go to work unless every woman present, from the youngest to the oldest, had been taken back and given her previous place after the strike." The women voted unanimously to join the strikers.[66]

By the end of the next workday, out of 850 employees, only about thirty were still working: "a few girls who are said to be afraid of losing their positions, and the new men who have since been hired." Claiming that there were over forty thousand pairs of unfinished shoes in the factory, the strikers announced that competitive pressures would soon lead to their victory over the firm.[67]

Thus far the story appears to follow the example of New England shoeworkers; though workers struck and presented grievances along the lines of occupations and sex, they seemed to be united in their efforts. This unity held throughout the two months of the strike, though cracks soon began to appear. Early meetings of the women strikers often featured speeches by local union activist Elizabeth Morgan, who urged the women to organize in order to prevent wage cuts and avoid being used as strikebreakers. Male strike leaders certainly supported this sentiment. However, Morgan also encouraged the women to affiliate with either the AFL or the Knights of Labor.[68] Male unionists, including Henry Skeffington of the AFL union, were unhappy with Morgan's ecumenical view of the women's organization, despite the fact that the women *did* eventually affiliate with the AFL union.[69]

The strikers' employer soon sought to take advantage of splits between male and female strikers, offering to take back all the women but only those men who had not been replaced already by strikebreakers. This offer would be repeated several times during the course of the strike; each time it would be refused by the women.[70] These women workers clearly agreed with the speaker who told them she saw their actions as "heroic": "You have not gone out for any grievances of your own, but you have gone out to help your brethren."[71] Several speakers also reminded workers that a strike the previous year in nearby Elgin, Illinois, had been lost because of the women's lack of unity. This memory clearly influenced the Chicago strikers in their efforts to fully include women in their activities.[72] Those efforts paid off, as the strikers won their battle in late May.[73]

In the Chicago strike, women walked off their jobs in a model of solidarity with their male co-workers. As one supporter addressing women strikers put it, "You are not united for your rights only, but also for the rights of the 600 men who work with you: for the rights of many wives and many children who are dependent on them for support. . . . I am glad that such a responsibility rests upon you, and I know you will prove yourself worthy of the confidence reposed in you."[74] The skilled lasters who began the strike were rewarded for the confidence they placed in their female co-workers. Perhaps because of the recent Elgin strike against the same company, these Chicago shoeworkers found that unity across gender lines worked much better than did the strict adherence to occupational craft unionism such as that practiced by Kearney's male mulespinners.

The example of the Chicago strike therefore supports Blewett's view of cross-gender craft cooperation in the shoe industry. Examining only this one strike would suggest that the shoe industry serves as the exception that can prove the rule of the limiting effects of gendered unionism. At the same time, the 1892 Chicago strike also sounds a warning to the historian: after all, this strike's positive conclusion appears to be based on the workers' absorption of a recent—and geographically close—counterexample. Furthermore, though the Boot and Shoe Workers' Union could successfully navigate the shoals of gender divisions in this particular strike, they based their very organizational structure on the sexual division of labor as it presented itself at the workplace. Would unity also prevail in strikes initiated by women workers? Would male workers prove themselves worthy of women's confidence?

In early August 1893, female stitchers in a shoe shop in Auburn, Maine, refused to sign the new, lower price list presented by their employers.[75] Workers held meetings along occupational (and therefore, gender) lines throughout the next week. All of the workers expressed sympathy with the skilled female stitchers, and most of them, belonging to the Boot and Shoe Workers' International Union, voted within the week to strike in support of the women. The male lasters, members of the Lasters' Protective Union, and male shoe cutters, members of their own Boot & Shoe Cutters' Union, took longer to decide finally to strike on behalf of the women.[76]

The lasters, whose union most closely resembled that of the mulespinners, walked out of their jobs only after the combined Auburn shoe manufacturers had escalated the strike considerably. When the lasters finally did strike, employers fought back in two ways: by importing immigrant Armenian lasters to work as strikebreakers and by installing new lasting machines in several of the shops.[77] Even more than the mulespinners, the reluctant lasters of Auburn and elsewhere increasingly faced this sort of technological and ethnic replacement over the following years.[78] The impact of this on the structure of the shoe unions and their gender relations would not be immediately obvious, however. The Auburn strike occurred just as the depression of the 1890s began. Even if the strikers had cooperated fully with each other, the quickly worsening economic conditions would have doomed the strike to failure. The unresolved gender issues of the Auburn strike lingered for years, until a combination of new technologies and a resulting new sexual division of labor within the shoe industry erased the efficacy of the nineteenth-century gender-based unions. Only examination of additional strike situations will reveal whether the shoe industry truly provides an exception or serves simply as a variant on the more usual rule of the limiting nature of gendered unionism.

This essay has outlined some of the ways in which gender and skill intersected in the strategies and definitions of the early AFL craft unions. In tailoring, cigar production, and mulespinning, skill—and therefore membership in craft unions—was defined and redefined as a male attribute. Even in the shoe industry, where craft unionism appeared to take a stance of greater cross-gender cooperation, we see the outlines of continuing problems of male workers' full acknowledgment of female workers' skills. The cross-gender strikes examined here thus begin to reveal the problems created by unions' gendered definitions of "skill." By defining some male workers as possessing "skill," the unions are de facto—and sometimes unwittingly—defining other workers, both male and more importantly female, as unskilled and therefore without recourse to the union.

In other words, the craft union notion of some workers' proprietorship of the socially constructed category of "skill" ensured continuing debate over the nature and content of that skill. In her important study of nineteenth-century American fraternalism, Mary Ann Clawson has argued that "fraternalism publicly affirmed the values of a patriarchal society in which social adulthood, proprietorship, and masculinity were inextricably linked."[79] Late nineteenth-century AFL unions shared this fraternal linkage and fraternalism's qualities of exclusion. Though union members would have argued that individuals were excluded merely because they were unskilled, not because they were members of any particular group (such as women, blacks, or immigrants), the unions' social construction of skill as an inherently gendered quality meant the exclusion of women from the nation's major craft unions.[80]

Craft unions based on workers' possession of the bundle of physical abilities known as skills had a number of implications for union strength and power. Whether they were custom tailors faced by the new "sweated" trades producing ready-made clothing, cigarmakers undermined by simple machines and tenement house production, shoe lasters confronting new technology and new immigrants, or mulespinners simply being mechanized out of existence, clinging to gendered definitions of skill ultimately undercut the economic power of all of their unions. A nongendered definition of skill still would have left these workers open to the threat of mechanization, but the intrinsic gendering of skill raised the specter of replacement by "mere women" as well. The concurrent racialization of skill turned immigrants and other racial groups into additional threats to these workers and their unions.[81] The problem faced by these unions therefore became much larger than Perlman and Taft's concern with "a solidarity with a quickly diminishing potency as one passed from the craft group."[82] The craft—and its cousin, the skill—became simultaneously the source of the AFL unions' economic power and the source of their greatest weakness. Appealing to male workers' sense of gendered skill could strengthen ties among union brothers, but it also implicitly excluded women workers and their concerns from most of the AFL unions. Nowhere is this clearer than in the stories of the cross-gender strikes told here. "To sit among men" proved a call to union brotherhood and solidarity— but also a call to exclusion.

Notes

1. *(Omaha) Daily Bee*, evening edition, 18 Mar. 1889, 8.

2. See, for example, Mary H. Blewett, *Men, Women, and Work: Class, Gender, and Protest in the New England Shoe Industry, 1780–1910* (Urbana: University of Illinois Press, 1988); Patricia A. Cooper, *Once a Cigar Maker: Men, Women, and Work Culture in American Cigar Factories, 1900–1919* (Urbana: University of Illinois Press, 1987); Carole Turbin, *Working Women of Collar City: Gender, Class, and Community in Troy, 1864–86* (Urbana: University of Illinois Press, 1992). See also many of the essays in Ava Baron, ed., *Work Engendered: Toward a New History of American Labor* (Ithaca: Cornell University Press, 1991) and in Laura L. Frader and Sonya O. Rose, eds., *Gender and Class in Modern Europe* (Ithaca: Cornell University Press, 1996).

3. The other recent work to take on a similar type of national study is Eileen Boris, *Home to Work: Motherhood and the Politics of Industrial Homework in the United States* (Cambridge: Cambridge University Press, 1994).

4. See, for example, an interview in the *Indianapolis Sentinel* with Gompers, 5 Jan. 1896, quoted in Samuel Gompers, *The Samuel Gompers Papers*, vol. 4: *A National Labor Movement Takes Shape, 1895–98*, ed. Stuart B. Kaufman, Peter J. Albert, and Grace Palladino (Urbana: University of Illinois Press, 1992), 112–13; American Federation of Labor, *Report of the Proceedings of the Thirteenth Annual Convention* (Bloomington, Ill.: Pantograph Printing and Stationery Co., 1893; reprint, 1985), 12.

5. Selig Perlman and Philip Taft, *History of Labor in the United States, 1896–1932*, vol. 4: *Labor Movements* (1935; reprint, [n.p.]: Kelley, 1966), 9.

6. This essay draws from a larger study examining strikes that involved both male and female workers—"cross-gender" strikes—in the decades immediately surrounding the turn of the twentieth century. The larger study looks at cross-gender strikes in four broad industries (boots and shoes, clothing, textiles, and tobacco) from 1887 to 1903. Together these four industries account for 80 to 86 percent of all women employed in manufacturing during these years.

7. My concern in this paper is with the AFL unions' de facto exclusion of women workers. During these same years the AFL also constructed parallel definitions based on race, ethnicity, religion, and age.

8. See Charles Jacob Stowell, *Studies in Trade Unionism in the Custom Tailoring Trade* (Bloomington, Ill.: Journeymen Tailors Union of America, 1913), 71–72, 88; Charles Jacob Stowell, *The Journeymen Tailors' Union of America: A Study in Trade Union Policy* (1918; reprint, New York: Johnson Reprint Co., 1970), 54–55.

9. Stowell, *Studies in Trade Unionism in the Custom Tailoring Trade*, 60, 100, 93–94; Samuel Gompers, *The Samuel Gompers Papers*, vol. 2: *The Early Years of the American Federation of Labor, 1887–90*, ed. Stuart B. Kaufman, Peter J. Albert, Elizabeth Fones-Wolf, Dolores E. Janiewski, and David E. Carl (Urbana: University of Illinois Press, 1987), 451.

10. See, for example, the "Secretary's Report" at 1889 JTUA convention. Lennon thanked Samuel Gompers, Adolph Strasser, and P. J. McGuire by name.

11. See, for example, "Women in the Tailoring Trade," *Tailor* 1 (Nov. 1888): 7 ["Frauen im Schneidergeschaft," 3] and ibid. 1 (Apr. 1889): 4.

12. Ibid. 3 (Aug. 1891): 2.

13. Alex S. Drummond, "The Eight Hour Question as Applied to Tailoring," *Tailor* 3 (Sept. 1891): 1.

14. The debate over this issue in the 1880s and 1890s is a variation of what Joan W. Scott found among Parisian tailors in the 1840s. She argues that, for French tailors in these years, "skill" became synonymous with "the shop" ("Work Identities for Men and Women," in *Gender and the Politics of History* [New York: Columbia University Press, 1988], 100).

15. United States Bureau of Labor, *Tenth Annual Report of the Commissioner of Labor*, vol. 1: *Strikes and Lockouts* (Washington, D.C.: Government Printing Office, 1896). The striking tailors argued that the cut was actually closer to 20 percent. See *Tailor* 1 (Apr. 1889): 4; *(Omaha) Daily Bee*, morning edition, 19 Feb. 1889, 2.

16. Letter from Beerman, in *Tailor* 3 (June 1893): 5.

17. "Constitution and By-Laws of the Journeymen Tailors' National Union, adopted Aug. 1887," *American Labor Unions' Constitutions, Proceedings, Officers' Reports and Supplementary Documents*, microform ed. (Ann Arbor, Mich.: U.M.I., 1986), 19–20.

18. Nebraska Bureau of Labor and Industrial Statistics, *Second Biennial Report of the Bureau of Labor and Industrial Statistics of Nebraska for 1889 and 1890* (Lincoln, Neb., 1890), 337.

19. *(Omaha) Daily Bee*, evening edition, 18 Mar. 1889, 8.

20. *Tailor* 2 (Mar. 1890): 4.

21. "Fillers" in the union's journal, the *Tailor*, often commented on the evils of home work. For example, "Tailors, is it not about time for you to place yourselves on a level with other mechanics and stop working in your homes?" (*Tailor* 1 [Nov. 1887]: 4). See also ibid. 1 (Oct. 1887): 3; 1 (Mar. 1888): 8; and 1 (Apr. 1888): 6.

22. See, for example, "Back Shops," *Tailor* 1 (June 1888): 4; and "Can the Workers of Our Trade Be Benefitted by the Eight-Hour Movement?" *Tailor* 3 (Oct. 1891): 4.

23. "Proceedings of the Sixth Convention of the Journeyman Tailors' Union of America, 1891," *American Labor Unions' Constitutions, Proceedings, Officers' Reports and Supplementary Documents.*

24. "Back Shops vs. Home Work," *Tailor* 1 (Dec. 1887): 4 ["Back-Shops gegen Hausarbeit," 2]; *Tailor* 1 (May 1888): 6.

25. "An Open Letter to the Chicago Drapers' and Tailors' Exchange and to the Public," *Tailor* 3 (Sept. 1892): 2.

26. "Back Shops," 4.

27. "On Back Shops," *Tailor* 3 (Nov. 1891): 1.

28. *Tailor* 2 (Dec. 1890): 4.

29. This was the unspoken rationale behind the "Wife's Funeral Benefit" and its unequal application. A male JTUA member's heirs received $100 on the member's death, and the member himself received $75 when his wife died. The heirs of female members of the union received only $75 on the member's death, and there was no "Husband's Funeral Benefit." Mrs. M. Shook, a member of the Beaver Falls, Pa., local, raised this issue in 1891, but was unsuccessful in her attempts to have it made more equitable at that year's union convention (*Tailor* 2 [Mar. 1891]: 6). Shook raised the issue again in 1893 (*Tailor* 3 [June 1893]: 3). When a married male tailor lost his wife, he lost an opportunity to add to his own salary as well as losing a cook and housekeeper. When a married female tailor lost her husband, on the other hand, she lost whatever income he might have been bringing in from his own job, but she did not lose any of her "own" earning capacity.

30. Letter from A. Todlenhausen, Knoxville, *Tailor* 1 (Mar. 1888): 7. The union was not, however, successful in bringing the men expelled from the union back into the JTUA.

31. Helpers appear to have comprised about 8 percent of the workers in the custom tailoring trade by the turn of the century (Stowell, *Studies in Trade Unionism in the Custom Tailoring Trade*, 24–25).

32. *Tailor* 1 (Jan. 1888): 7.

33. I am grateful to Grace Palladino for the initial research she did on this strike while annotating it for the *Samuel Gompers Papers*, vol. 2. References below to the *Daily Ohio State Journal* are from her notes.

34. *Tailor* 2 (Apr. 1890): 6; United States Bureau of Labor, *Strikes and Lockouts;* Ohio Bureau of Labor Statistics, *14th Annual Report of the Bureau of Labor Statistics, to the 69th General Assembly of the State of Ohio, for the year 1890* (Columbus, Ohio, 1891), 35; *Daily Ohio State Journal*, 16 Apr. 1890.

35. All quotes from *Tailor* 2 (June 1890): 4.

36. Thirty-five of the eighty men and twenty-five of the thirty-four women had reportedly been replaced by this date; twenty-five of these replacement workers came from outside of Columbus (United States Bureau of Labor, *Strikes and Lockouts*).

37. *Tailor* 2 (May 1890): 4.

38. Ibid. (Nov. 1890): 6.

39. "Proceedings of the Convention, Columbus, Ohio, August 12, 1889," *American Labor Unions' Constitutions, Proceedings, Officers' Reports and Supplementary Documents.* (Emphasis added.)

40. *Tailor* 2 (June 1890): 4.

41. "Proceedings of the Sixth Convention of the Journeyman Tailors' Union of America, 1891," *American Labor Unions' Constitutions, Proceedings, Officers' Reports and Supplementary Documents.*

42. Eileen Boris, "'A Man's Dwelling House Is His Castle': Tenement House Cigarmaking and the Judicial Imperative," in Baron, *Work Engendered,* 139.

43. Ibid., 119–20.

44. Ibid., 139.

45. Cooper, *Once a Cigar Maker,* 50–54.

46. *(Davenport) Evening-Democrat Gazette,* 16 Feb. 1888, 1.

47. George W. Perkins to Samuel Gompers, 23 Nov. 1898, *American Federation of Labor Records: The Samuel Gompers Era,* microfilm ed. (Glen Rock, N.J.: Microfilming Corporation of America, 1979), reel 139, frames 688–90.

48. Cooper, *Once a Cigar Maker,* 6.

49. Mary Blewett, *The Last Generation: Work and Life in the Textile Mills of Lowell, Mass., 1910–1960* (Amherst: University of Massachusetts Press, 1990), 12.

50. M. T. Copeland, *The Cotton Manufacturing Industry of the United States* (Cambridge, Mass.: Harvard University Press, 1912), 123; Mary H. Blewett, "Manhood and the Market: The Politics of Gender and Class among the Textile Workers of Fall River, Massachusetts, 1870–1880," in Baron, *Work Engendered,* 92–113.

51. United States Bureau of Labor, *Strikes and Lockouts; New York Times,* 9 Dec. 1890, 2; 10 Dec. 1890, 9; *Newark Daily Advertiser,* 9 Dec. 1890, 1; 10 Dec. 1890, 1.

52. *Newark Daily Advertiser,* 11 Dec. 1890, 1; 19 Dec. 1890, 1.

53. *Newark Daily Advertiser,* 12 Dec. 1890, 1. In 1888 the company's female employees had gone on strike complaining of the treatment they received from the same superintendent blamed for the 1890/91 mulespinners' strike. See *New York Daily Graphic,* 25 Jan. 1888, 614.

54. SG to AFL Executive Council (EC), 4 Feb. 1891, American Federation of Labor, *Letterpress Copybooks of Samuel Gompers and William Green, Presidents, 1883–1925,* microform ed. (Washington, D.C.: Library of Congress, Photoduplication Service, 1967), microfilm reel 4, vol. 5, frame 408 (hereafter *Letterpress Copybooks*); SG to Henry A. Woods, Kearney, N.J., 5 Feb. 1891, reel 4, vol. 5, frame 413. Boycott circular from AFL EC, *Tailor* 2 (Apr. 1891): 6.

55. See *Tailor* 2 (Apr. 1891): 6; *Seattle Post-Intelligencer,* 16 Mar. 1891, 8.

56. *Newark Daily Advertiser,* 18 Dec. 1890, 1; 22 Dec. 1890, 1; 23 Dec. 1890, 1; 5 Jan. 1891, 1.

57. *New York Times,* 16 Feb. 1891, 1; 12 Mar. 1891, 1; 19 Apr. 1891, 8; *Newark Daily Advertiser,* 16 Feb. 1891, 1; 12 Mar. 1891, 1.

58. *Newark Daily Advertiser,* 6 Jan. 1891, 1.

59. *New York Times,* 16 Feb. 1891, 1; 12 Mar. 1891, 1; 19 Apr. 1891, 8; *Newark Daily Advertiser,* 16 Feb. 1891, 1; 12 Mar. 1891, 1.

60. *New York Times,* 19 Apr. 1891, 8.

61. G. S. Gibb, *The Saco-Lowell Shops: Textile Machinery Building in New England, 1813–1949,* Harvard Studies in Business History 16 (Cambridge, Mass.: Harvard University Press, 1950), 261; Copeland, 73, 123.

62. Blewett, *Men, Women, and Work.*

63. Ibid., 226–29.

64. *Chicago Tribune*, 2 Mar. 1892, 6.

65. *Chicago Tribune*, 3 Mar. 1892, 9.

66. Ibid.

67. *Chicago Tribune*, 4 Mar. 1892, 8.

68. *Chicago Tribune*, 6 Mar. 1892, 3; 8 Mar. 1892, 7.

69. S. Gompers to E. Morgan, 11 Mar. 1892, *Samuel Gompers Papers*, vol. 3: *Unrest and Depression, 1891–94*, ed. Stuart B. Kaufman, Peter J. Albert, Grace Palladino, Ileen A. Devault, Elizabeth Fones-Wolf, and Dorothee Schneider, 154–55; S. Gompers to H. J. Skeffington, 21 Mar. 1892, *Letterpress Copybooks*, microfilm reel 6, vol. 7, frame 154.

70. *Chicago Tribune*, 16 Mar. 1892, 3; 19 Mar. 1892, 3; 20 Apr. 1892, 6.

71. *Chicago Tribune*, 6 Mar. 1892, 3. The speaker, a "Mrs. Brown," was probably Corinne Brown, a former teacher and principal in the Chicago schools, now married to a banker. Brown was, along with Elizabeth Morgan, one of the socialist trade unionist members of the Illinois Woman's Alliance (Meredith Tax, *The Rising of the Women, Feminist Solidarity and Class Conflict, 1880–1917* [New York: Monthly Review Press, 1980], 54, 66).

72. *Chicago Tribune*, 6 Mar. 1892, 3. I have been unable to uncover any additional material on the Elgin strike.

73. *Chicago Tribune*, 26 May 1892, 5.

74. *Chicago Tribune*, 6 Mar. 1892, 3.

75. *Lewiston Evening Journal*, 12 Aug. 1893, 7:1.

76. Cutters walked out on 25 August, lasters not until 25 September (*Lewiston Evening Journal*, 25 Aug. 1893, 7; 25 Sept. 1893, 7).

77. *Lewiston Evening Journal*, 25 Sept. 1893, 7; 26 Sept. 1893, 7; 2 Oct. 1893, 8; 26 Oct. 1893, 7.

78. John T. Cumbler, *Working-Class Community in Industrial America: Work, Leisure, and Struggle in Two Industrial Cities, 1880–1930* (Westport, Conn.: Greenwood Press, 1979), 82; Blewett, *Men, Women, and Work*, 268.

79. Mary Ann Clawson, *Constructing Brotherhood: Class, Gender, and Fraternalism* (Princeton: Princeton University Press, 1989), 46.

80. The category of "skill" was not only gendered, but was also a distinctly racialized concept. In the late nineteenth century, this racialization encompassed both racial and ethnic distinctions.

81. See David R. Roediger, *The Wages of Whiteness: Race and the Making of the American Working Class* (London: Verso, 1991).

82. Perlman and Taft, *Labor Movements*, 9.

Chapter 11

Charting an Independent Course

African-American Railroad Workers
in the World War I Era

ERIC ARNESEN

IT IS WIDELY recognized that the World War I era represented a watershed in African-American history. During these tumultuous years, unprecedented numbers of blacks migrated to the North and gained limited entry into the industrial sector for the first time; bloody race riots swept the nation's cities; and the emergence of the "New Negro" and Marcus Garvey's Universal Negro Improvement Association (UNIA) reflected a dramatic new orientation in black America.[1] The second decade of the twentieth century—and the war and postwar years in particular—also witnessed an upsurge in African-American labor activism that, until recently, has been largely invisible in much of the historiography of African Americans and American labor.

"It is a most commendable fact that the Negroes, instead of waiting for organized labor or any other body to speak for them, has organized itself [*sic*], and is now making this demand for equal and just treatment, not as individuals, but as an organization," the *New World* reported in 1918. "Let the Negro organize and then become conscious that he must contend for his own rights, not individually, but as an organization, he will get somewhere."[2] Though the piece was more an injunction than an accurate description, the author identified a significant wartime development. Unlike black ministers, editors, politicians, or other elites who believed that access to or security of employment took precedence above all else, black labor activists pursued an agenda that accorded considerable importance to challenging economic discrimination, winning rights or recognition, and attaining livable wages and better conditions.

Just as race necessarily constituted a lens through which African-American workers viewed their world and framed their demands, class and class strategies also proved central to black workers' thought and behavior in this period. Black workers (as well as black elites) participated in a wide-ranging debate over the desirability and feasibility of unionization. Should blacks unionize? Join the AFL? the IWW? Hold themselves apart and organize separately? And to what ends? To increase wages or improve working conditions? To court employer approval? To break strikes? These questions engaged the rhetorical and organizational energies of numerous black communities, with discussions taking place in churches, newspaper columns, neighborhoods, and on shop floors. The questions were not new; they extended back to Reconstruction. But the sheer scale of the northward migration in the World War I era, new opportunities born of critical labor shortages in both the South and North, and federal intervention in labor-management relations intensified that debate considerably.[3] The developments of the war and postwar years made the issue of blacks' relationship to organized labor more important than ever.

We remain more familiar with traditions of black anti-unionism and images of black strikebreaking than with black labor activism in this era. The reasons are complex. Before the early 1980s, labor historians paid relatively little attention to race relations and the African-American experience. And just as labor history has had something of a "race" problem, African-American history too has had its own "class" or "labor" problem. Failing to develop the scholarly tradition established by Charles Wesley, Abram Harris, Sterling Spero, Horace Cayton, and George Mitchell,[4] subsequent historians of the African-American experience often submerged black urban workers into the greater black community, thereby erasing distinctive class-related experiences. They focused instead upon the more literate black elites who left behind a paper trail that made their activities and ideologies easier to reconstruct.[5] With historians' attention further diverted from black workers' protest by the equation of the labor movement with white labor, the labor movement appeared less as an arena of contestation and struggle than as a hostile, alien force that excluded blacks from its ranks and from entire sectors of the economy. Yet in ceding the ground of labor activism to white trade unionists, these historians have rendered invisible black trade unionism and activism that does not fall neatly within the framework of race relations or middle-class activism. This "class" problem has had significant effects on the writing of black history, enabling authors to minimize or neglect entire areas of black protest. Only since the 1980s have labor and African-American history begun focusing on the subject of black labor, generating studies that cast light on both working-class race relations and African-American working-class experience.[6]

This essay explores several strains of an African-American union tradition in the railroad industry during and after World War I. Placing the rise of black labor activism in the context of the 1910s and early 1920s, it argues that the class and racial dimensions of the black experience cannot be divorced in any analysis of black workers' perspectives and movements. Black workers pursued workplace organizing for predictable economic reasons: they sought to increase wages, decrease hours, establish equitable work rules, win official recognition, and negotiate with employers. Yet black unions were not simply imitations of their white counterparts, because black railroaders labored in an industry characterized by sharp racial divisions and racist practices. Black trade unions or labor associations also constituted vehicles for pursuing black railroaders' distinct interests as *black* workers. Even their goals sometimes differed markedly from those of white unions, for blacks faced two distinct challenges to employment security: discriminatory job ladders that barred blacks from key positions while reserving most subordinate positions exclusively for them, on the one hand, and a fiercely hostile white labor movement that sought to advance its members' interests at blacks' expense, on the other. Formulating effective responses to those challenges, however, generated no single perspective or organizing approach. The black labor tradition of the World War I era not only differed from that of white labor, but itself reflected a remarkable diversity of visions and strategies.

Since the origins of American railroading, African Americans have constituted a vital part of its labor force. By the late nineteenth and early twentieth centuries, blacks worked as track layers, repair or maintenance-of-way crew members, and coach and car cleaners; as firemen and brakemen on board trains in the South; in service jobs as dining car waiters, porters and maids, and station red caps; and in railroad locomotive construction and repair yards. Yet for all of their skills and abilities, blacks confronted widespread employment discrimination. Everywhere they were barred from positions as conductors and engineers. In the North, blacks were also kept out of jobs as firemen and brakemen by the joint consent of white workers and managers; in the South, they worked as firemen and brakemen, but were subject to a wide range of discriminatory and racist practices, including seniority systems that favored whites, percentage agreements limiting their numbers, and a campaign by white labor—conducted at the contract negotiating table, in the halls of legislatures, and, from time to time, through outright terrorism—to reduce or eliminate them altogether.[7] The fictional Isaac Zachary, an African-American railroad firemen in Lloyd Brown's proletarian novel, *Iron City*, put it this way: "just remember this as long as you're black and live in Mississippi: there's three main things Cap'n Charlie won't 'low you to do, and that's mess with his women, vote in the elections, or drive a railroad train."[8]

Four developments prepared the ground for black labor associations in the early twentieth century. First, the 1910s witnessed unprecedented levels of working-class militancy, before, during, and after the war; black workers simply participated in the broader upheavals. Second, the emergence of the "New Negro"—in part born out of disillusionment with fighting a war for democracy abroad while being denied even a semblance of democracy at home—reflected a new assertiveness on the part of African Americans that proved conducive to organized and individual protest. The "New Negro," one observer noted, "asks no odds, but a square deal; . . . does not cringe or fawn . . . but demands his rights under the constitution—equal opportunities in the common affairs of life . . . in a word, justice."[9] This new attitude, prominently manifested in the flowering of black literature and arts in the 1920s, also found expression in the dramatic expansion of black protest organizations, including the nationalist UNIA, the civil rights oriented National Association for the Advancement of Colored People (NAACP), and a wide array of black labor groups. Third, white railroad labor's campaigns against black firemen, brakemen, switchmen, and porter-brakemen intensified after 1909; these black railroaders responded to campaigns for their elimination or restriction by organizing in self-defense. Fourth, and perhaps most important for the railroad industry, the federal government's increased involvement in managing class relations afforded black workers a valuable opportunity that they did not previously have. Whether testifying before the Commission on Industrial Relations in 1915, the Federal Wage Commission in 1918, or the U.S. Railroad Administration during and after the war, black workers now had a platform and an audience. Black organizations petitioned the government on behalf of their members, and rank-and-file black railroaders flooded the Railroad Administration with thousands of letters, outlining the abuses they endured and the inequalities they suffered. The advances made in this era were largely the result of a responsive federal government.

All African-American workers did not respond to workplace conditions and discrimination in the same fashion; their attitudes toward employers and white labor varied from organization to organization. Some sought organizational refuge through subordinate membership in the nation's largest and strongest working-class body, the American Federation of Labor (AFL). But while the black weekly *Washington Tribune* counted "many thousands of Negroes in organized labor as part and parcel of the existing Internationals,"[10] few of them were railroad workers. The independent white brotherhoods insisted upon jurisdiction over their crafts and simply wanted nothing to do with them. Far more common and significant was what the Tuskegee-based *Negro Year Book* called the "recent tendency" of black labor "to organize itself independent of white labor unions. The main reason . . . is that Negro labor feels that it is not receiving a square deal at the hands of white labor."[11] It was on the nation's vast rail system that such black workers' associations—both those affiliated with organized labor and those standing autonomously—first and most strongly developed.

Pullman porters remain perhaps the best known group of African-American railroaders. George Pullman made his mark and fortune by offering luxurious rail accommodations to long-distance travelers beginning in 1867. In addition to physical comfort, Pullman provided quality service. He drew upon a tradition of black service labor and brought into being the generic African-American porter—named "George"—to wait attentively upon Pullman car riders. By the late nineteenth century, the Pullman Company had become the single largest employer of African-American labor in the United States with some twelve thousand black porters on its payroll by World War I. Porters occupied a precarious and paradoxical position. An elite within the African-American working class, they traveled widely and earned wages that were comparatively good for blacks. At the same time they worked long hours, endured both managerial and passenger abuse, and had to assume a servile demeanor toward all whites. "Few workers in America are so low in the industrial world . . . [or] are as helpless," A. Philip Randolph once observed.[12]

Only after 1909 did organized and sustained porter discontent surface publicly. A number of independent porters' associations protested the long hours, lack of promotion opportunities, and low wages that employers justified on the grounds that tipping made higher wages unnecessary. In late 1912, porters in Oakland, California, formed a union to challenge the "oppressive actions of illiterate and ignorant conductors, the subserviency [*sic*] which they are obliged to show to anybody who is able to buy accommodations on their cars."[13] These porters' target was less railroad managers than white conductors and white riders who treated them with abuse. Yet in the prewar era, porters made few gains, despite the publicity provided by the black press and hearings of the U.S. Commission on Industrial Relations. Only when the United States government assumed operating control over Pullman cars in 1918 was progress forthcoming. Sleeping and parlor cars, the U.S. Railroad Administration argued, had "become an essential and indispensable part of our transportation system"[14] warranting government oversight. Federal administrators who assumed responsibility for labor relations in that field held hearings, heard porters' testimony, and finally ordered wage increases.

New unionization efforts produced porters' locals across the country. In New York, the Pullman Employees League, formed in June 1918, exhibited the spirit that "from now on," porters must "receive a living wage." "The agitation among these men," the socialist *New York Call* reported, "is being carried from New York to all parts of the country."[15] The following year, in July 1919, some five thousand people assembled in a Harlem auditorium under the aegis of the Brotherhood of Sleeping Car Porters Protective Union, which gathered to "lay a better foundation for future Colored Americans." "We are willing to work and at the same time be courteous," a porters' statement read, "but we are going to insist that we are men and as such entitled to a living wage. . . . We are men and added to this WE ARE UNION MEN."[16] Drawing on gendered language to establish their case for dignity, World War I era porters' protest anticipated by a decade the Brotherhood of Sleeping Car Porters' (BSCP) slogan of service, not servility. Along with the white railroad brotherhoods, porters' groups (as well as associations of dining car waiters and other black railroaders) testified before various railroad labor boards during the war, pressing the government with modest success to address long-standing grievances. "For the first time in all their existence as Pullman porters," Frank Boyd, a Minneapolis-based former porter and member of the BSCP later recalled, "they could speak their honest opinion on one of the most vital issues of life, security. For once their constitutional rights to this extent were not invaded. So Unionism became the topic of conversation among the porters."[17]

Such progress did not outlast the war and government control. Once the railroads reverted to private hands, the Pullman Company resumed its traditional anti-union stance. In the 1920s, it oversaw an elaborate system of surveillance, fired union activists, and maintained its own employee representation plan—in essence a company union—the Pullman Porters Benefit Association, effectively undermining porters' independent unions. Although a new Brotherhood of Sleeping Car Porters, headed by the socialist journalist A. Philip Randolph, was formed in 1925, it would take another decade—one marked by repeated defeats, a severe economic depression, and a new political environment—for the union to achieve official recognition and another two years to win its first contract.

Porters were hardly the only group of black railroaders to challenge economic hardship or racial oppression in this period. Black locomotive firemen and brakemen had formed numerous local and regional associations, including the International Order of Colored Locomotive Firemen (Savannah), the National Standard Order of Locomotive Firemen (Macon, Georgia), the Colored Trainmen of America (Texas), and the Grand United Order of Locomotive Firemen of America (Knoxville). The 2,000-member Interstate Association of Negro Trainmen of America maintained small chapters in Pennsylvania, Maryland, New York, Ohio, Mexico, Mississippi, Louisiana, Arkansas, Missouri, Kansas, New Mexico, and Texas. Aiming to perfect "a union of all unorganized colored employees of the railway lines of America, for their full protection in working conditions and wages," it sought to "maintain and insure standard working conditions and a uniform wage scale; to destroy caste and color prejudice that militate against justice as to these essentials; and to establish reciprocity between such other bodies of organized labor as shall be necessary for the promotion of the welfare of the Negro employees of the nation's railway." Its hope of becoming "one of the greatest labor unions in the United States, not less effective from a racial standpoint than the American Federation of Labor, in conserving the common rights of our trainmen" was never realized. But in the immediate postwar years, the *Norfolk Journal and Guide* praised its recent "phenomenal progress" which had inspired its "sponsors to believe that the association is to fill a large place in American history, far surpassing any previous effort to mobilize the thousands of Negro trainmen, who have needed only progressive leadership to obtain the rights and immunities due them."[18]

The largest and most impressive group—which brought many of these local organizations under its wing—was the Railway Men's International Benevolent Industrial Association (RMIBIA), founded in 1915 and led by dining car waiter Robert L. Mays. At its height in 1920, it claimed a membership of 15,000; Chicago alone boasted some seventeen chapters with about 1,200 members in 1922.[19] Aspiring to build a federation of all black railroaders, RMIBIA leaders recruited existing bodies of firemen, brakemen, and yard and shop workers, not just service workers. Before its slow demise in the early 1920s, Mays and other officials lobbied politicians for legislation prohibiting discriminatory contracts, testified before congressional and state legislative committees to publicize the plight of their members, and initiated lawsuits over wages, job security, and working conditions.

Though the RMIBIA began as an independent body, Robert Mays initially sought the protection, strength, and legitimacy that affiliation with the powerful AFL could bring. The ever ambitious Mays approached the federation with a plan to transform the RMIBIA into a huge industrial union of all black railroad workers. Accepting segregation as a given, Mays appealed to the Committee on Organization at the 1918 AFL convention for an international charter for a union embracing Pullman porters, dining car cooks and waiters, black brakemen, train porters, firemen, switchmen, yard engine men, shop workers, boilermakers and assistants, machinists and helpers, coach cleaners, laundry workers, and track laborers (among others). To his disgust, the committee rejected his request outright, on the grounds that such a union would trespass on existing craft unions' jurisdictional rights and that the AFL did not grant charters along "racial lines."[20] Even though some unions had "not yet opened their doors to colored workers," the committee anticipated "the day in the near future when these organizers will take a broader view of this matter"—hopeful thinking at best, willful duplicity at worst. The most the AFL was willing to do was to issue federal charters to individual groups of black railroaders.

His grand overture spurned by the AFL, Mays declared rhetorical war against the federation and the white railroad brotherhoods, now his main enemies. Black railroaders "must stand together," a RMIBIA bulletin declared in 1920, "in order first to prevent white unions from removing us completely from these jobs, second in order to get proper pay and working conditions from the Railroads." The crux of the issue, Mays informed the Chicago Commission on Race Relations in 1919, was this: "We agree with the policies and principles" of the AFL "so long as they are American and in the interests of the workmen, but if their practices are against Negroes, then we are against the American Federation of Labor unflinchingly."[21] Until the larger labor movement accorded blacks full equality, the RMIBIA vowed to continue steadfastly in its independent organizing.

Individual leaders and organizers crossed the South proselytizing on behalf of black organizational independence. Monroe James, a brakeman on the Gulf Coast Lines based in DeQuincy, Louisiana, conducted an organizing drive in the summer of 1920. He found the entire region "flooded with literature of the American Federation of Labor offering the black man membership in the A.F. of L. organization on the same terms offered to white men, color line having been abolished." James was dismayed to find the AFL attractive to the men with whom he spoke. "It was disgusting to me to see how many black men fell to such untrue propaganda, especially the maintenance of way men." Aggressively pushing membership in the RMIBIA, he waged a "determined fight" to convince the men "to stay out of the white man's organization, and stick to the black man's that has the interest of the black man at heart."[22]

The RMIBIA worked hard to persuade black railroad workers of the wisdom of its stance. In October 1920, its leaders went up against those of the AFL for the allegiance of the Brotherhood of Sleeping Car Porters Protective Union in Chicago. The five AFL representatives, which included a vice president of the Chicago Federation of Labor, a president of a Chicago union, and "many colored men who are members of the A.F. of L.," openly solicited the porters' affiliation. Actively opposed was Robert Mays. The RMIBIA did not reject "the fine principles of the Federation of Labor," he argued, but "rather [it] was an association of colored men formed for the purpose of protesting unfair treatment towards Negro Railway employes whether that treatment came from the employing companies or from the organized white labor unions." He expressed appreciation for "everything which had been done by the A.F. of L. to raise the status of labor as a whole." While "he was willing at all times to co-ordinate with the A.F. of L. to sustain the victories already won," Mays made clear that "still as long as there was an effort being made by any union of the A.F. of L. to keep the Negro laborer under the status of American workmen," his association would "direct all efforts against that union in a sincere and fearless attempt to correct that condition, and to give our people a square deal in industry." Mays's arguments carried the day, for not a single delegate of the porters introduced a motion to affiliate with the AFL.[23] But not all the porters actually affiliated with the RMIBIA. Some eventually did turn to the AFL, and when porters founded the BSCP in 1925, they quickly sought affiliation with that larger body of organized workers.[24]

The RMIBIA's accomplishments ultimately proved slight. If Mays received more positive press coverage from African-American journalists than he deserved, it was perhaps because his explicit stance on white labor unions echoed that of much of the black press, and the influential *Chicago Defender* in particular. Mays focused his anger far more on white labor than on white employers. After the war, his efforts failed to alter white brotherhood policies or break down corporate discriminatory barriers; and the small wage increases he helped win rendered him wholly dependent upon the U.S. Railroad Administration and subsequent Railroad Labor Boards. By the early 1920s, the favorable political environment that had permitted him to deliver the goods—however meager—to his constituents had grown far more hostile to black labor. In practice, Mays remained racially radical and economically conservative. After 1920, the RMIBIA dabbled in insurance and banking, sponsored conferences with Tuskegee Institute and Urban League representatives, and strenuously promoted a "program of racial economic unity" and "racial economic cooperation based on untrammeled opportunity for the Colored laborer and pyramiding into fuller race support of Negro business enterprises."[25] These failed to flower, and leaders resorted to bitter sectarian squabbling with those dissident members who questioned Mays's judgment or pursued a different agenda. Mays's appeals to dignity and racial pride—"Don't fear! Be Men! . . . Don't be an old-time Negro," a RMIBIA ad insisted in 1921—did not attract or retain adherents to the union cause.[26] By 1926, Mays was publicly blasting the upstart A. Philip Randolph, resentful of being ignored and pushed aside by a new group of organizers. He had built a movement with himself at the center, personally claiming credit for victories, blaming untrustworthy opponents for his failures. By the second half of the 1920s, the RMIBIA was no more, and Mays himself was reduced to accepting handouts from the Associate Negro Press's Claude Barnett, no fan of black unionization in this era. When the next upsurge of black railroad unionism took place in the 1930s, Mays would try to angle in on the action, but remained peripheral, ignored both by activists who had come of political age during the 1920s and by the generation that emerged during the Great Depression.[27]

Black workers in the railroad industry's operating division and switching yards faced the greatest challenges to their job security in the postwar years.

Their associations fought a drawn-out and ultimately unsuccessful battle to stem the tide of discriminatory rules and job loss. In contrast to Pullman porters who sought affiliation with the AFL or Mays's fiercely independent RMIBIA, these organizations neither found white allies within the organized labor movement nor issued quasi-nationalist statements of black autonomy and overt appeals to racial pride. Operating in the heart of the Jim Crow South, they accepted some limits on black employment, argued that past and current black loyalty warranted their retention in the labor force, and invoked the principles of American democracy and constitutional protections to advance their case against some forms of discrimination. The experiences of the Colored Association of Railway Employees (CARE)[28] illustrate how the specific constraints under which these black workers operated informed the development of a cautious, legalistic approach to black protest on the rails that both accepted and challenged Jim Crow.

By the early twentieth century, blacks in the operating trades and yard service faced growing hostility and competition from whites, particularly those enrolled in the Brotherhood of Railroad Trainmen (BRT), representing white brakemen and some switchmen, and the Brotherhood of Locomotive Firemen and Enginemen. These white unions had for decades sought to reduce the number of blacks working in their trades or to eliminate them altogether; at various times they employed threats, strikes, and terrorist violence to get their way. Although they had negotiated contractual restrictions on the percentages of blacks employed on specified rail runs by the 1910s, they remained unsatisfied. The fluid economic conditions of the war and immediate postwar years unsettled white unionists. "Never in its history has the organized labor movement been confronted with greater peril than at the present time," the white firemen's journal concluded immediately after the formal entry of the United States into the war.[29]

With somewhat less hyperbole, white brotherhood leaders predicted that labor market disruptions would allow railroad companies or the federal government to use alleged labor shortages as a pretext for hiring large numbers of African Americans to weaken the white unions' influence.[30] In fact, labor market conditions did lead to the employment of thousands of black migrants as construction and maintenance laborers on the Baltimore and Ohio, the Pennsylvania, the New York Central, and other northern lines. But the operating trades were not affected. The brotherhoods feared, but did not actually encounter, increased black competition. On the local level, however, unease about the present and uncertainty about the future produced heightened levels of white racial anxiety that could easily spill out into the open.

In the switching yards of Memphis, Tennessee, the conflict over the racial composition of the railroad labor force exploded shortly after the armistice. A five-day unauthorized hate strike against black switchmen and brakemen in January 1919 involved some 650 white switchmen and hundreds of sympathetic white firemen, engineers, flagmen, yardmasters, and conductors. White switchmen in the Memphis rail yards had charged for years that blacks threatened brotherhood fortunes. (In the late nineteenth century, white brakeman and union official S. J. Whitaker complained angrily that Memphis was "not a Brotherhood town" because it was "a 'nigger' town as far as train and yard men are concerned.") Now, in early 1919, they resolved to end the almost half-century tradition of black labor force participation. Drawing on the familiar themes of white railroadmen's past protests, spokesmen charged that blacks were incompetents who endangered the lives of their white counterparts. Strike chairman E. P. Tucker complained that blacks had "roundly cursed them" and at other times threatened them with violence; some blacks appeared "insolent, overbearing and vindictive, so that it is a menace to our lives to work with them;" they were "becoming rougher;" some were going around "armed" and "are more ready to use [their weapons] . . . than formerly."[31] But the conflict was less about the real or imagined disposition of black workers than about the racial distribution of available jobs. Always sensitive to the number of blacks and their distribution among yard crews, whites now fearful of rising unemployment proposed to extend their hold over jobs previously reserved for blacks. Over the next year or so, a new chapter in the history of racial exclusion in railroad employment would be written.[32]

During the war, the racial composition of the Memphis yard labor force fluctuated unpredictably and without serious objections from white workers. A regular yard crew customarily consisted of a white foreman, a white switchmen, and a black helper. Although the BRT's contract stipulated that promotion and layoffs would be governed by seniority, the uncontested twenty-five-year practice had been to rely upon two separate seniority lists, one for blacks and one for whites; that is, white foremen and switchmen were drawn from one seniority list, black helpers from another. But wartime labor shortages required some flexibility in the racial distribution of labor. As Railroad Administration official B. L. Winchell learned, it "has always been the practice when there was a shortage of colored helpers to temporarily fill the crew with white helpers and also if there was a shortage of white crewmen to put the second colored helper on the crew."[33]

Before the war's end, a shortage of black labor in Memphis rail yards allowed whites to make unexpected gains. In 1917 and 1918, expanding opportunities in war-related industries and other fields offered blacks a greater range of employment options than they had once had; similarly, the military draft reduced the number of available black workers. The Yazoo & Mississippi Valley railroad addressed this problem by occasionally employing a white switchman to fill in for an absent black helper. With the armistice, the number of black yard workers increased noticeably, their separate seniority list expanded, and the railroad removed those whites filling jobs customarily reserved for blacks.[34] This was not simply a matter of labor supply, for black workers' actions had prompted the restoration of the railroad's policy. "Finding that the positions formerly held by the colored switchmen were fast becoming filled by whites," the black yard workers' grievance committee had approached the terminal's yardmaster, who then ordered the discharge of some eighteen white men and their replacement by blacks.[35]

White workers rebelled. They now targeted the dual seniority system and the practice of reserving the helpers' position for blacks, demanding a unification of seniority lines as a means of displacing blacks. With certain positions off-limits to blacks, senior white switchmen would bid for helper's jobs, thus bumping black workers off the crews completely, while junior whites would take the now-vacated positions barred to blacks. Rail managers, however, held firm, maintaining that these men "had no right to any work on the colored seniority board." White workers were simply creating a "race question of giving the white man a position which he has not heretofore enjoyed."[36]

The January hate strike and subsequent brotherhood protests placed the issue of the postwar racial division of labor squarely before the U.S. Railroad Administration. White switchmen bombarded the Railroad Administration with telegrams listing their grievances against black co-workers, while BRT officials pursued white labor's agenda before federal officials and railroad managers. In the end, BRT persistence paid off handsomely, for the contract it secured settled the race question on the terms set by the white union men. Reiterating old restrictions on and establishing new barriers to black employment, contract provisions eliminated the dual seniority system, raised entrance requirements to key positions (to put presumably less-educated African Americans at a competitive disadvantage), and explicitly reserved for whites a number of jobs previously open to blacks.[37] "Nowhere in the long columns of fine print was the word Negro mentioned," novelist Lloyd L. Brown observed accurately in a fictional treatment of the era, "but to the black railroaders reading it every word was doom."[38]

Black railroaders immediately understood how the new rules worked against them. The seniority change, complained CARE president John Henry Eiland, was "apparently fair on its face," but "its enforcement unjustly and unfairly discriminates" against blacks. Whites with considerable seniority in job categories barred to blacks would voluntarily relinquish their positions, thus creating openings for junior white men. Then they would claim positions held by blacks, "rolling" them off their jobs. The application of what black railroaders termed the one-sided or Jim Crow seniority rule "would finally mean [blacks'] complete elimination."[39] The new rules, which were adopted for their "freeze-out and eliminating effects," complained black labor activist Thomas Redd on behalf of some sixty-nine black Kentucky brakemen in 1928, constituted nothing less than a "negro elimination program." The impact on black employment was devastating. As various railroads adopted the rules from 1919 to 1921, thousands of black workers lost their jobs.[40]

In their year-long quest for racially exclusionary provisions, the BRT received considerable assistance from top Railroad Administration officials. Among the most sympathetic to the white unionists' cause were labor division head W. S. Carter—the Texas-born former president of the firemen's brotherhood who had for decades championed restrictions on black labor—and C. S. Lake, the assistant director of the Railroad Administration's Division of Operations. Lake was a former general manager of the Seaboard Airline, a Virginian by birth, and a "typical southerner," in the opinion of the NAACP's Walter White. In a five-and-a-half hour meeting between Lake and black leaders in early January 1920 to discuss the new discriminatory contract provisions, White found it "exceedingly difficult to have Mr. Lake keep to a discussion of the matter which we came to discuss." (Among Lake's digressions were recollections of his "old black mammy" and expressions of his love for Negroes). Lake denied that the rules were designed to discriminate against blacks at all. Rather, they were "used for the purpose of protecting those Negroes now employed in the railroad service since there was determined effort to oust the colored man." Rejecting the detailed assessment of the rules' impact on black employment made by CARE president John Henry Eiland, Lake concluded that "there was no power in Heaven and earth which would convince the Railroad Administration that such a rule was discriminatory," for it "made no difference to them what colored trainmen thought about the matter."[41]

More than racial sympathies lay behind the Railroad Administration's easy capitulation to the BRT's demands. Concerns over the brotherhood's repeated demonstrations of militancy (on many issues), its demand for the permanent nationalization of the railroads, and labor unrest across the nation contributed to the government's decision. Facing radicalized unions on the rails and attempting to hold the line on wage increases, Railroad Administration officials sought to placate railway labor unions through nonmonetary concessions; in essence, they sought to trade the issue of white supremacy for others. B. L. Winchell, the Railroad Administration's southeastern regional director, confessed as much to CARE president Eiland in early 1920. Winchell's attitude was "that he had accepted the less of two evils,—that is, he had complied with the demands of the white trainmen rather than endure a strike. The crux of his opinion was that it was better to inconvenience a few men (colored) than to tie up the entire south for an indifinite [sic] length of time."[42] Given the balance of power—large, strong, and potentially disruptive white unions, on the one hand, and small, weak, and relatively powerless black workers on the other—and the absence of any federal commitment to African-American civil rights in the workplace or anywhere, Winchell's choice was logical and unsurprising. With the final settlements, government administrators managed to avoid a potentially devastating strike over the race issue in the months before returning the railroads back to private ownership and management.[43]

Black yard workers and brakemen did not stand idly by while white trainmen negotiated them out of work. Represented by the independent CARE, rank-and-file black workers formed yard committees, presented grievances to managers, provided affidavits, and attended mass meetings, while their union leaders presented complaints to company and government officials. These protests, however, were fundamentally cautious, seeking to persuade white elites to restore the earlier status quo, despite its racial inequities. Whatever the changes in disposition and expectation wrought by the war, African Americans in southern rail centers remained enmeshed in a system of racial subordination that made overt protest dangerous. The grievance committee of the Memphis branch of the CARE, for instance, petitioned the Yazoo & Mississippi Valley railroad for adherence to the long-standing tradition of separate seniority lists that offered some degree of protection to traditionally black jobs. But the committee did not—and likely could not—wage an aggressive public campaign. Nor could black workers bring economic pressure to bear on companies. Such action risked bringing down upon them the wrath of Memphis police, who were all too eager to engage in anti-black and anti-labor terror, and would have accomplished little. Gradually rising unemployment in the postwar years, coupled with white labor's covetous interest in traditionally black jobs, virtually guaranteed their complete replacement in the event of a walkout.

Black yard and train workers lacked two advantages available to their white counterparts. First, given the racial climate of the day, whites could stake a claim to black jobs—any jobs—while blacks could stake no legitimate claim to white jobs. And second, black workers could count on no extensive network of labor solidarity to bolster their claims. What made the threats of the white hate strikers in Memphis so compelling was the strong support received from other white, skilled, and hard-to-replace railroaders. The Railroad Administration's receptivity to white demands derived from the power of organized white railroad labor; the trainmen's union could cause disruption through a walkout of its own members allied with other white brotherhood men. Black workers, in contrast, possessed no such support. Indeed, despite the efforts of black firemen, trainmen, and service workers to form independent associations in the World War I era, their organizational reach remained limited by geography, their unity undermined by persistent craft divisions, their ideological outlook circumscribed by their belief in the need for caution, and their power weakened by their need to propitiate white railroad managers.

In their battle to preserve black jobs, African-American labor leaders appealed to Railroad Administration officials, mediators, and judges. Given the highly technical nature of the contract provisions and the bureaucratic procedures used to enact them, CARE logically turned for assistance to the NAACP.[44] The NAACP was no stranger to labor issues. In the pages of the *Crisis*, editor W. E. B. Du Bois repeatedly castigated white unionists for their racist attitudes and policies. During and after the war, NAACP officials challenged the AFL to live up to its name, embrace black unionists, and force recalcitrant white unions to drop their long-standing color bars. It had even publicly denounced the Railroad Administration in November 1918 for an order limiting the hiring of blacks on the northwestern railroads, which it succeeded in having rescinded. Now, it wasted no time in denouncing the Memphis strikers for depriving blacks of work. Over the next year, its officials occasionally advised black labor leaders in their dealings with government officials, and Walter White attended sessions with Railroad Administration personnel. But labor remained a side issue for the NAACP, despite the influx of working-class blacks into the organization after 1917. Other issues dominated its agenda. The association would take up the "question of discrimination shown towards Negro labor . . . as soon as it can possibly get to it," Walter White honestly admitted, warning that "our immediate fight at the present time is towards the abolishing of the lynching evil in America."[45] Only when white locomotive firemen and trainmen turned violent, carrying out an assassination spree in 1921 and 1922 did the NAACP temporarily assume a more aggressive role.

It fell to black labor organizations alone to carry on the fight to its conclusion. During 1919 and 1920, Eiland and other CARE leaders lobbied
railroad managers and federal officials, providing statistical information
collected by local activists and personal evidence in the form of letters,
petitions, and statements of fact about the impact of the white trainmen's
discriminatory rules. A great deal was at stake in the black struggle against
the white trainmen's "well laid and far reaching plan," Eiland argued.
Should the Railroad Administration comply with the white BRT's request
for the unification of racially separate seniority lines, "it will indeed be a
stab to my race," the "beginning of a move that will eventually mean the
complete elimination of our race from the railroads . . . [which] will spread
throughout the country into every industry where the Negro holds positions that amounts to anything financially."[46] By virtue of their long service in the railroad industry, African Americans should be allowed to "retain these positions formerly held by us, and that our right to earn an
honest living—our constitutional rights—should be considered, regardless of . . . Brotherhood contracts."[47]

If access to traditionally all-black jobs was a constitutional right, access
to all jobs apparently was not. Or rather, that wasn't a realistic demand.
Eiland believed, not without reason, that it would be simply impossible
for any African American to exercise that right in the context of post-
World War I American society. "No colored man in the employ of the
railroad company in any department and particularly the operating department," he informed the Railroad Labor Board in 1920, "would ever
dare to demand on account of seniority rights a place then filled and occupied by a white man. Both his life, liberty and property would be seriously endangered, in fact the law would simply invite him to commit suicide by doing what it apparently authorized."[48]

The caution that underlay Eiland's disclaimers of interest in traditionally white jobs led him further down the path of reinforcing black subordination in the job market. CARE went out of its way to reassure
southern whites, rail managers, and federal officials as to the essentially
conservative and highly limited nature of its goals. The association's
members, "individually and collectively," Eiland insisted in 1920, "do not
desire social equality with the white man. They ask for no rule or regulation which would enable them or any of them to take from the white
man the position which he occupies in the transportation service."[49] To
the president of the Illinois Central, C. H. Markham, Eiland had earlier disavowed any broader challenge to segregated job lines and prohibitions on blacks in more skilled positions. "The negro in this depart-

ment," he wrote in February 1920, "has never seeked [*sic*] promotion—furthermore, we have no special objections to the rule barring us from filling the position of flagman" (although they thought it to be "a poor rule"). Nor did they pursue "an equality of consideration of pay with the white man"—a surprising statement, given the popularity among black railroaders of the wartime General Order No. 27, which had equalized wages for blacks and whites performing comparable work.[50] Hoping to reassure the officials to whom he appealed, Eiland depicted a loyal, hard-working people: "As a rule," he noted, "the peculiarities under which the negro of the South has accustomed himself to . . . still enables him to labor hard in the face of oppression, unfairness and hardships, without complaining and, is one of the most docile facets in the fields of industry to deal with." The very "voices of thousands of black men protesting against this unfair ruling," Eiland concluded, referring to the unification of seniority lines, "is only a warning that they are, beyond a shadow of doubt, facing conditions which are unjust and Unamerican."[51] With bloody race riots less than a year in the past and with white brotherhood members in a particularly aggressive mood, Eiland navigated his association carefully between the shores of complete justice and the shoals of racial hatred. Pragmatically limited in what he could demand, he felt constrained to make a moral case on behalf of a racially unequal system that appeared preferable to the even more racially unequal system in the making.

However devastating the new rules were for black workers, many rank-and-file white railroaders remained dissatisfied with the speed of racial displacement. In the months following the unauthorized Memphis strike, black resistance to contractual restrictions initially slowed the progress of the brotherhood's leaders in convincing federal official and railroad managers to agree to contract changes; the subsequent drawn-out challenges by black unions before the Railroad Labor Board kept unresolved the ultimate fate of black labor.[52] As formal and informal negotiations proceeded slowly, the continued (if reduced) employment of black switchmen and brakemen suggested to some whites that they had not yet finished the job of ridding the railroads of black competition. With that goal in mind, they took matters into their own hands and invoked their most deadly weapon: racial terrorism.

The first blow, struck in March 1920 in Nettleton, Mississippi, was apparently an act of spontaneous racial violence. Declaring that "he would get all of the colored brakemen off the Frisco System," white brakemen Fred Lewis provoked an argument with black brakemen James Henderson. In "true Southern Barbaric style," the *Chicago Whip* reported, Lewis first mauled Henderson with his fists, shot him in cold blood, and "beat the brains out of the unfortunate Henderson with a club."[53] Racial violence escalated the following year. Yazoo & Mississippi Valley brakeman Horace Hurd—married, aged twenty-seven, a resident of Lake Cormorant, Mississippi, and a five-year veteran of the railroad—was the first victim in early 1921. While performing his duties on board train No. 59, he was shot and "literally torn to pieces by the terrific discharge of the weapon." Pinned to the coat of the murdered man was a note that read: "Let this be a lesson to all nigger brakemen." Next to die was Arthur Tyler, a twenty-seven-year-old brakeman employed by the railroad for eleven years, who was shot just five miles south of where Hurd had been killed, on 9 April. Twenty-three-year-old Henry Hager met an identical fate on 6 May, when whites ambushed him when his train stopped for water at Raines, Tennessee, just south of Memphis.[54]

Jesse Ficklin, a brakeman for the Gulf and Ship Island Railroad and a member of CARE Lodge Number 30 based in Hattiesburg, Mississippi, was a little luckier, for he escaped with a warning and his life. Two white men flagged down his train, which was en route from Laurel to Saratoraga, Mississippi, on 14 May 1921. These two armed assailants boarded the train, beat Ficklin, and "threatened to kill him if he ever came to Laurel again on that train." Reluctantly, Ficklin heeded their advice. The black brakemen, he later complained, were "being shot, beaten and white-capped off the railroads with threats of death, stating in their words, that the job is a white man's job, and they must not be caught on it again." The "men are being driven out of the service daily by this method," and unless some solution was found, the "colored men will soon be driven off of the railroad on the southern lines."[55]

By the summer of 1921, the black press openly wrote of an organized conspiracy to intimidate black workers into "voluntarily" relinquishing their positions. African-American railroaders, it appeared, were the targets of what Eiland called a "well laid plan" by "midnight assassins" to strike "terror to the hearts of the black men," thereby enabling whites to "come into possession of those positions which [the black brakeman] has been successfully filling for 50 years." The "carnival of blood," as the *Defender* called it, abated only when railroad companies appointed special agents to guard train employees. Sporadic terrorist attacks continued into the following spring.[56]

~⋺

The upsurge of black labor organizing on the nation's rail systems ran its course by the early 1920s. CARE's campaign to overturn discriminatory contracts failed, its appeals for justice largely rejected by employers and an indifferent Railroad Labor Board. Similarly, the RMIBIA lay in shambles, its appeals largely ignored by black workers more interested in results than ideology. Pullman porters' locals too collapsed in the face of hostile employer opposition; even the Brotherhood of Sleeping Car Porters, formed in 1925, would take over a decade to establish itself as a permanent fixture capable of transforming labor and race relations. If the wartime era produced a variety of African-American responses to the problems confronting black railroaders, ultimately, the varied black labor upsurge won few enduring victories. The larger political, social, and economic atmosphere proved increasingly inhospitable to black demands in the early 1920s, shifting the balance of power toward employers and white labor. Unable to strike because of their vulnerable position, some black workers sought to promote amicable relations with employers in the hope of securing a more solid place for blacks in the industry. But success remained dependent on the receptivity of the wartime Railroad Administration and the postwar Railroad Labor Boards. The imperative of reducing labor turnover vanished with the war's end, as did the government's need to meet basic black demands. In the postwar era, government and corporate officials took far more seriously threats from white labor, leading them to grant fewer black requests as time went on. Service workers from 1919 through the mid-1930s and operating trades workers from 1919 through the mid-1940s remained largely powerless on the job.

The rise and fall of a war-era black labor movement must be seen in the context of the rise and fall of a more general popular insurgency, both black and white. These were years of intensified social, class, and racial conflict, as different groups clashed over fundamental values and visions. Ultimately, the sense of new possibilities that had opened up for the labor movement and for many working-class African Americans had been crushed. The charting of such an independent course in the railroad industry provided only weak protection to black workers in the years following World War I. Neither appeals to employer paternalism, to racial pride, to white labor leaders, or to the black community proved sufficient to resist employer antiunionism and white union racism in the railroad industry. But if the postwar years saw few advances and many defeats, they also taught crucial lessons in organizing, producing a corps of aggressive local leaders who would emerge to take the leadership of black railroad unions in the 1930s.

Notes

1. See, for example, James Grossman, *Land of Hope: Chicago, Black Southerners, and the Great Migration* (Chicago: University of Chicago Press, 1989); Judith Stein, *The World of Marcus Garvey: Race and Class in Modern Society* (Baton Rouge: Louisiana State University Press, 1986); Steven A. Reich, "Soldiers of Democracy: Black Texans and the Fight for Citizenship, 1917–1921," *Journal of American History* 82 (Mar. 1996): 1478–1504.

2. "Something about the Negro," *Louisville News*, 9 Mar. 1918 (reprinted from the *New World*). On black labor activism during the war, see Eric Arnesen, *Waterfront Workers of New Orleans: Race, Class, and Politics, 1863–1923* (1991; reprint, Urbana: University of Illinois Press, 1994), 217–52; Earl Lewis, *In Their Own Interests: Race, Class, and Power in Twentieth-Century Norfolk, Virginia* (Berkeley: University of California Press, 1991), 48–61.

3. This debate is examined in Eric Arnesen, "Following the Color Line of Labor: Black Workers and the Labor Movement Before 1930," *Radical History Review* no. 55 (Winter 1993): 53–87; Arnesen, "'What's on the Black Worker's Mind?': African-American Labor and the Union Tradition on the Gulf Coast," *Gulf Coast Historical Review* 10 (Fall 1994): 5–18.

4. The older literature that focused on the role of African Americans in the labor market and their relationship to the labor movement includes Charles H. Wesley, *Negro Labor in the United States 1850–1925: A Study in American Economic History* (New York: Vanguard Press, 1927); Sterling D. Spero and Abram L. Harris, *The Black Worker: The Negro and the Labor Movement* (1931; reprint, New York: Atheneum, 1969); Horace R. Cayton and George S. Mitchell, *Black Workers and the New Unions* (Chapel Hill: University of North Carolina Press, 1939).

5. See Kenneth L. Kusmer, *A Ghetto Takes Shape: Black Cleveland, 1870–1930* (Urbana: University of Illinois Press, 1976); David Katzman, *Before the Ghetto: Black Detroit in the Nineteenth Century* (Urbana: University of Illinois Press, 1973); George C. Wright, *Life behind a Veil: Blacks in Louisville, Kentucky 1865–1930* (Baton Rouge: Louisiana State University Press, 1985).

6. A small sample includes Joe W. Trotter, Jr., *Coal, Class, and Color: Blacks in Southern West Virginia, 1915–32* (Urbana: University of Illinois Press, 1990); and Lewis, *In Their Own Interests*. Of the new wave of African-American history that explores the working-class experience, Robin Kelley's pays the greatest attention to class divisions within the black community (Robin D. G. Kelley, "'We Are Not What We Seem': Rethinking Black Working-Class Opposition in the Jim Crow South," *Journal of American History* 80 [June 1993]: 76; Robin D. G. Kelley, *Hammer and Hoe: Alabama Communists during the Great Depression* [Chapel Hill: University of North Carolina Press, 1990]). Also see Eric Arnesen, "The African-American Working Class in the Jim Crow Era," *International Labor and Working Class History* 41 (Spring 1992): 58–75.

7. For a more detailed background, see William A. Sundstrom, "Half a Career: Discrimination and Railroad Internal Labor Markets," *Industrial Relations* 29 (Fall 1990): 423–40; Eric Arnesen, "'Like Banquo's Ghost, It Will Not Down': The Race Question and the American Railroad Brotherhoods, 1880–1920," *American Historical Review* 99 (Dec. 1994), 1601–34.

8. Lloyd Brown, *Iron City* (New York: Masses & Mainstream, 1952), 153.

9. "The Negro Fourth Estate and Post-War Prosperity," *Chicago Whip*, 17 July 1920; "Symposium on 'New Negro—What Is He?'" *New York Age*, 7 Feb. 1920.

10. "Unionism Not Entirely New among Negroes," *Washington Tribune*, 7 Nov. 1925.

11. Monroe N. Work, ed., *Negro Year Book: An Encyclopedia of the Negro 1921–22* (Tuskegee: Negro Year Book Publishing Co., 1922), 36; Ira De A. Reid, Director, Department of Research and Investigations of the National Urban League, *Negro Membership in American Labor Unions* (New York, 1930), 118.

12. A. Philip Randolph, "The Case of the Pullman Porter," *Messenger* 7 (July 1925): 254. A very selected list of works on Pullman porters includes Brailsford R. Brazeal, *The Brotherhood of Sleeping Car Porters: Its Origin and Development* (New York: Harper & Brothers, 1946); M. Melinda Chateauvert, "Marching Together: Women of the Brotherhood of Sleeping Car Porters, 1925–1957" (Ph.D. dissertation, University of Pennsylvania, 1992); William H. Harris, *Keeping the Faith: A. Philip Randolph, Milton P. Webster, and the Brotherhood of Sleeping Car Porters, 1925–37* (Urbana: University of Illinois Press, 1977).

13. *New York Age*, 2 Jan. 1913; F. Boyd, "Previous Struggles of the Pullman Porters to Organize," *Messenger* 8 (Sept. 1926), 283–84.

14. *New York Age*, 14 Sept. 1918.

15. *Call*, 24 June 1918; *New York Age*, 20 June 1918; *St. Louis Argus*, 28 June 1918.

16. *Chicago Whip*, 25 July 1919.

17. *Tampa Morning Tribune*, 26 Feb. 1918; *New York News*, 4 Dec. 1919; Boyd, "Previous Struggles," 283.

18. *Norfolk Journal and Guide*, 24 June 1919; *Atlanta Independent*, 28 June 1919; *Crisis*, Aug. 1919, 205; *New York Age*, 4 Jan. 1919.

19. "R.R. Men Organize at Nashville, Tenn.," *Chicago Defender*, 30 Jan. 1915; "Railroad Men Organize," *Chicago Defender*, 18 Sept. 1915; Spero and Harris, *Black Worker*, 312; Reid, *Negro Membership*, 124; *St. Louis Argus*, 18 July 1919; Chicago Commission on Race Relations, *The Negro in Chicago: A Study of Race Relations and a Race Riot* (Chicago: University of Chicago Press, 1922), 409–11.

20. *Report of Proceedings of the Thirty-Eighth Annual Convention of the American Federation of Labor Held at St. Paul, Minn. June 10 to 20, Inclusive, 1918* (Washington, D.C., 1918), 263–64; Robert Mays, "Railway Association Head Charges Union with Subterfuge," *Chicago Whip*, 17 July 1920; "Want to Have Colored Men Organized," *Tacoma News*, 25 May 1918, in Tuskegee Institute News Clippings File (hereafter TINCF), reel 8; *New York Age*, 4 May 1918.

21. Robert L. Mays, Railroad Men's International Benevolent Industrial Association, Special Bulletin, All Locals, 21 Aug. 1920, in box 25, John Fitzpatrick Papers, Chicago Historical Society, Chicago, Ill.; Chicago Commission on Race Relations, *Negro in Chicago*, 410.

22. *Birmingham Times Plain Dealer*, 10 July 1920, in TINCF, reel 11.

23. *St. Louis Argus*, 29 Oct. 1920; *Chicago Whip*, 20 Oct. 1920; "Second Annual Convention of B.S.C.P.P.U.," *Brotherhood*, Nov.–Dec. 1920, in TINCF, reel 11; "Report on Convention Held in Chicago . . . September 20, 1920 . . ." in box 25, John Fitzpatrick Papers. Brailsford Brazeal has asserted that the Protective Union "was not a labor union; in some respects, it was more of a fraternal organization" (*Brotherhood*

of Sleeping Car Porters, 10–11). On Mays's arguments, also see *Chicago Whip*, 17 July 1920; *Chicago Defender*, 20 Mar. 1920.

24. *Chicago Defender*, 29 Dec. 1923. At least some porters, members of the Pullman car porters' organization, Local Union No. 268, numbering 3,000, did join the AFL in Chicago (*Chicago Defender*, 29 Oct. 1921).

25. *Buffalo American*, 26 Jan. 1922; *Chicago Defender*, 4 Feb. 1922, 21 Jan. 1922, 8 Jan. 1921.

26. *Chicago Defender*, 2 July 1921.

27. "Mays Charges Randolph with Misrepresenting Pullman Case," *Chicago Defender*, 27 Mar. 1926. On Mays's activities in the 1930s, also see author's interview with Truman Gibson, Dec. 1994.

28. This organization was founded in Knoxville in 1912; in the early 1920s, it changed its name to the Association of Colored Railway Trainmen. For the sake of clarity, the acronym CARE is used throughout this essay.

29. "Labor's Peril: Greater Dangers Have Never in the Nation's History Confronted the Workers of the United States," *Brotherhood of Locomotive Firemen and Enginemen's Magazine* 62 (1 June 1917): 3.

30. W. S. Carter, "The Negro Question," *Brotherhood of Locomotive Firemen and Enginemen's Magazine* 62 (15 June 1917): 9; "Railroads Eager to Employ Negroes in Train Service," *Brotherhood of Locomotive Firemen and Enginemen's Magazine* 63 (15 Aug. 1917): 11.

31. S. J. Whitaker, "Memphis, Tenn.," *Railroad Trainmen's Journal* 16 (Nov. 1899): 1040; "Illegal Strike, Memphis (Tenn.) Terminals," *Railroad Trainman* 36 (Mar. 1919): 200; "From Assistant President J. B. Connors," *Journal of the Switchmen's Union of North America* 21 (Mar. 1919): 138–39; "Memphis Terminals (File 7260)," Brotherhood of Railroad Trainmen, *Reports of Grand Lodge Officers. Year 1919*, 91–93; *Memphis Commercial Appeal*, 12–16 Jan. 1919; *Memphis News-Scimitar*, 13–18 Jan. 1919; Illinois Central Railroad Company, "Misunderstanding between Officers of the Brotherhood of Railroad Trainmen, and the Officers of the Yazoo and Mississippi Valley Railroad, on Seniority Rules," in Records of the Division of Labor. Case Files of G. W. W. Hanger, Assistant Director, Division of Labor, 1918–20, box 16, United States Railroad Administration, RG 14, National Archives, Washington, D.C. (hereafter Hanger Case Files). For background on labor and race relations in Memphis, see Michael Honey, *Southern Labor and Black Civil Rights: Organizing Memphis Workers* (Urbana: University of Illinois Press, 1993).

32. Hugh Reid, "The Labor Outlook for the Coming Year," *Railway Maintenance Engineer* 15 (Feb. 1919): 43; "A Year of Prosperity for Railway Labor," *Railway Age* 66 (3 Jan. 1919): 37.

33. Telegram, B. L. Winchell to W. T. Tyler, 30 Jan. 1919, and Carter, memorandum, 22 Mar. 1919, Hanger Case Files.

34. Connors, "From Assistant President J. B. Conners"; Brotherhood of Railroad Trainmen, *Reports of Grand Lodge Officers. Year 1919*, 93; telegram, B. L. Winchell to W. T. Tyler, 30 Jan. 1919, Hanger Case Files.

35. "In Re: Switchmen's Strike, Memphis Tennessee, Saturday, January 11, 1919 . . . Statement of Facts from the Grievance Committee of the Colored Association of Railway Employees, from the Illinois Central and Yazoo & Mississippi Railroads," in Administrative File, Subject File: Discrimination-Employment-Railroads,

1919, box C-272, Papers of the N.A.A.C.P., Library of Congress (hereafter NAACP Papers); A. E. Clift to William Blackman, 6 Feb. 1919, in Hanger Case Files.

36. Memorandum, W. S. Carter, 22 Mar. 1919; Illinois Central, "Misunderstanding," Hanger Case Files.

37. "Discrimination against White Trainmen," *Railroad Trainmen* 36 (Nov. 1919); Spero and Harris, *Black Worker,* 299–301; Brotherhood of Railroad Trainmen, *Reports of Grand Lodge Officers. Year 1919,* 21; "United States Railroad Labor Board, November 4, 1921, Decision No. 307 (Docket 138), Association of Colored Railway Trainmen vs. Illinois Central Railroad Company, Yazoo & Mississippi Valley Railroad Company," Subject: Association of Colored Railway Trainmen Petition" in Records of the National Mediation Board, Erdman Act Case Files, RG 13, Washington National Records Center, Suitland, Md. (hereafter ACRT Petition).

38. "Report of the President W. G. Lee," in Brotherhood of Railroad Trainmen, *Reports of Grand Lodge Officers. Year 1919,* 101–3; Brown, *Iron City,* 162.

39. "In and before the United States Railroad Labor Board, The Colored Association of Railway Employes, Petitioner, vs. The Illinois Central Railroad Company, and the Yazoo & Mississippi Valley Railroad Company, Defendants," 2 June 1920; J. H. Eiland to C. H. Markam, 24 and 26 Feb. 1920; and Thomas Redd to IC Railroad, 4 May 1920, in ACRT Petition.

40. Petition to the Illinois Central Railroad Company, 18 May 1928, Records of the Illinois Central Gulf Railroad, Selected Personnel Department Files, box 8, Labor-Management Documentation Center, Martin P. Catherwood Library, Cornell University, Ithaca, N.Y.; L. C. Going to Judge R. M. Barton, 25 Aug. 1921, ACRT Petition.

41. Walter F. White, "Memorandum Re Railroad Trainmen's Case, January 4th & 5th, 1920," in Subject File: Unions-Railroads-Jan. 3–Dec. 23, 1920, box C414, NAACP Papers.

42. W. S. Lovett to Walter F. White, 27 Jan. 1920, in Subject File: Unions-Railroads-Jan. 3–Dec. 23, 1920, box C414, NAACP Papers.

43. "Seniority, Etc., of White and Colored Trainmen," *Reports of Grand Lodge Officers, Year 1919. Brotherhood of Railroad Trainmen,* 101–7; Walker D. Hines, *War History of American Railroads* (New Haven: Yale University Press, 1928), 175–81; Charles Hamilton Houston, "Foul Employment Practice on the Rails," *Crisis* 56 (Oct. 1949): 269.

44. R. R. Church to James W. Johnson, 17 Jan. 1919, Subject File: Unions-Railroads, Jan. 17–Dec. 1, 1919, box C414, NAACP Papers.

45. Press Release, 21 Jan. 1919, and White to J. H. McConico, 17 Mar. 1919, in Subject File: Labor-General-Jan.–Apr. 1919, box C319, NAACP Papers.

46. R. R. Church to James W. Johnson, 17 Jan. 1919, Subject File: Unions-Railroads, Jan. 17–Dec. 1, 1919, box C414; Eiland to W. D. Hines, 26 Jan. 1919, in Subject File: Labor-General-Jan.–Apr. 1919, box C319, both in NAACP Papers.

47. Eiland to C. H. Markham, 24 Feb. 1920, in ACRT Petition.

48. J. H. Eiland to U.S. Railroad Labor Board, 9 Feb. 1920, in ACRT Petition.

49. "In and before the United States Railroad Labor Board. The Colored Association of Railway Employees, A corporation, PETITIONER, vs. The Illinois Central Railroad Company, A corporation, and the Yazoo & Mississippi Valley Railroad Company, a corporation, DEFENDANTS," 2 June 1920, in ACRT Petition.

50. Eiland to Markham, 24 Feb. 1920, in ACRT Petition.
51. Eiland to Markham, 26 Mar. 1920, in ACRT Petition.
52. Eiland to R. R. Church, 9 May 1921, Subject File: Unions-Railroads-Jan. 5–Aug. 21, 1921, box C414, NAACP Papers; "Report of the President W. G. Lee," *Reports of Grand Lodge Officers. Year 1919*, 104.
53. "Brakemen Murdered in Cold Blood in Mississippi," *Chicago Whip*, 13 Mar. 1920. Also see Walker James to the *Crisis*, 8 Mar. 1921, in Subject File: Unions-Railroads-Jan. 5–Aug. 21, 1921, box C414, NAACP Papers.
54. Nathan Hopkins, "'Get Off!'—Death Signal to Trainmen in the South," *Chicago Defender*, 4 Mar. 1922. On the campaign of terror, also see *Chicago Defender*, 4 and 11 June, 10 Sept., 15 Oct. 1921, 28 Apr. 1922; *Jackson Daily News*, 21 and 22 Sept. 1921; "Heroes of the Railroad," *New York Age*, 20 Aug. 1921; *New York Age*, 6 Aug. 1921; "Intimidating Our Railroad Workers," *Norfolk Journal and Guide*, 24 Sept. 1921; *Birmingham Reporter*, 3 Dec. 1921; "Discrimination," *Crisis* 23 (Mar. 1921), 212.
55. Jesse Ficklin, Member lodge #30, Hattiesburg, Miss., to Eiland, 17 May 1921, in Subject File: Unions-Railroads-Jan. 5–Aug. 21, 1921, box C414, NAACP Papers.
56. Eiland to Church, 9 and 11 May 1921, in Subject File: Unions-Railroads-Jan. 5–Aug. 21, 1921, box C414, NAACP Papers; Hopkins, "'Get Off!'"; *Jackson Daily News*, 21 and 22 Sept. 1921.

Chapter 12

Boring from Within and Without

William Z. Foster, the Trade Union
Educational League, and
American Communism in the 1920s

JAMES R. BARRETT

IN THE MIDST OF a sharp turn to the right in domestic politics, the end of the cold war, and the collapse of Communist regimes around the world, historians have rediscovered American Communism. An older anti-Communist historiography, which describes the Party as a "creature given life and meaning by its umbilical ties to the Soviet Union," has found new adherents. In this view the Party's industrial organizing was as much a product of Soviet intrigue as any other element of its work. Most recent, sympathetic work, however, views the Party as an indigenous form of American radicalism responsible for successful mass organizing and achieving important reforms.[1] Is it possible now to integrate the international and indigenous dimensions of American Communism, to relate changes in the American party's policies and practices, its breakthroughs and failures, to the factionalism in the Party and the Communist International without losing the nuances of the more recent social histories?

The life of William Z. Foster, the best known Communist in the United States, offers the context for such an integration. Foster's story is central to the history of American radicalism because his life exemplifies so much about the movement—its social basis, rise, and ideological transformation during the early twentieth century and the depression years, and its ultimate isolation and destruction in the post–World War II era. As Theodore Draper writes, "Foster personified the American proletariat as few radical leaders have ever done."[2]

Born in 1881 and raised in Philadelphia's slums, Foster left school after the third grade and drifted around the country and around the world, working at a wide variety of jobs and developing a sensitivity to workers' mentalities and problems that made him a brilliant organizer. He joined the Socialist party just after the turn of the century, identifying always with its proletarian, revolutionary left wing, and the Industrial Workers of the World (IWW) in 1909. He taught himself to read German and French and traveled in Europe, studying labor movement ideas and strategies there. Influenced particularly by French syndicalism, he split with the IWW over its dual unionism, establishing a succession of small syndicalist groups. Foster earned national prominence orchestrating successful World War I organizing campaigns in the open shop bastions of meatpacking and steel and leading the great 1919 Steel Strike. He joined the Workers' party in 1921 and shaped its industrial work for a generation. Eclipsed by Earl Browder's rise in the mid-1930s, Foster reemerged with Browder's 1945 expulsion and remained the Party's leading figure until his death in Moscow in 1961.[3]

Foster and many of those with whom he created Communism in the United States were veterans of the Socialist party, the IWW, and the bitter strikes of the early twentieth century. Thus, America's own radical traditions and the persistence of class inequality and violence shaped Foster and his party. But there was another dimension of Communism in the United States and of Foster's own career. From the day the Bolsheviks seized power, radicals throughout the world had their eyes on Russia. The politics of the Soviet party and the Communist International, and the reflection of these struggles in the American party's own factionalism constrained individual Communists in their everyday organizing. This tension between Communism as a reflection of social inequalities and conflict and Communism as the product of Soviet policy initiatives and Comintern politics is crucial to understanding the Party's history.

In Foster's case, the tension between his own distinctive brand of Communist activism, heavily influenced by his earlier industrial experiences and contacts, and the exigencies of political life in a highly centralized international Marxist-Leninist movement developed in the midst of the catastrophic labor defeats and Red Scare of the early 1920s. This timing vastly complicated his project of radicalizing the labor movement. Given this hostile political climate, his successes in the early to mid-twenties constituted a genuine achievement. Thoroughly intertwined with that of the Communist movement, Foster's story suggests a great deal about the potential and limits of radicalism during the conservative 1920s. Rather than an eventuality, the Communists' ultimate failure is a historical problem understandable in terms of Foster's own background and experiences, indigenous and international Communist politics, and labor's own conservatism in these years.

From Syndicalism to Communism

While Foster offered the Communists their most visible and talented working-class leader, his Trade Union Educational League (TUEL) brought them "into the daylight of actual contact with American workers." Foster formed the TUEL in November 1920, *before* becoming a Communist, to coordinate the activities of left-wing militants throughout the labor movement. To avoid any association with dual unionism, the league was loosely structured, with neither dues nor formal membership.[4] Local industrial committees, perhaps as many as five hundred in forty-five to fifty cities during the early twenties, were each affiliated with one of the league's fourteen national industrial groups. Four district committees coordinated activities on a regional basis. An annual conference elected the national committee, and at the international level, the TUEL was affiliated with and subsidized by the Red International of Labor Unions (RILU). At its height in the mid-1920s, the league relied on thousands of local militants, but the key group was in Chicago—a core of veterans from the steel and stockyards organizing campaigns, the IWW, and Foster's syndicalist leagues. The whole operation revolved around Foster. "Not often does one find an organization so completely dominated by the philosophy and personality of one man," wrote Earl Beckner.[5]

The league's program was radical, reflecting both Foster's thinking and Soviet influence: class struggle over class collaboration, industrial unionism, organization of the unorganized, a shop delegate system of local union representation, an independent labor party, affiliation with the RILU, recognition of Soviet Russia, abolition of capitalism, and establishment of a workers' republic. Yet in their daily work TUEL activists emphasized practical issues, often developing reputations as honest, progressive trade unionists.[6]

Foster's radicalism revolved around two key concepts, both heavily influenced by French and British syndicalist models: the *militant minority* and *boring from within*. In the early 1920s both these elements of what contemporaries sometimes called "Fosterism" provided ideological links between Foster's earlier syndicalism and his later Leninism. Foster's notion of the militant minority, which he embraced at least as early as 1909, lent itself easily to a revolutionary elitism that helps to explain his attraction to Communism. Left to their own devices, he wrote in early 1922, the great mass of rank-and-file workers were "ignorant and sluggish." The key to making the labor movement "an instrument of working class emancipation" lay in organizing "the thinking and acting part of the working class, the very soul of labor." The TUEL provided a channel through which these militants could coordinate their activities, educate the rank and file, and transform the unions. "Revolutions are not brought about by the sort of far-sighted revolutionaries you have in mind," he told the economist Scott Nearing in 1924, "but by stupid masses . . . goaded to desperate revolt by the pressure of social conditions . . . led by straight-thinking revolutionaries who are able to direct the storm intelligently against capitalism."[7]

Boring from within likewise represented a strategic link between Foster's syndicalist past and his early Communist career. Like British and French syndicalists, Foster believed that prospects for a revolutionary movement lay within the conservative unions that the militants must transform into effective class weapons. Foster and his followers struggled against what he called "the disease of dual unionism," first in the IWW, then through a series of syndicalist groups, and finally in the TUEL during the 1920s. Foster's persistent syndicalism in the context of the Communist Party suggests more continuity between Communism and earlier labor radicalism than might normally be assumed.

Communist industrial policy in the twenties falls into three periods. From its foundation in 1919 through 1921, a period of huge strikes and lockouts, the Party had little base in the labor movement. When he joined in late 1921, Foster brought with him the TUEL, its program and contacts, and several experienced activists. From late 1921 through late 1923, the TUEL made significant headway by building united front opposition movements in some unions. By the mid-twenties, however, the organization foundered on both factional conflict within the Party *and* attacks from conservative trade union leaders. Over the course of the late twenties, the Party settled into a dual union strategy dictated by both the official Comintern line and the bitter conservative opposition to the TUEL within the unions.

In his project to radicalize the American labor movement, then, Foster found his efforts blocked on one side by labor conservatives and on the other by opponents within the Party. His interests and genius lay in the practical trade union world, but life as a Communist leader drew Foster into another world where decisions relied as much on party politics, in New York and ultimately in Moscow, as they did on conditions and events in the coalfields of Pennsylvania and West Virginia. Pursuing his chosen strategies depended on maintaining his leadership in the Party, which drew him into intense factional conflicts and positions that isolated him from the labor movement he had long seen as the proper focus for his own and other radicals' efforts.

The Chicago Movement, the Labor Party, and the Amalgamation Campaign

The TUEL achieved its greatest influence with two central demands—for amalgamation of existing craft unions and for a labor party based on the unions. The labor party movement sprang from union organizations throughout the United States—in Seattle, Minneapolis, and industrial towns in Pennsylvania, Ohio, and Connecticut. But Chicago, where President John Fitzpatrick put the full weight of the labor federation behind the idea, was the heart of the movement. Here a November 1919 national conference established the National Labor party, later renamed the Farmer-Labor party (FLP).[8] Originally skeptical of this venture on syndicalist grounds, Foster gradually became active in the Illinois movement during 1920, long before visiting Russia. His change of heart lay in his experiences in meatpacking and the steel strike where he saw the implications of corporate control over local government in devastating legal and physical assaults on unions and strikers. Foster later recalled, "my old Syndicalist anti-politics had started to collapse." Yet he still placed more emphasis on industrial activity and apparently saw the political effort as a product of industrial conflict.[9]

Meanwhile, the international Communist strategy of a "united front" moved the Party in the United States in Foster's direction. Lenin's *Left-Wing Communism: An Infantile Disorder* vindicated Foster's arguments against dual unionism and provided a blueprint for radicalizing the labor movement. At the Comintern's 1921 Third Congress, which Foster attended as an observer, Lenin prescribed united fronts for parties throughout the advanced capitalist world. As the postwar revolutionary tide receded in the year following Foster's Russian journey, the united front proved more and more attractive, particularly to activists like Foster who prized their contacts with the broader movement. His personal political trajectory, based on the concepts of the militant minority and boring from within, intersected with that of international Communism. Foster recalled, "It appeared that our ten-year fight for work in the conservative unions was at last going to be successful."[10]

In early 1922 union, farm, socialist, and Farmer-Labor party delegates met to constitute the Conference for Progressive Political Action (CPPA) and develop a common program. That fall the Workers' party sought to implement Lenin's united front vision by formally supporting Fitzpatrick's FLP, which came into the CPPA's second national convention pushing for the immediate formation of a national labor party. When moderates refused to commit to this plan and opposed the demand for railroad nationalization, Fitzpatrick's FLP withdrew and laid plans for a national convention at Chicago in July 1923. Fitzpatrick actually created the united front by inviting the Workers' party to this convention. Still, he was wary. "Let's get this straight," Fitzpatrick told the group at its first meeting, "we are willing to go along, but we think you Communists should occupy the back seat." The remark underscored a contradiction that came back to haunt the Chicago militants: They prided themselves on being a vanguard, but to enter the mainstream, they had to acknowledge the leadership of people like Fitzpatrick. Foster and other well-connected trade union Communists who countenanced this arrangement found in such progressives influential allies. By the spring of 1923, Communists were an integral part of the labor party movement.[11]

This labor party work helped to put the TUEL on the map, but Foster's plan for transforming the labor movement ultimately depended on success in the unions. Here the campaign for amalgamation—the integration of craft unions in the major industries—provided the TUEL with prospects for a broad-based movement. League activists struck a responsive chord with the motto "amalgamation or annihilation," which reflected workers' growing enthusiasm for industrial union organization. Foster started the campaign in March 1922 at the Chicago Federation of Labor meeting, where his first TUEL amalgamation resolution passed overwhelmingly.[12] When the AFL's Samuel Gompers claimed Foster aspired to be "the Lenin of America," Fitzpatrick remained loyal—even when the AFL cut financial support for the Chicago federation. In the eighteen months following the March 1922 CFL meeting, TUEL activists succeeded in getting the same resolution adopted by sixteen international unions, seventeen state federations, scores of city labor councils, and thousands of local unions, organizations representing perhaps one-half of organized labor in the United States. If the TUEL were properly funded, Foster wrote Solomon Lozovsky, he expected "a tremendous overturning of the American labor movement in the near future."[13]

Rank-and-File Rebellions

TUEL policy and practice grew in part from Foster's own experiences and represented a logical extension of his thinking: develop rank-and-file opposition groups; organize the unorganized; fight strikes over key industrial issues. They focused on struggles over the most fundamental questions facing the movement in the twenties: What was the purpose of unions? Was it possible to work out compromises with employers? Should the labor movement steer clear of politics or develop its own independent political voice? How would the Communists' program relate to these questions, which had emerged from the prolonged crisis of the unions in the 1920s?

In the context of Communist deliberations on such questions, a different impulse was at work: the central planning and direction characteristic of a vanguard party. Increasingly, the TUEL's program and actions had to be squared with not only the Party executive but also the Comintern's international line. More than other parties, American Communists turned repeatedly to the Comintern to settle their factional struggles. Foster became increasingly embroiled in these disputes, spending considerable time arguing his case in New York and Moscow. Factionalism in both places, the class struggle in theory, shaped TUEL policy as much as conflicts in the workshops and streets.

Finally, the mainstream union leadership, generally conservative and on the defensive during the twenties, had a major impact on Communist fortunes in the labor movement. In particular situations, TUEL activists might make alliances with local, district, or even national leaders; more often, and particularly from the mid-1920s on, they faced attacks from union leaders.

The TUEL's fortunes are best understood, then, in terms of the interaction among three factors: workers' resistance to employers' efforts to rationalize work and industrial relations in various industries; Communist strategy and factional politics; and union officials' responses to the TUEL challenge. Throughout the twenties, Foster dominated the Party's industrial work, and his policies reflected all these influences. The force of each emerges clearly from an analysis of the league in particular situations.

The TUEL mobilized in more than a dozen industries but built its strongest and most durable movements in the needle trades and coal mining. In each industry, economic problems and competition led to dramatic confrontations with employers, while conservative union policies precipitated rank-and-file opposition movements. League militants built united fronts with these groups by addressing genuine industrial problems and confronting unpopular leaders.

In the International Ladies Garment Workers' Union (ILGWU), the Amalgamated Clothing Workers of America (ACWA), and other needle trades unions, workers' activism sprang from deep roots in radical immigrant subcultures, particularly in Yiddish-speaking enclaves like New York's Lower East Side.[14] In the ILGWU left-wing opposition dated back to at least 1917 when radical dressmakers organized a Current Events Committee and agitated against the union's conservative socialist leadership. The committee soon disintegrated, but loosely knit opposition groups remained in a number of locals, merging in the fall of 1919 into a shop delegate movement modeled on the British Shop Stewards and Workers Committee Movement. This group, which sought to shift organization and authority from the union's leadership to its rank and file in the shops, spread throughout the ILGWU, attracted early Communists, socialists, syndicalists, anarchists, and others who saw it as a way to build a more militant and democratic union. By 1922 shop delegates formed an indigenous base for the TUEL, controlling several large New York locals and the union's joint boards in Philadelphia and Chicago. Comparable movements developed in other sections of the industry, particularly among fur workers where the left wing won control in 1925 after leading a successful strike.[15]

In the ACWA the league cooperated with Sidney Hillman, who had supported Foster's 1919 steel strike and underwritten a 1920 speaking tour he made in the wake of the strike. Hillman, whom Foster judged "the most skillful bureaucrat in the American labor movement," tended to line up with the left in its disputes with old-line socialists in the Jewish community. Hillman's strongest bond with the left was undoubtedly his consistent support for the Soviets. The ACWA contributed large sums for famine relief and established a cooperative manufacturing venture in the Soviet Union. Despite rank-and-file grievances, Foster and other Party leaders counseled against any open break and invoked Party discipline against those who resisted such advice.[16]

In America's coal mines, trade unionism had a compelling, almost desperate quality that invested United Mine Workers of America (UMWA) factional conflicts with an endurance and intensity seldom matched in other organizations. As in the needle trades, the coal industry felt severe pressure to cut costs, and as in the ILGWU, the UMWA radicals attached themselves to an indigenous rebellion with deep roots and built their program on issues of greatest concern to miners. The union itself was at stake. In 1920, more than half of America's 785,000 miners belonged to the UMWA. In the following decade, employer attacks decimated the organization, while factional conflicts tore it apart.

John L. Lewis, the union's autocratic president, typically crushed any opposition. Between 1919 and late 1921, he revoked more than one hundred local union charters and expelled thousands of miners in Illinois and Kansas. When British Columbia miners voted to join the radical One Big Union movement, he expelled their leaders and reorganized the union's entire western Canadian district.[17] In 1923 TUEL activists united these and other disparate opposition groups in the Progressive International Committee. By the time the UMWA assembled for its tumultuous 1924 convention, the league was rallying the opposition around a clear set of demands, most of which related to greater union democracy. Others included nationalization of the mines and Foster's pet project of a miners'-railroad workers' alliance. The delegates defeated each of these, but the left garnered significant support. The Communist presidential candidate won almost a third of the votes in the union's December 1924 elections, despite apparent ballot irregularities.[18]

On the railroads, where Foster maintained widespread contacts, TUEL activists played active roles during the 1922 shop crafts strike, involving more than eighty thousand machinists and maintenance workers in a long and bitter struggle. The segmented character of the industry's craft unions doomed the strike, which Foster called "the greatest single defeat ever suffered by the workers in this country." The sixteen railroad brotherhoods generally failed to support the machinists, providing a dramatic rationale for the league's demand for amalgamation and fueling opposition movements in both the International Association of Machinists (IAM) and the brotherhoods. In late 1922 the TUEL sponsored a successful national amalgamation conference, which drew over four hundred machinists and railroad workers to Chicago and laid out a plan for linking the unions. In the IAM, whose membership had plummeted from 273,000 in 1921 to 97,300 in 1923, the TUEL supported William Knudsen, a non-Communist who endorsed the league's entire program and won 30 percent of the vote in his 1922 run against president William H. Johnston. TUEL groups also thrived in some building trades, particularly in New York City, Chicago, and Detroit, where a Communist was elected carpenters' district president and vice president of the city labor federation.[19]

In creating alliances with non-Communist progressives, Foster was impatient with Communists who thought they would win the masses "with talk" and urged them to do more "day-by-day detail work." "Let the militants offer a practical program," he counseled, "participate in labor's everyday struggles with concrete demands, let them learn how to handle the masses and his [*sic*] task will be accomplished soon."[20]

Repression

Building on Foster's strategy, the TUEL had sunk deep roots in the labor movement throughout the country by the middle of 1923. Yet by the end of 1924 Foster himself conceded that the TUEL was declining. If successes in the early 1920s suggest that Communist efforts to build progressive blocs in the unions were not preordained to fail, then what explains the league's eclipse? In part, the raids, arrests, firings, blacklisting, and expulsion of activists and whole local unions made it increasingly difficult for the league to operate. This political atmosphere clearly shaped the Party's and Foster's own politics. In 1920 federal agents arrested an estimated ten thousand people, including most of the leaders of the Young Communist movement, deporting hundreds of foreign-born radicals and shutting down political organizations and publications in raids throughout the country. The TUEL was under attack from its inception. Justice Department agents worked with business groups to identify and blacklist activists. In August 1922 state's attorney's agents raided the TUEL's Chicago headquarters, wrecking the place and carting away documents and subscription lists. A few weeks later police raided the group's first national conference, arresting some of the delegates.[21]

In August 1922, Colorado state rangers seized Foster at his hotel room and handed him over to Wyoming authorities, who dumped him out on the open range. The Cheyenne sheriff threatened to send him home "in a box" should he ever return. The following year a gunman attempted to assassinate Foster as he addressed a crowd of Chicago garment workers. Within a few days of the Colorado kidnapping, Michigan state police raided a secret Communist Party convention near Bridgman, Michigan, arresting fifteen Party leaders and again seizing a large quantity of documents. The most important discussion at the convention had involved liquidation of the secret, underground party and the formation of a program to help the Communists establish links with the mainstream labor movement. Ironically, the arrests of the Communist leaders coincided with their decision to work openly. Foster, a crucial link in this new strategy, spoke in a forest, illuminated by torches and lanterns, and "made a tremendous impression," arguing that union work should be at the very center of the Party's program. Police arrested him in Chicago shortly afterward on suspicion of planning a train wreck. This charge was dropped quickly, but Foster and ten other Communist leaders were then indicted for criminal syndicalism under an extremely broad Michigan conspiracy law. They faced up to ten years in prison, $45,000 fines, or both, if convicted.[22]

Foster received impressive support from progressive, non-Communist labor activists. Until Foster's arrest, the Chicago Federation's *New Majority* noted, the Palmer Raids had "seemed something remote" but the raids on the TUEL and the Michigan convention were a "direct attack upon the labor movement as a whole, particularly upon the progressive trade union movement." CFL leaders denounced the arrests, organized protests, and helped establish a series of local labor defense councils in cities throughout the country. The councils, which included prominent liberals and labor progressives as well as Workers' party activists, formed the basis for the International Labor Defense that provided legal assistance to radicals throughout the twenties and thirties. Fitzpatrick regularly attended the trial himself and arranged for brilliant labor attorney Frank Walsh to serve as Foster's defense counsel. The Michigan Federation of Labor demanded repeal of the criminal syndicalism law. Eugene Debs, who had publicly endorsed the TUEL, wrote warmly in Foster's support. The American Civil Liberties Union also supported Foster, who served briefly on its national board.[23]

When he stood trial in spring of 1923, the *New York Herald* claimed that Foster, the "ablest and most vicious Red," posed the greatest threat because of his potential as a labor leader. Although he had secretly joined the Party, the defense maintained that Foster had not, and federal authorities, working with the state and local prosecutors, never succeeded in proving the point. Foster estimated that Communists represented only 10 percent of the TUEL's membership, but when asked about his relationship to the Party, he admitted that he "fully sympathized with its aims." The jury deadlocked, and Foster was acquitted.[24]

Factionalism: The TUEL and the Party

The success of these attacks suggests a second factor contributing to the TUEL's decline, which grew from the character of Communist industrial policy and the position of Foster's "trade union Communists" in the

Party. Some Party initiatives, often with origins in the Comintern's and the Americans' own closely related factional conflicts, isolated TUEL activists and facilitated union officials' attacks.

The Party's original division of authority between Foster's direction of trade union affairs and Party secretary Charles Ruthenberg's control of the political apparatus allowed Foster an unusual autonomy during his first two years as a Communist. The Chicago-based TUEL Communists, with their emphasis on industrial work, remained quite distinct from the more theoretically grounded group at the Party headquarters in New York. Foster himself served as chair of the CFL's organization committee. Protecting his connections with the mainstream, he preferred to deal with the New York group through intermediaries, notably Earl Browder.

Yet Party influence became increasingly intrusive. Throughout the mid-twenties, Foster chaired both the Party's trade union committee and the TUEL meetings. This created a close relationship between the two organizations in the persons of Foster and his colleagues. Since Foster also sat on the Party's Central Committee almost from the moment he joined, he dealt regularly with the professional revolutionaries in the Union Square headquarters. Through frequent correspondence with Solomon Lozovsky, director of the RILU, he was also in close contact with the Comintern, even as he toured coalfields and directed organizing efforts and strikes around the United States.[25] On the trade union committee, Foster focused on practical work, taking special interest in precisely how to raise issues with the union rank and file and how to build alliances with non-Communist progressives. On the political committee, he criticized Party activists for ineptitude and slighting industrial work. At times he clearly felt that politics interfered with this work.[26]

Thus, Foster could not remain aloof from factionalism, and the Party positions that increasingly shaped his industrial work were products not of revolutionary science but of politics, within the Party in the United States and ultimately in Moscow. Chronic factionalism meant that Foster was usually under siege from one or another opponent as he planned and executed the Party's trade union program. Three related periods of conflict suggest how factionalism constrained his work.

Foster's first involvement with factional conflict grew out of the struggle over the Communists' labor party policy. The debate and its results drew him deeply into the political life of the Party, cut him off from many of his most valued union connections, and opened the league to charges that it was simply an arm of the Party rather than a genuine rank-and-file movement. Foster viewed the Farmer-Labor party as an opportunity to link the Communists with a genuine mass movement, and in early 1923 prospects seemed bright for a strong united front with the Communists playing a key role. Two factors destroyed these prospects and isolated Foster and the Communists from their base of support. First, the AFL leadership launched an attack aimed at separating the Communists from Fitzpatrick and other labor progressives. At the same time, the Communists' own internal conflicts actually facilitated this attack and cost radicals the alliances they had painstakingly created in the previous two years.

Throughout early 1923, Gompers placed increasing pressure on Fitzpatrick and other AFL progressives and Farmer-Labor party supporters. In June he cut the CFL's subsidy in half and threatened to reorganize the federation unless it abandoned the Communists. Fitzpatrick asked the Party to postpone the convention until he could ensure strong union support.[27]

While the Chicago Communists proceeded with caution, the Party's New York leadership forced the issue. Foster's main protagonist was John Pepper, a Hungarian Comintern representative who had enjoyed a meteoric rise during his one year in the country. Pepper demanded that Communist unionists identify more closely with the Party and abandon the CFL group unless Fitzpatrick acted immediately. This could only be done, Foster argued, if the Party generated enough labor support without Fitzpatrick, but a majority of the Party's executive committee supported Pepper, who appeared to have the Comintern's blessings. Fitzpatrick, believing perhaps that he could still muster a majority at the convention, refused even to meet with Workers' party representatives.[28]

The Split with the Labor Progressives

When the moment arrived, it seemed Foster was mistaken. The July 1923 Farmer-Labor party convention represented a humiliating defeat for John Fitzpatrick and, on the surface at least, a great victory for the Communists. Fitzpatrick had bolted the CPPA convention when the body refused immediately to establish a national labor party. Now he fought the majority of Farmer-Labor party delegates from the opposite side of precisely the same issue. When the Communists, well-organized and represented through a variety of radical labor, fraternal, and farm groups, easily defeated Fitzpatrick on the convention floor, he walked out, losing even some of his old supporters. The Communists controlled the new Federated Farmer-Labor party (FF-LP) which emerged from the convention, and Foster hoped that "the split had been practically avoided."[29]

But Foster and others with experience soon understood that this was a hollow victory. Although organizations representing six hundred thousand members had voted to form the FF-LP, those actually voting to affiliate with the new party numbered only 155,000, and most of these came from organizations close to the Workers' party. As Foster himself concluded, the FF-LP amounted to "a united front with ourselves." Though he publicly supported the decision, Foster was enraged. He understood how much it would cost in organizational terms, and he had been made to look foolish in the eyes of old and trusted labor friends. Fitzpatrick complained that the Communists' betrayal was "on the level of a man being invited to your house as a guest and then once in the house seizing you by the throat and kicking you out of the door." The Communists attacked him publicly, apparently confirming Gompers' characterization of them as devious disrupters. Fitzpatrick turned against the Communists and most other progressive causes, throwing his enormous prestige behind conservative labor politics.[30] The Communists' strategy had done more to kill progressive labor politics than to promote it.

The AFL leadership took the split with Fitzpatrick as the signal for an attack. The September 1923 Illinois Federation of Labor convention, which Foster described as "one of the bitterest clashes that has yet taken place between revolutionaries and reactionaries," showed how far the breach between the Communists and the labor progressives had widened.[31] Delegates resoundingly defeated resolutions supporting Soviet Russia and even Foster's amalgamation resolution, which the CFL had endorsed only a few months earlier. Attacking the TUEL, Fitzpatrick bitterly opposed his own earlier resolution calling for AFL support of an independent labor party. When conservative delegates argued that the resolution was a Communist ploy, Foster reminded them that the Illinois federation had a reputation for facing issues squarely. "Let us say whether we are for a labor party or against it. . . . We must consider this resolution on its own merits." Miners, machinists, and Chicago teacher unionists supported him, but the delegates voted seven to one against the labor party resolution, another clear reversal of the federation's earlier position.[32] The channels through which Foster had operated successfully were now closing.

At the AFL's national convention the following month, Phil Murray of the UMWA made a motion to unseat William F. Dunne—Foster's close associate and a duly elected Montana delegate—strictly on the grounds of his Workers' party membership. After two hours of red-baiting hyperbole aimed largely at Foster, William Hutcheson, a frequent TUEL target, insisted that every delegate rise for a roll call vote. The result was what David Montgomery terms "a lynch-mob atmosphere" and a vote of 27,837 to 108 against Dunne. The delegates overwhelmingly rejected all progressive resolutions including those supporting industrial unionism and independent labor politics. The AFL leadership demanded that Seattle, Minneapolis, Detroit, Cleveland, and other city central bodies cleanse themselves of Communist influence or face revocation of their charters. In the CFL, where Foster's group had once stood at the heart of a powerful, progressive movement, Communists were clearly on the margins, discredited and distrusted. Now the middle ground gave way and progressive trade unionists found themselves forced to choose between going to the left with Foster or back to the right with Gompers.[33]

By 1924 conservatives in one union after another turned on the TUEL with increasing fury. Because most of the ILGWU leaders were members of the Socialist party, Foster enlisted Eugene V. Debs, an early TUEL supporter, in his efforts to end the union's right/left warfare, but the ILGWU leaders refused to have anything to do with the Communists. In the ensuing struggle, the ILGWU leadership proscribed TUEL membership and launched an all-out attack, expelling individual activists, unseating convention delegates, and reorganizing the union's largest locals to reassert control. Foster claimed that conservative leaders employed strategies ranging from stacking conventions and vote fraud to physical intimidation and murder to purge their unions.[34]

Where the TUEL generated considerable rank-and-file support, the attack drove it in the direction of dual unionism. The ILGWU's left wing created a Joint Action Committee comprising, in effect, a parallel union structure that collected dues, negotiated with employers, called strikes, and continued to attack the leadership. The committee filled Yankee Stadium with forty thousand cloak- and dressmakers to protest the union leaders' attacks on the left wing. At the 1925 convention, the left wing won control of the New York joint board and the following year led a giant but disastrous strike of New York's needle trades workers. Foster consulted directly with the strike leaders, while simultaneously locked in a growing factional conflict with Jay Lovestone that shaped the strike's outcome. Neither man wished to weaken his position by supporting a compromise settlement. The protracted strike drained the union's treasury, ending in a weak contract. The socialists regained control in the midst of this defeat, though New York's Communist needle trades workers remained an organized force within the union and an important base of Foster's support within the Party for a generation.[35]

Attacks on left-wing activists were more damaging in the UMWA, where the executive demanded the expulsion of all Communists. Here and elsewhere the term was used rather loosely to describe various opposition elements. To defend the alliance between the TUEL and other dissidents, Foster formed the "Save the Union" movement. In early 1926 he spent five months in the coalfields building the movement that aimed to salvage unionism by breaking Lewis's control and reversing his policies. In 1926–27 the movement rallied TUEL activists and other dissidents behind the candidacy of John Brophy, a Pennsylvania progressive who agreed to support a labor party, nationalization of the mines, and other league positions. Brophy mistrusted the Communists, but had considerable respect for and worked closely with Foster. Brophy took more than one-third of the votes amidst claims of massive vote fraud.[36]

The collapse of the UMWA in the spring of 1927 precipitated a bitter strike in the soft coal regions of Pennsylvania and Ohio. Foster toured the fields for months, directing league activists, speaking to miners, and erecting a large system of commissaries modeled on those he had established during the 1919 steel strike. Such support earned the Communists a solid reputation amongst some miners and the Party established branches throughout the region. But after more than a year, the strike was defeated with considerable violence, and Lewis once again purged the Communists and their allies, expelling thousands of miners and revoking dozens of charters. Surviving progressives distanced themselves from the Communists. The Save the Union movement died.[37]

Conservatives crushed the TUEL in one union after another, often taking the opportunity to rid themselves of all dissidents with or without league connections. Carpenters' Union president William Hutcheson expelled some opponents immediately but gave others the option of saving themselves by promising in writing to "in no way affiliate with or give support, assistance or comfort to the Trade Union Educational League, or any similar . . . organization."[38]

This rout had profound implications for Foster's notion of boring from within. In the Party, the TUEL's decline undercut Foster's arguments against independent Communist unions. In nearly every trade union throughout the country, Foster later concluded, the attacks had left the TUEL virtually "an underground organization." More and more, the left found itself boring from without.[39]

Minneapolis and Moscow

The labor party movement declined in parallel to these escalating attacks. At the beginning of 1924, Foster publicly repudiated Fitzpatrick, claiming he had committed "treason to the labor party movement."[40] His bitter tone suggests that the split represented a personal as well as a political crisis, confronting Foster with a conflict between Party discipline and personal judgment.

Events in Minnesota offered one last chance to salvage some connection with progressive labor and broaden the base of the FF-LP. Here William Mahoney, an influential labor editor, led a regional Farmer-Labor party with strong roots in the unions and the Farmers' Non-Partisan League. He agreed to work with the FF-LP to create a national Farmer-Labor party with progressive Wisconsin senator Robert M. La Follette as its standard-bearer. Foster regarded La Follette and other middle-class reformers with antipathy, but he welcomed the prospect of bringing the Communists back into a broad, labor-based coalition. Once again, international Communist politics intervened.[41]

In the spring of 1924, with the Farmer-Labor party convention fast approaching, Foster and Pepper went not to Minneapolis but to Moscow to resolve their conflicts. Both men supported some form of third party initiative, but once in Moscow, they found that the emerging struggle between Stalin and Trotsky had produced an abrupt shift in the Comintern line away from the united front. Each tried to use the Comintern struggle to enhance his own position. Foster asked the Comintern leaders to sanction the emerging third party strategy and remove Pepper, who was "gambling with the life and health of the Party through a reckless struggle for power." The Comintern recalled Pepper, but sided with Trotsky on the labor party issue, denouncing any cooperation with La Follette.[42]

Foster accepted the inevitable break with La Follette and even proposed a separate Communist slate. Why did he relent so readily to the termination of a third party strategy after devoting so much effort to it? One possible explanation is opportunism. Certainly, this turn of events best served Foster's own interests. Rather than fight the emerging line, he accepted it in exchange for Pepper's removal. Yet his decision was not inconsistent with his earlier thinking. He had always envisioned the labor party as a "class party" based largely on the unions. The Minnesota movement relied heavily on farmers, and La Follette's emerging campaign included numerous middle-class reformers and a moderate program, elements for which Foster had a profound distaste. La Follette's plans left little room for a labor party to develop in his wake. He saw himself as an independent and refused to tie his candidacy too closely to any particular constituency, least of all radical labor. If it were impossible to have a "real" labor party, perhaps it was better for the Communists to run their own slate. La Follette simplified things for the Communists by denouncing them and refusing to associate himself with the Minnesota group that he saw as contaminated by its association with the Workers' party.[43] Between them, La Follette and the Comintern ended any chance for the Minnesota group to form a viable party.

In the wake of this failure, the Minnesota movement disintegrated as its constituents flocked to La Follette, while the Workers' party quickly nominated a slate reflecting its factional divisions, with Foster for president, and liquidated the FF-LP. Like Fitzpatrick before him, Mahoney felt betrayed and was thereafter suspicious of the Communists. Foster attacked not only La Follette and Mahoney but also Eugene V. Debs, the great symbol of American Socialism, whose reluctant support for La Follette was "capitulation" to "petty-bourgeois reformism." When Debs responded that he had "no Vatican in Moscow," Foster was unrepentant: "We make no apology for accepting the guidance of the Third International. . . . Our party is proud to be a section of the revolutionary world organization."[44] The new turn brought disastrous election results and further isolation for Foster and the Party. He polled 33,316 votes; La Follette, whose movement turned out to have fairly strong labor support, just under five million. Opposing La Follette, Foster later conceded, had been a serious error.[45]

At the end of 1926 the left-wing labor journalist J. B. S. Hardman took stock of the relationships of Foster, the TUEL, and the Party, assessing the damage inflicted by sectarianism: "the TUEL is not a party unit. . . . The league was to be a clearinghouse for *all* progressives in the movement, . . . Foster himself permitted the Communists . . . to make him responsible for the very things he has steadfastly opposed. . . . The immense value of his reputation and the access his former achievements and name gave him . . . was largely blotted out by party tutorship over an effort that should have been kept off party tracks." It is difficult to exaggerate the significance of this failure for the Party's development or for Foster's. Its importance lies in both the short-term destruction and the enduring isolation it produced. A broad left movement based on the unions, like the labor party campaign, offered the best chance for translating local standing, considerable in Chicago and a few other places, into national influence. This prospect depended heavily on Foster's judgment, instinct, and reputation as well as his extensive contacts. Until the fall of 1923 the labor party movement and the TUEL's leadership in rank-and-file insurgencies offered the Communists a home in the labor movement and an opportunity to build a radical base. The strategy dictated by the Party and ultimately followed by Foster destroyed their credibility and cut them off from valued allies. As Paul Buhle concludes, "American Communism had bungled its first attempt at sustained influence."[46]

"Trade Union Communists" and "City College Boys"

The labor party debate drew Foster into the heart of a chronic factionalism that had characterized the Party from its birth. Operating with rare autonomy in the early twenties, Foster was reluctant at first to become involved in factional politics, perhaps because he lacked the intellectual confidence of the New York leadership. Yet the collision between Party dictates and Foster's long-term goal of building a radical labor movement presented him with a dilemma: Factionalism had created the break with Fitzpatrick, yet it was only through such a struggle that he could preserve the union work he saw as the key to building a revolutionary movement. Whatever hopes he held for the FF-LP vanished in the months following the convention, as he saw his political space in the labor movement close and his TUEL work washed away in a flood of expulsions. Yet with his proletarian credentials and labor experience, Foster was not without assets in his conflicts with the more intellectually sophisticated New York group.[47]

Convinced that Pepper's reign would kill any prospects for a mass movement but lacking the experience and confidence for a sustained factional struggle, Foster and his group of union-minded Communists turned to James P. Cannon, the Party's chairman, another former Wobbly and ally on the Central Executive Committee (CEC). In November 1923 the two produced a remarkably lucid postmortem on the Labor party debacle, assessing the damage and laying responsibility at the door of Ruthenberg's majority on the CEC. Their dogmatic position, Foster and Cannon argued, had destroyed much of the Party's influence. It was essential to rebuild united front alliances with progressive elements, especially in the labor movement. The new faction, which Cannon carefully crafted from diverse Party elements, moved Party headquarters to Chicago, the heart of the Party's union work, after winning control of the executive committee and installing Foster as chair in early 1924.[48]

To call the "Fosterites" syndicalists, as their opposition often did, is an oversimplification. Yet their union experiences certainly shaped their political orientation; they valued the industrial over the electoral. Many of Foster's early supporters were old colleagues with roots in the unions, the IWW, or syndicalist groups. For them, the class struggle lay in the nation's factories and mines. Foster's faction "prided itself on being proletarian . . . they were always denouncing the others as petit-bourgeois and intellectual (a term uttered with scathing contempt)." More commonly, the Fosterites referred to Jay Lovestone and the other young intellectuals around Ruthenberg as "the City College boys." Ironically, Foster's early experiences and later commitment to research and writing suggest a great respect for learning. His deep animosity toward "the City College boys" may have derived in part from a frustration with his own meager education. But he was also impatient with the abstract quality of much of the theory he saw about him, a grievance he shared with many Communists involved in mass organizing. The Ruthenberg faction dismissed Foster and his colleagues as politically inarticulate, "half-educated workers." One of Foster's opponents recalled that "Ruthenberg made a much better impression than Foster," whom she found "overwrought, easily provoked, and contentious." Alexander Bittelman, the Foster group's theoretician and the odd man out among these proletarians, agreed that those around Foster "were a rather rough-and-ready group . . . four letter exclamations were a dime a dozen," as were loud drinking parties. Ironically, Foster himself was a revolutionary ascetic, a vegetarian who neither smoked nor drank. But the parties, language, and mannerisms all symbolized the cultural chasm between Foster's group and the intellectual New York leadership who resented the Fosterites' lifestyles as much their policies. The first meeting of James P. Cannon, a former midwestern Wobbly, and Max Bedacht, a Swiss immigrant steeped in European socialist traditions, represented a classic confrontation of this sort. What bothered Bedacht more than thirty years later was that Cannon was chewing tobacco as they spoke.[49]

Such cultural differences accentuated policy fights, as with the labor party question, which remained a major source of contention. Ruthenberg's group continued to support the idea, while the Fosterites considered it a dead issue. To break the cycle of factionalism, the Comintern set up an American commission whose report repudiated Foster's position but remained inconclusive on the vital question of Party control. It appeared to give Ruthenberg an edge, but Foster maintained his leverage with support from RILU chief Solomon Lozovsky, who ensured an endorsement of the TUEL.

On the eve of the Workers party 1925 convention, the Comintern finally intervened to settle the question of Party control, appointing a parity commission with the old Bolshevik Sergei Gusev as impartial chair. Foster emerged with a clear majority of the convention delegates and prepared to consolidate his hold on the Party by removing Ruthenberg and Jay

Lovestone, Ruthenberg's young, college-educated protégé, from the top leadership and assuming control of the *Daily Worker*, the Party's new paper. But Gusev obliterated Foster's plans by simply reading a telegram from Moscow that accused Foster's group of "ultra factional methods," declared the Ruthenberg Group "more loyal to decisions of the Communist International," and demanded shared control of the Central Committee and the *Daily Worker*. "Those who refuse to submit," Gusev concluded, "will be expelled."[50]

Enraged, Foster refused to serve on the Central Committee under these conditions, but Cannon and a majority of Foster's caucus deserted him. Once again, he yielded publicly to Party discipline. "[L]ike soldiers we must obey the CI," he concluded, "if the Comintern finds itself criss-cross with my opinions, there is only one thing to do and that is change my opinions to fit the policy of the Comintern."[51] Ruthenberg reassumed the chairmanship from Foster, Party headquarters moved back to Union Square, district functionaries and organizers were reshuffled. Apparently, Party control depended more on Comintern support than on a majority.

As the TUEL declined, becoming more isolated during 1924 and 1925, Foster's opponents sought to absorb its remnants into the Party. This personal threat also meant abandoning any notion of boring from within. In Foster's view, Party control of trade union work in its own name would cut any remaining ties with non-Communist labor progressives. In late 1925, as Foster traveled once again to Moscow for support, Ruthenberg's majority assumed direction of the Party's union activity. In Moscow, the Comintern refused to give Foster leadership of the Party, but restored his control of union work and endorsed the TUEL.[52]

The next round of factionalism, again reflecting Comintern politics, resulted in the expulsion of several key Foster allies. American Communists keyed their own positions in relation to Stalin's emerging campaign against Trotsky. As early as September 1925, Foster warned a radical writer that "One can easily break his political neck on the Trotzky [*sic*] issue." But some of Foster's closest associates showed sympathies for Trotsky's position, placing Foster himself in a rather awkward situation. "Why, in spite of repeated warnings," Stalin later demanded, did Foster "not repudiate them at the time? Because he behaved first and foremost as a factionalist." When Stalin demanded Trotsky's expulsion in 1928, Cannon sided with Trotsky and Foster himself preferred charges against his former partner. Cannon took perhaps only one hundred activists with him when he was expelled in late 1928, but this number included prominent pro-Foster labor activists in Chicago and Minneapolis. The expulsions undoubtedly weakened Foster in the midst of a major factional confrontation with Jay Lovestone.[53]

When Charles Ruthenberg died suddenly in March 1927, he advised his comrades to "close the ranks and build the party." Instead, American Communists turned on one another with renewed vigor. The ascendancy of Lovestone, who embodied the Party's cerebral, urbane wing that held Foster in such low regard, brought with it the most bitter stage of factional conflict. Foster termed him a "professional factionalist and intriguer." Not above rifling an opponent's mail for political improprieties, Lovestone *was* the consummate factionalist, closely watching Comintern politics to maximize his leverage in the American struggle.[54]

Lovestone is commonly associated with the concept of American exceptionalism, the notion that class relations were unique and the prospects for revolution dimmer in the United States due to the stability of its economic system. Comparable ideas had been around for years and influenced the Party's program long after Lovestone's demise. The Comintern line was always based on the notion of *general* characteristics of capitalism and the class struggle worldwide, but their actual experiences always seemed to lead American Communists back to the unique characteristics of the United States. Foster himself had bordered on exceptionalism in discussing the weakness and conservatism of labor in the United States. Earl Browder likewise argued during the Popular Front era that the Party must base its policies on the unique character of the United States. The same tension between international line and domestic realities reemerged in later efforts to democratize the Party.[55]

Lovestone's argument came at a fateful moment. Stalin now turned 180 degrees to the left, attacking his remaining opponents for "right opportunism." The new line defined a third period of capitalist crisis and revolutionary ferment in which parties must take a "class against class" position—uncompromising independent Communist leadership in mass organizations and attacks on social democrats and other "social fascists." Usually sensitive to the nuances of Comintern politics, Lovestone blundered by aligning himself with Nicolai Bukharin, Stalin's new target.[56]

As late as March 1929, Lovestone held the support of more than 90 percent of the Party's convention delegates and fended off Comintern efforts to install Foster as general secretary. In April 1929, however, the Comintern once again established an American commission and summoned leaders from both factions to Moscow. Foster attacked Lovestone's CEC as petit bourgeois and his southern organizers as racist, while Lovestone read aloud embarrassing passages from Foster's personal correspondence. Speakers shouted profanities at one another, ignoring the chair. Lozovsky lectured each side on proletarian civility but with little effect.[57]

The significance of American factionalism in the context of Comintern politics is suggested by the fact that Stalin himself and seven other prominent Russian leaders served on the new American commission. Stalin's first appearance as an international leader came in his confrontations with Bukharin over the nature of American capitalism, and the tiny American party's problems furnished the context for another major turn in the history of world Communism. The commission's report criticized both factions, but effectively stripped Lovestone and his followers of control. They were labeled "right opportunists," and the Party soon expelled them. In his official analysis of Lovestone's revisionism, Foster quoted at length from Stalin's *Speeches on the American Communist Party* but not from those portions criticizing him.[58]

"The Disease of Dual Unionism"

The new line confronted Foster with his own dilemma. It required independent revolutionary unions, a concept Foster had fought throughout his life. His aversion to dual unionism rose not from theory but from experience and was deeply embedded in his politics. Despite the fact that his mentor Lozovsky had designed it, Foster vigorously resisted the new line throughout the spring and summer of 1928, risking his political future and facing one of the bitterest experiences of his life. Lozovsky, having supported the boring from within strategy for years, now repudiated Foster's opposition as a "fetish." Foster found himself isolated. He had always acknowledged the viability of radical unions where there was no organization at all. At least as early as May 1928, he also justified dual unions where organization was extremely weak, as in textiles, or where mass expulsions excluded the strategy of boring from within, as in mining. But he still saw these as unusual, regrettable situations, not the beginning of a new policy. Otherwise, he said, "Our basic trade-union policy remains the same. It was right in the past and it is right now."[59]

Under enormous pressure, Foster finally caved in, concluding in January 1929 that building new revolutionary unions was the Party's "main task," but this was not good enough. Foster's theory was "a very dangerous one," wrote Max Bedacht, editor of *The Communist*, "[it] is in reality an opportunist conception, a Right deviation from the correct line of the Communist International." Bedacht's language was particularly damning in light of Stalin's campaign against Bukharin. At the end of February

Foster resigned himself to "a prolonged period of dual unionism." By the summer he saw the main danger arising from "rightists" advocating work in the reformist unions. In assessing the Party's ten years of union work, Foster included a long list of TUEL errors, most related to the "basic error" of "trade union legalism." Foster emerged as national secretary of the Party's new Trade Union Unity League (TUUL).[60]

To some degree, the new strategy responded to a real challenge. Vast areas of industry remained unorganized, and the AFL showed little inclination to undertake the task. In auto, food processing, and other mass production industries, there would be little competition with mainstream unions simply because there was so little union activity of any kind. Many Communists argued, rightly as it turned out, that new industrial unions were required to do the job. In some industries with union organization, mass expulsions and other attacks had made it virtually impossible for radicals to function. Such conditions produced a base for radical organizations in coal mining and the needle trades, for example, by placing thousands of unionists outside the mainstream unions. Thus, both the labor movement's own weakness and conservatism and the new Comintern line were responsible for the TUUL's origins.[61]

On a personal level, Foster's acceptance of dual unionism represented the final stage in his shift from "Fosterism," a sort of syndicalist Communism, toward a more orthodox Stalinist position. It also suggests the struggle that raged within him when Party policy contradicted his experience and seemed to threaten the industrial work he saw as the focal point for his radicalism. Foster's reversal, conditioned as it was by the AFL's attacks, indicated that he now saw little choice but to subordinate his own instincts to the Party's will. Within a year, Foster was denouncing UMWA radicals Powers Hapgood and Alex Howath as "fascist tools."[62]

In later years Foster maintained that "a constructive process" beneath the maelstrom of factional conflict in the 1920s raised the Party's ideological level "through the tireless instruction of the Comintern," and "ideological unification" purged "harmful, non-Communist elements from the ranks." Expulsions "broke down the factional walls practically overnight."[63] The Party had indeed purged itself of factionalism, but at the expense of most of its membership and its influence in the labor movement. The fights engendered deep enmity among people who might otherwise have put their efforts into more constructive pursuits. Many of those not expelled simply dropped out in disgust. By the end of 1929 only seven thousand members remained, most of them separated from the mass of American workers. On the eve of capitalism's greatest crisis, the Communist Party was once again a small sect.

Like many Communist labor activists who followed them, Foster and his colleagues were indeed indigenous radicals, working within the mainstream and building on older traditions. But they worked within an organization where international and party politics shaped their options in crucial ways. Sometimes, as in the Popular Front years and World War II, the international line might facilitate their work; in the 1920s, it more often constrained them. Yet the failures of the 1920s were not preordained but rather the result of political repression and Communist factionalism, in Moscow and in the United States. If Foster's story represents a tragedy, it is a tragedy made as much at home as in Moscow, one that resides at the center of the American labor movement's story.

Notes

Thanks to David Roediger, David Montgomery, Diane Koenker, the volume editors, and the University of Illinois Social History Group for their comments and to Randi Storch, Toby Higbie, and Kathy Mapes for research assistance.

1. Theodore Draper, *The Roots of American Communism* (New York: Viking, 1957), and *American Communism and Soviet Russia: The Formative Period* (New York: Vintage, 1986); Irving Howe and Lewis Coser, *The American Communist Party: A Critical History, 1919–1957* (Boston: Beacon Press, 1957); Harvey Klehr, *The Heyday of American Communism: The Depression Decade* (New York: Basic Books, 1984); Harvey Klehr and John Earl Haynes, *The American Communist Movement: Storming Heaven Itself* (New York: Twayne, 1992); Maurice Isserman, *Which Side Were You On? The American Communist Party during the Second World War* (1982; reprint, Urbana: University of Illinois Press, 1993); Roger Keeran, *The Communist Party and the Auto Workers' Unions* (Bloomington: Indiana University Press, 1980); Mark Naison, *Communists in Harlem During the Depression* (Urbana: University of Illinois Press, 1983); Robin D. G. Kelley, *Hammer and Hoe: Alabama Communists during the Great Depression* (Chapel Hill: University of North Carolina Press, 1990); Fraser Ottanelli, *The Communist Party of the United States from the Depression to World War II* (New Brunswick: Rutgers University Press, 1991); Theodore Draper, "American Communism Revisited," *New York Review of Books* 32 (9 May 1985) and "The Popular Front Revisited," *New York Review of Books* 32 (30 May 1985); Maurice Isserman, "Three Generations: Historians View American Communism," *Labor History* 26 (Fall 1985); quotes, Harvey Klehr, John Earl Haynes, and Fridrikh Igorevich Firsov, *The Secret World of American Communism* (New Haven: Yale University Press, 1995), 17.

2. Draper, *Roots of American Communism*, 62.

3. Edward P. Johanningsmeier, *Forging American Communism: The Life of William Z. Foster* (Princeton: Princeton University Press, 1994); Arthur Zipser, *Working Class Giant: The Life of William Z. Foster* (New York: International Publishers, 1981). During the 1920s, the American Communist Party was known as the Workers' party.

4. *New Majority*, 24 Dec. 1921, 8; William Z. Foster, *From Bryan to Stalin* (New York: International Publishers, 1937), 58–85; quote, Bert Cochran, *Labor and Communism: The Conflict That Shaped American Unions* (Princeton: Princeton University Press, 1977), 21.

5. Earl Beckner, "The Trade Union Educational League and the American Labor Movement," *Journal of Political Economy* 33 (Aug. 1925): 410; Jack Johnstone, "The League in Chicago," *Labor Herald* 1 (Apr. 1922): 29; Earl Browder, interview with Daniel Bell, 22 June 1955, Addendum, box 1, folder 20, 50, Daniel Bell Papers, Tamiment Institute, New York University, New York (hereafter Bell Papers); Johanningsmeier, *Forging*, 187; Klehr, Haynes, and Firsov, *Secret World*, 28.

6. William Z. Foster, *The Bankruptcy of the American Labor Movement* (Chicago: Trade Union Educational League, 1922); Foster, *Bryan to Stalin*, 165–67; "The Principles and Program of the Trade Union Educational League," *Labor Herald* 1 (Mar. 1922); David M. Schneider, *The Workers' (Communist) Party and American Trade Unions* (Baltimore: Johns Hopkins University Press, 1928), 1–7.

7. Foster, *Bankruptcy*, 24; cf., Earl C. Ford and William Z. Foster, *Syndicalism* (Chicago: Syndicalist League of North America, 1912), 43–44; David Saposs, "What's Back of Foster?" *Nation* 116 (17 Jan. 1923): 70; David Saposs, *Left Wing Unionism: A Study of Radical Policies and Tactics* (New York: International Publishers, 1926), 50; Philip S. Foner, *History of the Labor Movement in the United States*, vol. 9: *The TUEL to the End of the Gompers Era* (New York: International Publishers, 1991), 121; "A Statement of the Aims of the Trade Union Educational League," Fund 615, Opis 1, Delo 86, Listki 5–7, William Z. Foster Papers, Center for the Preservation and Study of Documents of Recent History (hereafter RTsKhIDNI), Moscow; "Foster's Reply to Nearing," *Daily Worker,* 10 May 1924, quoted in Draper, *American Communism and Soviet Russia*, 123.

8. James Weinstein, *The Decline of Socialism in America, 1912–1924* (New York: Vintage, 1967), 222–29, 274; John Keiser, "John Fitzpatrick and Progressive Labor, 1915–1925" (Ph.D. dissertation, Northwestern University, 1965), 106–33; Foner, *TUEL*, 339–43.

9. Johanningsmeier, *Forging*, 156; Foster, *Bryan to Stalin*, 160–61, quote 140.

10. Foster, *Bryan to Stalin*, 137–38, quote 138; Edward Hallett Carr, *The Bolshevik Revolution, 1917–1923*, vol. 3: *Socialism in One Country* (New York: Macmillan, 1953), 383–425; Foster's testimony before the American Commission, Communist International, 6 May 1929, p. 6, Fund 495, Opis 72, Delo 66, Listok 96, RTsKhIDNI.

11. Weinstein, *Decline*, 275–78; Arne Swabeck, "From Gene Debs to Mao Tsetung," box 8, Charles H. Kerr Papers, Newberry Library, Chicago, Ill.; Draper, *American Communism and Soviet Russia*, 39, 41, cf. n. 29 on 487.

12. Draper, *American Communism and Soviet Russia*, 71; Eugene Staley, *History of the Illinois State Federation of Labor* (Chicago: University of Chicago Press, 1930); *Labor Herald* 1 (May 1922), 16.

13. Saposs, *Left Wing Unionism*, 52; *American Federationist*, Apr. and May 1922; *Chicago Tribune*, May 1922; Edward B. Mittelman, "Basis for American Labor Opposition to Amalgamation and Politics at Portland," *Journal of Political Economy* 32 (Feb. 1924): 90; Philip Taft, *The AF of L in the Time of Gompers* (New York: Harper, 1957), 453–54; Foster to Lozovsky, 16 Dec. 1922, Fund 534, Opis 7, Delo 457, Listok 141, Profintern Papers, RTsKhIDNI.

14. Irving Howe, *World of Our Fathers: The Journey of the East European Jews to America and the World They Found and Made* (New York: Harcourt, Brace, Jovanovich, 1976); Paul Buhle, "Jews and American Communism: The Cultural Question," *Radical History Review* 23 (Dec. 1980): 9–33; Foner, *TUEL*, 269–310; Schneider, *Workers' Party*, 60–104.

15. Rose Wortis, "The Shop Delegate League in the Needle Trades," *Labor Herald* 1 (May 1922), 26; David Gurowsky, "Factional Disputes within the ILGWU, 1919–1928" (Ph.D. dissertation, SUNY Binghamton, 1978), xxvi–xxvii, 49–51; James Hinton, *The First Shop Stewards' Movement* (London: G. Allen & Unwin, 1975).

16. J. B. Salutsky, "Constructive Radicalism in the Needle Industry," *Labor Herald* 1 (May 1922): 10–13, 19; Steve Fraser, *Labor Will Rule: Sidney Hillman and the Rise of American Labor* (New York: Free Press, 1991), 178–83; Foner, *TUEL*, 302–7; Joseph Schlossberg to Lozovsky, 1 June 1922, Profintern Papers, Fund 534, Opis 7, Delo 457, Listki 109–13; quote, William Z. Foster to A. Lozovsky, Moscow, 13 June 1926, Profintern Papers, 534, Opis 7, Delo 472, Listok 100, RTsKhIDNI.

17. David Montgomery, *The Fall of the House of Labor: The Workplace, the State, and American Labor Activism, 1865–1925* (New York: Cambridge University Press, 1987), 338–39; William Goldsmith, "Notes on interview with John Brophy, November 11, 1955, CIO headquarters, Washington, D.C.," section 2, box 7, Bell Papers; Alan Singer, "Communists and Coal Miners: Rank and File Organizing in the United Mine Workers of America during the 1920s," *Science and Society* 55 (1991): 135–39; Schneider, *Workers' Party*, 38–59; Foner, *TUEL*, 208–68; Johanningsmeier, *Forging*, 185–86; Foster, *Bryan to Stalin*, 196–200.

18. Selig Perlman and Philip Taft, *Labor Movements*, vol. 4 of *History of Labor in the United States* (New York: Macmillan, 1935), 562–71; William Z. Foster, "The Left Wing and the Trade Union Elections," *Workers' Monthly* 4 (Feb. 1925): 147–48; Foner, *TUEL*, 259–65; Singer, "Communists and Coal Miners," 139–43; notes on mining in box 1, vol. 3, new series, Bell Papers.

19. Colin J. Davis, "Bitter Conflict: The 1922 Railroad Shopmen's Strike," *Labor History* 33 (Fall 1992): 433–55; William Z. Foster, *Misleaders of Labor* (New York: Trade Union Educational League, 1927), 143; Schneider, *Workers' Party*, 9–25, 29–35; Johanningsmeier, *Forging*, 182–85, 215–16; Robert Christie, *Empire in Wood: A History of the Carpenters' Union* (Ithaca: Cornell University Press, 1956), 253–54; Richard Schneirov and Thomas J. Suhrbur, *Union Brotherhood, Union Town: The History of the Carpenters' Union of Chicago, 1863–1987* (Carbondale: Southern Illinois University Press, 1988), 94–108; Foner, *TUEL*, 170–207; Morris Rosen, manuscript autobiography, 25–27, 130–31, 89–90, 104–10, 118–21, 183–84, Tamiment Institute, New York University, New York.

20. *Worker*, 22 Apr. 1922, 2, quoted in Draper, *American Communism and Soviet Russia*, 72–73.

21. *New York Times (NYT)*, 21 Aug. 1922, 1; *Labor Herald* 1 (Oct. 1922), 14; *Voice of Labor*, 18 Aug. 1922; *New Majority*, 16 Sept. 1922, 3; Edward P. Johanningsmeier, "William Z. Foster: Labor Organizer and Communist" (Ph.D. dissertation, University of Pennsylvania, 1988), 474–75.

22. *New Majority*, 9 Aug. 1922, 4, 5; Foster, *Bryan to Stalin*, 75–76; William Z. Foster, *Pages from a Worker's Life* (New York: International Publishers, 1939), 217–18, 224–28; *NYT*, 8 Aug. 1922, 2; 23 Aug. 1922, 1; 24 Aug. 1921, 1; *Voice of Labor*, 18 Aug. 1922, 11; Earl Browder interview, Columbia University Oral History Research Office, *Columbia University Oral History Collection*, microfiche ed. (Glen Rock, N.J.: Microfilming Corporation of America, 1973), 206–8; quote, Benjamin Gitlow, *The Whole of Their Lives: Communism in America—A Personal History and Intimate Portrayal of Its Leaders* (New York: Charles Scribner's Sons, 1965), 100–104.

23. *Labor Herald* 1 (Oct. 1922), 14, 16; 2 (Apr. 1923), 3; *New Majority*, 16 Sept. 1922, 3; 23 Sept. 1922, 1, 6; *Chicago Tribune*, 29 Mar. 1923, 5; Lillian Herstein interview with Elizabeth Balanoff, transcripts, 60, 67, Labor Oral History Project, Roosevelt University, Chicago; Labor Defense Council, Chicago, *Eight Questions and Seven Answers about the Michigan "Red Raid" Cases* (Chicago, [1922?]); Foner, *TUEL*, 142–46.

24. Foner, *TUEL*, 207–9; *Chicago Tribune*, 13 Mar. 1923, 2; 16 Mar. 1923, 3; 28 Mar. 1923, 1, 12; 4 Apr. 1923, 16; 5 Apr. 1923, 1; 6 Apr. 1923, 12; *New York Herald*, 4 Dec. 1922, 1; Robert Minor, "The Trial of William Z. Foster," *Liberator* 6 (Apr. 1923): 8–11; William Z. Foster, "On Trial in Michigan," *Labor Herald* 2 (May 1923): 3–6, 25–27; correspondence and newspaper clippings, scrapbooks, vol. 16, Frank Walsh Papers, New York Public Library, New York.

25. The Red International of Labor Union (RILU) collection (Fund 534) at RTsKhIDNI contains detailed correspondence between Foster and Lozovsky.

26. Political Committee Meeting Minutes, 13, 14 June 1928, box 1, folder 1, Bell Papers.

27. Johanningsmeier, *Forging*, 196; Beckner, "Trade Union Educational League," 90; Keiser, "John Fitzpatrick," 101–2.

28. Earl Browder interview with Theodore Draper, 29 Sept. 1953, 2, box 1, folder 3, Draper Papers, Woodruff Library, Emory University, Atlanta, Ga.; Jay Lovestone to Ella [Wolfe], 8 Jan. 1923 [1924], box 9, folder 74; Jay Lovestone to Bert and Ella [Wolfe], 11 Oct. 1923, box 9, folder 73, Bertram Wolfe Papers, Hoover Institution Archives, Stanford University, Stanford, Calif.; James P. Cannon to CEC, 25 May 1923, Profintern Papers, Fund 534, Opis 7, Delo 458, Listki 121–23, RTsKhIDNI; Malcolm Sylvers, "Pogany/Pepper: Un représentative du Komintern après du Parti Communiste des Etats-Unis," *Cahiers d'Histoire de l'Institut de Recherche Marxiste* 28 (1987): 119–31; Swabeck, "From Gene Debs to Mao Tse-tung," 149–50; Theodore Draper, notes of an interview with Max Bedacht, 1 June 1954, box 1, folder 15, Draper Papers.

29. Foster to Lozovsky, 7 Nov. 1923, Profintern Papers, Fund 534, Opis 7, Delo 460, Listok 105, RTsKhIDNI; *Voice of Labor*, 14 July 1923; Keiser, "John Fitzpatrick," 133–35; John Pepper, "The Workers' Party and the Federated Farmers' Labor Party," *Liberator* 6 (Aug. 1923): 10–14; "The World We Live in" *American Labor Monthly* 1 (Aug. 1923): 3–15.

30. Jay G. Brown, "The Farmer-Labor Side" *American Labor Monthly* (Sept. 1923): 33–37; William Z. Foster, *History of the Communist Party of the United States* (New York: International Publishers, 1952), 217; Swabeck, "From Gene Debs to Mao Tse-tung," 150–51; Weinstein, *Decline*, 284–88, 288–89; *New Majority*, 14 July 1923, 2, quoted in Keiser, "John Fitzpatrick," 135; Herstein interview with Balanoff, 63–67; Foster quote, Johanningsmeier, *Forging*, 210.

31. William Z. Foster, "The Decatur Battle," *Labor Herald* 2 (Nov. 1923), 6.

32. Illinois State Federation of Labor, *Proceedings*, 1923 (Springfield: Illinois State Federation of Labor, 1923), 404.

33. Taft, *AF of L*, 457–58; American Federation of Labor, *Proceedings*, 1923 (Washington, D.C.: American Federation of Labor, 1924), 256–59; Foster, *Bryan to Stalin*, 183–84; Browder interview, *Columbia University Oral History Collection*, 158; Montgomery, *Fall of the House of Labor*, 433–34; CFL minutes, *New Majority*, 10 Nov. 1923.

34. Schneider, *Workers' Party*, 48–49; Foster, *Misleaders*, 271–305; exchange of letters between Foster and Debs, 25 Sept. 1923 to 8 Nov. 1923, reprinted in J. Robert

Constantine, ed., *Letters of Eugene V. Debs*, vol. 3: *1919–1926* (Urbana: University of Illinois Press, 1990), 393–94, 397–99, 402–4, 406–8, 411, 415–16.

35. Gurowsky, "Factional Disputes within the ILGWU," 151–73, 175–79, 236–46; Saposs, *Left Wing Unionism*, 53–58; Schneider, *Workers' Party*, 91–104; Howe and Coser, *American Communist Party*, 249–51.

36. "Save the Union, an Open Letter by John Brophy to Officers and Members of the UMWA," 24 Sept. 1926, leaflet, Fund 515, Opis 1, Delo 911, Listki 47–48, Communist Party of the USA Papers, RTsKhIDNI; Schneider, *Workers' Party*, 54–59; William Z. Foster, "A Dangerous Situation," *Workers' Monthly* 5 (Sept. 1926): 493–95; Goldsmith, "Notes on interview with John Brophy"; Foster, *Misleaders*, 291–94; Foster, *Bryan to Stalin*, 196–200.

37. Foster, *Bryan to Stalin*, 199–200; John Brophy, Pat Toohey, Powers Hapgood, "'Save-the-Miners' Union Call," *Communist* 7 (Mar. 1928): 175–80; William Z. Foster, "Tasks and Lessons of the Miners' Struggle," *Communist* 7 (Apr. 1928): 195–200; William Z. Foster, "Two Mine Strike Strategies," *Communist* 7 (May 1928): 279–83; William Z. Foster, "The Mining Crisis Deepens," *Communist* 7 (June 1928): 323–26; William Z. Foster, "Proposals for Work in the Coal Mining Industry, n.d., [spring, 1927]," box 2, "Miners," closed series; [William Z. Foster], "Proposals on Mining Situation, April 30, 1928," box 1, folder 1, open series; "Draft of Plan for Work in Miners Union and Agenda for National Miners Conference, Chicago May 8–9, 1928 (Submitted by Foster to the T.U. Committee, May 6, 1928)," box 1, vol. 5, closed series; [William Z. Foster], "Proposals for Policy in the Mining Industry, May 16, 1928," box 1, folder 2, open series, all in Bell Papers.

38. Christie, *Empire in Wood*, 256–66; Saposs, *Left Wing Unionism*, 53–58; Foster, *Misleaders*, 296–99; Schneider, *Workers' Party*, 4–6, 30–37.

39. William Z. Foster, "Party Industrial Methods and Structure," *Workers' Monthly* 4 (June 1925): 351.

40. William Z. Foster, "An Open Letter to John Fitzpatrick," *Labor Herald* 2 (Jan. 1924): 6, 8, 26–27.

41. Weinstein, *Decline*, 290–313.

42. *Daily Worker*, 19 May 1925, 1; Browder interview, *Columbia Oral History Collection*, 151–56.

43. *NYT*, 19 June 1924, 3; Weinstein, *Decline*, 313–14; Draper, *American Communism and Soviet Russia*, 110–13; Johanningsmeier, *Forging*, 209–10.

44. William Z. Foster to Eugene V. Debs, 15 July 1924; Eugene V. Debs to William Z. Foster, 23 July 1924, quoted in David Shannon, *The Socialist Party of America* (Chicago: Quadrangle Books, 1967), 178; William Z. Foster, "The Significance of the Elections: Three Stages of Our Labor Party Policy," *Workers' Monthly* 4 (Dec. 1924): 51–54; *Daily Worker*, 31 July 1924, 1, reproduced in Constantine, *Letters of Debs*, 431.

45. Weinstein, *Decline*, 313–23; Foster, *History of the CPUSA*, 219, 220.

46. Paul Buhle, *Marxism in the USA* (London: Verso, 1987), 132.

47. Pepper, "Workers' Party and the Federated Farmer-Labor Party"; John Pepper, "Facing the Third American Revolution," *Liberator* 6 (Sept. 1923): 9–12; John Pepper, "Shall We Assume Leadership?" *Liberator* 6 (Oct. 1923): 9–11, 28.

48. James Cannon and William Z. Foster, "Statement on Our Labor Party Policy," Nov. 1923, in "Farmer-Labor Party Maneuvers," Bell Papers; Foster to Lozovsky, 10 Sept. 1923, Profintern Papers, Fund 534, Opis 7, Delo 460, Listki 8–14, RTsKhIDNI.

49. Benjamin Gitlow, *I Confess* (New York: E. P. Dutton & Co., 1940), 106, 313; Vera Buch Weisbord, *A Radical Life* (Bloomington: Indiana University Press, 1977), 95, 98–99; Gitlow, *Whole of Their Lives*, 106; Alexander Bittelman, "Things I Have Learned," manuscript autobiography, 398–99, 407–8, 434–35, Tamiment Institute, New York University, New York; Joseph Freeman, *An American Testament* (New York: Farrar & Rinehart, 1936), 295; Max Bedacht to Theodore Draper, 9 Dec. 1954, box 10, folder 15, Draper Papers.

50. Foster and Bittelman to G. Zinoviev, 15 Dec. 1925, Fund 515, Opis 1, Delo 423, Listok 44, CPUSA Papers; Charles Krumbein, Phil Aronberg, Joseph Zack, "Appeal to the EC of the Communist International" [1925], Fund 515, Opis 1, Delo 423, Listki 67–70, CPUSA Papers, RTsKhINDI; Carr, *Socialism in One Country*, 408, 406–13; Foster, "Significance of the Elections"; Alexander Bittelman, "In Retrospect," *Workers' Monthly* 4 (Dec. 1924): 51–54, 77–79, 85–90; Browder interview, Columbia Oral History Project, 164–66; Howe and Coser, *American Communist Party*, 159; Draper, *American Communism and Soviet Russia*, 127–52; James P. Cannon, *The First Ten Years of American Communism* (New York: Lyle Stuart, 1962), 131–38; Foster, *History of the CPUSA*, 223.

51. *Daily Worker*, 8 Oct. 1925, quoted in Draper, *American Communism and Soviet Russia*, 149; Howe and Coser, *American Communist Party*, 159–60; C. E. Ruthenberg, "The Tasks of the Party in the Light of the Comintern," *Workers' Monthly* 4 (July 1926): 401–5.

52. Foster, "Party Industrial Methods and Structure"; Browder interview, Columbia Oral History Project, 167.

53. Foster to Calverton, 8 Sept. 1925, box 5, V. F. Calverton Papers, New York Public Library, New York; Foster, *History of the CPUSA*, 269–70; Cannon, *First Ten Years*, 222–26; Draper, *American Communism and Soviet Russia*, 357–76; Carr, *Socialism*, 52–22; C. E. Ruthenberg, "From the Third through the Fourth Convention of the Workers (Communist) Party," *Workers' Monthly* 4 (Oct. 1925): 531–38; *Stalin's Speeches on the American Communist Party* (New York: International Publishers, 1929), quoted, Philip J. Jaffe, *The Rise and Fall of American Communism* (New York: Horizon Press: New York, 1975), 31.

54. Foster's remarks before the American Commission of the Comintern, May 1929, transcript, Fund 495, Opis 72, Delo 66, Comintern Papers, RTsKhIDNI.

55. Foster, *Bankruptcy*; James G. Ryan, *Earl Browder: The Failure of American Communism* (Tuscaloosa: University of Alabama Press, 1997); Maurice Isserman, *If I Had a Hammer: The Death of the Old Left and the Birth of the New Left* (1987; reprint, Urbana: University of Illinois Press, 1993), 3–34.

56. Franz Borkenau, *World Communism: A History of the Communist International* (Ann Arbor: University of Michigan Press, 1962), 436–37, 439; William Z. Foster, "The Growing World Offensive against Capitalism," *Communist* 9 (Mar. 1930): 199–203.

57. American Commission, Communist International, May 1929, Fund 495, Opis 72, Delo 66, RTsKhIDNI; H. M. Wicks to "Louis" (Weinstock?), Helsingfors, Finland, 29 May 1929, box 6, folder 8, Draper Papers.

58. "The Significance of the Comintern Address," *Communist* 8 (June 1929): 291–302; Draper, *American Communism and Soviet Russia*, 405–30; Earl Browder to Philip Jaffe, 31 Aug. 1954, box 1, folder 3, Philip Jaffe Papers, Woodruff Library, Emory University, Atlanta, Ga.; Foster, *History of the CPUSA*, 273–74.

59. "Proposals for Policy in the Mining Industry, Submitted by William Z. Foster, May 16, 1928," box 1, folder 2, open series, Bell Papers; William Z. Foster, "The Tasks and Lessons of the Miners' Struggle," *Communist* 7 (Apr. 1928): 198–99; "Old Unions and New Unions," *Communist* 7 (July 1928): 404–5.

60. William Z. Foster, "The Decline of the American Federation of Labor," *Communist* 8 (Jan.–Feb. 1929): 47–58; Max Bedacht, "The Decline of the American Federation of Labor," *Communist* 8 (Jan.–Feb. 1929): 44, 46; William Z. Foster, "Right Tendencies at the Trade Union Unity Congress," *Communist* 8 (July 1929): 369–74; "The Party Trade Union Work During Ten Years," *Communist* 8 (Nov. 1929): 609–18; *Daily Worker,* 11, 22 Feb. 1929; Goldsmith interview with Earl Browder, 6 July 1955, 17–18, section 2, box 8, Bell Papers.

61. Foster, *Bryan to Stalin,* 209–13; Gurowsky, "Factional Disputes within the ILGWU," 278–315.

62. *Daily Worker,* 4 June 1930, 1.

63. Foster, *Bryan to Stalin,* 299–300.

Chapter 13

The Dynamics of "Americanization"

The Croatian Fraternal Union
between the Wars, 1920s–30s

PETER RACHLEFF

THE "AMERICANIZATION" of immigrants and their children has received increased attention from working-class historians. While we have not yet constructed a full paradigm of the process, we have begun to generate some hypotheses and sketch out some patterns. This process is no longer depicted in a simplistic, top-down fashion, in which such external agents as teachers, social workers, and politicians refashion ethnic cultures in their own middle-class, patriotic images. Rather, it is now viewed as a dynamic process, in which immigrants and their children respond not only to these influences but also to pressures from middle-class leaders within their groups and from labor and radical organizers of various backgrounds, while trying to sort out their lives in a challenging and changing American society. Thinking and acting on their own behalf, immigrants and their children have shaped themselves as much as they were shaped, transforming American society while altering their own ethnic subcultures.

These cultures were built out of old country values and experiences that were already in transition, since emigrants typically left from regions that were undergoing fundamental social and economic change. While immigrants and their children organized themselves, built such institutions as churches, mutual benefit associations, and political organizations, and constituted themselves as communities, they did not live within self-contained cultural bubbles. As they evolved in the United States, they incorporated elements of both mainstream American culture and other ethnic cultures around them. They were also influenced by their own ethnic entrepreneurs and activists, who promoted diverse agendas, ideologies, and organizations. Out of this process emerged dynamic, changing ethnic identities that ought to be understood as "invented" rather than "essential" or "inherited."[1]

As with most of the "new" social history, our understanding of these social processes is being built through case studies of particular groups in specific historical contexts.[2] Only on this firm empirical ground can a new paradigm be pieced together. This essay—which uses the experience of the Croatian Fraternal Union (CFU) in the 1920s and 1930s as a window—is intended to contribute to this ongoing discussion. It revolves around three related themes: the cultural struggle of the immigrant generation to attract their children to the CFU; the repercussions of political upheaval and turmoil in Yugoslavia; and the economic impact of the Great Depression. The CFU provides a window through which to view the "Americanization" of Croatian immigrants and their children, maintaining cultural values and adjusting to new circumstances. While shaped by particular circumstances, values, and events, the Croatian experience was similar to that of many other immigrant groups, especially where the dynamics of "Americanization" were concerned, as we shall see.

Croatia, and the other provinces that would later constitute Yugoslavia, had long been part of the Austro-Hungarian Empire. By the 1870s and 1880s, economic and social changes had begun to shake the regime's centralized authority. Along the Dalmatian coast, in the peasant-dominated Slavonian countryside, and in the mountains of Hercegovina and Bosnia, these changes disrupted everyday life while putting political freedom on the historical agenda for the first time in a millennium. Two popular responses to these new dynamics developed: emigration to the United States, but also to Canada and Australia, which took on "exodus" proportions of nearly half a million between 1905 and 1914, and a variety of political movements, seeking to shape the configurations of a new nation.[3]

Until the outbreak of World War I, Croatian emigration fit the model of a "labor migration." Men outnumbered women almost six to one, most were in their prime working years, and as many as half of them returned home after a sojourn abroad. Mostly peasants and farm laborers, they were drawn to those expanding industries in the United States with a high demand for unskilled labor: coal, iron, and copper mining, steelmaking, and meatpacking. In 1914, 42 percent of Croatian men were in the iron and steel industry, 35 percent in mining, and 15 percent in meat processing, accounting for 93 percent of the male immigrants. They settled in the heavily industrialized cities of Pittsburgh, Cleveland, and Chicago; in the smaller industrial towns around these cities; the industrial frontier of northern Michigan, Wisconsin, Minnesota, and Montana; and the coal towns of Pennsylvania, West Virginia, Ohio, and Colorado. The women who did come played important roles contributing to family income. In steel and mining towns, they ran boardinghouses, and in cities like Chicago, Omaha, Kansas City, and South St. Paul, they worked in the processing departments of the meatpacking industry.[4]

These immigrants worked long hours as unskilled laborers in this country's most dangerous industries. They needed to provide for their own and their families' needs in case of injuries or even death. Commercial insurance was unavailable. Thus, early on, like many immigrants before and after them, they organized mutual benefit societies. Members paid dues, were eligible for benefits, and participated in the organizations' governance and social activities. In the late nineteenth and early twentieth centuries, most of these benefit societies were local in nature, and they grouped men who often came from the same village or region in the homeland.[5]

Among these organizations, the Hrvatska Bratska Zajednica (Croatian Fraternal Union) gradually took on national proportions and subsumed the others. Started as the Croatian Society in the Pittsburgh region in 1894, it became the National Croatian Society in 1897, incorporated diverse independent local organizations, and then merged in 1924 with regional organizations such as the Croatian League of Illinois, the New Croatian Society of Indiana, and the St. Joseph Society of Kansas City, assuming the name of the Croatian Fraternal Union and encompassing sixty thousand adult and thirty thousand child members in nine hundred local lodges across the United States. In addition to providing death benefits and insurance, the CFU maintained orphans' and old people's homes, a network of "junior nests," and a weekly national newspaper, *Zajedničar* (Unity).[6]

The CFU—popularly known as "Zajednica" (the Union)—sought to unify Croatian Americans. To do so, its activists promoted a "Croatian" ethnic identity that had existed primarily as a political ideology among romantic, "illyrian," and nationalist activists back in the homeland. Ironically, it was in the diaspora that this "Croatian" identity would first find a popular base. At the same time, the CFU's immigrant activists promoted a Pan-Slavism ("Yugoslavism"), which reflected newer movements and ideologies in the homeland. Over the next decades, this identity would evolve further, incorporating more elements of the immigrants' American experience yet still based upon their Croatian foundation.[7]

Organizationally, the CFU brought together diverse elements of the Croatian diaspora—Dalmatian sailors in New Orleans and San Pedro; Licani, Bosnians, and Hercegovinians among coal, iron, and copper miners in Pennsylvania, Michigan, Montana, Minnesota, and Colorado; former peasants and soldiers, now steelworkers and packinghouse workers in industrial cities. In many of its local lodges, Slovenes, Serbs, and other Slavs were welcomed as members. Village loyalties, regional dialects, and provincial identities were submerged within the CFU's slogan of "One for All—All for One" and its symbol of two hands clasped in fraternity.[8]

The CFU both provided a bridge to the old country and assisted its members in adapting to their new lives in America. Delegates to the 1894 founding convention pledged "to encourage their members to be true sons of their nation and to become good citizens of the U.S." In the early twentieth century, it launched a campaign to teach Americans—*and* Croatians in the United States—not to "call the Croatians strange names such as Austrian, Hungarian, etc., but give them their proper name, Croatian." The CFU organized English classes for the immigrant generation and provided Croatian language classes for their children. Its activists also promoted knowledge of the Croatian homeland and respect for its heritage.[9]

Even when Croatian immigrant workers organized themselves around their immediate self-interests within the United States, homeland politics remained a prime concern. At the turn of the century, immigrants supported a number of Croatian-language newspapers, whose titles suggest their continuing interest in political conflict in their homeland: *Velika Hrvatska* (Great Croatia); *Hrvatska Rodoljub* (Croatian Patriot); *Hrvatska Republika* (Croatian Republic); *Sloboda* (Liberty); *Hrvatska Zastava* (Croatian Flag); *Hrvatska Sloboda* (Croatian Liberty). The National Croatian Society engaged in substantial fund-raising on behalf of movements challenging the Austro-Hungarian regime. By 1904, its convention advised each lodge to contribute to the opposition, generating some $5,900. Between 1912 and 1915, immigrants (mostly unskilled laborers who earned $1.00 a day) sent more than $200,000.[10]

On the eve of World War I, "Croatian," "Croatian-American," and "Yugoslav" identities intermingled among the immigrant generation, often overlapping and reinforcing each other. Infused with ideas of democracy and self-government, returning immigrants played prominent political roles in homeland movements. Some immigrants built organizations in the United States with the express purpose of influencing the political situation in Croatia. In 1912, a group of activists came together in Kansas City to organize the Hrvatski Savez (Croatian League) to promote the "destruction" of the Austro-Hungarian empire and the establishment of a "South Slavic state." A year later, a Pittsburgh-based organization sent one of its members back to Croatia to assassinate the royal commissar. He failed, but his venture created an uproar on both continents.[11]

Immigrant attention to the political affairs of the homeland reached a peak during World War I. The war itself broke out in the heart of the old country and sounded the deathknell of the Austro-Hungarian empire. Two issues dominated political debate within the Croatian communities in the United States: What should be the geographic configuration of the new state to be created? And what should its political character be? These questions were posed in the ethnic press, in mass public meetings and lecture tours, and in local fraternal lodge meetings.[12]

Out of this debate, a consensus emerged that said as much about the evolution of Croatian ethnic identity in the United States as it did about the political solution to the destruction of the Austro-Hungarian empire. It reflected the deep traditions of peasant populism and Pan-Slavism as well as the influence of years spent in the United States. Croatian immigrants articulated a vision of a "United States of Yugoslavia," with Croatia, Serbia, Hercegovina, Bosnia, Dalmatia, Macedonia, Montenegro, and Slovenia enjoying a status comparable to Pennsylvania, Illinois, or Minnesota in the United States. In March 1915, a "national congress" of 563 Croatian, Serbian, and Slovenian delegates meeting in Chicago sought to combine cultural autonomy, political federalism, economic unity, and democracy. They urged that the Hapsburg monarchy be replaced with a system in which "everybody may understand what it means to be a free man, in a free country, and how to respect and use this liberty." On this basis, Croatian immigrants and exiles lobbied President Woodrow Wilson and other world leaders, urging that this model be adopted after the war.[13]

World War I was a turning point for Croatians in Europe and the United States. While it spelled the demise of Austria-Hungary, the new state of Yugoslavia fell short of the expectations held by Croatians, both in the homeland and in the United States. Rather than the political and cultural democracy they had envisioned, the new regime was a monarchy with a Serbian line of succession. In the United States, the war, followed by restrictive immigration quotas, cut off the stream of Croatian immigration. More and more of the immigrants decided that they were here to stay. They married, brought over family members, and began to raise children. By the 1920s, their American-born children reached adolescence or young adulthood, speaking English, playing American sports, and listening and dancing to American music.[14]

Meanwhile, like all immigrant groups, the Croatians were subjected to intensive "Americanization" campaigns in the 1920s. Recent historical scholarship has demonstrated the complexity of these campaigns and of the overall process of cultural change in the 1920s. In *Making a New Deal*, Lizabeth Cohen presents a convincing argument that the "mass culture" of chain stores, chain movie theaters, and commercial radio had a limited impact on ethnic cultures in the twenties, and that ethnic groups were even able to use elements of this culture, such as the phonograph, to celebrate and maintain their own cultural expressions. Gary Gerstle, in *Working-Class Americanism*, explores the political lessons that French-Canadian immigrants drew from "Americanization," which they injected into their struggles to improve their standard of living and expand their rights at work and in the community. In *Becoming Mexican-American*, George Sanchez shows that while working-class Mexican immigrants in 1920s Los Angeles were subject to pressures from both Anglo "Americanizers" and middle-class advocates of Mexican nationalism tied to the Mexican government and the local consulate, immigrants selected elements of both these agendas and interwove them with their own values and practices to, ultimately, make their own culture. Cohen, Gerstle, and Sanchez provide strong evidence that "Americanization" did not turn out the way that the "Americanizers" wanted it to.[15]

CFU activists played a key role in redirecting this process of "Americanization." On the one hand, they realized by the late 1920s that they were in a war for the loyalties of the American-born generation, and that if they lost this war, they would lose the entire organization that they had built. They made two critical adjustments: the creation of "English-speaking lodges" (ESL's) and the publication of an English language section of *Zajedničar*, the CFU's weekly newspaper. On the other hand, they renewed their efforts to build support for political movements in Croatia. They helped form several new organizations for this purpose, encouraging CFU members to participate. The constitution of one of these organizations, the Croatian Republican League of the United States, articulated the cultural dualism that informed these activities. It pledged "to diffuse a more intimate knowledge of Croatian history and the history of the Croatian people in America, and stimulate a just pride of Croatian ideals and achievements, thus enabling our people to contribute in the highest degree to the enrichment of American culture."[16]

CFU activists redoubled their efforts after the dramatic assassination of peasant leader Stjepan Radić on the floor of the Yugoslav parliament in 1928. They participated in the formation of yet another organization, the Hrvatsko Kolo (Croatian Circle). Kolo's political program relied on concepts of "self-determination" and "liberty," while drawing a parallel between American Prohibitionism and "Jugo-slavism" as "twins born out of wedlock, unwanted and despised." They appealed to Croatian immigrants and their children to be *more* "American," since "according to the best traditions of American citizenship, a good American means, in the first place, a man or a woman with a backbone, not a jellyfish!" As part of their organizing efforts, they planned to fight anything that promoted "inferiority complexes" among Croatian-American youth, by teaching Croatian history, culture, and language, and by making their homeland a source of pride.[17]

In the very year they were sanctioned by the CFU, forty ESL's were created. At one level, we might see the English-speaking lodges and the English section of *Zajedničar* as steps towards "assimilation." Some older members of the CFU opposed these measures precisely on these grounds, especially since these lodges did even more than conduct business in English. Where entertainment for the old lodges consisted of lectures, gymnastics, and an occasional play or concert, the new lodges played American sports, such as bowling, baseball, basketball, football, and hockey, and sponsored social events popular among American teens and young adults, such as weenie roasts, beach parties, and outings to amusement parks.[18]

A close look suggests that more than "assimilation" was going on within these new lodges. They offered Croatian language classes and taught Croatian history, geography, and culture to the "average younger CFU member, whose knowledge of conditions over there is somewhat limited." Croatian folk songs like "Oj ti vilo, vilo Velebita" and traditional games like "Igraj kolo" were popular, and plays about the old country were performed by lodge groups. Many lodges organized tamburica orchestras, which became an absolute rage among the second generation in the 1930s.[19]

Likewise, the English-language section of *Zajedničar* reached the American-born generation with substantial content about their parents' history and culture. To be sure, it reported news of interest to the younger generation, and its pages were full of accounts of ESL activities as well as the academic and athletic accomplishments of Croatian-American youth. But it also included regular features about Croatian history and culture. *Zajedničar* sponsored essay contests in which younger members were asked to write on such topics as "Impressions of Yugoslavia" and "Why Should

Every Child of Croatian Parentage Be in the Croatian Fraternal Union?" The English section of *Zajedničar* was particularly active in promoting the 1930s renaissance of tamburica music. Matt Gouze, the key national figure in this musical movement (born to Slovene parents in Ely, on Minnesota's Iron Range, in 1911), wrote a regular column, "On Tamburica Interests," which quickly became one of the paper's most popular features. This column "is read and re-read in hundreds of towns and cities in this country," Gouze noted,

> not only by our older people who are more closely linked to the instrument because of their birth in the old country, but also by the younger people, who were born and raised in this country, far away from the origin of the tamburica. . . . Day after day, they can be found in wide-awake Croatian colonies, strumming tunes of the land, of their parents, national airs, folk dances, kolos. And these seem to kindle in the hearts and minds of these youngsters a certain measure of love and respect for the land, the country, and the people from whence they came. We know of nothing better that will link our American-born youth to the traditions of their people than the strumming of native instruments, the singing of age-old songs, and the recitation of Croatian verse so familiar to their parents.[20]

Recent historical study of other ethnic groups suggests that such musical activities in the 1930s were more complicated than just the "singing of age-old songs" by the American-born generation. Indeed, they often incorporated new elements, forms, and dynamics from the American setting. In his examination of the making of Mexican-American culture in Los Angeles in this period, George Sanchez demonstrates that the roots of ethnic music lay in musical forms that were already in transition before emigration, and that the American-born youth chose elements from the Anglo music around them to blend with their already fluid "Mexican" musical styles. Victor Greene, in his fascinating study of the evolution of polka music, shows that ethnic performers drew creatively from the commercial recording and radio business in developing styles that would appeal to their rapidly evolving audiences. Greene argues that polka music is better understood as "new" than as "traditional." In her study of Polish "goral" string bands in 1930s Polish-American communities, Mary Cygan finds not a "traditional" form of music "imported" into the United States but a form newly created out of reaction to American urban culture, "Americanization" pressures, and the impact of the Great Depression.[21]

These studies give us added insight into the tamburica "craze" among American-born Croatian youth in the 1930s. Three hundred and thirty orchestras were organized, consisting almost entirely of young men and women whose introduction to this "traditional" music came through commercial recordings. Participants came from Slovene and Serbian as well as from Croatian families. Gouze's meteoric career took him from Minnesota's Iron Range to the metropolitan Twin Cities, to Texas, and then, in 1937, to a position at Duquesne University in Pittsburgh, where he organized the highly professional "Duquesne Tamburitzans." "Orchestras" in the United States were smaller in size than in the old country, and the accompaniment was often changed to include an accordion. The "folk traditions" of tamburica music were soon intermingled with all aspects of the American music business, from recordings to radio to commercial tours. Its identification with things "Croatian" and its function as a pathway for the second generation to their parents' "culture" was in no way undercut by these developments. But its dynamic, evolving character, its intermingling of "old" and "new" elements, typified the evolution of Croatian-American ethnic identity—and that of other immigrant groups—in the 1930s.[22]

As these studies suggest, the Great Depression was a crucial context for the transformation of the second generation's culture and identity. It had a major impact on Croatian industrial workers, as layoffs, short hours, and wage cuts reduced their incomes. The consequences were severe, not only for them but also for the CFU, which depended on their dues to pay out their insurance benefits. *Zajedničar* emphasized the values of mutuality as they had been practiced in the village and the extended family: "In this period of depression, every true member of the CFU should be like a great rock in the weary land, under whose shelter the way-worn traveller—the unemployed member—may rest from his journey and find a helping hand."[23]

But CFU activists discovered all too soon that efforts at self-help, from the informal efforts of families and communities to the structured efforts of their organization, amounted to little more than stretching inadequate resources to meet rapidly deepening needs. The English editor of *Zajedničar* eloquently captured the severity of the situation: "We find today an army of destitute men and women, shorn of their life's savings, jobless and penniless, with nothing to look forward to in the twilight of their life except the stark reality of want and privation." A stopgap measure to help members keep up their dues led to a hemorrhage, first of money in the treasury and then of members themselves. In December 1930, the CFU Supreme Board announced that unemployed members could draw on their accrued insurance policies in order to keep up their dues. Within two years, twenty thousand men and women—one-third of the organization's adult membership—were doing so. Some unemployed members requested the pay-out of their policies for the immediate income they so desperately needed. Instead, as the deficit of pay-outs to dues received worsened, the CFU was forced to levy special assessments and cut the payment of benefits by 50 percent. But the treasury continued to shrink, as did the membership ranks. By 1934, the paid-up adult membership of the CFU had fallen by more than half, down to twenty-seven thousand.[24]

As the crisis worsened, CFU activists changed their outlook. They began to look outside their own organization's limited—and shrinking—resources. "It needs no argument to prove," some contended in late 1931, "that if anything is to be done to help the unemployed and the needy, it must be done by strong government action and assistance. Charity and voluntary contributions will not suffice."[25]

The crisis of the Great Depression was driving CFU activists into American politics. A decade earlier, they sought to influence Woodrow Wilson's foreign policy toward Yugoslavia but, during the 1920s, Croatian immigrants and their children had evinced little interest in American politics. This changed rather quickly. In March 1933, following Franklin D. Roosevelt's election as president, *Zajedničar* called for protests against the McLeod-Norris Bill, which would have allowed cities to scale down their debt to municipal bondholders. *Zajedničar* noted that while organized participation in American politics might be a new experience for many CFU members, it was becoming a necessity. In the summer of 1933, *Zajedničar* urged its readers to campaign for legislation to restrict the use of child labor and sweatshops. Over the next five years, the CFU would champion one New Deal measure after another. "More and more, we are led to believe," *Zajedničar* opined at the time of the 1936 elections, "that there is a spark of justice in the demands for old age pensions, for unemployment insurance, so that men, after their three score years in the mines, factories and forests of this country may cease bending their backs to fill the bottomless coffers of the money barons."[26]

When CFU activists looked outside the parameters of their own organization for responses to the Great Depression, they did not only look to the federal government. They had a long tradition of supporting participation in the labor movement and promoting the more militant and radical elements within it, including the Industrial Workers of the World and the Trade Union Unity League. Delegates to the 1926 CFU convention gave *Zajedničar* responsibility to "publish accurate accounts of the struggles of union labor for its rights and especially strikes of workingmen's organizations." The CFU's bylaws promised that "a justified struggle and the demands of the workingmen for accomplishment of their rights shall be supported." While strikers could apply to the Culture and Enlighten-ment Fund for support, strikebreakers faced summary expulsion. The 1929 convention of the CFU adopted a resolution that urged the American labor movement "to develop in the direction of modern industrial union-ism, regardless of trade, nationality, or race, and encompass more unskilled workers, including members of the CFU who work in factories and mines."[27]

Given the concentration of Croatian and Croatian-American workers in unskilled jobs in mass production industry, it is not surprising that CFU activists should have encouraged industrial unionism. They were "aware that the old and primitive form of trade and professional organization was not in the best interest of labor in a modern, highly centralized industry," explained a group of activists in a report to the 1947 CFU convention.

> In those great struggles which took place particularly between 1919 and 1933, sentiment and movement grew for a new and modern form of labor union and for industrial organization, which was to encompass all the work-ers in one industry. . . . Far-sighted members of the CFU knew that indus-trial unions would obtain better wages for workers, which would ease the payment of membership dues. They knew that industrial unions would im-prove working conditions . . . [which] . . . would better protect workers' health and thus the members would be healthier and . . . reimbursements would be lower. They knew that industrial unions would be in a position to instigate laws regarding work safety which would mean fewer accidents for their members and accordingly smaller compensation payments.[28]

And so CFU activists threw themselves into the developing labor conflicts of the mid-1930s. In the summer of 1932, delegates to the CFU national convention decried "the very unfavorable situation existing among the working class in the present industrial depression, the reduc-tion of wages and the extension of working hours." A resolution placed the convention on record as "favoring the formation of militant labor unions, so that they may compel their employers to offer better working conditions and greater earnings." In 1933 and 1934, *Zajedničar* criticized the inadequacies of the National Industrial Recovery Act, reported on the working conditions in the clothing, textile, and steel industries, and called for support of the unionization campaign in these industries. Widespread unionism would be in the best interests of the national economy, the pa-per argued, since higher wages would increase demand, which would in turn stimulate production and employment.[29]

Through convention resolutions and *Zajedničar* editorials, the CFU urged members to participate in the resurgent labor movement. They trumpeted Roosevelt's famed pro-union statements in the spring of 1933, the promises of section 7A of the National Industrial Recovery Act, and the creation of the Committee for Industrial Organization in the summer of 1935. "CIO" appeared again and again in page one headlines in *Zajedničar*. Individual lodges were encouraged to pay out strike benefits and to expel strikebreakers and company police. Fraternal halls were used as meeting places by organizing committees, and some became directly involved in strikes. "Hundreds of CFU members became volunteers and unpaid organizers," noted a report a decade later. "Lodge meetings became organizing caucuses."[30]

The Steel Workers Organizing Committee (SWOC) drive attracted the participation of thousands of Croatians and, especially, Croatian Americans. "News of the Workers Movement" became a new front page column in *Zajedničar*, which continually hailed the successes of the SWOC and CIO drives. Letters from lodges bore witness to the intensity of prounion feelings. "The poor working man," one member wrote, "realizes today, better than ever before, that only through efficient organization can he cope with the might of money." Another called the Wagner Act "the modern version of Lincoln's Emancipation Act." Yet another urged CFU members to "sign the blue card. Be proud to say you are not only a MAN, but a UNION MAN." The CFU Supreme Board formally endorsed the SWOC drive and called "upon its members who work in the steel industry to join that union, and it also calls upon all other members and lodges to help them in their organizing." The board pledged "moral and, if possible, financial support . . . so as to accomplish a complete organization of steel workers into one union as soon as possible." When the SWOC formed its Fraternal Orders Committee to mobilize rank-and-file lodge members, CFU president John Butkovich was elected chairman.[31]

It was at this point that CFU activists undertook their most imaginative exercise in cultural and political syncretism. They not only contributed their support to the union campaign at all levels but they also launched their own membership drive. Focusing on the second generation, primarily via the vehicle of English-speaking lodges, they concentrated on those industrial cities like Steelton, Aliquippa, and Lackawanna, where the Croatian-American communities were already in motion from the union organizing drive in steel.[32]

Labor issues were not the exclusive focus of these campaigns. CFU activists placed considerable emphasis on the predicament of Croatians in Yugoslavia and, indeed, in an ever worsening Europe. All of these concerns—the social and cultural world of the second generation, the resurgent labor movement, Roosevelt's reelection campaign (which was seen as a veritable referendum on the New Deal), and the struggle against political absolutism, fascism, and starvation in Croatia—were woven into this 1936–37 CFU campaign.[33]

Despite the continuing economic hard times, enthusiasm and optimism swept Croatian-American communities. CFU activists set ambitious goals—to reach a membership of one hundred thousand, to unionize basic industry, to reelect Roosevelt and expand New Deal programs, and to bring democracy and justice to Croatia. Reports from local lodges voiced the explosion of rank-and-file energies. Blue-collar Croatian Americans were building a new pride and self-respect out of the ashes of the Great Depression. "Casting off the cloak of oppression and submission he has worn for the past half century," wrote one correspondent, "the Man of Steel has finally awoke and come into his own."[34]

CFU activists utilized a variety of strategies to reach their goals. In city after city, they sponsored rallies where speakers urged the audiences to join both the CIO and the CFU. CFU halls served as union meeting places, soup kitchens and commissaries for strikers, and organizational centers for political campaigns. English-speaking lodges stepped up their social activities, including dances, picnics, holiday parties, athletic teams, and the sponsorship of radio shows. By promoting activities that were already popular among the second generation, the CFU was successfully incorporating them under its widening umbrella. Cleveland's American Croatian Pioneers, who consistently attracted more than one thousand members to such events as their annual anniversary dance, their spring frolic and other dances, were held up as a role model for other ESL's.[35]

At the height of the summer of 1936, these lodges organized community-wide outings called "Croatian Day" or "Fraternal Day," an invented holiday that blended the celebration of ethnic heritage with participation in the forms of American popular culture so enjoyed by the second generation. Held at an amusement park, the festival provided Croatian-American (and other ethnic) youth an opportunity to go on rides, swim, dance, and hear music. Much of the food, music, and dance was Croatian, and the day provided an opportunity to sit around and swap stories. For "those of our people who left their homesteads many years ago," explained an organizer of Pittsburgh's Croatian Day festivities at Kennywood amusement park, it would "bring pleasant old memories," while, for the American-born it would encourage a "realization that there is something noble and honorable in giving thought to the country of one's origins." Michael Horvath, the English editor of *Zajedničar*, described it as an undertaking by "American-born youth" to "entwine the sacred national characteristics of their own people with the ideals and principles of America." Croatian Day celebrations included speeches, too, in which CFU activists presented their messages about the CIO, the CFU, the New Deal, and the political situation in the old country. The theme of most speakers at Pittsburgh's August 1936 "Fraternal Day" celebration "was the laboring man's determination to organize into unions," *Zajedničar* reported. They were well received. "A mere mention of the workers' cause and a mere mention of the CIO brought down the applause."[36]

CFU activists did not limit their energies in the 1930s to building industrial unions and rebuilding their fraternal organization. They had been frustrated by the political situation in Yugoslavia ever since the establishment of the Serbian monarchy after World War I, and they had been dealt another blow by Stjepan Radić's assassination in 1928. In the 1930s, the rise of fascism in Europe further altered the prospects for Croatian movements for peasant empowerment, cultural pluralism, and representative democracy. Even as they dealt with the challenges of material and cultural survival in their adopted home in the United States, CFU activists also sought to have an impact on events in Yugoslavia. Their successes on this side of the ocean—in the CIO, in New Deal politics, in ties with other ethnic groups, and in reenergizing the CFU—gave them more opportunities and resources to have a positive impact abroad. At the same time, grappling with these homeland issues would provide an important ingredient in the continuing evolution of Croatian-American ethnic identity.

As in the 1920s, activists participated in diverse political organizations and made use of the CFU's resources, from *Zajedničar* to internal communications networks. Their resolutions condemning the "Belgrade dictatorship" were overwhelmingly endorsed by CFU delegates in 1929 and 1932. Some joined the Croatian Franciscan Commissariat, which continued to promote Pan-Slavic republicanism, while others rejuvenated branches of Radić's Croatian Republican Peasant party. The Croatian Circle, or Kolo, founded in the aftermath of Radić's assassination, adamantly repudiated all Pan-Slavism. Its name echoed the popular folk dance and also reflected the notion that all Croatians were linked together. Indeed, this was a theme that Kolo activists consciously pushed, even as they recruited among the American-born generation. In 1931, they put out a call for an "All Croatian Congress": "This is not and should not be a convention of old country partisans. This is a Croatian convention, a convention of Croatians in America, children of one mother—Mother Croatia— and as such we pledge ourselves to work for the good of us all, immigrants as well as those in Croatia."[37]

CFU activists participated in this convention, and they were soon using the pages of *Zajedničar* to educate other CFU members about the looming fascist threat in Europe. Local lodges sponsored lectures on the implications of European politics for Yugoslavia. The Kolo and the Croatian National Council (another broad organization formed to address international issues) circulated petitions, held plebiscites, and sent memoranda to Hoover, the League of Nations, and, after his election, Roosevelt. Activists raised widespread protests on several occasions when homeland public figures, including Stjepan Radić's son, were detained, arrested, or deported upon arrival in New York for scheduled speaking tours. These protests, of course, became opportunities to educate wider audiences about Yugoslav political issues. Another vehicle was provided by Louis Adamic, the Slovenian-born writer who had gained significant popularity in the United States. In 1932, he made a pilgrimage to Yugoslavia, sending back stories that appeared in mainstream publications such as the *Nation*, the *Atlantic Monthly*, and the *American Mercury*, as well as the ethnic press. These stories were collected and published in 1934 as *The Native's Return*, which reached even more readers. The CFU itself bought thousands of copies, which it sold to its members.[38]

The great power conflict shaking Europe had rapidly subsumed the 1920s struggle between Croatian peasants and the Serbian monarchy. In the early 1930s, Mussolini made it clear that he had designs on the Dalmatian coast. His promises of "liberation" from the Serbians struck some responsive chords in Croatia. One leader, Ante Pavelić, organized the Uštaša, along the Mussolini model. He called himself "Duce" and urged his followers to wear blue shirts. The Uštaša launched a terrorist campaign, initiated an unsuccessful uprising in Lika, and masterminded the assassination of King Alexander in 1934.[39]

Like earlier homeland organizations, the Uštaša sent its organizers and fund-raisers to the American "colonies." They sponsored a new organization, the Hrvatski Domobran (Home Defenders). Like the Uštaša, their members wore blue shirts and modeled themselves after Mussolini's fascist legions. Cloaking themselves in the mantle of Croatian nationalism, the Uštaša and the Domobran claimed that the very concept of a Yugoslav nation had been flawed from the start, that Croatian separatism was necessary as an end as well as a means, and that Mussolini would serve as a responsible agent in this direction. The Domobran played on Croatian-American frustrations with the failure of Yugoslavia to respect Croatian aspirations, while they sought to raise funds for the Uštaša.[40]

But Croatian immigrants and their children largely rejected this approach. Labor activists, local political organizers, fraternal order leaders, and even some priests openly challenged the Domobran. While they continued to advocate a "free" Croatia, they argued that subordination to Mussolini was no way to achieve it, and that fascism was contrary to the political thinking of citizens of the United States and to the political traditions of the Croatian peasant movement. In 1933, the Croatian National Council, having gathered delegates from all over the United States into Youngstown, Ohio, sent a memorandum to Roosevelt urging "the reestablishment of Croatia as a completely free, completely sovereign, and completely independent nation." Two years later, Kolo bluntly resolved: "Much as we want independence for the mother country, we must not look to Italy for help."[41]

The Croatian Fraternal Union also made its stance clear. Its convention in the summer of 1935 opened with a moment of silence for Stjepan Radić, who had been dead for seven years. Resolutions to support the Domobran and the Uštaša generated heated debates. A *Zajedničar* columnist referred to them as "a battle royal between opposing factions." When the debate ended, every pro-fascist resolution had been soundly defeated. In the winter of 1936, when news of widespread hunger in the homeland reached the United States, the CFU Supreme Board sent $5,000 in immediate aid and urged local lodges to raise additional funds. All the money was sent to the Croatian Republican Peasant party (the Uštaša's chief Croatian adversary) to distribute. *Zajedničar* praised Dr. Vladko Maček, the leader of the Peasant party, noting that he has "the task of leading our people to the point where someday soon they may be recognized as a free people, unoppressed and unmolested by anyone."[42]

A year later, CFU president John Butkovich led a delegation of two hundred members to Yugoslavia on a "fact-finding" mission to look into government persecution of political prisoners. Shortly after they laid flowers on Stjepan Radić's grave, the Yugoslav government expelled them. Over the following months, President Butkovich traveled the United States, informing local lodges that Yugoslavia was now ruled by an unholy merger of Serbian monarchy and Italian fascism. He received an enthusiastic reception.[43]

Even as they were protesting the treatment of their fellow Croats in the homeland, these lodges were celebrating CIO victories and the CFU's organizing drive success. "The working people are winning their demands for better working conditions," Butkovich reported to the Supreme Board. "Recognition of labor unions, better wages and conditions are a big step for the working class, in which most of our members are included." In December 1937, CFU lodges around the country celebrated the tenth anniversary of the creation of English-speaking lodges, giving them the lion's share of the credit for having restored the CFU to financial stability. "Our organization has gone through what may very well be termed a life-threatening experience," noted Michael Horvath. "Some of the mightiest financial structures of this, the richest country on earth, have gone tottering down to ruination."

> Think if you will of the thousands upon thousands of our members who were literally driven out of the mills, mines, and factories in the early days of the 1930s. Think if you will that many thousands of these have been without any gainful occupation during all these years, and then add the thousands upon thousands who have been compelled to draw upon the reserve accumulations of their policies of insurance in order to maintain their fraternal protection, plus the large number of members who took advantage of loan privileges to save themselves and their families, lest they be driven into the cold and cruel out-doors.
>
> And in spite of all these most unfortunate experiences, our organization today [January 1939] is as sound and as stable as one could expect it to be. Its financial condition is excellent and its membership, during all these years, has been maintained.[44]

The CFU's membership and financial success reflected its activists' ability to provide a framework through which immigrants and their children could weave together the traditions of the Croatian peasant movement (including democracy, folklore and music, ethnic pride, and Pan-Slavism) with their experiences in the United States (industrial labor, unionization, commercialized mass leisure, political participation, and the New Deal). This process shaped the overwhelmingly negative response to the Domobran and the Uštaša. In mid-1936, the CFU played the central role in the organization of the Antifascist Front of the American Croats, which included members of Kolo, the Croatian Catholic Union, the Croatian Peasant party, and the Alliance of Croatian Workers' Clubs. This broad organization not only opposed fascism but it also lent its support to industrial union drives and Croatian Day celebrations. The CFU helped organize the All-American Slav Congress in 1938 and endorsed its call for "all Slavs and all liberty-loving people to unite as one great body" to defeat fascism the world over.[45]

CFU activists saw this struggle as domestic as well as international. In 1939 and 1940, the CFU Supreme Board and *Zajedničar* pointed to the suppression of labor rights, attempts to revive nativism and xenophobia, the Dies Committee on "Un-American Affairs" and the Father Coughlin movement as serious threats "to the cultural and civil rights of our members." "We, too, as Americans, are faced with a crisis," the Supreme Board resolved in July 1940, "a crisis that challenges the loyalty and devotion of every resident of this country to the sacred ideals and principles of America." Three months later, they circulated a resolution for the endorsement of all local lodges that synthesized their domestic and international concerns into a single identity: "As Americans, we shall never give up our democratic institutions, our homes, our liberties, and our sacred principles, without a struggle to the very end of our lives. As Americans, we shall continue to cherish the sanctity of a country which has outreached its arms of welcome and helpfulness in the dark and dreary days, when the early immigrants reached American shores to escape oppression and tyranny in their native lands."[46]

As we reflect on the "Americanization" of Croatian immigrants and their children, we might do well to imagine a bowling alley in an industrial city on a Thursday night in the fall of 1939. A team from the CFU lodge is wearing tee-shirts with "Hrvatski Dom" on the back and caps bearing "PWOC" (Packinghouse Workers Organizing Committee) dues buttons. The jukebox mingles tamburica music with polkas and jazz. Between frames, the men's discussion ranges from the baseball pennant race and the local Croatian boys playing on the university football team to the unionization of the "Big 4" meatpacking companies and the Hitler-Stalin pact. While the conversation is in English, it is peppered with Croatian expressions, especially expletives. After the game is over, the men retire to the Croatian Hall for a plate of sarma and cabbage and a glass of beer. The conversation turns to plans for the local Democratic party campaign and the next round of fund-raising for the Croatian Peasant party.

And so, on the eve of World War II, we can take stock of the "Americanization" process as Croatian immigrants and their children experienced it, particularly as it was shaped by the Croatian Fraternal Union. One might say that it involved a "both/and" rather than an "either/or" process. Croatians combined senses of coming from peasant roots, of being industrial workers, of being particularly Croatian but also Slavic, of being Croatian-American, American, and hyphenated American. They expressed these senses in their music, their organizations, and their political ideologies. At times, these different elements reinforced each other; at other times, they contradicted each other. In the specific historical context of the 1930s, they brought Croatian Americans into the labor movement, the New Deal, emerging forms of commercialized leisure, and broad antifascist formations. And, in turn, these experiences left an indelible mark on Croatian-American identity.

Notes

1. Kathleen Neils Conzen, David A. Gerber, Ewa Morawska, George E. Pozzetta, and Rudolph J. Vecoli, "The Invention of Ethnicity: A Perspective from the USA," *Altreitalie* 3 (Apr. 1990): 37–62; Werner Sollors, *The Invention of Ethnicity* (New York: Oxford University Press, 1989); Eric Hobsbawm and Terence Ranger, eds., *The Invention of Tradition* (Cambridge: Cambridge University Press, 1983); James R. Barrett, "Americanization from the Bottom Up: Immigration and the Remaking of the Working Class in the United States, 1880–1930," *Journal of American History* 79 (Dec. 1992): 996–1020.

2. Gary Gerstle, *Working-Class Americanism: The Politics of Labor in a Textile City, 1914–1960* (New York: Cambridge University Press, 1989); Lizabeth Cohen, *Making a New Deal: Industrial Workers in Chicago, 1919–1939* (New York: Cambridge University Press, 1990). See the essays collected in Dirk Hoerder, ed., *"Struggle a Hard Battle": Essays on Working-Class Immigrants* (DeKalb: Northern Illinois University Press, 1989); and Marianne Debouzy, ed., *In the Shadow of the Statue of Liberty: Immigrants, Workers, and Citizens in the American Republic, 1880–1920* (Paris: PUV St.-Denis, 1988). See also George Sanchez, *Becoming Mexican-American: Ethnicity, Culture, and Identity in Chicano Los Angeles, 1900–1945* (New York: Oxford University Press, 1993); John Bodnar, *Lives of Their Own: Blacks, Italians and Poles in Pittsburgh, 1900–1960* (Urbana: University of Illinois Press, 1992); Joseph Barton, *Peasants and Strangers* (Cambridge, Mass.: Harvard University Press, 1975); Matjaz Klemencic, *Slovenes of Cleveland* (Novo Mesto, Slovenia: Tiskarna Novo Mesto, 1995).

3. Charles Jelavich, "The Croatian Problem in the Habsburg Empire in the Nineteenth Century," and Bogdan Krizman, "The Croatians in the Habsburg Monarchy in the Nineteenth Century," in *Austrian History Yearbook*, vol. 3, pt. 2, 1967; Ivan T. Berend and Gyorgy Ranki, *Economic Development in East Central Europe in the 19th and 20th Centuries* (New York: Columbia University Press, 1974); Johann Chmelar, "The Austrian Emigration, 1900–1914," *Perspectives in American History* 7 (1973); Gunther E. Rothenberg, *The Military Border in Croatia, 1740–1881* (Chicago: University of Chicago Press, 1966); Edward Zivich, "From Zadruga to Oil Refinery: Croatian Immigrants and Croatian Americans in Whiting, Indiana, 1890–1950" (Ph.D. dissertation, State University of New York at Binghamton, 1977), 11.

4. On "labor migration," see Dirk Hoerder, ed., *Labor Migration in the Atlantic Economies* (Westport, Conn.: Greenwood Press, 1985). On the Croatian immigration, see Walter F. Wilcox, ed., *International Migrations* (New York: National Bureau for Economic Research, 1929), 887; U.S. Department of Commerce, *U.S. Census of Population: 1930* (Washington, D.C.: Government Printing Office, 1930), 2:347–69; U.S. Department of Labor, *Eleventh Annual Report of the Secretary of Labor* (Washington, D.C.: Government Printing Office, 1923), 133; *Yugoslavs in America and Austria-Hungary: Immigration and Emigration* (San Carlos, Calif.: Ragusan Press, 1978), 40, 57, and 146; Branko Colakovic, *Yugoslav Migrations to America* (San Francisco: R & E, 1973), 52; Frances Kraljic, *Croatian Migration to and from the United States, 1900–1914* (Palo Alto, Calif.: Ragusan Press, 1978), 43–44; Ivan Cizmić, "The Experience of South Slav Immigrants on Ellis Island and the Establishment of the South Slavonic Immigrant Society of New York," in Debouzy, *In the Shadow of the Statue of Liberty;* Frank J. Sheridan, "Italian, Slavic, and Hungarian Unskilled Immigrant Laborers in the United States," *Bulletin of the Bureau of Labor* 72 (Sept. 1907); Ivan Mladineo, "The Southern

Slavs in America," *Our World* 2 (Dec. 1923); Emily G. Balch, *Our Slavic Fellow Citizens* (New York: Charities Publications Committee, 1910); Louis Adamic, "A Bohunk Woman," *American Mercury* 14 (July 1928); Louis Adamic, "Manda Evanich from Croatia," in *From Many Lands* (New York: Harper, 1936); John Modell and Tamara Hareven, "Urbanization and the Malleable Household: An Examination of Boarding and Lodging in American Families," *Journal of Marriage and the Family* 35 (Aug. 1973); Corinne A. Krause, "Urbanization without Breakdown: Italian, Jewish, and Slavic Women in Pittsburgh, 1900–1945," *Journal of Urban History* 5 (May 1978).

5. Joseph Stipanovich, "Collective Economic Activity among Serb, Croat, and Slovene Immigrants in the United States," in Scott Cummings, ed., *Self-Help in Urban America* (Port Washington, N.Y.: Kennikat Press, 1980), 16; Ivan Cizmić, *History of the Croatian Fraternal Union of America 1894–1994* (Zagreb: Golden Marketing, 1994); John Badinovac, "The Croatians as Pioneers in the Field of Fraternalism," *American Slav*, Sept. 1939; Margaret Galey, "Ethnicity, Fraternalism, Social and Mental Health," *Ethnicity* 4 (1977); George J. Prpic, *The Croatian Immigrants in America* (New York: Philosophical Library, 1971); George J. Prpic, *South Slavic Immigration in America* (Boston: Twayne, 1978); Zivich, "From Zadruga to Oil Refinery"; Stjepan Gazi, *Croatian Immigration to Allegheny County, 1882–1914* (Pittsburgh: Zajedničar, 1956); Clement S. Mihanovich, *Americanization of the Croats in St. Louis* (St. Louis: St. Louis University Press, 1936); Anthony W. Rasporich, *For a Better Life: A History of the Croatians in Canada* (Toronto: McClelland and Stewart, 1982); John Bodnar, "Materialism and Morality: Slavic-American Immigrants and Education, 1890–1940," *Journal of Ethnic Studies* 3 (Winter 1976).

6. "Statement of Purpose of Croatian Union of the U.S." (1894), reproduced in Prpic, *Croatian Immigrants*, 126; *By-Laws and Rules of the National Croatian Society of the U.S.* (Pittsburgh: National Croatian Society, 1918); *Constitution and By-Laws of the Croatian Fraternal Union of America* (Chicago: CFU, 1926); Cizmić, *History of the Croatian Fraternal Union*, chaps. 2 and 7.

7. Dinko Tomašić, "Ethnic Components of Croatian Nationhood," *Journal of Croatian Studies* 3–4 (1962–63); Aurelio Palmieri, "The Growth of Croatian Nationalism," *Catholic World* 109 (June 1919); *In Memory of the 1000th Anniversary of the Croatian King Tomislav's Coronation* (Allegheny, Pa.: n.p., 1903); Mario Spalatin, "The Croatian Nationalism of Ante Starčević, 1845–1871," *Journal of Croatian Studies* 16 (1975).

8. Bonifačić Sorić, *The Life and Work of the Croatian People in Allegheny County, Pa., 1847–1947* (Pittsburgh: Croatian Historical Research Bureau, 1947); CFU, *A Brief Historical Review, 1894–1947* (Pittsburgh: CFU, 1947); Joseph Stipanovich, "'In Unity is Strength': Immigrant Workers and Immigrant Intellectuals in Progressive America: A History of the South Slav Social Democratic Movement, 1900–1918" (Ph.D. dissertation, University of Minnesota, 1978); Peter Rachleff, "The Croatian-American Left," in Paul Buhle, Mari Jo Buhle, and Dan Georgakas, eds., *Encyclopedia of the American Left* (1990; reprint, Urbana: University of Illinois Press, 1992); Cizmić, *History of the Croatian Fraternal Union*, chap. 3.

9. "Statement of Purpose of Croatian Union of the U.S." (1894), reproduced in Prpic, *Croatian Immigrants*, 126; *By-Laws and Rules of the National Croatian Society*; *Constitution and By-Laws of the Croatian Fraternal Union*; *Citanka* (Pittsburgh: Nakladom, 1923); *Abečedarka* (Pittsburgh: CFU, 1932).

10. *Izvješće o primitiku; izdatku NHZ od i kodovbza* (Pittsburgh: CFU, 1915); J. Strizich, "A Brief Historical Review of the First 50 Years," *Zajedničar*, 15 Apr. 1987.

11. Colakovic, *Yugoslav Migrations*, 32; Kraljic, *Croatian Migration*, 78–81; George J. Prpic, "The Croatian Press in the U.S. before 1939," unpublished paper, n.d., 17–18; Stjepan Radić, *Javna Politicka Poraka* (Zagreb: Croatian Peasant Party, 1913).

12. Jozo Tomasevich, *Peasants, Politics, and Economic Change in Yugoslavia* (Stanford: Stanford University Press, 1955); Victor S. Mamatey, *The United States and East Central Europe, 1914–1918* (Princeton: Princeton University Press, 1957); Philip Lukas, "A Geopolitical Analysis of Croatian Territory," in Antun S. Bonifačić and Clement S. Mihanovich, eds., *The Croatian Nation in Its Struggle for Freedom* (Chicago: Croatia Publishing Company, 1955).

13. Ivan Mestrović, "The Yugoslav Committee in London and the Declaration of Corfu"; A. Palmieri, "The Growth of Croatian Nationalism," in Bonifačić and Mihanovich, *Croatian Nation;* James P. Krokar, "The 1915 Yugoslav Immigrant Conference and the Chicago Immigrant Community," unpublished paper, 1983; Slovenian-Croatian Union, *Proceedings of the 9th Session, Eveleth, Minnesota, August 1918*. See also David Montgomery, "Nationalism, American Patriotism, and Class Consciousness among Immigrant Workers in the U.S. in the Epoch of WWI," in Hoerder, *Struggle a Hard Battle*.

14. A. Dragnich, *The First Yugoslavia* (Stanford: Hoover Institute, 1978), 18–21, 34–49; Vladko Macek, *In the Struggle for Freedom* (New York: Praeger, 1960), 42; Charles Beard, ed., "Autobiography of Stephen Raditch," *Current History* 29 (1928–29): 105; Basil Pandzic and Steven Pandzic, *A Review of Croatian History* (Chicago: Croatian Publishing Company, 1954), 37; U.S. Department of Labor, *Eleventh Annual Report*, 130; *U.S. Census of Population: 1930*, vol. 2, 347–69; Prpic, *Croatian Immigrants*, 99.

15. Cohen, *Making a New Deal*, esp. chap. 3, "Encountering Mass Culture"; Gerstle, *Working-Class Americanism*, 183–218; Sanchez, *Becoming Mexican-American*, 97–187. Also, John Bukowczyk, "The Transformation of Working-Class Ethnicity: Corporate Control, Americanization, and the Polish-American Middle-Class in Bayonne, N.J., 1915–1925," *Labor History* 25 (Winter 1984); Ewa Morawska, "The Internal Status Hierarchy in the East European Immigrant Communities of Johnstown, Pa., 1890–1930s," *Journal of Social History* 16 (Fall 1982); David Montgomery, "Immigrants, Industrial Unions, and Social Reconstruction in the U.S., 1916–1923," *Labour/Le Travail* 13 (Spring 1984).

16. "Report of the English editor of *Zajedničar*," *Izvješča* (Milwaukee, Wis.: CFU, 1935). Karlo Mirth, ed., "The Constitution of the Croatian Republican Peasant League of the United States," *Journal of Croatian Studies* 20 (1979); Stjepan Gazi, "Beginning of the Croatian Peasant Party: A Historico-Political Study," *Journal of Croatian Studies* 3–4 (1962–63).

17. Joseph Kraja, "The Croatian Circle, 1928–1946: Chronology and Reminiscence," *Journal of Croatian Studies* 20 (1979): 147; "Declaration of the Croatian Circle," *Croatian Review* 1 (1931): 24, 37. The president of the CFU played a key role in the establishment of the Kolo (Prpic, *Croatian Immigrants*, 267).

18. *Zajedničar*, 5 Sept. and 11 Nov. 1928; 4 Sept. and 6 Nov. 1929; 18 June 1930; 7 and 28 Jan. 1931; 22 June 1932; 29 Aug. 1934; 2 Jan., 4 and 25 Dec. 1935.

19. *Zajedničar*, 23 Oct. 1929; 7 Jan. 1931; 13 July 1932; 22 Jan., 25 Mar., and 6 May 1936; *Zapisnik Treče Konvenčije* (Gary, Ind.: CFU, 1932), 29, 74–77, and 229–300; *Abečedarka*.

20. *Zajedničar*, 14 Mar. 1934; 6 and 13 May, 10 and 24 June, 30 Dec. 1936; 22 Dec.

1937; James R. Baldrica, "Tamburitza Music, History and Origin on the Iron Range of Minnesota" (M.A. thesis, University of Minnesota, 1978).

21. Sanchez, *Becoming Mexican-American*, 177–87; Victor Greene, *A Passion for Polka* (Berkeley: University of California, 1992), 12–48, 77, 91–92; Mary Cygan, "Inventing Polonia: Cultural Activists and the Polish-American Community," unpublished paper, 1986; William J. Schereck, ed., *The Peoples of Wisconsin: Scripts of the Ethnic Radio Series* (Madison, Wis.: State Historical Society, 1956).

22. Baldrica, "Tamburitza Music"; Zivich, "From Zadruga to Oil Refinery," 90.

23. *Zajedničar*, 10 Dec. 1930.

24. "Report of M. J. Horvath, English Editor of *Zajedničar*," *Izvjesca: Glasnik Odbornika, Odborai Casnika HBZ* (Gary, Ind.: CFU, 1932). "Hard Times," *Croatian Review* 1 (Dec. 1931): 31–32; *Historijsko Statiščki* (Cleveland: CFU, 1935), 56–57; *Zajedničar*, 10 Dec. 1930; Cizmić, *History of the Croatian Fraternal Union*, 222–27. In the first five years of the depression, the CFU paid out $6.5 million.

25. "Hard Times," 36; Prpic, *Croatian Immigrants*, 284–91; *Zajedničar*, 14 Sept. 1932. For a valuable comparison, see Cecilia Bucki, "Workers and Politics in the Immigrant City in the Early Twentieth Century U.S.," *International Labor and Working Class History* 48 (Fall 1995); Cecilia Bucki, "The Pursuit of Political Power: Class, Ethnicity, and Municipal Politics in Interwar Bridgeport, 1915–1936" (Ph.D. dissertation, University of Pittsburgh, 1991).

26. *Zajedničar*, 27 Mar. and 7 June 1933; 29 May and 11 Dec. 1935; 4 Mar., 6 May, and 11 Nov. 1936.

27. Resolution of the 1929 convention, reprinted in "The CFU and the American Labor Movement," in CFU, *Brief Historical Review*, 22–23; *Zajedničar*, 13 July 1932; James Barrett, Rob Ruck, and Steve Nelson, *Steve Nelson: American Radical* (Pittsburgh: University of Pittsburgh Press, 1981); Anthony Rasporich, "Tomo Cačić: Rebel without a Country," *Canadian Ethnic Studies* 10 (1978); Ivan Cizmić, "Yugoslav Immigrants in the U.S. Labor Movement," in Dirk Hoerder, ed., *American Labor and Immigration History* (Urbana: University of Illinois Press, 1983); Cizmić, *History of the Croatian Fraternal Union*, chap. 5; Hyman Berman, "Education for Work and Solidarity: The Immigrant Miners and Radicalism on the Mesaba Range," unpublished paper, 1963; Peter Friedlander, "The Slavic Immigrants and SWOC," unpublished paper, 1972.

28. "CFU and the American Labor Movement," in CFU, *Brief Historical Review*, 22–23; Barrett, Nelson, and Ruck, *Steve Nelson*, 45.

29. *Zajedničar*, 13 July 1932; 7 June 1933; 20 June 1934; 29 May 1935.

30. *Zajedničar*, 20 and 27 May, 17 June 1936; "CFU and the American Labor Movement," in CFU, *Brief Historical Review*, 26–27; Friedlander, "Labor and Society," unpublished paper, 1972, 37; "A Steel Unit Becomes Tempered," *Party Organizer* 10 (Jan. 1937): 7–9. For similar stories of other ethnic groups, see Thomas Gobel, "Becoming American: Ethnic Workers and the Rise of the CIO," *Labor History* 29 (Spring 1988); Thomas Bell, *Out of This Furnace* (Pittsburgh: University of Pittsburgh Press, 1976), esp. 259–413.

31. *Zajedničar*, 20 and 27 May 1936; "CFU and the American Labor Movement," in CFU, *Brief Historical Review*, 26.

32. *Zajedničar*, 1936–37, passim.

33. Ibid.

34. *Zajedničar*, 13 Jan. 1937

35. *Zajedničar*, 23 Jan. and 4 Dec. 1935; 22 Jan., 15 Apr., 6 and 20 May, 28 Oct. 1936; 25 Jan. 1939.

36. *Zajedničar*, 13 July 1932; 7 June 1933; 3 July 1935; 9 Sept. 1936; 11 and 18 Aug., 9 Sept. 1936; 21 July, 18 Aug., and 8 Sept. 1937; 8 June 1938; 12 July and 30 Aug. 1939.

37. "Declaration of the Croatian Circle," 37; Croatian Franciscan Commissariat, *The Yugoslav National Defense* (n.p.: Croatian Franciscan Commissariat, 1930); Mirth, "Constitution of the Croatian Republican Peasant League"; "All Croatian Congress," *Croatian Review* 1 (Dec. 1931); Prpic, *South Slavic Immigration*, 99–110.

38. "Declaration of the Croatian Circle," 24–37; Kraja, "Croatian Circle," 147; *Zajedničar*, 27 Mar., 7 June, 15 Nov. 1933; 10 Jan. 1934; 29 May and 4 Dec. 1935; 4 Mar., 29 Apr., 20 and 27 May, 22 July, 11 Nov. 1936; Prpic, *Croatian Immigrants*, 109–10, 283–84; Louis Adamic, *The Native's Return* (New York: Harper's, 1934) and review in *Zajedničar*, 17 Jan. 1934.

39. Kraja, "Croatian Circle," 152–57; Prpic, *Croatian Immigrants*, 271ff.; Prpic, *South Slavic Immigration*, 109ff.; Stanko Guldescu, "The Background of the Croatian Independence Movement," *South Atlantic Quarterly* 56 (Summer 1957); Stephen Clissold, *Croat Separatism, Nationalism, Dissidence, and Terrorism* (London: Institute for the Study of Conflict, 1979), 3–4; Dragnich, *First Yugoslavia*, 89–99; Dinko Tomašić, "The Struggle for Power in Jugoslavia," *Journal of Central European Affairs* 1 (1941); Maček, *In the Struggle for Freedom*.

40. Prpic, *Croatian Immigrants*, 284; *Zajedničar*, 29 Aug. 1934; Kraja, "Croatian Circle," 194–95.

41. Kraja, "Croatian Circle," 197; Prpic, *Croatian Immigrants*, 284; *Zajedničar*, 30 Jan. and 26 June 1935; George J. Prpic, *Croatia and the Croatians: A Selected and Annotated Bibliography in English* (Scottsdale, Ariz.: Associated Book Publishers, 1982), 101–2.

42. *Zajedničar*, 26 June and 31 July 1935; 12 Feb., 18 Mar., 6 May, 8 July, 5, 12, and 29 Aug., 14 and 28 Oct., 30 Dec. 1936.

43. *Zajedničar*, 15 and 22 July 1936; 14 Oct. 1936; 31 Mar., 23 June, 1, 8, and 22 Sept. 1937; 12 Jan., 8 June, and 23 Nov. 1938.

44. *Zajedničar*, 14 Apr. (Gary), 28 Apr. (Joliet), 12 and 26 May (Pittsburgh), 2 June (Youngstown), 8, 15, and 22 Dec. 1937. Horvath report in *Zajedničar*, 3 Jan. 1939. Three months later, the CFU Supreme Board announced that the organization's financial condition was so secure that it was waiving four assessments for senior lodge members and five for junior members.

45. *Zajedničar*, 11 Aug. 1937; 23 Nov. 1938; Cizmić, *History of the Croatian Fraternal Union*, 245. The participants included the CFU, the Slovene National Benefit Association, the National Slovak Society, the Slovak Union Sokol, the Greek Catholic Union, the Carpatho Russian Democratic National Committee, and the United Bohemian Societies.

46. *Zajedničar*, 5 July, 16 and 23 Aug. 1939; 14 Feb., 29 May, and 17 July 1940. Resolution appeared in South St. Paul *Daily Reporter*, 10 Sept. 1940.

Contributors

ERIC ARNESEN received his Ph.D. from Yale and is an associate professor of history and African-American Studies at the University of Illinois at Chicago. His book, *Waterfront Workers of New Orleans: Race, Class, and Politics, 1863–1923*, received the American Historical Association's John H. Dunning Prize in 1991. His articles on race, class, and African-American labor history have appeared in the *American Historical Review, Radical History Review, Labor History, Labor's Heritage*, the *International Review of Social History*, and *International Labor and Working-Class History*. He is completing a study of black labor and employment discrimination entitled *Brotherhoods of Color: African-American Railroad Workers' Struggle for Equality*.

JAMES R. BARRETT is professor of history and chair of the Department of History at the University of Illinois at Urbana-Champaign. Author of *Work and Community in the Jungle: Chicago's Packinghouse Workers, 1894–1922* (1987) and coauthor of *Steve Nelson, American Radical* (1981), he is currently completing a biography of William Z. Foster and beginning a book on the mentalities of immigrant workers.

CECELIA F. BUCKI teaches labor and political history at Fairfield University, Fairfield, Connecticut. An active public historian, she has also published in *Social Science History* and *International Labor and Working-Class History*. Her study of workers, unions, ethnicity, and city politics in interwar Bridgeport is forthcoming from University of Illinois Press.

ILEEN A. DEVAULT is an associate professor of labor history at the Cornell University School of Industrial and Labor Relations. She received her M.A. from the University of Pittsburgh and her Ph.D. from Yale University. Her book, *Sons and Daughters of Labor: Class and Clerical Work in Turn-of-the-Century Pittsburgh*, was published by Cornell University Press in 1990.

JULIE GREENE is an assistant professor of history at the University of Colorado at Boulder. She received her Ph.D. from Yale University in 1990, and is the author of *Pure and Simple Politics: The American Federation of Labor and Political Mobilization, 1881 to 1917*, to be published by Cambridge University Press in 1998.

TERA W. HUNTER received her B.A. degree from Duke University and Ph.D. from Yale University. She is an associate professor of history at Carnegie Mellon University. She is the author of *To 'Joy My Freedom: Southern Black Women's Lives and Labors after the Civil War*, published by Harvard University Press in 1997.

REEVE HUSTON received his Ph.D. at Yale University in 1994 and teaches American history at the University of Arizona. He is currently writing a book on the New York Anti-Rent Wars.

BRUCE LAURIE received his Ph.D. from the University of Pittsburgh in 1971. He is professor of history at the University of Massachusetts at Amherst. He is the author of *Working People of Philadelphia, 1800–1850*, published by Temple University Press in 1980, and *Artisans into Workers: Labor in Nineteenth-Century America*, published by Hill & Wang in 1990 and reprinted by the University of Illinois Press in 1997. He is also co-editor of *Class, Sex, and the Woman Worker*, published by Greenwood Press in 1977.

KATHRYN J. OBERDECK received her Ph.D. in American Studies from Yale University. She held a postdoctoral fellowship at the Michigan Society of Fellows and is currently an assistant professor of history at the University of Illinois at Urbana-Champaign. She has published in *American Quarterly, Radical History Review*, and *Labor History* and is completing a book that uses the lives of Alexander Irvine and Sylvester Poli, a vaudeville entrepreneur, to explore cultural class conflict in the United States at the turn of the century.

GUNTHER PECK teaches comparative labor, immigration, U.S. western, and twentieth-century cultural history at the University of Texas at Austin. He is currently revising his dissertation, "Reinventing Free Labor: Immigrant Padrones and Contract Laborers in North America, 1880–1920," which won the Porter Prize at Yale in 1995, for publication. His writings have appeared in the *Western Historical Quarterly*, the *Journal of Social History*, and the *Journal of American History*.

KIMBERLEY L. PHILLIPS teaches African-American history at the College of William and Mary. She received both a M.A. in Afro-American Studies and a Ph.D. in American Studies from Yale University. Her articles on migration and southern gospel quartets have been published in the *Journal of Social History* and a forthcoming volume on the history of emotions edited by Peter Stearns. Her book, *AlabamaNorth: African American Migrants, Community and Working-Class Activism in Cleveland, 1915–1945*, will be published by the University of Illinois Press.

PETER RACHLEFF earned his Ph.D. from the University of Pittsburgh in 1981. Since 1982, he has taught at Macalester College, in St. Paul, Minnesota, where he is currently professor of history. His major publications include *Black Labor in Richmond, Virginia, 1865–1890*, published by the University of Illinois Press in 1989, and *Hard-Pressed in the Heartland: The Hormel Strike and the Future of the Labor Movement*, published by South End Press in 1993. He has recently contributed essays to *"We Are All Leaders": The Alternative Unionism of the Early 1930s*, edited by Staughton Lynd and published by the University of Illinois Press in 1996, and *Unionizing the Jungles: Labor and Community in the Twentieth Century Meat-Packing Industry*, edited by Shel Stromquist and Marvin Bergman and published by the University of Iowa Press in 1997.

SHELTON STROMQUIST is professor of history and chair in the Department of History at the University of Iowa; he is author of *A Generation of Boomers: The Pattern of Railroad Labor Conflict in Nineteenth-Century America*, published by the University of Illinois Press in 1993, and *Solidarity and Survival: An Oral History of Iowa Labor in the Twentieth Century*, published by the University of Iowa Press in 1993. His current research focuses on class and Progressive Era politics.

Index

Wilson, Christopher, 203
Wilson, Henry, 62
Wilson, Leola B. ("Coot Grant"), 167–68
Wilson, Woodrow, 72, 344, 349; and
   USCIR, 101–2, 118
Winchell, B. L., 295, 298
"Wisconsin Idea," 103, 105, 113
Wisconsin Industrial Commission, 104,
   115
Wisconsin school of labor history, 1
Wise, Stephen, 101
Wobblies. *See* Industrial Workers of the
   World
Women: in African-American religion,
   245, 246–47; as domestic workers, 153–
   74; exclusion of, from political process,
   58; help for migrants from, 236; as im-
   migrants, 342; in manufacturing, 266–
   71, 280n.6; subordination of, 27; suffrage movement for, 138; and
   ten-hour-day movement, 49, 52, 58;
   unions' exclusion of, 9, 11, 13, 259–83;
   unions' inclusion of, 12–13, 262–63. *See
   also* "New Woman"; Strikes: cross-gender; Work
Women's National Committee, 217
Wood, Keziah, 158
Woodson, Carter G., 237
Worcester (Massachusetts), 54, 56–58,
   68n.72
Work: by cigarmakers' families, 269, 270;
   dancing as, 167–68; nonwage domestic,
   154, 156–57, 180, 181, 183; opposition
   to, for wages, 51, 52, 211; peonage as,
   207, 208, 220; by tailors' families, 263–
   66, 268; valorization of women based
   on their abstinence from, 167; for wages
   among African-American women, 154–
   56, 159–60, 164–67; for wages in antebellum North, 19–44. *See also* Equal pay
   issue; Unions; *Specific industries and occupations*
Work camps, 244
"Workers' Bill," 142, 148n.53
Workers Committee Movement, 316
Workers' party, 310, 314, 319, 321, 322,
   326, 328
Workers Unemployment and Social Security Act, 142
Work gangs, 179–81, 184

Working class: as agents in their history,
   3–6, 9, 83–84, 125–43, 340, 345; consciousness by, 203; culture of, 8–9; current conditions for, 1–2; and domesticity, 12, 221, 222; employers' attempts to
   influence, 71–96; institutions among,
   10–13; physical vigor associated with,
   201, 205, 206, 209, 213–14; racial and
   ethnic ramifications of, 126, 202; and
   religion, 230–56; self-construction of
   identity of, 202; themes in history of, 2.
   See also Ethnicity; Immigrants; New labor history; Race; Unions
Working-Class Americanism (Gerstle), 345
Workingman's party, 40n.13
Workingmen's Protective Association
   (WPA), 79, 82–83, 85–86
Workmen's Sick and Death Benefit Society (Bridgeport), 133
World's Work magazine, 211
World War I: black railroad workers in,
   284–308; idea for trade-union armies
   in, 118; impact of, on Bridgeport, Con-
   necticut, 126, 129; War Chests in, 130;
   and Yugoslavia, 344
WPA. *See* Workingmen's Protective Asso-
   ciation
Wright (judge), 36
Wright, Elizur, Jr., 49–53, 55–57, 59, 60,
   62–64
Wright, Eric Olin, 3
Wunderlin, Clarence, 115

Yale University, 49, 50, 204, 205, 214
Yazoo & Mississippi Valley railroad, 296,
   298, 302
YMCA, 213
You May Plow Here (Brooks), 230
Young, John, 36
Young, Owen D., 146n.24
Young, William Field, 64
Young America (newspaper), 26
Young Communist Movement, 318
"Your Mama's Baby Child" (song), 245
Yugoslavia, 341, 344, 349, 351–54
YWCA, 135

Zajedničar, 342, 348, 349–56; English language section of, 345, 346–47
Zamora, Emilio, 184

The Working Class in American History

Power at Odds: The 1922 National Railroad Shopmen's Strike *Colin J. Davis*
The Common Ground of Womanhood: Class, Gender, and Working Girls'
Clubs, 1884–1928 *Priscilla Murolo*
Marching Together: Women of the Brotherhood of Sleeping Car Porters
Melinda Chateauvert
Down on the Killing Floor: Black and White Workers in Chicago's
Packinghouses, 1904–54 *Rick Halpern*
Labor and Urban Politics: Class Conflict and the Origins of Modern
Liberalism in Chicago, 1864–97 *Richard Schneirov*
All That Glitters: Class, Conflict, and Community in Cripple Creek
Elizabeth Jameson
Waterfront Workers: New Perspectives on Race and Class *Edited by*
Calvin Winslow
Labor Histories: Class, Politics, and the Working-Class Experience *Edited by*
Eric Arnesen, Julie Greene, and Bruce Laurie